MORAL PHILOSOPHY

MORAL PHILOSOPHY

A CONTEMPORARY INTRODUCTION

Daniel R. DeNicola

broadview press

BROADVIEW PRESS – www.broadviewpress.com
Peterborough, Ontario, Canada

Founded in 1985, Broadview Press remains a wholly independent publishing house. Broadview's focus is on academic publishing; our titles are accessible to university and college students as well as scholars and general readers. With over 600 titles in print, Broadview has become a leading international publisher in the humanities, with world-wide distribution. Broadview is committed to environmentally responsible publishing and fair business practices.

Library and Archives Canada Cataloguing in Publication

DeNicola, Daniel R., author
    Moral philosophy : a contemporary introduction / Daniel R. DeNicola.

Includes bibliographical references and index.
ISBN 978-1-55481-354-4 (softcover)

    1. Ethics. I. Title.

BJ1012.D46 2018   170   C2018-905575-8

Broadview Press handles its own distribution in North America:
PO Box 1243, Peterborough, Ontario K9J 7H5, Canada
555 Riverwalk Parkway, Tonawanda, NY 14150, USA
Tel: (705) 743-8990; Fax: (705) 743-8353
email: customerservice@broadviewpress.com

Distribution is handled by Eurospan Group in the UK, Europe, Central Asia, Middle East, Africa, India, Southeast Asia, Central America, South America, and the Caribbean. Distribution is handled by Footprint Books in Australia and New Zealand.

Canada Broadview Press acknowledges the financial support of the Government of Canada for our publishing activities.

Edited by Robert M. Martin
Book Design by Em Dash Design

PRINTED IN CANADA

Contents

Preface and Acknowledgments

An anonymous reviewer of this text began the review with wise words: "The author of an introductory textbook for ethics has an essentially impossible task: to strike a balance between being careful, technical, and accurate enough to please professional philosophers, and being intelligible, unassuming, and readable enough for an undergraduate with perhaps no technical background in the subject." I have not resolved this dilemma, but that is certainly my aim.

About the form of this book: Each chapter opens with a real case or fictional scenario related to the issues of that chapter and intended to provoke thought, discussion, and application. Reference to these cases often recurs later on. I have included questions for discussion at the end, along with a few questions for personal reflection. Terms in **bold** are defined in the Glossary at the end. I have included dates for each philosopher upon their first mention.

I have taught ethics classes many times over the span of a career of nearly five decades. My students—the brilliant, the honestly struggling, the skeptical, the eager, the witty, the reticent—all have contributed so much to the shape and content of this book. My own ethics teachers were Stanley Grean at Ohio University and John Rawls and Roderick Firth at Harvard University. They were inspirational.

Our world very much needs serious reflection about the right and the good. My hope is that this text will be useful in provoking such reflection, in clarifying ethical thinking, deepening moral understanding, and awakening moral imagination.

I have deep gratitude to Stephen Latta of Broadview Press for his invitation, his encouragement, his intelligent critiques of earlier drafts, and his patience. Professor Lisa Tessman, once an anonymous reviewer of this text, gave me a great gift: an offer to pilot-test the book by using a draft typescript in her class. She is a distinguished ethicist and a most supportive critic; she and her students provided invaluable comments, for which I give grateful acknowledgment. The final text benefited greatly from the copy-editing of philosopher Bob Martin. I alone bear responsibility, however, for any remaining infelicities, errors, and omissions.

Finally, to my wife Sunni, whose love and encouragement helped keep even this consuming project in perspective. She is a force for good.

Dan DeNicola
Gettysburg College

CHAPTER ONE
Ethical Theory, Moral Concerns

Olivia's was among the earliest cases identified in the United States: she had contracted the Zika virus during the early stages of pregnancy. She and her boyfriend Michael had enjoyed a memorable beach vacation in Latin America. She didn't know then that she was pregnant; and she had no symptoms of the virus until she returned home.

She quickly learned the implications: the Zika virus is linked with scarily high rates of neurological birth defects, including microcephaly, which is characterized by an abnormally small head, underdeveloped brain, and cognitive disability. Severe forms result in death. But even milder forms may produce significant disabilities that necessitate continual monitoring and medical care.

From a sample of the amniotic fluid and a genetic test, she has learned that Zika has now infected the fetus. But unfortunately, according to medical authorities, microcephaly cannot be detected until very late in the second trimester (perhaps twenty weeks).

Olivia is surprised that Michael downplays the risks. He points out that despite a scary correlation, scientists haven't yet identified a specific causal link between the virus and microcephaly. So, they should wait until the ultrasound evidence could determine if the baby has a visible birth defect. Then they could talk and make a decision.

But Olivia is not sure. It isn't that she wouldn't want a child with Michael—though she hadn't really thought about it. She had imagined motherhood was years away. It's that she is not prepared—they are not prepared—for a newborn with severe disabilities or a brief and tragic life. Nor can she in good conscience pass the responsibility for such an infant to others. Most of all, she is horrified at the quality of life she'd being giving her child. Although she has thought of herself as "pro-life," she is now reluctantly considering whether to terminate her pregnancy. She knows that the longer she waits the more difficult in many ways an abortion would be. Every alternative seems to require moral courage. She wants to do "the right thing"—if only she could be sure what that is.

1.1 MORALITY AND LIFE

Morality is the foundation of social life, an essential aspect of culture. We acquire ethical sensibilities as we mature; we try to inculcate moral conduct in our children; and we rely on the ethical behavior of others. In complex societies, we often entrust our very lives to the ethics of strangers. Yet morality is not only foundational and implicit: moral considerations can compel our attention—as in the case of Olivia and Michael—and they can trouble or ease our minds, move us to action, and become the explicit reasons for the choices we make. To give attention to ethics is to consider what is right and wrong, what is good and bad, what is just and unjust, what sort of person one should be, and what sort of life and relationships one should have. When we discuss ethics, as Plato (c. 427–347 BCE) said, "We are discussing no small matter, but how we ought to live."

Ethical concerns, because of their multiplicity and pervasiveness, are familiar aspects of our lives. We encounter them in public life, where they often become issues of controversy, scandal, outrage, and the reach of law—vexed issues, such as abortion or capital punishment or the rights of immigrants; and clearly wrongful practices such as human trafficking, domestic abuse, animal cruelty, bribery, and corruption. They also pervade our personal relationships and our self-images, surfacing in moments of reflective questioning: *Should I have lied to her about my plans for the weekend? Am I really a compassionate person or a dupe? Should I move and advance my career or stay to care for my elderly mother?*

But however fundamental and familiar ethical issues may be, they are often difficult to resolve. Life may not be as melodramatic as a soap opera or a reality show, but neither is it always simple. We may confront dilemmas in which any alternative seems wrong. Even when one faces a clear choice between right and wrong, doing what is right can sometimes test one's will and courage. That is not, however, how Olivia saw her situation: she was trying to determine what the right thing to do is. *Should she violate her previous beliefs and terminate the life of her unborn, who is at serious risk for a devastating birth defect? Should she bring such a child into the world and accept the likely burden of such a tragedy—or pass it to others? Should she wait for the most reliable confirmation, at which point the baby would be further developed and an abortion would be more difficult— or perhaps legally questionable because of its lateness? Or is she morally obligated, because of the preciousness of all life, to carry the child to term and see what life brings?*

A person's moral values can sometimes conflict, in which case keeping faith with one means violating the other. Say you value both honesty and loyalty to friends. Imagine you and your friends attend an event at which something controversial or illegal happens. Being honest about what happened may well conflict with your loyalty to your friends who were participants. The choice is painful because a betrayal of something you value seems unavoidable, and we yearn for a way to be faithful to both.

Even when we are confident in our moral beliefs and think the issue is clear-cut, we may find that conscientious people disagree about what is right. *Should someone who murders his family be executed?* Moreover, in a contested issue like this, thoughtful people may even disagree about whether something is *relevant* to deciding the issue. For example, *is the fact that the murderer was fifteen years old at the time of the killing relevant to the matter—or the fact that his IQ is quite low?*

Sometimes, it is hard to know whether something is morally significant. Suppose someone is considering whether to purchase a certain product. *Should she reject the product for moral reasons because the company's CEO has made homophobic comments, or because the company does not pay its workers fairly, or because another product from the same company is produced by child labor? Would any of those factors make the purchase of, say, a pair of socks a morally significant act?*

Finally, we may be stymied by new, unexpected ethical issues that emerge from technological developments, issues that could not have been imagined in earlier years. *Is cloning a human being morally acceptable? Should androids have rights?*

All of these life circumstances make it challenging to achieve moral clarity. Yet there is more to morality than anguished decisions. We may be moved by acts of compassion or courage and admire the qualities of character they display. We may also be outraged at conduct or policies that we find cruel or unfair. We may have satisfaction, even joy, when justice triumphs. And we may work to become more like some people and less like others. All these are also features of the moral life.

1.2 THE VALUE OF ETHICAL STUDY

In the introductory scenario, Olivia wants to do "the right thing." She is seeking moral clarity and guidance for her situation. If only there was an authoritative handbook for morality, one could simply consult it to learn what is right for any situation.

The old Donald Duck comic book stories featured a fictional book called *The Junior Woodchuck's Guidebook*. It was issued by a Scout-like organization called the Junior Woodchucks, to which Donald's little nephews—Huey, Dewey, and Louie—belonged. The book was an invaluable guide, and they would regularly consult it to extricate themselves and others from embarrassing or dangerous predicaments. Supposedly compiled by "the Guardians of the lost Library of Alexandria," the volume contained the essence of all knowledge. Astounding in the breadth and detail of information it contained, it magically provided just the required information for every situation—if you were adept at using the massive index. And yet it was somehow small enough to fit into a Junior Woodchuck's backpack. Ah, the Disney magic!

Unfortunately, there is no such guidebook for ethics. Alas, no moral code can specify precisely what should be done in every possible situation. The philosophical study of ethics (what is often called *moral philosophy* or simply *ethics*) cannot offer this either, but it does offer assistance. Through the philosophical study of ethics, you can: (1) better articulate your own ethical beliefs and moral intuitions about cases, (2) come to understand different visions of morality as expressed in various ethical theories; (3) test your moral beliefs in dialogue with philosophers who hold quite different positions; and (4) reflect upon and thereby refine your own views.

The goal of moral philosophy—and the goal of this book—is not to settle once-and-for-all the wide range of ethical questions we face. That is an impossible task. Nor is the goal to convince you to adopt specific moral beliefs or a certain ethical code. Rather, the ultimate goal is for you to achieve what the philosopher John Rawls (1921–2002) called **reflective equilibrium**, a state of moral coherence in which the ethical beliefs you have (your ethical principles or theory) and your intuitions about specific cases (or your considered judgments) coincide.

Olivia is conflicted. Her ethical principles included the belief that abortion is morally wrong; but now she seems to have the moral intuition that it may be right in this case—not just acceptable, but right. Actual situations, with all their unique complications, test both our moral intuitions and our ethical beliefs. Our moral equilibrium is disturbed if, in a given situation, we find ourselves saying something like, "According to my professed ethical principles, this is wrong, but now ... it just seems like the right thing!" At such a moment, we (like Olivia) have a choice about how to resolve the conflict and restore the equilibrium, our moral coherence: we can either reject or change our principles or we can change our judgment of the matter. Olivia can decide that her prior beliefs were wrong: at the very least, abortion is not wrong in all circumstances. Or, she can make her judgment conform to her earlier beliefs: she was correct, and abortion is wrong—even in her case.

This process demands serious reflection upon both one's beliefs or principles and one's judgments, a back-and-forth examination of theory and practice that is perceptive in analysis, alert to implications, responsive to criticism, and sensitive to moral values. And once achieved, the process is not finished. Maintaining reflective equilibrium is an ongoing task, because new issues, additional insights, and unexpected problems can disrupt the balance and prompt further reflection.

There are additional ways in which the philosophical study of ethics can be of help. You can study moral questions and dilemmas at a reflective, psychic distance; you can examine issues without the pressure or immediacy of actually being in their throes (unlike Olivia and Michael). And these studies can also be preparatory; for instance, thinking through the moral dimensions of an issue like euthanasia may help prepare you for difficult end-of-life decisions. In studying ethics, you are an independent thinker, but you are not alone: you will examine the considered arguments and conclusions of philosophers over the centuries, and you do so with the guidance of an instructor and in tandem with other students who may share their thoughts. If you engage this study with an open mind, you will join a lively and challenging dialogue, an interplay of ethical viewpoints, diverse experience, and varying intuitions. This study will furnish you with intellectual resources and a precious period to think about your life and what life should be.

Let's begin the study with the first, but crucial, philosophical step: clarifying central concepts.

1.3 THE MORAL SPHERE

Some thinkers make a subtle distinction between "ethics" and "morality." "Ethics" and "ethical" (derived from the Greek, *ethos*, "character," "habit") seem to refer to matters related to structured, public, even professional, codes of conduct. "Morality" and "moral" (derived from the Latin, *mores*, "customs," "manners," "morals") tend to point to the deeper principles and values on which the codes or rules are based. Thus, we talk about the professional *ethics* of a physician or financial auditor, not their professional *morality*. The violation of a campaign law may be an *ethics* violation, but we might not call it a *moral* lapse. But we are more likely to refer to greed or courage as *moral* traits, not *ethical* traits. Slavery seems to be a *moral* problem, not an *ethical* problem. This distinction is not universal or consistent, however; nor is it sharp. So unless we encounter the need for such a nuanced distinction, I will take these terms to be interchangeable.

The word "moral" (like the word "ethical") is systematically ambiguous. It may refer to a sphere of human experience, specifically to those matters to which moral judgments apply. Everything outside that sphere is neither moral nor immoral, but is *nonmoral*.[1] Deciding whether to lie or tell the truth is a *moral* matter; choosing the color scheme for your room is a *nonmoral* matter. But the word "moral" also means "morally good." We may describe someone as a *moral* person and someone else as *immoral*. (For "ethical," the parallel contraries are "non-ethical" and "unethical.") Thus, a phrase like "a moral act" might mean either an action that falls within the purview of morality or an action that is morally good. Usually the context will clarify the sense intended, but it is smart to be alert to this ambiguity in reading and writing about ethics. "Morality" and "ethics" may also designate the views and codes of conduct of a particular group, such as "ancient Greek ethics" or "Puritan morality." So much for the important ambiguities.

I referred to ethics as a "sphere of human experience." It is helpful to contrast it with other such spheres, such as law, custom, and etiquette. It is true that moral values undergird much of the law: think of the laws against murder, rape, enslavement, theft, and so on. There is no doubt that the legal and ethical spheres overlap, but they are not the same. Some moral concerns, such as being honest with and loyal to your friends, are not legal matters. And some laws, such as those that legislate whether cars are to drive on the left or right side of the road, are clearly nonmoral. Moreover, some laws may be judged *immoral*. Jim Crow laws, for example, may have had the full force of the law, but they legitimated immoral treatment.

Custom refers to social traditions: it is customary in the United States to play the national anthem before an athletic event—but note that it is not generally taken to be a moral requirement. Similarly, using a salad fork correctly is a matter of *etiquette* or politeness; it is neither illegal nor immoral to use the incorrect fork. What all these spheres of experience have in common, however, is that they *prescribe* our conduct.

There are other comparable domains, of course, such as the economic, the therapeutic, and the aesthetic. You might also wonder about the religious sphere and its relation to moral. That will be the topic of Chapter 2. For now, I can note that the spheres are not identical: religions have components that are not considered to be moral matters even by their followers. For example, within the Christian tradition, the authority given to bishops by Roman Catholics and Methodists is quite different; these are doctrinal matters for each denomination—but not moral concerns.

We may also change the metaphor and think of all these "spheres" or domains as different perspectives or points of view. For example, we may examine a policy or an action from a legal, economic, etiquette, or moral point of view. In adopting one of these perspectives—for example, in determining whether something is legal, economically efficient, or morally good—we would attend to different aspects, ask different questions, invoke different values, and employ different criteria and standards of judgment. But one of the distinctive features often claimed for morality is that *moral concerns always override all others*; so something may be legal, customary, economically efficient, and so on, but if it is also immoral, it should not be done.

1.4 IDENTIFYING THE MORAL

But what *is* the moral sphere? What *is* the moral point of view? Intuitively, morality concerns the sort of lives and relationships we should have. It seems to involve not only what sort of person I should be and how I should act, but also how I should respond to others, and even what sort of social practices and policies we should create.

As a starting point, we can identify dimensions of our lives that typically are of moral concern.[2] *Care* and *harm* form such an axis. What we deeply care about sets our moral profile. Helping and hurting others are acts that are morally relevant; and therefore kindness, compassion, and cruelty are morally relevant traits. A related axis is the *pleasure* and *pain* that our actions can produce in ourselves and others. Issues of justice are related to our concern for *fairness* and *unfairness*. We blame and punish cheaters and violators who claim more than is due them; we seek policies that are fair to all involved.

Loyalty and *disloyalty* to family, friends, and groups as large as one's nation are also of moral concern. Our children, for example, seem to deserve our special moral consideration. Solidarity, fidelity, nurturance, and patriotism spring from this concern; betrayal, treachery, and treason are morally freighted acts. Similarly, *honesty* and *dishonesty* in our communications and treatment of others comprise a basic moral concern. Our duties may also carry a moral charge: being *dutiful* or *irresponsible* are traits that carry a moral judgment.

The components of *happiness* and *a flourishing life* for oneself and others, along with concerns about *freedom* and *oppression* are moral matters. The actions of bullies and conditions that prevent human flourishing are morally negative. A concern for *human dignity* underlies these issues and gives rise to the concept of *human rights*. Morality weighs against anything that degrades a human life. It draws a line indicating some things that are morally unacceptable.

Although this is by no means a complete list, these are the sorts of things with which morality is concerned. When a decision or an act or a policy or practice involves one or more of these (and related concerns), it indicates that we have entered the moral sphere. The matter requires moral judgment.

We experience such moral concerns from different perspectives. In the first place, we are **moral agents**; that is, we are beings capable of acting morally and immorally, creatures who may bear moral responsibilities. Who is "we"? Normal adult humans are clearly included. But, conventionally, not most animals: we don't think fish can act morally or that cows have moral responsibilities, though we may be uncertain about dogs and chimpanzees. Perhaps there is a "gray area" of the more "advanced" species. Even among humans, neither infants nor adults with severe mental disabilities nor those in comas are capable of moral or immoral acts. So there is another gray area as various human moral capacities develop or disappear. A moral agent can examine her own choices and actions from an ethical perspective: *Is it really bad to slightly fudge the experimental data if I am sure the actual data are misleading? Is it right to let go my reliable, long-term employees in order to hire replacements at lower wages? Is eating animals morally wrong?*

Often, however, we are on the receiving end of someone else's action; we are implicated then as **moral patients**. We might be, for example, the victim of a racist insult, the recipient of an apology, or the beneficiary of a life-saving response. We might be the one harmed, not the one harming. We are "patients" because we are on the receiving end of actions; we are the objects of others' moral responsibilities. And we are "moral" because we have moral standing; we are entitled to moral consideration. Note that all moral agents may be moral patients, but not all moral patients can be moral agents. Moral patients form a much larger group than moral agents. Cows and infants and comatose adults may not be able to act morally or immorally, but others can do things that are morally right or wrong *to* them—animal cruelty and infant abuse are acts that are commonly judged to be morally wrong.

The term "patient" seems to imply a creature, a being, perhaps one that is conscious and can feel pain. Exactly what quality or capacity gives something moral standing is an interesting question, however. Is it the capacity to suffer? A rock can't feel pain—and that's a reason why we can't do anything immoral to a rock. But perhaps there are objects that deserve moral consideration even if they are not "patients." Many people condemned as immoral the wanton destruction of an iconic sandstone formation, "the Duckbill," in Oregon's Kiwanda State Park. Might a stone that is a sculpture or an ancient work of art, for example, have a kind of moral stature? Vandalizing such "rocks" would then be immoral. We will not resolve this question here, but my point is that the class of things that deserve moral consideration is quite large, and moral standing may admit of degrees.

There is, I think, a third perspective. We occasionally find ourselves thrust into the role of **moral bystander**, unexpectedly witnessing a situation of moral concern. We come upon a stranded motorist, see an apparent assault, hear an offensive remark, or encounter a homeless woman begging for money. I say we "find ourselves" in such a situation because we are keenly aware that we did not create it; at least initially, we don't feel like an agent or a patient. Perhaps we are a little of both. But, of course, as we wonder what we should *do*—whether to avert our eyes or ears or to do or say something—we become agents, reluctantly or willingly assuming the responsibilities of our agency.

1.5 PHILOSOPHICAL ETHICS

There are four different types of studies regarding ethics, three of which are philosophical in nature, and it is important to distinguish them. **Descriptive Ethics** comprises empirical studies of moral behavior and beliefs, including accounts of the evolution of ethical capacities and codes of conduct. Sociologists and anthropologists, for example, describe the ethical beliefs and practices of certain populations, and the ways in which moral requirements function in society. Historians may describe the moral views of individuals or groups in the past. Psychologists attend to the process of developing moral capacities; they may map the brain's operations during moral decision-making or survey factors that affect moral judgment. All these studies are aimed at describing the facts about actual beliefs and behavior. These are not philosophical concerns.

Normative Ethics is not directly concerned with what people believe (or have believed) is right or wrong, but with what they *should* believe. It attempts a general account of what things—states of affairs, experiences, qualities—are *genuinely* good or bad, what acts or practices are morally right or wrong, and which traits of character are moral virtues or vices. It is a philosophical enterprise that proposes norms or standards. In other words, it prescribes what *should be* done—which might differ greatly from what actually *is* done.

Metaethics, also a philosophical enterprise, analyzes moral concepts, judgments, and arguments. It studies the meaning of ethical terms like "right" and "obligation," and the justification of ethical claims like "incest is morally wrong." In addition, metaethics considers moral knowledge and the issue of whether there are moral facts.

Applied Ethics involves the application of ethical theory to specific cases or practices. It employs philosophical analysis to make moral judgments about such issues as capital punishment, abortion, warfare, plagiarism, dilemmas within medical ethics, and so on.

Philosophical ethics (also called "moral philosophy"), a major branch of philosophy, comprises the last three forms of inquiry. This book is primarily devoted to normative ethics and metaethics, though we will discuss specific applications to cases. Once again, when I say this approach is **normative**, not descriptive, I mean that it is not focused on what *is*, but on what *ought to be*. As ethicists, we pursue an understanding of what truly is right (how people *ought to act*), and it is quite a different pursuit from determining what people *believe* to be right. It assumes that being mistaken in our moral beliefs is a possibility.

Perhaps you are wondering: *Are the actual facts of human life, the reality of human morality, ignored by ethicists?* No. So I will highlight two important points of reality-grounding: The first is that ethicists adhere to the maxim, *"Ought* implies *can."* This means that to say one *ought to do* something implies that one *can* do it. We cannot be morally obliged to do the impossible, nor may we rationally prescribe it. For example, I cannot be obligated to attend a funeral that was held yesterday, if I first learned about it today. Reality restricts what actions are possible; and what is possible for humans restricts what we can morally require. The second is that facts are relevant to the achievement of norms or goals. Just as the facts of nutrition are relevant to the goal of good health; so facts about humans and the world may be relevant to the achievement of human flourishing, to acting rightly in a situation, or to becoming a virtuous person and living a morally good life.

You may also be wondering: Who is to judge what is truly right or wrong, or to prescribe how people ought to act? Isn't it arrogant to claim that prerogative? By studying ethics, we are not appointing ourselves as moral authorities and claiming an expertise not available to others. Moreover, to frame the question as a "who" question suggests that moral judgments are to be made by someone in authority, someone who makes a pronouncement. But it is not really a matter of "Who is to decide what is right and wrong?"—that is a misguided approach—but rather of "What is right and wrong?" That question is open to anyone who can reflect and reason; it responds to intellectual inquiry. Philosophical ethics values conceptual clarity, reasoned argument, consistency with relevant facts, and sensitivity to the broader implications of a claim. It attempts to justify its claims. And thinking through how one properly justifies a moral judgment—that's the business of metaethics. (Metaethics will be the topic of Chapter 13, though we will deal with some metaethical issues as they arise in this study.)

When we examine normative questions philosophically, reasoning our way to a conclusion, the result is taken to apply to everyone—everyone, that is, in morally similar circumstances. This is known as the **Principle of Universalizability**: *any valid moral principle or judgment applies to anyone and everyone who is in morally similar circumstances.* It entails that no one can make herself or himself a special exception without having a morally relevant difference, and also that one should have consistency in one's own judgments. Note that universalization does *not* prescribe the conditions or differences that are morally relevant—they might include a wide range of circumstances, as we shall see, including culture, relationships, foreseeable consequences, and many others. It merely requires that, whatever the morally relevant aspects of situation, if those conditions are the same, the moral conclusion should be the same. So, when Olivia and Michael struggle to determine what they should do, they are reasoning for all couples in a similar situation, not giving themselves a special moral exception.

Over the centuries, philosophers have developed ethical theories, which are the products of systematic inquiry in normative ethics and metaethics. They present accounts of morality; they both theorize ethics and prescribe moral conduct. My plan is to examine each of the influential theories in turn, sympathetically and critically, and to offer comparisons and some syntheses. Be forewarned: some ethical theories will seem more like challenges to the whole enterprise of philosophical ethics—the philosophical equivalent of wolves in sheep's clothing.

Having a clear understanding of each theory is basic; using these accounts to think through your own views, however, is the ultimate goal. As we shall see, each of these theories has vigorous advocates and sharp critics; they each harbor (explicit or implicit) views of human nature and moral agency; they privilege certain human traits and have implications for moral education; and they seem to be specially apt for certain situations and relationships—and to be somewhat ill-suited for others. As normative theories, they offer guidance to behavior—and their guidance may lead us in different directions. They may even imply different views of what it is to "do ethics." These major ethical theories are enormously influential; they have shaped thought and practice. What is at stake in their debates is a vision of what we value and much that we hold dear.

1.6 EVALUATION OF ETHICAL THEORIES

Theories are systematic conjectures that comprehend a specific domain of phenomena. A scientific theory—indeed any descriptive theory that attempts to explain actual events and phenomena—can be judged by whether it fits or explains the known facts. But since philosophical ethical theories are not descriptive, one might wonder how they can be evaluated. They are not attempting to explain actual moral codes or ethical behavior in any culture. How does one judge a theory that is normative, that claims to account for what should be?

There are, I think, certain tests that an ethical theory should meet. They include both tests of logic that may apply to any type of theory, and criteria that relate specifically to the domain of ethics. These tests are applicable before we adopt a theory, before we seek reflective equilibrium.

TESTS FOR AN ETHICAL THEORY

TESTS OF LOGIC

Is the theory:

a. *clear?* (Are its key concepts and relationships clear?)
b. *coherent?* (Is it internally consistent, free from self-contradiction?)
c. *consistent with facts?* (Is it consistent with established facts?)

TESTS OF PLAUSIBILITY

a. *Can the theory serve to guide practice?* Moral theory should prescribe conduct. If a theory is so complicated or restrictive that it cannot be used to guide practice, it has failed in one important respect.
b. *Does the theory rest on a plausible account of human nature and psychology?* All ethical theories rest on a view of human nature; they imply human capacities and options for action. No adequate account of morality can assume an unrealistic account of what it is to be human, including differences among humans.
c. *Does the theory give a plausible account of common "moral phenom-ena"?* Any ethical theory attempts to interpret or give place to familiar moral phenomena. These include moral concepts, practices, relationships, and institutions within the moral sphere. Theories may give crucial or controversial roles to such phenomena, but if a theory distorts or dismisses a particular phenomenon, it should offer special justification. **Figure 1** presents a suggestive list of such moral phenomena.
d. *Does the theory provide guidance and help harmonize the various spheres of our lives?* Our public life (civic relationships), private life (familial and intimate relationships), and professional life (rela-tionships with colleagues, clients, patients, etc.) all have moral dimensions. A strong moral theory helps us live a coherent life within and among these aspects of our lives.

FIGURE 1   MORAL PHENOMENA

1. *a moral point of view*, a kind of conscientiousness, that markedly differs from other perspectives, such as the economic, the aesthetic, or the legal points of view

2. *moral agency*, including an account of what it is to be a *moral agent*

3. *moral stature*, including an account of what it is to be a *moral patient* or to be entitled to *moral consideration*

4. *moral judgments* about acts and policies (right/wrong), things (good/bad), and people (blameworthy/praiseworthy)

5. *moral deliberation* with others or with oneself

6. *moral differences and disagreements* with others, which may persist even after deliberation

7. *changes in moral beliefs*, that is, individuals and societies alter their moral judgments over time, often interpreted as *moral reform or advancement*

8. *morally-related emotional/ psychological phenomena and "moral sentiments,"* such as care and compassion, guilt and remorse, shame, gratitude, etc.

9. *moral dissent* from social practices, laws, religious teachings, and other received principles or patterns of conduct

10. the giving and receiving of *moral advice*

11. personal *sacrifice* for moral reasons

12. *supererogation*, that is, action above and beyond duty; and *moral saints*, that is, individuals who live lives of extraordinary moral commitment and who are revered as morally inspirational

13. *rules, principles, maxims*, and *precepts* which prescribe moral behavior

14. *moral education*, the deliberate attempt to inculcate moral values and educate people to adhere to moral standards of conduct

15. diverse kinds of *moral practices and related roles*, almost institutions themselves, such as promising, taking a vow or oath, punishing, rewarding, and so on— including the roles of promisor, oath-taker, judge, etc.

16. *moral virtues*, traits of character which are admired, praised, and fostered as relevant to living a moral life, related to moral ideals, such as justice, duty, well-being, etc.

17. practices or rituals of *moral repair*, including apologizing, forgiving, making amends, etc.

18. *moral dilemmas and conflicts*, inescapable situations of choice

1.7 CASES, THOUGHT-EXPERIMENTS, AND COUNTEREXAMPLES

There are three tools philosophers use to explicate and critique ethical theories. *Cases* are stories or brief narratives, factual or fictional, which present moral issues, dilemmas, or situations that illustrate moral conduct. They invite moral judgment and justification. The introductory case of Olivia and Michael is a fictional case. Here is a true case that generated public controversy and is ethically complex:

> Sharon Duchesneau and Candy McCullough wanted to have a child, and planned to seek a sperm donor. But because both women are deaf and wanted a child who was like themselves, they sought and found a sperm donor who came from five generations of family deafness. Their plans were successful: their son Gauvin was born deaf. When their story became public, they were vilified. Letter writers had so many points of outrage: they are lesbian partners who had "designed" the child they conceived by means of a sperm donor and a turkey baster, and they had deliberately inflicted a serious disability on an innocent baby. Duchesneau said, "We feel whole as deaf people and we want to share the wonderful aspects of our community—a sense of belonging and connectedness—with children. We truly feel we live rich lives as deaf people."[3]

This case generates many ethical questions: *Is it wrong to produce deafness in a child deliberately? Is the fact that the parents are deaf morally relevant? Should we see deafness as a disability—an affliction or harm—or as a cultural identity? Is it wrong to "design" any child by picking significant features? Are the values that motivated this decision morally worthy? Do the rights of parents include choosing the capacities of the child to be conceived?* Cases like this inspire moral reflection by raising provocative questions. It can be insightful to apply an ethical theory to such a case, to see how these questions are answered and what guidance is offered, and to check one's own intuitions.

Sometimes, philosophers turn to invented scenarios, *thought-experiments* that are designed to illuminate or test a specific aspect of an ethical issue. They are like cases, but they have less narrative detail and tend to be more stylized, even cartoonish. Here is a version of a famous example:

> Suppose you are the hapless driver of a runaway train, which is barreling down the tracks and heading for a group of five workers. It will

*surely kill all five, who are unaware of the impending threat. You could
throw a switch that would deflect the train onto a spur. Unfortunately,
it would then run over a man who is walking on that siding. You have
only a moment to act.* Would you (should you) pull the switch?[4]

Thought-experiments also provoke many acute questions. *Is it always
better for one person to die than for many? Is intentionally causing the death
of a person always wrong?* Would you be responsible in this situation if
you just let events happen? Plus, with a thought-experiment like this, one
can vary different aspects of the scenario to highlight what is morally relevant: *What if the lone person on the siding was your son? Would you push
someone into the path of the trolley if that would stop it from killing the five
workers?* Though these scenarios may be far-fetched, they can serve to
reveal and sharpen moral reasoning. (We will examine this thought-experiment more fully much later in the book.)

A third technique is the use of examples and counterexamples. An
example illustrates a claim by citing an instance; a challenging response
is to offer a *counterexample*, another instance that serves to contradict
or oppose the claim. Suppose someone claims, "It is always wrong to lie
to a child, that is, to tell the child something you know isn't true, in order
to deceive them." One might offer as a counterexample: *What about telling your child about Santa Claus?* The effective deployment of examples
and counterexamples is an important technique for presenting, testing,
and sharpening moral claims and theories.

In succeeding chapters, I will employ all three of these techniques in
the unfolding of various ethical theories. Every chapter will open with a
case or thought-experiment that is salient to the topic. These three tools—
cases, thought-experiments, and counterexamples—do not compose an
ethical theory, but they help test and shape our intuitions and support
our efforts to construct a theory.

1.8 THE POINT OF IT ALL

Ethical theories prescribe moral conduct; they lead us to what is right and
good. They often articulate principles or rules that moral agents should
follow. They mark some actions as morally required—that is, actions that
are our **obligations** or **duties**.[5] They also mark some actions as wrong,
things that should not be done, and so are morally prohibited. Not meeting our moral obligations would, of course, be among the **prohibitions**.

Not all actions are morally required or prohibited, however: there is a range of *permissible* actions. Choosing a car, going to the gym, meeting a friend for lunch, investing money in a business—none of these is in general morally required or forbidden. There are also permissible actions that have moral worth: the term **supererogation** refers to acts that are morally good and are *above and beyond* what is required. A supererogatory act exceeds what we ethically owe; it might be a gift, a special favor, or a saintly act. The fact we are not obliged to do such acts, that they are not our duties, means that their goodness is freely given. Repaying more than we owe or granting mercy are clear, if modest, examples.

How high is the bar of morality? How much do ethical theories expect of us? Is it just to avoid serious wrongdoing? Or must we act in certain ways, live in a certain way, to advance the good? How much of our lives should be driven by moral motives? These are questions you should keep in mind as we consider various moral visions. We will return to them in the final chapter. For the moment, we might observe that most moral theories value both who we are now and the motive to become a better person than we are now. Perhaps, though we are inspired by extraordinary acts and lives of moral goodness, we cannot all be moral saints. But we can be decent people, and we can often do more and do better than we have done. And that is not always easy. There is an undeniable uplift, a call to act or to be better, that we will encounter in this philosophical study. Of course, studying ethical theory does not make one ethical. It can only propose what that would involve.

As we examine influential ethical theories, your first task is to understand the moral vision of the theory. Only then is a valid critical response possible. While you should seek the best theory—the one you can defend over others as sound and true—it is wise also to seek whatever truth is embodied in each theory.

1.9 SOURCES OF MORAL VALUES

When I am unsure of what is right, where should I turn to find the answer? The normative theories we will examine all require a metaethical source or ground for the values, principles, or judgments they advocate. Broadly speaking, there are five possible sources or grounds for our moral affirmations, each presenting a different domain of facts, each framing normative ethics in a different way. It will helpful to offer a brief, annotated list of them now for they represent the larger architecture of the book; but elaboration and critique of these theories will be the subjects of later chapters. The five sources are:

1. **God.** Many people take God to be the source of moral values, the only source, the only possible source. Some cannot conceive of morality unless it is derived from God. Such a believer, therefore, must turn to God's will as the ground of moral judgment—divine will, that is, as revealed in sacred texts, by a religious authority figure, or even by direct revelation. Judging whether charity is good and abortion or capital punishment or torture is wrong is, then, grounded in an understanding of God's will.

2. **Nature, especially Human Nature.** Natural laws apply to everything in the cosmos, including human beings. Those who reject the supernatural may emphasize that we are part of the natural order and look to Nature as the source and determinant of human values. Or they may narrow the focus from Nature to human nature. As it is revealed in history, biology, psychology, or neurophysiology, human nature may direct us and present limits on realistic moral prescriptions. For example, it may be morally significant if we are naturally selfish or altruistic, trusting or distrusting, jealous or generous, aggressive or pacific.

3. **Culture.** Alternatively, we might ground our moral affirmations in our culture, its mores and traditions, or its current practices. One's culture might be taken not merely as a formalized expression of morality, but as the source of morality. Morality does not, in this view, transcend culture; there is no morality outside culture.

4. **Reason and Its Instruments.** Some thinkers believe that morality is a practical form of rationality, that Reason itself is the source or ground of morality. Moral deliberation is not only an exercise in reasoning; it is an inquiry into what is rational. Other philosophers look more directly to specific artifacts of our reason, especially to contracts and agreements, which they suppose are rationally desirable. For them, morality is rooted in what we owe each other as a result of a Social Contract or special agreements we may have made, such as marriage vows.

5. **The Self.** Some theorists claim that the only valid source of morality is within oneself. Perhaps it is the emotions one feels, our moral

sentiments, shaped by our capacity for empathy. Maybe it resides in our individual moral intuitions or our conscience. Or perhaps morality is created through the personal and existential choices we make as free selves.

This is the widest spectrum of potential sources of morality, from God to the depths of our individual souls. Because it may prove useful to schematize these theories in a consistent way, I will introduce a common definitional formulation as a shorthand. Using "X" to stand for a moral act or practice, we can schematize the five sources of moral facts (in order) as follows:

1.   "X is right" = "X is willed by God"
2.   "X is right" = "X is in accord with human nature"
3.   "X is right" = "X is approved by my culture"
4.   "X is right" = "X is in accord with Reason" (or "... with a rational contract")
5.   "X is right" = "X is commended by my conscience" (or "... by my sentiments")

This schema can also be used for "X is wrong" as well as for other moral terms. Of course, these initial formulations give only one simple version for each source, and various theories will refine the right-hand formulation. For our purposes, this sort of schema will provide only a convenient and comparative encapsulation of a theory.

We will begin by examining the view that morality derives from God, one of the oldest and most familiar of moral theories.

QUESTIONS FOR DISCUSSION

1   Discuss my claim that the "Who is to decide?" question is a misguided question to ask when we engage in philosophical ethics.

2   "Reflective equilibrium" is both a method and a goal for the study of philosophical ethics. Does it have any liabilities of which we should be cautious?

3   The contents of the moral sphere change over time. Do you think smoking has become a moral matter? Is economic inequality a moral matter? Homosexuality was considered a significant moral matter—but isn't it now moving outside of the sphere of moral concern? Is our moral sphere growing or shrinking—that is, are

more issues or fewer now considered to be of moral concern? Can you apply the "axes of moral concern" to reach your judgments?

4 What "axes of moral concern" mark the situation of Olivia and Michael as an ethical dilemma? What elements of the situation make their decision a moral one?

5 Share your views regarding the case of the couple who arranged for a child to be deaf like them. Try to be as precise as you can about what aspects of this case make the parental actions morally permissible or morally wrong, in your view.

6 Try to construct a counterexample to this claim: It is always better for one person to die than for several.

QUESTIONS FOR PERSONAL REFLECTION

1 Have you had an experience that challenged a previous moral belief you held? Did you resolve it by changing your judgment of the situation or by rejecting your earlier belief?

2 Consider the list of "moral phenomena." Can you give an example of each?

3 In your personal life, to which of the "sources of morality" do you tend to turn for moral guidance, to determine what is right or wrong?

SUGGESTED SOURCES

Baggini, Julian, and Peter S. Fosl. *The Ethics Toolkit: A Compendium of Ethical Concepts and Methods.* Oxford: Blackwell, 2007.

Frankena, William. *Ethics.* Englewood Cliffs, NJ: Prentice-Hall, 1988.

LaFollette, Hugh. *The International Encyclopedia of Ethics.* 9 vols. New York: Wiley-Blackwell, 2013.

Singer, Peter, ed. *A Companion to Ethics*. Oxford: Blackwell, 1997.

Williams, Bernard. *Morality: An Introduction to Ethics.* Cambridge and New York: Cambridge UP, 1993.

On-line Reference Sources

The Internet Encyclopedia of Philosophy: http://www.iep.utm.edu/home/about/

Stanford Encyclopedia of Philosophy: http://plato.stanford.edu/about.html

NOTES

1 The word "amoral" is sometimes used to mean "outside the sphere to which moral judgments apply"; but it also means "indifferent to or unconcerned with moral rightness or wrongness." It is better to reserve this term for that latter use.

2 The "axes of moral concern" approach I use here draws on, but does not mirror, the work of Jonathan Haidt, including his *The Righteous Mind: Why Good People Are Divided by Politics and Religion* (Vintage, 2013).

3 This case was reported by the *Washington Post Magazine* in an April 1, 2002, story titled, "A World of Their Own." The reporter, Liza Mundy, went on-line to field questions. A transcript of her discussion may be read at http://www.washingtonpost.com/wp-srv/liveonline/02/magazine/magazine_mundy040102.htm. A search of the Web will reveal the barrage of global news coverage that followed.

4 The original version of this thought-experiment was introduced by Philippa Foot in a 1967 paper titled, "A Problem of Abortion and the Doctrine of the Double Effect," published in the *Oxford Review*. She used the term "tram" rather than "trolley." But her scenario has spawned so many variations and so much discussion that this literature is now referred to as "trolleyology." See my discussion in Chapter 12.

5 Some philosophers distinguish between these terms, restricting the term "obligation" to requirements derived from roles, while "duty" is more generic. I will use them interchangeably.

CHAPTER TWO

Morality and Religion

Genesis 22: Some time later God tested Abraham. He said to him, "Abraham!"

"Here I am," he replied.

2 Then God said, "Take your son, your only son, whom you love—Isaac—and go to the region of Moriah. Sacrifice him there as a burnt offering on a mountain I will show you."

3 Early the next morning Abraham got up and loaded his donkey. He took with him two of his servants and his son Isaac. When he had cut enough wood for the burnt offering, he set out for the place God had told him about. 4 On the third day Abraham looked up and saw the place in the distance. 5 He said to his servants, "Stay here with the donkey while I and the boy go over there. We will worship and then we will come back to you."

6 Abraham took the wood for the burnt offering and placed it on his son Isaac, and he himself carried the fire and the knife. As the two of them went on together, 7 Isaac spoke up and said to his father Abraham, "Father?"

"Yes, my son?" Abraham replied. "The fire and wood are here," Isaac said, "but where is the lamb for the burnt offering?"

8 Abraham answered, "God himself will provide the lamb for the burnt offering, my son." And the two of them went on together.

9 When they reached the place God had told him about, Abraham built an altar there and arranged the wood on it. He bound his son Isaac and laid him on the altar, on top of the wood. 10 Then he reached out his hand and took the knife to slay his son. 11 But the angel of the Lord called out to him from heaven, "Abraham! Abraham!"

"Here I am," he replied.

12 "Do not lay a hand on the boy," he said. "Do not do anything to him. Now I know that you fear God, because you have not withheld from me your son, your only son."

New International Version (NIV)

2.1 THE RELIGIOUS CONTEXT

Of the nearly 7.5 billion people in the world, roughly 85% claim a religious identity. This includes over 4,000 different religions, distinguished by a great diversity of belief and practice. Of the 19 major world religions, Christianity is by far the largest, with over 2.3 billion followers, or just under a third of all people (31%). Islam is second with about 1.8 billion (24%); 16 million identify with Judaism (.02 %). These three Abrahamic religions—Judaism, Christianity, and Islam—therefore account for well over half the world's population (nearly 56%).[1] All three recognize Abraham ("Ibrahim" to Muslims) as a tribal patriarch and the founder of their religious tradition. They are sometimes known as "religions of the book" because they elevate certain ancient texts, the oldest of which they share. Thus over half the world reveres the Abraham of Genesis and regards the story of Abraham and Isaac as sacred text.

The account of God's test of Abraham's faith is a vivid and dramatic episode, and it has generated a huge literature of interpretation, commentary, and critique. The need for all this explication is obvious: *Why would a good God command a good man to kill his only son, his precious son, as a sacrifice? Why would a good man willingly murder his only son, whom he loved?* If any act is morally wrong, surely it is the killing of one's own child. The story provokes questions about the nature of God and the bounds of faith. But our interest here is philosophical, not theological: the episode prompts us to examine ties between morality and religion, and to scrutinize the prospect of grounding moral judgments in religious commitments.

2.2 RELIGION AND MORALITY

The connection between religion and morality seems natural and historic. Religions prescribe a way of life, reflect a view of human nature, portray the human predicament, and envision human destiny. It thus appears obvious that religion would have a deep influence, perhaps a defining influence, on morality.

One theory, derived from anthropological study, is that morality emerged from religion; which, in turn, developed from primitive superstitions, myths, and rituals of contact with supernatural powers. If this historical account were true, one would expect that, as religions became "organized" and increasingly distinct, they would likely establish increasingly diverse moral codes. But the challenging fact is that the world's religions vary more widely in their beliefs, rituals, and practices, than they do in the moral codes of their societies.

Indeed, the world's religions are enormously diverse. They differ in the number of gods they recognize: they can be monotheistic, polytheistic, or even non-theistic. Some affirm that the soul survives in eternal afterlife, while others believe in reincarnation and a pilgrimage through many lives; and there are religions that are confident only of this one, earthly life. Religions have quite different views of human nature. Abrahamic religions give humans "dominion" over other creatures and the natural world; but others deify certain animals. Yet despite such profound differences in metaphysics, cosmology, and practice, there is a remarkable convergence regarding basic moral values.

In 1993, thousands gathered in Chicago for a Parliament of the World's Religions. During that event, 200 religious leaders representing over forty of the world's religions endorsed a document declaring their common morality. The report, *Declaration Toward a Global Ethic*, affirmed the universality of the principle most people know as the Golden Rule ("What you do not wish done to yourself, do not do to others." Or in positive terms: "What you wish done to yourself, do to others!"). These religious leaders also affirmed values like truthfulness, compassion, and respect; they rejected selfishness, violence, theft, corruption, and other moral negativities.[2] This uplifting declaration of unity may paper over doctrinal differences, but it does express a genuine consensus about deep moral values that should be surprising if one assumed that morality derived primarily from religion.

Today there is an ascendant, alternate view that morality emerged as a product of biological and social evolution; in particular, it arose from the need for cooperation and trust among social primates. The demands of social living and the advantages of social cooperation favored the taming of selfishness, the extension of trust, and the punishment of rogue behavior and freeloading. Thus, by the gradual extension of cooperation and reciprocity, a sense of fairness and justice emerged. This account suggests that the origins of morality are independent of religion, though it is quite possible that this sort of advantageous social behavior received supernatural sanction early on.[3]

In any event, these two accounts concern the historical origins of morality; they do not settle the conceptual questions: *Is religion necessary for morality? Does morality require specific religious beliefs—for example, the belief that morally good behavior will be rewarded by God in the afterlife, while immorality will be punished?* They are our concern, along with questions about the impact of religion, such as: *Is religion a boon or a threat to morality? Does religion do more harm than good in the world?* I will address the questions of doubters, but let us begin by considering the perspective of believers for whom morality is fully dependent on religion, especially on the goodness of God.

2.3 DIVINE COMMAND THEORY

Many religious traditions offer lofty ideals to guide our lives, such as living in harmony with the Tao (Taoism), or living a life of renunciation and harmlessness to all life (Jainism). The Abrahamic religions focus on living in accordance with God's will. Judaism, Christianity, and Islam are mono-theistic religions in which God is the omnipotent, omniscient, all-perfect Creator of the world and all that is therein, a domain that thrives under his providence. God's will for human beings is expressed in a holy book, or rather a compendium of texts; the oldest texts are shared, but each religion has a distinctive sacred text as well: the Tanakh (the Hebrew Bible), the New Testament, the Qur'an. They have developed separate traditions of translation, commentary, and interpretive scholarship. Over the centuries, they have branched into different sects and have developed offshoots such as the Rastafari and Bahá'í from Christianity. As Abrahamic religions, their roots are in tribal societies, in which the distinction between one's own people and all others is basic to identity. Especially for Christianity and Islam, membership is defined by one's beliefs. They form communities of *believers* who declare their shared beliefs in creeds.[4]

For many in the Abrahamic religions, the will of God provides the source, the ground, the authority, the sanction, and the content of morality. To do what is right is to follow God's will. When formalized, this view is called the **Divine Command Theory**. In simple schematic form, it claims that:

"X is right" = "X is willed by God"; and

"X is good" = "X is commended by God."

In addition,

"X is wrong" = "X is forbidden by God"; and

"X is permissible" = "X is not forbidden by God."

God's will may be discovered by reading the sacred text, especially those commandments and instructions that are addressed to all believers—though God's special directives to individuals like Abraham and Moses are also instructive. Sanctified religious leaders may also express a mediated version of God's will; but prayer and revelation, which are direct communion with God, may convey the divine will also. The will of God is, of course, separate from the will of any person; and it is our task to accept and follow whatever God wills.

According to Divine Command Theory, Abraham's willingness to kill his own son was morally right because he was faithfully following God's command. Indeed, Abraham was obligated to take his son's life. This assessment is clearly endorsed by Augustine of Hippo, known as St.

Augustine (354–430 CE). One section of his great work, *The City of God*, is titled "Of the cases in which we may put men to death without incurring the guilt of murder." In that passage, although Augustine acknowledges that "Thou shalt not kill" is God's commandment, he allows that there are special cases:

> However, there are some exceptions made by the divine authority to its own law, that men may not be put to death. These exceptions are of two kinds, being justified either by a general law, or by a special commission granted for a time to some individual.... Abraham indeed was not merely deemed guiltless of cruelty, but was even applauded for his piety, because he was ready to slay his son in obedience to God, not to his own passion.[5]

Over eight hundred years later, Thomas Aquinas (1225–74) concurred: "When Abraham consented to slay his son, he did not consent to murder, because his son was due to be slain by the command of God, Who is Lord of life and death...."[6] It would, for Aquinas, have been murder if Abraham had attempted to slay his child on his own—that is, without God's command. The phrase "Lord of life and death" reminds us that Isaac was a child promised to Abraham in his old age by God: God gave him life and may—as with all humankind—take it away. God ultimately takes the life of all humans, and that is not murder; so neither is this case in which God's will was to be carried out by Abraham. Thus, the Qur'an notes that Abraham "is surely among the righteous" because "When his Lord said to him, Submit, he said: I submit myself to the Lord of the worlds."[7]

Divine Command Theory has been adopted by notable philosophers through the ages, including William of Ockham (1287–1347) and Søren Kierkegaard (1813–55). Ockham's position is that morality turns on one's will—not on the act itself—and a will that is morally good is one that yields to God's will.[8] The Danish Christian philosopher Kierkegaard, through his pseudonym Johannes de Silentio, honored Abraham with a "panegyric" (a public speech of praise) in *Fear and Trembling*.[9] Indeed, the entire book is a meditation on the story of Abraham and his son. Abraham is, for Kierkegaard a "knight of faith" who "suspends" conventional ethics, acts against reason in fear and trembling, and displays an astonishing leap of faith in God and God's will. For Kierkegaard, God's commands transcend conventional ethics, and one always faces an existential choice of whether to obey God.

2.4 IMPLICATIONS

Let us begin our evaluation of this theory by considering some of its philosophical implications. These are not critiques, but facets of the theory that should be unfolded for understanding.

1. Divine Command Theory identifies God as the source and ground of morality. Because it offers answers to the questions of what basic ethical terms mean and how moral judgments are justified, it is a metaethical theory. "Right" means "commanded by God" and moral judgments are justified when they accord with God's will. But it gains normative ethical content as one starts spelling out just what God requires of us. It implies that all conflicts of values are only apparent—matters of ignorance and error. Genuine moral deliberation, which is interpreted as dutiful attempts to discern God's will, can lead us to find a resolution of any dilemma.

2. The elevation of a text as God's sacred word transforms the supernatural into the textual, which is certainly more accessible. The "religions of the book" thereby give rise to **fundamentalism**. A fundamentalist is someone who believes that (a) morality is a matter of following God's will; (b) a specific text is the revealed will of God, and the believer should interpret it literally and grant it absolute inerrancy; and (c) this moral viewpoint is the only valid one. Fundamentalism, so defined, is a special version of Divine Command Theory. Since the relevant texts are ancient, it is not surprising that this approach is ill-suited for complex, contemporary moral issues like cloning or robot ethics, but more at home with issues like the obligations of marriage and the wrongs of theft or deception. Of course, many followers of these religions are not fundamentalist. Although they consider the relevant text(s) sacred, they may have different interpretations of what that sacredness implies for a non-literal or even critical interpretation and for the ways in which reading may provide appropriate guidance.

3. Although these religions emphasize the essential role of belief, most versions see morality as fundamentally a matter of the will. Both the deepest tension and the most profound moral accord are to be found in the relationship between our individual wills and the will of God. Imperatives, commandments, laws, and rules are the forms in which divine will is expressed.

4. For most advocates, this theory implies that, exempting personal instructions like those given to Abraham, God's generic commands have universal application. Ethical prescriptions are *universal* when they apply to all people at all times. The contrasting view is that what is right or good is *relative*, which means that what is morally right for one might be wrong

for another—so, normative moral judgments might vary according to time or place or culture or circumstance. Divinely ordained prescriptions for a moral life are usually understood to be universal, not relative to specific believers. This means that believers apply the morality that is God's will with full force to non-believers, even though non-believers do not acknowledge it. The Decalogue (the Ten Commandments given to Moses) would apply to atheists, agnostics, Buddhists, deists, and all others—not just to Jews, Christians, and Muslims. It is this view that inspires proselytizing and missionary work aimed at religious conversions.

5. But if morality is centered on one's will, then non-believers do not behave ethically because they refuse the guidance of God's will. Though they are subject to the moral commands; they cannot act morally. They may accidentally (or for non-religious reasons) act in a way that conforms to God's will, but without that intent. Even John Locke (1632–1704), in his progressive *Letter on Toleration*, urged the extension of tolerance toward believers in religions other than one's own—but not to atheists. Locke writes: "Those are not at all to be tolerated who deny the being of God. Promises, covenants, and oaths, which are the bonds of human society, can have no hold upon or sanctity for an atheist. The taking away of God, even if only in thought, dissolves all."[10] Atheists are moral renegades.

6. The will of God is supreme; it overrides all other considerations. Advocates recognize, of course, that there is a potential for apparent conflict between what God commands and conventional morality, the laws of the state, or rationality. Some seek to ease the tension by claiming that there is always a convergence of reason (God's gift to humans), good laws, and proper morality, with God's will. As a consequence, there would be no distinction between the morally wrong and the sinful. Nonetheless, this opens the door for conflicts with other authority, whether parental, medical, educational, or legal. The believer is obligated to refuse to comply with any law or practice that flouts God's will, which is "a higher law." Recently, this view has been argued by people who refuse to comply with same-sex marriage recognition or the requirement for employee medical coverage that includes birth control and abortion procedures. The controversy is sometimes framed as the conflict between "God's law" and "human law." Radical religious advocates prefer the state to be established as a theocracy, thereby precluding conflicts of authority. As the concept of the nation state took hold, the proper distinction between "church and state" and the separation of their domains became a preoccupation of many Enlightenment thinkers, such as Locke and George Berkeley (1685–1753).[11]

7. Divine Command Theory, in its normative dimension, is an example of a *deontological* ethical theory. **Deontology** (from *deon*, Greek for

"duty") is a type of ethical theory in which doing the right thing is a matter of doing one's duty. For deontologists, doing what is morally right is not about making people happy or relieving pain, but about fulfilling our moral obligations. It is the nature of the act itself, not its consequences, that gives moral value to the act. Conversely, an act is wrong if it violates our moral obligations and principles (whatever their source). Under Divine Command Theory, however, our moral duty is specifically to follow God's commands; acts that comply with those duties—like Abraham's—are morally right, without reference to their circumstances or consequences. If I took the view that Abraham was morally wrong and argued that we have an inviolable moral obligation never to take a human life except in self-defense, I would be expressing a deontological view of a different sort. Both views are deontological because of their reference to duties; but they differ in the source and content of our duties.

2.5 CRITIQUE OF DIVINE COMMAND THEORY

Of course, the Divine Command interpretation of morality will immediately be rejected by those who do not believe such a God exists. The theory requires not only the existence of a god, but only one God, one who meets specific requirements, such as having all perfections, having the capability of issuing "commands," and having concern for the individual and collective fates of human beings. Without such a God, the entire theory falls.[12] Arguments concerning the existence of God are beyond the scope of this book, but there are other serious objections to the theory that do not depend on denying the existence of an Abrahamic God.

A first caution concerns the identity of God. Though some believers, in an ecumenical spirit, affirm that all monotheistic religions pray to the same God, many reject that idea. In early 2016, officials at a Midwestern Christian college threatened to discipline its first tenured, black, female faculty member, Larycia Hawkins, because she wore a hijab in solidarity with Muslims. She also had posted online that Christians and Muslims worship the same God. This was not acceptable to the College's senior administrators. In the end, she and the college signed a separation agreement. Thus, despite common Abrahamic roots, many believers, especially evangelicals, believe that Christians and Muslims do not worship the same God. So, one might ask, which god is the true God, the one that issues the commands of morality?

A more probing critique is as ancient as Plato. In a dialogue named *Euthyphro*, Socrates asked whether the good is good because the gods approve of it; or whether the gods approve of it because it is good. Advocates of Divine Command Theory have often asserted that *whatever* God wills is good, because his command creates goodness. Thus, if God were to command murder, rape, or any other imaginable act, it would be morally good purely because it was his will. But if this were true, we would surely lose all stable sense of right and wrong, since such commands would violate our deepest moral intuitions. Just as "Because I say so!"—the parental retort that asserts authority over the child—refuses explanation or reason, this interpretation denies reason and is infantilizing. Another consequence of this view is that statements like "God is good" or "God's will is good" become empty tautologies; we might as well say, "God is God"—since there is no concept of goodness independent of God, the predicate "good" adds no information.

Others have asserted that God *could* not command such evils, because God is love, and this would be contrary to God's divine nature. But that seems to limit God's power, to contradict his omnipotence, since such actions are seen as *impossible* for him. Even the reference regarding God's nature, however, begins to pry open a conceptual distinction between goodness and God. That takes us to Plato's view: God *would* not do evil, though he is free to choose. And if God commands and acts as he does *because it is good*, then goodness may (and must) be conceived independently from godliness. Goodness and righteousness become a moral ideal or standard which God meets. We must then analyze moral ideals as conceptually independent from religion. "X is right" cannot then be *defined* as doing God's will, even if God always wills only what is right. We would still need to supply a separate account of the meaning of moral concepts like "right."[13]

Another important concern involves the problem of knowing what exactly God's will is. When Benjamin Franklin's lightning rods were first installed, some theologians denounced them because they deflected the lightning and thereby defied God's will. While some religious groups believe God wills us to relieve suffering; others reject medical interventions, such as the use of anesthetic or blood transfusions, as forbidden by God. Throughout history, religious groups have engaged is mass violence claiming it was God's will. Today, we witness fanatical believers announcing that their rapes, bombings, beheadings, and tortures are done in God's name (despite vehement rejection by mainstream religious authorities). Locke warned that "some have been very apt to pretend to revelation, and to persuade themselves that they are under the peculiar guidance of heaven in their actions and opinions, especially in those of them which they cannot account for by the ordinary methods of knowledge and the principles of reason."[14] Although many claim to know God's will, passionate assurance is not adequate evidence. The uncertainty can lead to either extreme: a defensive certitude about God's will or a skeptical denial that one can ever know the will of God. The former often reflects a fundamentalism that claims to honor the text but ironically ignores its critical history and its internal contradictions or inconsistencies. Since the sacred text is viewed as "timeless," it is presumed to speak to every era, even to people living in a world very different from the tribal context of the ancient Middle East and facing quite different problems and prospects.

The root of this problem of knowing God's will leads us to an important distinction: **objective** versus **subjective**. As I will use these terms, a moral judgment is **objective** if the evidence or basis for it is independent of the judge; if it is, in principle, open to scrutiny by others. A moral judgment is **subjective** if the relevant evidence or basis is private, dependent upon the judge, and not available to scrutiny by others. Note that this is quite different from the distinction between *universal* and *relative*. So, for example, the theory that "*X* is right" = "*X* is approved by my culture" is a theory that produces objective judgments, because what one's culture approves is a public matter, factually independent of any single judge, available to scrutiny by others.[15] Its judgments are also relative, because they will vary among cultures. In objective theories, one may be sincere but mistaken in one judgments. The difficulty for Divine Command Theory is that, although it seems to be objective, in the sense that the basis for moral judgments is publicly available in sacred texts and pronouncements by religious authorities, it is really subjective: it ultimately relies on individual interpretations of text, along with claims of private revelation in prayer. Morality becomes tied to the unpredictable mediation of one who "speaks with God" or "to whom God speaks." And its judgments are universal. Unfortunately, when a theory gives subjective judgments a universal validity, when any individual claims to know God's will and requires all others to accede to it, we risk the sort of moral aggrandizing that produces repressive and authoritarian cults, tyrants, and regimes.

Yet another line of criticism concerns the necessity of yielding to God's will. If we think of moral agents as beings who can act autonomously, of their own free will, and on the basis of reasons, then anyone who adopts Divine Command Theory forfeits their moral agency. The theory requires the moral agent to yield her will in deference to the will of God, to renounce her own desires and intentions, and to dispense with the need for reasoning. (This is, of course, the very aspect that Kierkegaard so values: "Only at the moment when his [Abraham's] act is in absolute contradiction to his feeling is his act a sacrifice."[16]) According to this line of criticism, absolute submission to the will of another being—even to God—relinquishes one's moral agency, abrogates one's reason and autonomy, and surrenders the very capacity for morality.[17] It is not possible to act morally when one's will is enslaved.

2.6 THE TWO FACES OF RELIGION

Regardless of the status of the Divine Command Theory, religion has been such a powerful force in the world, it is reasonable to assess its moral impact. To such a query, religion reveals two faces: one benevolent, one malevolent. Even a quick perusal of human history shows that religion has done much good and much harm. Which is greater is debatable.

Of great moral value are the ways in which religion has presented the world with moral exemplars: individuals who have performed inspiring acts of kindness, mercy, compassion, sacrifice, and courage. It privileges these and related virtues in moral education—by which, of course, is meant a religious education. The accounts of saints, martyrs, and heroes elevate our sense of what a moral life may be and enrich our moral imagination with possibilities for supererogation. While we may question the actions of some—Abraham, for example—we encounter these religious figures as people for whom the right and the good matter enormously.

Religions, especially the Abrahamic religions, offer a promise of judgment and justice for the life one has lived. The world we live in is not fair: the good often suffer and fail, while others luxuriate and succeed. But there is the hope, sustained by faith, that one's true worth is recognized and rewarded, at least ultimately, at least in an afterlife. This affirmation of an ultimate justice, this sense that the universe has a moral arc, sustains the moral life. It offers an answer to the question, *Why should I be moral?* Faith in God has helped untold numbers to accept a loss, to survive a crisis, to endure great burdens, and simply to make it through the night.

Even nonbelievers might recognize that religion has benefits to society in its promotion of morality. This line of reasoning, articulated during the Enlightenment and popular in the 1880s, goes like this: religious dogma may be suspect or nor longer credible, but organized religion offers important benefits to society, including the inculcation of a basic morality that has a transcendental authority. Keeping the moral order is a great social good—even if it relies on appeals to self-interest, such as a reward in Heaven or eternal torment in Hell; or on superstition and dubious belief, such as the occurrence of miracles or the providence of a Good God. Thus, religiosity should be promoted within society.

When advanced by non-believers, this sort of argument seems condescending and corrupting to me. In the first place, it is usually advocated by intellectuals as important for the unenlightened masses: *We are not believers, of course, but it is a good thing that others are, so let's promote religious membership.* Second, it advocates a belief one takes to be false. It is not a "vital" lie—something *I myself* believe because I need to believe it. Rather, like Plato's "Noble Lie," it is the deliberate promulgation of a falsehood, something *others* should believe, for social benefit. And third, either it violates that venerable principle of ethics, universalizability— the standard that any valid ethical principle applies to everyone—or it requires the advocate to believe something that she also believes to be false; or worse, to pretend to believe hypocritically.

Through vast networks of charity and support, organized religions have provided a social net to support the poor, the most alone, the infirm, and the sick and wounded; basic education for many; and enrichment activities for young and old. It is also true that religion has sustained and enhanced our cultures; religion has inspired great works of art, masterpieces of the visual arts, music, poetry, and architecture. One might, in a chary frame of mind, question examples of all these great positives; no doubt, many saints have feet of clay, some charities have ulterior motives, and many soaring spires are built from offerings of the poor. But it remains true that religion has a face of benevolence.

John Stuart Mill (1806–73), a nonreligious man, examined this "social benefit" argument in three essays, the central one called "The Utility of Religion." Mill thought the force of this argument was waning as society became more secular. He writes, "If religious belief be indeed so necessary to mankind, as we are continually assured that it is, there is great reason to lament, that the intellectual grounds of it should require to be backed by moral bribery or subornation of the understanding."[18] The power that religion has had to motivate good behavior arises, at least in part, from the human desire for a transcendent ideal that can sustain us. It would be better, he opined, if this ideal would be humanity as a whole, rather than a God.

There are, of course those who believe that religion has done more harm than good; that liberating morality from religion would be a genuine advancement. Those who think God is a delusion would of course rejoice, but the acerbic argument for religion's malevolence does not depend on atheism. The claim is historical: religion has done so much harm that it is reasonable to declare it a threat to morality.

It is true that a great deal of violence and oppression can be traced to religious zealotry and doctrinal differences. The Crusades, the many persecutions and genocide of Jews, the forced conversion of indigenous peoples by missionaries, "the Troubles" in Ireland, the conflicts between Sunni and Shia Muslims, the genocide of Yazidis and Christians by ISIL, and on and on through the centuries. The caustic remark made by Nobel Prize-winning physicist, Steven Weinberg, (b. 1933) too often seems true: "With or without religion, good people can behave well and bad people can do evil; but for good people to do evil—that takes religion."[19] One thinks of so many public figures killed by religious zealots: Hypatia by Christians, William of Orange by a Catholic, Mohandas Gandhi by a Hindu, Anwar Sadat by a Muslim, Yitzhak Rabin by a Jew, to name just a few. In addition to individual and mass violence, we must add the weight of oppression: all the religious acts that ban, censor, excommunicate, shun, denounce, repudiate, persecute, and execute. The targets are those who believe otherwise, those who are different, those who do something forbidden by doctrine.

The view that religion is a drug was famously advanced by Karl Marx (1818–83). His concern was not so much extremism and violence as it was a subtle but severe form of oppression: "Religion is the sigh of the oppressed creature, the heart of a heartless world, and the soul of soulless conditions. It is the opium of the people."[20] Religion comforts those who suffer, just as opium does, but it also produces "an illusory happiness" that prevents the masses from seeing their (economic) oppression clearly and rising against it.

In 1927, the British philosopher and logician, Bertrand Russell (1872–1970), delivered a talk he titled, "Why I Am Not a Christian." After discussing his negative views of God's existence and of the divinity of Jesus, he discussed his concerns with religion in general. Russell said:

> Religion is based, I think, primarily and mainly upon fear. It is partly
> the terror of the unknown and partly, as I have said, the wish to feel
> that you have a kind of elder brother who will stand by you in all
> your troubles and disputes. Fear is the basis of the whole thing—
> fear of the mysterious, fear of defeat, fear of death. Fear is the
> parent of cruelty, and therefore it is no wonder if cruelty and reli
> gion have gone hand in hand.[21]

Since the turn of the century, a spate of atheistic manifestoes has appeared; as a barrage against religion, they have been so influential that many bookstores have introduced a new section on atheism. While the authors are atheists, they attack religion from different but converging perspectives. In 2004, Sam Harris (b. 1967), a philosophical neuroscientist, authored *The End of Faith: Religion, Terror, and the Future of Reason*, in which he argued that religious faith is the greatest threat to contemporary civil society.[22] In 2006, in a book titled *The God Delusion*, evolutionary biologist Richard Dawkins (b. 1941), attacked the range of arguments for God's existence and reviewed the harm that acting in God's name has done—and continues to do.[23] Surprisingly for an evolutionary theorist, Dawkins never adequately considers why religion has persisted among humans for millennia if it has no survival advantage. But in that same year, the secularist philosopher and cognitive scientist Daniel Dennett (b. 1942), produced *Breaking the Spell: Religion as a Natural Phenomenon.*[24] Dennett calls for the scientific examination of religion, for the study of the survival value—if any—of religious belief. The "spell" Dennett wants to break is the notion that religion itself is "sacred" and should not be subject to investigation. Harris had explicitly argued that point as well: given the enormously negative impact of religion on public life, it should not be off limits for examination and critique. Harris and Dennett do recognize the beneficent aspects of religious faith, but Harris would replace religion with "spirituality." Christopher Hitchens (1949–2011), a journalist, essayist, and provocateur, released *God Is Not Great: How Religion Poisons Everything* in 2007.[25] His is an unrelenting recital of the history of religious extremism, violence, and oppression. Hitchens argues that these negatives are not simply a function of anomalous religious excesses: they are embedded in the sacred texts and thus imbued even in mainstream religious faith.

Moreover, it is not only atheists who are concerned about the harm done by religion. In a 2008 book titled *The Religious Case Against Belief*, James Carse (b. 1932) argues that organized religions have abandoned their grounding in religious experience, becoming instead "territories of belief."[26] Defining one's religion in terms of a specific belief-system creates a believer/non-believer dichotomy, discourages open-mindedness, creates a hyper-concern for heresy, and leads to a psychology of denial when reality conflicts. If this is accurate, religion discourages the deliberation, the pursuit of reflective equilibrium, the attention to reasoning that ethics requires.

2.7 ETHICS WITHOUT GOD

"God is dead. God remains dead. And we have killed him. How shall we comfort ourselves, the murderers of all murderers?"[27] So pronounced Friedrich Nietzsche (1844–1900). His claim is that God or religion or the supernatural can no longer be a credible source for morality. The ethical foundations of the past, especially those of traditional Christian ethics, have crumbled under the weight of human progress. For most of history, the meaning and value of our lives have been imported from outside the natural world; they have been bestowed upon us. God the Creator established the world order, crafted humans in his image, and steered the direction of history and our individual fates. The advances of civilization have eroded this dependency: the scientific method and the resulting growth of knowledge; the rise of the secular nation state; individualism and its component values of autonomy and freedom. Religion persists, but only as hollow rituals without vitality. Nietzsche prophesied: "God is Dead; but given the way of men, there may still be caves for thousands of years in which his shadow will be shown. And we—we still have to vanquish his shadow, too."[28] This is our collective passage from a protective juvenescence to a mature and heroic adulthood.

We are now alone, and our loneliness is terrifying. There is a sense of overwhelming loss: without God, the universe has no purpose; history has no plot; nothing is *meant to be*. Our existence is accidental, our lives without a discoverable meaning. The ground of morality has vanished, so there are no valid moral prohibitions. This reaction is expressed by Ivan in *The Brothers Karamazov*: "Without God and the future life? It means everything is permitted now, one can do anything?"[29] The result may be a sense of rootlessness, absurdity, *angst*, futility.

It is a fair, if broad, generalization that philosophy has spent a few centuries now pursuing an adequate response: *How are we to proceed without God?* That predicament has accelerated the turn to other sources for moral meaning.

Nonetheless, even for those who remain faithful believers, there is reason to ground ethics in something other than God's will. We have noted the confusing conflicts of religious authority, the irrelevance of ancient tribal texts to many contemporary ethical problems, along with the conceptual reasons for an independent conception of morality. Moreover, we—at least those in liberal democracies—live in pluralistic societies and ought to have reasons that can be shared with one another and that don't depend on premises unique to our faith.

The great Prussian philosopher, Immanuel Kant (1724–1804), a principal figure of modern philosophy, addressed these issues as a central concern. Greatly influenced by his Pietistic religious upbringing (Pietism being a movement to refocus Lutheran practice on simple piety), Kant could not reject the existence of God. But he also knew that virtue (righteousness) and happiness often do not coincide in this world. Yet virtue is what makes a person *worthy* of happiness. If the universe is just, he concluded, if we are to be assured that those who deserve happiness will ultimately achieve it, we must presume an afterlife of the soul. Kant writes:

> Therefore, morals is not really the doctrine of how to make ourselves happy but of how we are to be *worthy* of happiness. Only if religion is added to it can the hope arise of someday participating in happiness in proportion as we endeavored not to be unworthy of it....
>
> [The postulate of immortality] derives from the practically necessary condition of a duration adequate to the perfect fulfillment of the moral law.[30]

Despite this invocation of religion, Kant made a rather dramatic move. In 1793, he wrote a tract called *Religion within the Limits of Reason Alone*, in which he affirmed that, indeed, many moral concepts, and the authority of morality itself, culminate in a God who is Good. But Kant believes that morality is a practical aspect of rationality; to be moral is to be rational and *vice versa*. He does not derive morality from religion; he derives religion from morality. (Kant's moral philosophy will be the primary subject of Chapter 7.) Thus, in the end, Kant's morality has its grounding in Reason; it ultimately stands independent from religion.

Most philosophers since Kant have agreed that moral philosophy should be separate from theology; that ethics must be grounded in something other than religion. Religion—at least many religions, and especially the Abrahamic religions—divide believers from non-believers. This creates a tension between these divisions and the hope of a morality that speaks to all, that can resolve conflicts rather than provoke them. Finding such a broader basis for morality is our task ahead.

QUESTIONS FOR DISCUSSION

1 Why do you think so much violence over the centuries has been done "in the name of God"—whether Allah, Jesus, or Yahweh?

2 Is it unfair to judge religions by the beliefs and actions of their zealots? Is it unfair to evaluate the Divine Command Theory on the basis of ancient examples and extreme cases like that of Abraham and Isaac? What should be the basis for evaluation?

3 The historian of religions, Martin Marty (b. 1928) has argued that the important religious conflict of the modern world is not between one religion and another; it is between fundamentalism (in all

religions) and more modernist and ecumenical forms. What are the implications of this claim for ethics?

4   What might Mill mean when he says that the argument that we need religion for its social usefulness in promoting moral conduct is "backed by moral bribery or subornation of the understanding"? How would you respond?

5   Explain these two distinctions: objective vs. subjective, and universal vs. relative.

6   There have been numerous cases recently in which religious believers have refused to serve those with a non-heterosexual orientation—refusing to sell wedding cakes, to approve marriage licenses, to find real estate, etc.—in defiance of the law. They believe they are doing God's will. When should such claims for exemption on religious grounds be honored? Is this a moral issue or simply a legal issue?

QUESTIONS FOR PERSONAL REFLECTION

1   Have you had an experience that made you question your belief as to God's existence (or non-existence)?

2   Do you think that "without God, everything is permitted"? Why or why not?

SUGGESTED SOURCES

Austin, Michael. "Divine Command Theory," *Internet Encyclopedia of Philosophy*: http://www.iep.utm.edu/divine-c/ (accessed April 2016).

Declaration Toward a Global Ethic, Parliament of the World's Religions, September 4, 1993. Available at: http://www.urbandharma.org/pdf/ethic.pdf (accessed April 2016).

Mill, John Stuart. "The Utility of Religion" in *The Collected Works of John Stuart Mill*, Vol. X: *Essays on Ethics, Religion and Society*; ed. J.M. Robson (Toronto: U of Toronto P, 1969).

Quinn, Philip L. *Divine Commands and Moral Requirements* (Oxford: Oxford UP, 1978).

Wainwright, William J. *Religion and Morality* (New York: Routledge, 2005).

Zagzebski, Linda Trinkaus. *Divine Motivation Theory* (Cambridge: Cambridge UP, 2004).

NOTES

1   The statistics on world religions in this paragraph are drawn from "The Future of World Religions: Population Growth Projections, 2010–2050," a report of the Pew Research Center. It is available on the Pew Forum website: http://www.pewforum.org/2015/04/02/religious-projections-2010-2050/ (accessed July 2018). Approximate extrapolations have been made from the 2010 figures.

2   *Declaration Toward a Global Ethic*, Parliament of the World's Religions, September 4, 1993. Available at: http://www.urbandharma.org/pdf/ethic.pdf (accessed July 2018).

3   For a critical discussion of the origins of morality, see Richard Joyce, *The Evolution of Morality* (Cambridge, MA: MIT P, 2007).

4   The global influence of the Abrahamic religions is shown, ironically, in the fact that the 1993 Parliament of the World's Religions expressed its unity in a "declaration" of ethical principles. The draft of the document was, in fact, prepared by Hans Küng, a Catholic priest and Swiss theologian.

5   Saint Augustine, *The City of God*; translated by Marcus Dods (New York: Modern Library, 1950), I.21 (pg. 27).

6   Thomas Aquinas, *Summa Theologiae. Prima Secundae* trans. Fr. Laurence Shapcote (Lander, WY: The Aquinas Institute for the Study of Sacred Doctrine, 2012), I–II, q.100, a.8, ad 3; p. 299.

7   *The Holy Qur'an*, Part 1, Section 16, 130–31.

8   William of Ockham, *Quodlibetal Questions: Quodlibets 1–7*; translated by Alfred J. Freddoso and Francis E. Kelley (New Haven, CT: Yale UP, new edition, 1998), Third Quodlibet, Q4, pp. 211–14.

9   Søren Kierkegaard, *Fear and Trembling* and *The Sickness Unto Death*; translated by Walter Lowrie (New York: Doubleday Anchor, 1954), 30–37.

10 John Locke, *A Letter Concerning Toleration*; edited by Kerry Walters (Peterborough, ON: Broadview P, 2013), 81.

11 Ibid.; and George Berkeley, *Passive Obedience, or the Christian Doctrine of Not Resisting the Supreme Power*, 2nd ed., available at: https://quod.lib.umich.edu/e/ecco/004899015.0001.000/1:1?hi=0;rgn=div1;view=fulltext;q1=Passive+Obedience.

12 Or perhaps it could be seen as version of an Error Theory, in which, although the Divine Command Theory is valid, there is no God or no God who gives commands.

13 For a recent book that attempts to resolve this problem, in part by moving from divine commands to divine motives, see: Linda Trinkaus Zagzebski, *Divine Motivation Theory* (Cambridge: Cambridge UP, 2004).

14 John Locke, *An Essay Concerning Human Understanding* (Kitchener, ON: Batoche Books, 2001), 584.

15 In this interpretation, the speaker carries the judgment of right and wrong from the home culture to all others. One could alter the definition to read, *"X is right"* = "X is approved by the culture in which X occurs." In this case, it may be a different culture from one's home culture. Both interpretations are objective, since the approval or disapproval is available for all to test empirically.

16 Kierkegaard, *op. cit.*, 84.

17 This point has led to controversy—even to the claim by James Rachels that it disproves the existence of God. For a review of this controversy and a modest proposal for reconciling Divine Command Theory with moral agency, see Chan Coulter, "Moral Autonomy and Divine Commands," *Religious Studies*, 25; 117–29.

18 John Stuart Mill, *Collected Works of John Stuart Mill*, Vol. X: *Essays on Ethics, Religion and Society*; ed. J.M. Robson (Toronto: U of Toronto P, 1969), 404. Originally published posthumously (1874) in J.S. Mill, *Three Essays on Religion: Nature, The Utility of Religion, and Theism*.

19 Steven Weinberg, "A Designer Universe?," *The New York Review of Books*, October 21, 1999; available at: http://www.nybooks.com/articles/1999/10/21/a-designer-universe/ (accessed July 2018). This sentiment preexisted Weinberg's utterance. In my undergraduate class notes from many years earlier is this: "It is not difficult to get good people to do good things. It is easy to get bad people to do bad things. But if you want to get a lot of good people to do bad things, it requires religion."

20 Karl Marx, *Critique of Hegel's* Philosophy of Right; translated by Annette Jolin and Joseph O'Malley (1844, unpublished; Cambridge: Cambridge UP, 1971), 1–2.

21 Bertrand Russell, *Why I Am Not a Christian and Other Essays on Religion and Related Subjects*; ed. Paul Edwards (1957; New York: Simon & Schuster, 1967), 22.

22 Sam Harris, *The End of Faith: Religion, Terror, and the Future of Reason* (New York: W.W. Norton, 2004).

23 Richard Dawkins, *The God Delusion* (New York: Houghton Mifflin Harcourt, 2006).

24 Daniel Dennett, *Breaking the Spell: Religion as a Natural Phenomenon* (New York: Viking, 2006).

25 Christopher Hitchens, *God Is Not Great: How Religion Poisons Everything* (New York: Twelve, 2007).

26 James P. Carse, *The Religious Case Against Belief* (New York: Penguin, 2009).

27 Friedrich Nietzsche, *The Gay Science*, tr. Walter Kaufmann (New York: Vintage Books, 1974), Section 125, p. 181.

28 Ibid., Section 108.

29 Fyodor Dostoevsky, *The Brothers Karamazov*, trans. Richard Pevear and Larissa Volokhonsky (San Francisco: North Point P, 1990), 589.

30 Immanuel Kant, *Critique of Practical Reason*, trans. Lewis White Beck (Indianapolis, IN: Bobbs-Merrill, 1956), 134, 137.

CHAPTER THREE

Relativism

Shafilea Ahmed, a 17-year-old student who planned a career in law, disappeared from her home in Warrington, England in September 2003. Five months later, her dismembered corpse was found in the River Kent. The murder investigation gradually revealed her plight.

Earlier in 2003, on a trip with parents to their native Pakistan, Shafilea had swallowed bleach. It was an apparent suicide attempt, though her father claimed it was a mistake made during a power outage. But she had refused treatment for the injury. She had written an emotional poem titled "I Feel Trapped." She had been reported missing twice previously, and had been found with friends. Interviews with her friends suggested that "Shafi" had been arguing with her parents about an arranged marriage.

Six years later—long after the coroner's report, the inquest, and an inconclusive investigation—Shafilea's younger sister contrived to be arrested; in custody, she told police that her parents, Iftikhar and Farzana Ahmed, had killed her sister by suffocating her. It seems she had adamantly refused to accept the arranged marriage to a much older man; the intense pressure from her parents had driven her to despair. For them, her refusal and rejection of the intended husband would bring great dishonor to the family; and the deliberate damage to her throat had so weakened her that she was no longer desired as a bride. An honor killing was the solution.

At their trial, Justice Roderick Evans said: "You chose to bring up your family in Warrington, but although you lived in Warrington, your social and cultural attitudes were those of rural Pakistan and it was those you imposed on your children." He added, "She was being squeezed between two cultures: the culture and the way of life she saw around her and wanted to embrace, and that they wanted to impose upon her." Both parents were sentenced to life in prison.[1]

3.1 FORMS OF RELATIVISM

"Squeezed between two cultures"—Judge Evans's description implies a well-known truth: different cultures often have different customs or mores. While some variations concern the merely customary, such as traditional clothing or the color appropriate for funerals; others may constitute conflicts in what practices are seen as morally right and wrong, which acts are obligatory and forbidden. Anthropologists have provided vivid accounts of exotic moral practices from across the globe; along with historians, they have often done the same regarding cultures of the past. From their work, we have learned just how wide this variation is, including approved practices such as polygamy, slavery, abandonment of infants, pederasty, cannibalism, modification of the human body, ritual sacrifice, and the eating of creatures we find disgusting or that we embrace as pets. In her classic work, *Patterns of Culture*, pioneering anthropologist Ruth Benedict (1887–1948) declared that great cultural diversity is evident even in moral matters where we might well expect human beings to agree.

> We might suppose that in the matter of taking life all peoples would agree on condemnation. On the contrary, in the matter of homicide, it may be held that one kills by custom his two children, or that a husband has a right of life and death over his wife or that it is the duty of the child to kill his parents before they are old. It may be the case that those are killed who steal fowl, or who cut their upper teeth first, or who are born on Wednesday. Among some peoples, a person suffers torment at having caused an accidental death, among others, it is a matter of no consequence. Suicide may also be a light matter, the recourse of anyone who has suffered some slight rebuff, an act that constantly occurs in a tribe. It may be the highest and noblest act a wise man can perform. The very tale of it, on the other hand, may be a matter for incredulous mirth, and the act itself, impossible to conceive as human possibility. Or it may be a crime punishable by law, or regarded as a sin against the gods.[2]

Few would deny that moral judgment and ethical practices do in fact differ from one culture to another—despite the affirmation of shared values by religious groups (in the previous chapter). These differences are both temporal and geographic: they are matters of both time and place. No doubt, the culture of ancient Greece differed markedly from the culture of Greece today, which in turn differs from the culture of, say, distant Bhutan.

Differences among people, especially differences in perception, opinion, judgment, practices, and forms of life, lead us to *relativism*. In its most general and abstract form, **Relativism** is the doctrine that a particular property, and therefore correct judgments about that property, vary in relation to something else. Fashion is a relativistic concept, for example, because what is fashionable varies in relation to time and place. This doctrine stands in contrast to **Universalism**, which asserts that the property is the same in all times and places. (The concepts of relative and universal judgments introduced earlier are the foundation of these doctrines.) The ethical theory we will now examine is called **cultural relativism**, because it asserts that morality is relative to culture.[3]

But now we come to a crucial distinction: relativism may be descriptive or normative. What historical and anthropological studies have shown us is that moral practices and judgments about what is right and wrong in fact vary in relation to time and culture. But that form of moral cultural relativism is *descriptive* only; it details actual differences in conduct and judgment. As such, these are facts about the world. There is a contrasting form of cultural relativism that is *normative*: it is the doctrine that what is *genuinely* right and wrong—not what people believe and do—varies in relation to culture. It is this normative form that is of interest in moral philosophy.

It is easy to imagine this distinction being invoked by advocates of Divine Command Theory, for example. They might acknowledge that cultures differ in their moral beliefs, but affirm nonetheless that there is a genuinely correct view, which is to adhere to God's commands, using their particular interpretation. Cultures which have different views are simply misguided and morally wrong or sinful, they might say.

The theory that most concerns us in this chapter, however, not only acknowledges the fact that cultures differ, but distinctively claims that *the genuinely correct, normative doctrine* is that morality is relative to culture. (Where needed for clarity, I may use the term *moral cultural relativism* as a reminder that we are discussing this normative form; but in most contexts, the focus on morality is obvious and I will simply refer to *cultural relativism*.)

3.2 MORAL CULTURAL RELATIVISM

Cultural relativism is not the only form of moral relativism, as we shall see; but we will focus on it because of its predominance in the social sciences, and much of the analysis would apply to other variations that may arise. In stark form, moral cultural relativism claims:

"*X* is right" = "*X* is approved of by one's culture"; and

"*X* is wrong" = "*X* is disapproved of by one's culture."

Also:

"*X* is good" = "*X* is valued by one's culture"; and

"*X* is bad" = "*X* is disvalued by one's culture."

The notion of "approval" and "disapproval" here refer to affirmation (and rejection) within the moral sphere of one's culture. Thus, right and wrong, good, and bad, the permissible and the forbidden are all determined by one's own culture—or by "my culture," where the "my" refers to whoever is making the judgment or claim.[4]

The first implication of this theory (as with all forms of moral relativism) is that there is no absolute or universal standard of right or wrong to which one may appeal. Culture creates and defines morality; there is no morality that transcends culture. There is no culturally-independent way in which one might define "*X* is right." The moral judgments of my culture have no force in a different culture—and *vice versa*. Second, it is essential to know one's cultural identity if one is to avoid moral confusion. Third, the same act or practice may be morally right or wrong depending on time and culture. So, slavery may have been morally acceptable in ancient Greece, but it is not in contemporary democracies; forced marriages may be morally acceptable in some cultures, such as rural Pakistan, but not in Warrington, England, today. To reiterate: this means that for moral cultural relativism, the same practice can be *genuinely* right *and* wrong, not just thought to be so.

Yet moral cultural relativism is an objective theory: what a culture approves is a public matter; it can be determined by empirical research: ethnographic studies, surveys and polls, and studies of morally-grounded laws are among the sources one might consult. Thus, a person who claims that a certain practice is approved of in a specific society makes a claim that is either true or false. Someone who is sincere in her moral judgment could nevertheless be wrong—even about her own culture. But although an individual or a group may be mistaken, the collective population of a society cannot be wrong.

There are many factors that contribute to the attractiveness of cultural relativism. The first is that the facts of cultural diversity *are* impressive. True, we cannot simply argue that because cultures differ, they must all be morally correct. But given such variety, it is surely a prejudice to believe that one's native culture owns morality, and all other societies are simply wrong. Perhaps in the days when cultures were isolated and travel was difficult, it was natural to believe that one's own morality was a universal morality. In today's global society, however, anyone who travels widely or even reads broadly encounters societies that seem quite content with moral standards different from the homeland's. Among this profusion, there seems to be no neutral and universal way of determining which cultures are morally correct.

Second, an open-minded person wants to avoid *ethnocentrism*, the judging of other cultures by the customs and standards of one's own. One who acknowledges the moral equality of cultures shows respect for difference. Moreover, it often seems that the meaning of an act or a practice is understandable only within the context of its particular culture. (This view was articulated by one of the founders of anthropology, Franz Boas (1858–1942); it became a guiding principle of the field.) Relativism seems to promote *tolerance* and *understanding* in cultural interactions. These attitudes are so important, because intolerance and misunderstanding often lead to repression, conflict, and violence between cultures. Those who are skilled at conflict resolution, negotiation, and peace-making know how fundamental is the first step of giving each party a seat—an equal status—at the table. And the equal moral status of cultures is a fundamental claim of cultural relativism.

In addition, the theory seems initially plausible because our moral values are undeniably shaped by the culture in which we live. We imbibe the values of our society from infancy; even the terms in which we come to think about morality are culture-bound. Cultures are not just givens; they are formative in the shaping of moral agents and the ethical systems in which they think and act. It is questionable whether one could transcend one's culture, even if one earnestly wanted to and tried fervently to do so.

Shedding the absolutism and arrogance that we often associate with claims to a universal standard, relativism still offers an objective reference point, a ground for morality. Psychologically, this places responsibility for moral judgments not on individuals, but on an abstract function of a large group: culture. The individual need only conform to cultural norms. Yet it also urges personal sensitivity to cultural context when making moral judgments of others.

3.3 CRITIQUE OF CULTURAL RELATIVISM

Despite the attractions of cultural relativism, it has serious flaws. These include both conceptual difficulties and problems that arise in its application. It is even possible to challenge the descriptive moral diversity thesis which undergirds the theory. Let us survey these issues, beginning with the problematic key phrase: "one's culture."

(1) The first problem is *the ambiguity of "culture."* Cultural relativism seems to visualize a world in which tribal cultures are simple, homogeneous, and relatively distinct or isolated from each other. "One's culture" is the tribe within which one grew up and lived in adulthood. This does not describe the contemporary world. Today, cultures exist within and across nation states. Nation states are unifying political forces for their

citizenry, but they can remain culturally divided or multicultural: divisions may occur between urban and rural, between liberal and conservative religious groups, between socio-economic classes, between immigrants and residential groups, and between racial, ethnic, linguistic, and heritage groups. *Which culture is my culture?* Canada has certainly felt the cultural divisions among French-speaking Quebecois, the Inuit and Métis, the many First Nations (aboriginal groups), immigrants, and English-speaking others. In the United States, for example, the culture of Utah is certainly different from that of New York City. The point is that such divisions can represent moral differences, disparities in the approval or disapproval of certain practices. The natural move is to look to what the majority believes, what the dominant value of the culture is. Yet an American who wishes to know whether abortion is right or wrong will find that there is great division within the culture—many approve or at least find it permissible under certain circumstances, while many others disapprove under any circumstance. In such a case, where a culture is split over a morally significant issue, cultural relativism leaves us with no helpful answer.

Moreover, in a complex society, cultures are "nested": one person holds membership in a set of expanding spheres of culture. A single individual may be a member of Wall Street financial culture, the New York City culture, the Chinese-American culture, the culture of the United States, and the culture of a major world religion. The values and ethical judgments of these cultures are likely to differ in important ways. *Which culture's judgments are the morally relevant ones under cultural relativism?*[5]

In developed nations, many subcultures thrive within a single pluralistic culture: the Amish and ultra-Orthodox Jews, for example, live according to their respective lights as distinct subcultures within American culture. But what about cults? Are they morally relevant cultures? Consider two examples. Jim Jones was the leader of "The People's Temple," a cult formed in Indiana that launched an agricultural commune with socialist beliefs in Jonestown, Guyana. Under Jones's direction, 909 American members of the cult committed suicide by drinking cyanide on November 18, 1978. David Koresh believed himself to be the last prophet of the Branch Davidians; in his fortified commune in Waco, Texas, he gathered 80 men, women, and children. He practiced polygamy, including "spiritual marriages" involving forced sexual acts with underage girls. In a controversial move, federal authorities raided the commune, resulting in the deaths of four agents and six cult members. Koresh bargained for time to complete his religious writings, while the federal authorities treated the matter as a hostage crisis. *Can a charismatic leader establish not only a religious cult but a (moral) culture?*

There is a special problem, of course, for those who grow up in a bicultural family. *Intersectionality* is the term used to describe the interconnecting and overlapping identities one might have—for example, in being a Black, Jewish, gay man. The thrust of these complications is that cultural relativism is ambiguous and incomplete—at least in its basic and standard form. It lacks determinacy in specifying which culture is morally definitive. Our multicultural world is, in fact, problematic for cultural relativism, and further precision in specifying which is "one's own culture" seems somewhat arbitrary and will not remove the remaining problems.

(2) Even with further clarification, the theory presents *problems for travelers, refugees, and immigrants.* The old saying, "When in Rome, do as the Romans do," is easy advice, aimed no doubt at diplomatic politeness and respect. It seems to advocate temporarily replacing the practices of one's own culture with those of one's current location. But such encountered differences may be more than matters of custom: the local culture may violate one's own ethical principles and moral values. *How does one prioritize or integrate one's home culture and the local culture? Which culture was Shafilea Ahmed's culture?*

A professional woman from North America who must travel today to Saudi Arabia today will find that she cannot shop, eat in most restaurants, or even enter the country without a male escort. Saudi women are pressured to wear an *abaya* (an ankle-length, long-sleeved garment, preferably black). Those who stay with a Saudi family may not leave the country without the permission of the male head of household. Movie theaters and alcoholic beverages are prohibited. Until recently, females weren't permitted even to ride a bicycle, but as of 2018, women became eligible for automobile driver's licenses. Gender separation requires separate lines, counters, and eating areas in fast-food outlets.[6] In 2008, an American living in Riyadh with her husband and children sat in Starbuck's with a male business partner, drinking coffee in the "family section," which is the only section in which men and women may sit together. She was arrested and, she claimed, strip-searched and forced to sign false confessions. The local authorities were adamant: The Commission for the Promotion of Virtue and the Prevention of Vice publicly said her actions violated the country's Shariah law. "It's not allowed for any woman to travel alone and sit with a strange man and talk and laugh and drink coffee together like they are married," it said. It also accused her of wearing makeup, not covering her hair, and of "moving around suspiciously" while sitting with her colleague. Though her husband strongly defended her innocence, they soon needed to relocate for their own safety.[7] Male guardianship is a basic ethical principle: a female must be accompanied by her *mahram*, a male chaperone, usually an older relative. In 2006, when a Saudi teenager reported she had been gang-raped, she was punished with a sentence of ninety lashes—more than her rapists received—because she had been in a car without a *mahram* when she was assaulted.[8]

On the other hand, a Saudi woman traveling in North America might well be appalled at the gratuitous display of the female body in advertising, at the harassment and sexual assault that women face in many workplace environments, and the disrespect for women this conveys. She might find shameful the attitude toward old age and the treatment of the elderly. She might be disgusted by the preoccupation with celebrity and pop culture icons, and by the crude discourse and commercialism of public life. She might be astounded at the numbers of people we incarcerate in various types of prisons. She might be baffled by our love of guns and the rate of gun violence. She would likely be anxious at the bigoted treatment many Muslims have received in the West, especially in the United States. Today, she might well be mistrusted or mistreated by customs or immigration officers, or even be insulted or harangued by bystanders.

How much of one's own culture—one's own moral commitments—should one retain regardless of local culture? Seasoned travelers expect different practices in exotic locations, and it is usually possible to tolerate them for short stays. Refugees and immigrants have a more difficult time: whether by choice or not, their stay is likely permanent. They can easily become, as the judge said, "squeezed between two cultures."

This problematic fact of cultural mobility, along with the first problem of multiculturalism and divided cultures has prompted the literary scholar Stephen Greenblatt (b. 1943) to issue a "manifesto," urging the establishment of "Mobility Studies." Indeed, he thinks these issues have been part of human life long before our Information Age society. He observes, "There is no going back to the fantasy that once upon a time there were settled, coherent, and perfectly integrated national or ethnic communities." It would be unwise to adopt a theory that assumed this fantasy to be true. Yet, "At the same time we need to account for the persistence, over very long time periods and in the face of radical disruption, of cultural identities for which substantial numbers of people are willing to make extreme sacrifices, including life itself."[9] This tension between actual communities and cultural identities suggests great difficulty in attaching the meaning and justification of morality to cultures.

(3) The theory has *a problem with theoretical coherence*, because it contains a paradox that has a baffling practical impact. It seems that the cultural relativist must accept ethical universalism as equally valid for

those cultures that advocate it in some form. The practical impact is that we must, it appears, tolerate the intolerant.

Imagine two interacting cultures that differ severely in their normative judgments: Culture A, which holds a relativist ethic and views the morality of other cultures as equally valid for its members; and Culture B, which holds a universalist ethic, believing that only its own moral view is correct for all cultures everywhere. Members of Culture B may disapprove of Culture A; they may send moral missionaries to convert those in A to B's beliefs; if they are aggressive, they may colonize or seek to destroy A's culture. Culture B might be a racist culture, a terrorizing culture of religious fanaticism, or a culture that embraces slavery, sexism, homophobia, or cannibalism. It appears that the relativists of Culture A must accept all of this as morally valid, since they recognize no transcultural principle that would restrain B. If it came to warfare, Culture A's self-defense could be characterized merely as a defense against an equally justified cause.

Attempting to escape the paradox of tolerating the intolerant would only create a meta-paradox: treating relativism as a universalism. Suppose the advocate says: "Of course, relativism prescribes relativism, not universalism; tolerance advocates tolerance in others, not aggression." But that is to prescribe relativism for everyone, for all cultures: it is the universalist claim that anyone advocating universalism is wrong. There is a meta-paradox in claiming that relativism is a universalist principle. Thus, under either view—whether one claims relativism is right for my culture (but not necessarily for another culture), or one claims it is right for everyone in all cultures—one encounters threats to theoretical coherence.

(4) A general concern that follows from the above three is this: *cultural relativism offers no way to resolve cultural differences and conflicts.* How, besides violence, could Culture A and Culture B resolve their severe differences? It is true that an integration and unification of previously divergent cultures would resolve their conflicts, but this takes a long time and usually requires enormous patience in the face of residual conflict and injustice. Moreover, there is no moral basis for the relativist to advocate such mergers. Perhaps they reject resolution and simply avoid contact because of their moral hostility.

(5) Cultural relativism seems unable to absorb the internal dynamism of societies; *it cannot accommodate or motivate moral reform.* Western societies once accepted dueling as an honorable method of settling disputes between gentlemen, denied women suffrage, burned witches, enslaved Africans, displaced and devastated indigenous peoples, exploited child labor, and denied basic civil rights to many, including the LGBTQ population. These practices were "approved of" by our past cultures. Those who

then advocated change—the reformers, the suffragettes, the abolition-ists, the civil rights activists—were in the minority, and so, according to cultural relativism, *they were in the wrong.* They persisted in their "wrong-ness," which would seem to deepen their immorality; however, they grew in numbers and influence, successfully translating their moral judgments into the protection of the law. We normally consider those who sustain a fight for moral reform to be among our most admirable people—not as advo-cates who urged others to adopt a wrong-headed belief. Once a majority was reached, according to cultural relativism (Voila!), *they suddenly were in the right!* But this transformation is very odd: the person whose added support shifted the balance of approval above fifty per cent changed the morality polarity from wrong to right!

Moreover, cultural relativism offers no support for reforming one's society. The Saudi women who risk their lives to protest social restrictions and advance women's rights simply do not have the sanction of morality—worse, they are immoral, violating the morality of their culture. The utter rejection of the effort at moral reform (until it is culturally embraced) is a serious defect. We might put the metaethical question this way: *Isn't what is morally right and wrong more stable than the latest poll?* Normatively speaking, *Are we wrong until we get a majority to agree with us? Don't we want to credit moral reformers with being pioneers in discerning the right—not just morally lucky in holding views that prevailed?*

(6) Finally, it is unclear how someone who holds moral cultural relativ-ism can distinguish the merely customary from the moral. The customary and the moral both prescribe practices, and—according to the Cultural Relativist—both are created and defined by culture. On what basis could the two be distinguished *using only factors internal to the culture*? Why are capital punishment and gender separation moral matters and not simply customs? While the lines that describe the moral sphere may vary by culture—the eating of dog meat may be considered merely customary in one culture and a moral matter in another—the identification of the moral usually implies features that are transcultural.[10] Yet, for Shafilea's Pakistani parents, an arranged marriage was more than customary; it was a deeply moral issue. But breaking with custom and engaging in immorality are normally different; it is not merely that the latter is likely a more serious offense. They have different sorts of sanctions; punishment has differ-ent justifications. In short, while custom is clearly grounded in culture, morality seems to point beyond the traditions of culture.

For all of these reasons, cultural relativism has not been in favor among philosophers, and that has remained the case over the years despite many attempted replies by relativists to these concerns.

3.4 SUBJECTIVISM

There is yet an additional concern: the difficulties involved in individuating cultures tend to produce a cascade of ever finer-grained, like-minded subcultures, risking a slide down the slippery slope to **subjectivism**. Subjectivism features the smallest "group" of all: the individual. It is the theory that affirms:

"X is right" = "X is approved of by me."

"Me" is whoever is making a moral judgment. Technically, this is *individual relativism*, yet because what someone sincerely approves is not objectively verifiable by others, the theory is subjective. We might imagine several variations of subjectivism, hinging on the interpretation of "approval." The phrase "approved by me" might refer to my thoughts, beliefs, emotions, or feelings about X. But in all these variations, the implication is that the rightness of X is not about X at all; it is about me. One's "approval" (as variously interpreted) defines its rightness. As long as one is sincere, one cannot be morally mistaken.

The theory does not mean that "what is approved of by *me*" applies to *all other* individuals. That would be a monomaniacal version of giving oneself an exceptional moral status! The theory means "what is approved of by me is right *for me*" and "what is approved of by you is right *for you*," and, by implication therefore, "what is approved of by *anyone* is right *for that person*." This explication reveals an odd sort of egalitarianism: each person creates morality, but only for him- or herself. Subjectivism resolves the problem of cultural individuation by giving up the attempt to identify one's culture. Indeed, it ignores the influence of culture on the determination of what is right and wrong, privileging instead the narrowest and unique identity: individuality.

Except for avoiding the problems associated with the concept of culture, subjectivism inherits and, in some cases, magnifies all the other problems associated with cultural relativism. For example, it exacerbates the problems of conflicting beliefs and tolerating the intolerant—since individuals are greater in number and diversity and brush against each other exponentially more frequently than cultures do. It offers no guidance or interest in resolving conflicts. It also provides no motivation for moral education or self-improvement. Changing one's mind is fine, but one stance is as good as another.

In truth, subjectivism ultimately represents the abandonment of the enterprise of moral philosophy. Reason, deliberation, consistency, universalizability—none of these matter, because anyone's and every-one's moral views are correct as long as they are sincere and honest with themselves. Subjectivism endorses the absurd conclusion that our most inspiring moral figures and our icons of evil held equally valid moral views. Gandhi and Hitler are equally correct in their moral visions and judg-ments—and no one has ever accused either of being insincere.

Subjectivism is thus the most extreme version and the dead-end of relativism. Avoiding this slippery slope is an important task for moral relativism in any form, and especially for cultural relativism.

3.5 THE CASE OF AN HONOR KILLING

Given the strong and normally affectionate bonds between parents and their children, the moral obligation to kill one's child must surely require a strong sanction, one that overrides all other moral concerns. Abraham thought his obligation was created by a command from God. The parents of Shafilea Ahmed apparently thought they were obligated by their cultural mores—though in actuality they never admitted their guilt. Her tragic case displays many of the critical issues with cultural relativism.

The problem of cultural identification looms large in this case. Let us assume that arranged marriages are common in Pakistan and even stan-dard practice in its rural areas. Assume also that, in the rural areas, a breach of such an arrangement, a refusal to marry, dishonors the family. Further, assume that an honor killing is considered the obligatory response to such dishonor. Pakistan is changing, of course, and these practices are not condoned in more urban, sophisticated areas, so we also need to presume that we can identify "rural Pakistan" as a viable culture. If we make all these assumptions, then such honor killings would be morally justified according to a relativism of culture. Shafilea's parents were simply doing what is right, fulfilling their moral obligations, in murdering their daughter—according to their home culture.

But of course, they lived in England. Shafilea was born in England and grew up there, though she was reared in a Pakistani home that prized its heritage culture. At least in some significant ways—such as marriage—Shafilea identified as British, as a member of a Western democracy. She rejected the institution of arranged marriages and all that follows from it. She clearly imagined a different, autonomous status for herself as a woman. Her family culture—her parents' culture—was not the culture with which she identified. At least, not fully.

About 55 per cent of the marriages in the world today are arranged unions in which two consenting adults are linked as a couple by a third party. They have a low divorce rate—globally, it is just 6 per cent. But *arranged* marriages are to be distinguished from *forced* marriages, in which one or both parties are married against their will. The United Nations claims forced marriage affects 15 million girls around the globe each year.[11] Refusals of marriage may precipitate honor killings. Force, coercion, and deception are usually involved, and in some cultures the bride may be selected by outright abduction, kidnapped off the street. In the Kyrgyz Republic, it is estimated, about one in three married women became a bride against their will through "bride kidnapping." They were forced to marry a man whom they often did not know, someone who abducted them, often violently.[12] Although these practices are considered sex crimes under the law in most countries, they occur on all continents; they are "traditional," however, in Central Asia, where the legal prohibitions and punishments are seldom enforced.

In any event, Shafilea Ahmed was killed in England, not Central Asia. The fact that her parents hid and denied their deed, forced family members to keep silent about it, and dismembered and sank her corpse, certainly suggests that they knew well they were doing something disapproved by the culture in which they lived as immigrants, the culture in which they had *chosen* to live.

Immigrants and first-generation children have a difficult time moving from one moral system to another. Cultural relativism endorses both cultures, even if one is repressive. In "tolerating the intolerant," we often find that intolerance involves the denial of equal status to women, certain races, and to homosexuals and transgendered people. This has led many— even anthropologists who elevate the equal status of cultures—to assert a principle of basic human rights as transcendent and universal. (We will discuss this view in the next chapter.) From this perspective, Shafilea was deprived of her right to make fundamental decisions that affect her future, to seek a mate of mutual choice, ultimately of her right to life. In murdering their daughter, therefore, her parents did something wrong in any culture—whatever rural Pakistanis may believe. But this assertion of human rights as the universal ground of acceptable cultural practices is essentially an abandonment of cultural relativism: it stakes the claim that morality is independent of culture.

On the one hand, cultural diversity like biological diversity makes the world a richer place. The preservation of threatened cultures can be a noble enterprise, on par with saving endangered species. On the other hand, the clash of cultures can destroy lives and oppress whole populations.

From a moral perspective, how much assimilation to their new culture should one demand of immigrants? What sorts of practices from the old country should immigrants be encouraged to retain? Does voluntary immigration entail acceptance of the moral values of the adopted culture?

One might argue that my account has been unfairly stacked against relativism. To open the discussion with such an outrageous practice of a non-Western culture immediately arouses antipathy and the need to defend ourselves against "barbarism." The account thus has focused on situations of extreme, even violent conflict, whereas cultural conflicts about the most fundamental moral values are rare. In the last chapter, I spoke of the surprising ways in which divergent religions converge regarding moral values; here, that point seems abandoned, as I have focused on deep differences. I would reply that no one has exclusive rights to the charge of "barbarism." Others may find some of the West's practices as "barbaric" as Westerners find theirs. But many of today's most pressing conflicts do derive from cultural differences regarding moral matters; that immigration and displacement raise acute concerns; that these problems have no solution from standard forms of relativism; and that violence is all too often the result.

3.6 RELATIVISM AND PLURALISM

Despite the criticisms of cultural relativism, its deepest concerns do reso-nate with aspects of contemporary life. We live in a postcolonial age that rejects and responds to the legacies of *imperialism*, the imposition of the values of colonizing cultures upon indigenous cultures. At the same time, an ascendant intercultural dynamic has raised ethical concern regarding *cultural appropriation*, the eager adoption and exploitation of aspects of one culture by another, more dominant culture. Instead of colonizing a native culture by asserting political control, global corporate powers simply take its music, clothing, art, and artifacts, turning them into fashionable commodities for the marketplace. Add to these two movements a third: *globalization*. Among the many meanings of this term—digital intercon-nectedness, a global marketplace, a focus on global problems, the rise of transnational agencies, and so on—there is the controversial notion that we are inexorably evolving a single, dominant culture. Various cultures use the same technology, the same media, hear the same music, see the same movies, and use versions of the same products. Major international cities look more and more alike, hosting the same retail stores and hotels. Cross-cultural marriages increase; more children are multicultural. The result is a gradual, global, cultural integration. For many, this process threatens existing cultures that should be preserved and undermines the value of cultural diversity; it foreshadows a rootless, bland, uncultured life of global consumerism. For others, it is the emergence of a cosmopolitan culture that unites humanity. These three trends may reveal our deep concern for the status of distinct cultures; yet they also suggest the need for our moral practices to have a transcultural, transnational foundation.

Alongside the resonance of "culture," there is the resonance of "relativism." The American philosopher Richard Rorty (1931–2007) described our contemporary plight as one of irony: we are committed to the values and judgments of our culture, our community; but we also know full well that our community and our place in it are contingent. Had we been born in a different community, we would have acquired its values and judgments. We must hold both insights simultaneously. But it is culture in which we act; the language of our culture in which we describe our actions; the institutions of culture in which we frame moral meanings. This tension is expressed in an attitude of irony. Living in a world without God, we know that "finite, mortal, contingently existing human beings might derive the meanings of their lives from [nothing] except other finite, mortal, contingently existing human beings."[13]

There is another phenomenon that leads us to relativism. David B. Wong (b. 1949) has called this phenomenon *moral ambivalence*. He writes:

> We see that reasonable and knowledgeable people could have made different judgments than we are inclined to make about ... [moral] conflicts, and any prior convictions we might have had about the superiority of our judgments get shaken. Moral ambivalence is the phenomenon of coming to understand and appreciate the other side's viewpoint to the extent that our sense of the unique rightness of our own judgments gets destabilized. In other words, the most discomforting kind of moral disagreement is not simply one in which both sides run out of reasons that are persuasive to the other but is also a disagreement in which coming to the other side brings along an appreciation of *its* reasons.[14]

Perhaps you have had this experience with religion: you grow up within a particular religious tradition, absorbing its doctrines and rituals, and other religions and maybe even their sacred structures seem uncomfortably alien. But as you get older and learn about other religions, perhaps through close friends, perhaps attending weddings or funerals or worship services, you learn something of their doctrines and experience their rituals—and despite the difference, you come to appreciate their way, or to see some beauty in their practice. Wong allows that there are universal constraints on adequate moral systems, but these are rather loose, he believes, and allow for diverse views within an acceptable range. Among these are constraints that arise from a common human nature. Richard Rorty also proposed general constraints on moral communities: the rejection of cruelty, for instance, and the relief of suffering.

These reflections lead us away from a stark and simple moral relativism toward *moral pluralism*. Cultural relativism grounds morality in culture, and defines "goodness" (and other moral terms) in relation to one's culture. Moral pluralism is the view that there is more than one "correct" morality; that morality cannot be captured by any one universal or absolute morality. Pluralists need not, however, accept every culture's moral system, or even identify moral systems with cultures; rather, they impose certain tests or filters which any acceptable moral system must pass. They would separate the values that must be shared from those that can vary. These required filters are grounded in something other than culture itself. Abjuring cruelty might be one such test. Respecting human rights might be another: a pluralist would then tolerate any moral systems that respect certain basic human rights.

Nonetheless, the move to a filtered pluralism would require moral constraints that are universal, that apply to each and every culture's system of morality. David Wong terms his version a "nuanced relativism" or "pluralistic relativism." In such an account, the acceptable range of diversity may be very wide, but "adequate" moral systems would need to endorse the same essential moral core. Not needing to justify a comprehensive, universal moral system admittedly would make the task simpler, but it would still require a universal grounding. (Wong proposes this grounding is found in aspects of human nature—an issue for Chapter 4.)

One last point—and it is a consideration that bears on the possibility of a universal moral core. I said earlier that it might even be possible to challenge the *descriptive* thesis of moral diversity. Though the facts about moral differences, the sort that Ruth Benedict recited, are impressive, we should be cautious about the meaning of such differences. If we probe an exotic practice, even one that seems bizarre, we may discover that the difference is more a matter of non-moral beliefs than of moral values. Consider the case of the Toraja people of Indonesia, who have elaborate funeral practices, including a ritual called Ma'Nene that takes place each year in August: they exhume the bodies of fellow villagers, especially those that died away from home; they retrieve those stored in "the house of the dead"; the corpses are cleaned and groomed, dressed

CHAPTER THREE: RELATIVISM 57

in new clothes, and ceremonially walked home and paraded around the village.[15] We likely find this a macabre desecration of human bodies; but the Toraja understand it as an act of deep respect and homecoming. These seem to be vast moral differences. Notice, however, that although we and the Toraja have conflicting beliefs—different beliefs about death and the proper treatment of dead bodies—we seem to share the deeper moral value that our family and friends deserve respect and should be honored, even in death.

I have noted that core moral values seem to be more convergent than religious beliefs and practices; they may be more convergent than cultural practices. American anthropologist Donald Brown (b. 1934) compiled a list of hundreds of "human universals"—features of culture and human psyche for which there are no known exceptions.[16] Mourning the dead is one such universal. We value life and grieve the loss of those who are close to us, though our grieving practices vary widely.

My point is that we need both to appreciate and to study our differences. There are many ways, various levels of thought, in which differences can mask similarity—and *vice versa*. When we encounter judgments and practices that are strikingly different, careful attention and dialogue may reveal that this difference is rooted in different beliefs about the world; we may approach the moral sphere with different facts. Differences in non-moral beliefs may be resolved differently—or at least debated differently—from differences in moral values.

QUESTIONS FOR DISCUSSION

1 What accommodations to their adopted culture should immigrants be required to make?

2 What is the best way to determine whether a culture finds a practice morally right, permissible, or wrong? Use as examples such practices as abortion or euthanasia.

3 Are the practices of Saudi Arabia described above matters of custom or matters of morality? Explain your reasoning.

4 Science fiction is a genre that abounds with plots that involve complex relations between cultures, usually human and alien cultures. Usually, the humans operate under ethical imperatives. The Star Trek series, for example, has explorer crews that operate under the "Prime Directive" of non-interference. The books in the Enders series by Orson Scott Card describe the interactions between humans and various aliens; in The Speaker for the Dead,

the "xenologists" work with the Porquinhos (the "Piggies") and struggle with the imperative of non-interference issued by the Starways Congress. Why does it become so difficult in such encounters to comply with an ethic of non-interference?

5 When, if ever, do you believe we would be morally obligated to intervene in another culture in order to discourage, prevent, or prohibit a practice which is approved by that culture? (Intervention might be through "educational programs," incentives, diplomacy, or military action.) How would you justify such an intervention?

6 If you were to adopt ethical pluralism, what filters or tests would you require of any morally acceptable culture? Suppose a critic claims that these constraints only represent your own cultural biases. How would you respond?

QUESTIONS FOR PERSONAL REFLECTION

1 You might wonder why Shafilea did not report her situation to the British authorities. Discuss her situation, and for background, read and this article by Emily Dugan in the *Independent* for July 16, 2015, on forced marriages in Britain: http://www.independent.co.uk/news/uk/crime/forced-marriage-how-hundreds-of-terrified-british-victims-of-the-tradition-are-being-failed-every-10394985.html.

2 What are your "nested cultures"? In your own life, which ones are more influential in guiding your decisions?

3 Is Rorty correct? Do you hold strong moral commitments of your own, but also know full well that, had you been born elsewhere, you would have believed something else just as strongly? Does this tension undermine the strength of your own commitments? What attitude do you think it promotes—irony, amorality, tolerance, uncertainty, confusion?

SUGGESTED SOURCES

Appiah, Kwame Anthony. *The Ethics of Identity* (Princeton: Princeton UP, 2005).

Audi, Robert. *Moral Value and Human Diversity* (Oxford: Oxford UP, 2007).

Benedict, Ruth. "A Defense of Moral Relativism," *The Journal of General Psychology*, 10 (1934): 59–82.

Hampshire, Stuart. *Morality and Conflict* (Cambridge, MA: Harvard UP, 1983).

Locke, John. *A Letter Concerning Toleration*, ed., Kerry Walters (Peterborough, ON: Broadview P, 2013).

Wong, David B. *Natural Moralities: A Defense of Pluralistic Relativism* (Oxford: Oxford UP, 2006).

——. "Pluralism and Ambivalence." In M. Krausz, ed., *Relativism: A Contemporary Anthology* (New York: Columbia UP, 2010).

NOTES

1 The case and quotations from Mr. Justice Roderick Evans reported in *The Guardian*, "Shafilea Ahmed's parents jailed for her murder," August 3, 2012; available at: http://www.theguardian.com/uk/2012/aug/03/shafilea-ahmed-parents-guilty-murder (accessed April 2016).

2 Ruth Benedict, *Patterns of Culture* (1934; New York: Houghton-Mifflin, 2005), 45–46.

3 Confusingly, forms of relativism are named in two different ways. (1) Relativism may take its name from the particular property that is being characterized: So *aesthetic relativism* refers to the view that beauty and related terms are relative concepts; *ethical relativism* refers to the view that ethical judgments and practices are relative. But, of course, one may ask, "Relative to what?" (2) To answer that question, relativism may also be named by the domain in relation to which the property varies. Thus, *cultural relativism* indicates the view that something, perhaps ideas of beauty or moral judgments, varies according to culture. To be precise in reference, one needs both names—though the context often makes the first obvious. To be precise, therefore, we have been speaking of *moral cultural relativism*: morality varies in relation to culture.

4 We could replace "culture" with "society" and call the theory Social Relativism. If one distinguishes between culture and society, this would be a different, but related theory. We could also vary this formulation as "X is right" = "X is approved by the culture in which the act occurred" with divergent results.

5 A related problem concerns the giving of moral advice to someone from a different culture: should one advise according to one's own moral beliefs or in terms of the advisee's culture?

6 Pressure from activist Saudi women and from the international community has grown, and with the additional incentive of economic factors, a new Crown Prince has begun to introduce reforms that may modify some of these policies. The situation is developing at this writing, but resistance and reversals are also possible.

7   For this incident, see: http://abcnews.go.com/International/
    story?id=4261213.

8   Donna Abu-Nasr, "Rape Case Roils Saudi Legal System,"
    Washington Post, November 21, 2006. Available at: http://
    www.washingtonpost.com/wp-dyn/content/article/2006/11/21/
    AR2006112100967.html (accessed April 2016).

9   Stephen Greenblatt, "Cultural Mobility: An Introduction," in *Cultural
    Mobility: A Manifesto*, eds. Stephen Greenblatt and Ines Županov
    (Cambridge: Cambridge UP, 2010), 2.

10 One could claim that this distinction between custom and morality
    is itself a cultural artifact of Western Culture; but, regardless, the
    problem of defining the boundary of the moral sphere exists for all
    cultures.

11 "Ending Child Marriage: Progress and Prospects," UNICEF, 2014;
    available at: http://www.unicef.org/media/files/Child_Marriage_
    Report_7_17_LR..pdf (accessed May 2016).

12 See the astonishing report, "My Husband Kidnapped Me," by
    Daniel Burgui Iguzkiza; available at: http://www.dburgui.com/01/
    noviasKG_ENG.html (accessed May 2016).

13 Richard Rorty, *Contingency, Irony, and Solidarity* (Cambridge:
    Cambridge UP, 1989); quotation from p. 8. The original has a doubly
    negative usage, which I have altered by my insertion.

14 David B. Wong, *Natural Moralities* (Oxford: Oxford UP, 2006), 5.

15 For an account of Toraja rituals, see "The Toraja people and
    the most complex funeral rituals in the world," *Ancient Origins*,
    January 24, 2014; available at: http://www.ancient-origins.net/
    ancient-places-asia/toraja-people-and-most-complex-funeral-
    rituals-world-001268?nopaging=1#sthash.MzUZtc9P.dpuf (accessed
    April 2016).

16 Donald Brown, *Human Universals* (New York: McGraw-Hill, 1991).
    A summary of the list is available at: https://condor.depaul.edu/
    mfiddler/hyphen/humunivers.htm (accessed April 2016).

CHAPTER FOUR
Moral Naturalism

In the 1980s, Canadian businessman Winston Blackmore became the leader of a small settlement in British Columbia that embraced plural marriages. Claiming the community was organized on the original principles of Mormonism, Blackmore used the title, "Bishop of the Fundamentalist Church of Jesus Christ of Latter Day Saints."[1] He named the settlement "Bountiful." He and his community lived up to its name: by 2014, Blackmore had at least 24 wives and fathered over 130 children.

After a long and complex series of legal battles, a direct criminal charge of polygamy was brought in 2011. Blackmore's attorney argued that the ban on polygamy was an unconstitutional infringement of his right to religious freedom and an imposition of Christian values.

A professor of law, testifying for the prosecution, stated that polygamy has been defined as a crime in the Western cultures for centuries because it has been considered "unnatural and dangerous." He noted that from Roman times polygamy has often been seen as a crime as serious as rape and incest. Because it has been viewed as harmful to those who practice it and to society, both religious and secular laws in the West have consistently prohibited polygamy and promoted monogamy.

In a 355-page ruling, Chief Justice Robert Bauman of the Supreme Court of British Columbia stated that, although the ban against polygamy does infringe on the right to religious freedom, it is justified as a reasonable limitation intended to prevent harm to women, children, and society at large. Blackmore appealed the ruling and was denied; in 2014, additional criminal charges were filed. In 2018, Blackmore was given a conditional sentence for six months to be served in the community and 12 months' probation.

4.1 THE NATURAL AND THE GOOD

Moral naturalism is the doctrine that there is a moral order embedded in the natural world; thus, what is good is determined by nature; and thus, what is good for humans is established by the facts of human nature. This often includes the idea that morality is directed to the fulfillment of our nature, the perfection of the sort of creature we are—a view known as moral **perfectionism**. Just as what is good for the roses is whatever helps the roses thrive, so goodness for humans is whatever is conducive to our flourishing.

In schematic form, moral naturalism asserts:

"X is good" = "X is in accord with human nature"; and

"X is right" = "X is directed toward the perfection of human nature."

Of course, variant readings of just what is "in accord with human nature" permit strikingly different normative judgments, not only about what is natural and good, but also about what is unnatural and bad—such as fathering over 130 children with 24 wives.

These elements of naturalism produced **Natural Law Theory**, which holds that moral principles and proper laws are prescribed by Nature and may be discerned by an application of right reason. Laws enacted by humans may be good or bad, and that evaluation is made by testing them against natural law. The Natural Law tradition is traceable to Classical Greek thought, but it was later adopted by Christianity with the supplementary view that Nature is God's handiwork; to find God's will, we need only read his creation. In the eighteenth century an important claim was added: human beings have **natural rights** that are grounded in human nature (moral rights that should be protected by law). For theistic thinkers, natural rights are God-given ("endowed by their Creator"); for secular thinkers, they are simply an inherent aspect of the dignity of humanity.

There is yet another strain of moral naturalism: it is the broad affirmation of the goodness of Nature. Nature not only reveals moral goodness; it embodies the good. This is best understood in contrast with the view that the physical world contains nothing of ultimate worth; or that it is only a vale of tears and a distraction from true goodness; or that Nature is indifferent, a silent universe in which moral value is absent, or at best must be constructed. A contemporary version of this affirmative approach is an ecological ethic in which the natural order is the source of value. Moral worth therefore transcends the human species; it is the preciousness of our biosphere that yields our special human moral obligations.

Part of the attractiveness of moral naturalism from all these angles is that it proffers an objective, rational, and universal ethic that is grounded in the natural order. Grounding our morality in a common human nature would avoid the divisions and conflicts entailed by Divine Command Theory or cultural relativism. In addition, naturalism gives us a view of morality as inherent, correlated with basic but distinctive human capacities, not alien or imposed from without. Moreover, all moral theories make assumptions about human nature; naturalism brings these more sharply into focus and sets them front and center.

To better understand these forms of moral naturalism, let's look to some of their most prominent exponents—first, ancient and medieval; then, contemporary. All are thinkers whose views are rich and complex; necessarily brief summaries will allow me only to highlight illustrative aspects of their naturalistic theories. Following these, I will turn to the unfolding of implications and critique.

4.2 PRE-MODERN ADVOCATES OF NATURALISM

Epicurus (341–270 BCE) developed the clearest early version of moral naturalism. In his *Letter to Menoeceus*, he identifies the good with pleasure: "We call pleasure the alpha and omega of a blessed life. Pleasure is our first and kindred good. It is the starting-point of every choice and of every aversion, and to it we come back, inasmuch as we make feeling the rule by which to judge of every good thing."[2] The view that pleasure is the good is called **hedonism**. But one can easily be misled about Epicurus' doctrine by taking this single affirmation out of context. Epicurus quickly adds:

> And since pleasure is our first and native good, for that reason we do not choose every pleasure whatsoever, but ofttimes pass over many pleasures when a greater annoyance ensues from them. And ofttimes we consider pains superior to pleasures when submission to the pains for a long time brings us as a consequence a greater pleasure. While therefore all pleasure because it is naturally akin to us is good, not all pleasure is choice-worthy, just as all pain is an evil and yet not all pain is to be shunned....

> When we say, then, that pleasure is the end and aim, we do not mean the pleasures of the prodigal or the pleasures of sensuality, as we are understood to do by some through ignorance, prejudice, or willful misrepresentation. By pleasure we mean the absence of pain in the body and of trouble in the soul.[3]

Ultimately, for Epicurus, the good is a type of serenity of mind and body, a secure tranquility that the Greeks called *ataraxia*. Through prudential reason, one could vanquish or at least limit life's two great sources of pain: fear, especially of the gods and of death, and the needy pain of desire. Note that Epicurus claims that pleasure is good because it is "naturally akin to us." Note also that Epicurus acknowledged that we have natural desires like thirst and hunger that must be met to sustain life; we also have natural desires that aren't really life-or-death matters and can be controlled, such as sexual desire. His concern, however, was with unnatural, and hence unnecessary, desires. He spoke of desiring fine wine and gourmet food as examples.[4] These examples still apply in our day, but we might also think of unnecessary desires for all the various products that are marketed to us every day. We face a whole industry—advertising—devoted to *creating* desires for products that are, in his sense, unnecessary. Every desire we acquire is a superfluous need for gratification, a recurring and painful wait for satisfaction. Epicurus enjoined us to eliminate all such unnatural desires and live a simpler, gentler, more serene life. He established a kind of gated community—"the Garden"—in which he and his followers could live a tranquil, pleasant life. While never preponderant, Epicurean communities developed all around the ancient Mediterranean, and his philosophy attracted devotees for centuries.

At about the same time, across the globe, the Chinese philosopher Mengzi (371–289 BCE), known in the West as Mencius, also advocated moral naturalism. He wrote:

> What I mean by saying [human nature] is good is that there is that in our nature [xing] which is spontaneously part of us and can become good. The fact that we can become bad is not a defect in our natural endowment. All men possess a sense of commiseration; all men possess a sense of shame; all men possess a sense of respect; all men possess a sense of right and wrong. The sense of commiseration is the seed of humanity; the sense of shame is the seed of righteousness; the sense of respect is the seed of ritual; the sense of right and wrong is the seed of wisdom. Thus humanity, righteousness, ritual, and wisdom are not welded to us from outside. We possess them inherently; it is simply that we do not focus our minds on them.[5]

Mencius refers to a human potential and propensity that is part of our natural endowment, not to an inevitable or necessary state. Poor upbringing, negative influences, weakness of will, bad luck, dire life circumstances— these and other negativities can prevent us from flourishing, from our best life.

The Natural Law tradition took shape in the Greek debate that centered on the contrast between nature (*physis*) and culture (*nomos*), and their respective roles in human affairs. It is prominent in the works of Aristotle (384–322 BCE). The great philosopher wrote landmark treatises on every field known in his day and even invented a couple of fields himself (such as logic)—an accomplishment never to be equaled. He saw the world as a biologist might: a wondrous place of intricate order, full of marvelous living things that experience cycles of birth, development, and death. Everything in the cosmos has a ***telos***, a purpose or fulfillment toward which it naturally moves or develops; this approach is called *teleological* (from the Greek *telos*, meaning "end, purpose, or goal"). For living things, the ***telos*** is a healthy and mature flourishing. For an acorn, it is a sturdy, spreading oak. Culture—crafted tools, institutions, aesthetic objects, and forms of government, and many other things—have imposed, artificial, purposes. But every type of natural object possesses an inherent norm discernible by observation and rational analysis. It is clear, for example, that the natural *telos* of a chicken egg is to become a healthy, full-grown chicken—not to become my omelet, a purpose which I may impose upon it.

For Aristotle, like Mencius, ethics is the study of the means for perfecting our nature, the path to fulfill our distinctive *telos*, which is the highest human good. He fully acknowledges our animality, the demands and potentials of our bodies and our brains, but he focuses on what is distinctively human: our ability to reason. It is this capacity for reasoning that is our special feature and the key to our *telos*. Put succinctly, Aristotle finds that the highest human good is not pleasure or wealth or fame, but the wise use of our reasoning. We actualize our highest potential when we achieve wisdom in practical matters (making decisions, reaching judgments) and, even more, in theoretical matters (contemplating the workings of the cosmos). The term he uses for this human *telos* is **eudaimonia**, which is often translated as "happiness." It is better understood, however, as *fully-human flourishing*. There will be more to say about Aristotle (see Chapter 9), but here the relevant point is that he infers his normative ethics from an analysis of human nature. And our nature is continuous with biological and physical nature; it is in harmony with the inchoate aspirations of everything in the cosmos.

The concept of natural law was given its classic formulation by Marcus Tullius Cicero (106–43 BCE), a Roman lawyer and philosopher. He proclaimed:

> The law is right reason in agreement with nature: it is of universal application, unchanging and everlasting: it summons to duty by its commands and averts from wrongdoing by its prohibitions ... And there will not be different laws at Rome and at Athens, or different laws now and in the future, but one eternal and unchangeable law will be valid for all nations and all times, and there will be one master and ruler, that is, God, over us all, for he is the author of this law, its promulgator, and its enforcing judge. Whoever is disobedient is fleeing from himself and denying his human nature, and by reason of this very fact he will suffer the worst penalties, even if he escapes what is commonly considered punishment....[6]

Centuries later, this philosophy was adapted to Christianity by Thomas Aquinas, the Italian priest and theologian. Although an advocate of Divine Command Theory (Chapter 2), Aquinas also became the foremost exponent of *natural theology*, which claims that truths about God may be derived from observations of nature, his creation. In Aquinas's Christian interpretation, that which Aristotle had viewed as inherent human nature became God-given; our natural *telos* became God's purpose for us. But this is moral naturalism nonetheless, since it looks not simply to revelation or sacred textual authority, but to Nature. Good and evil may be derived from the rational nature of human beings. Aquinas declares:

> Since, however, good has the nature of an end, and evil, the nature of a contrary, hence it is that all those things to which man has a natural inclination, are naturally apprehended by reason as being good, and consequently as objects of pursuit, and their contraries as evil, and objects of avoidance. Wherefore according to the order of natural inclinations, is the order of the precepts of the natural law.[7]

For Aquinas, the natural basis of morality also determines the fundamental principles of jurisprudence and the law. Governments may adopt bad laws, but we should know them to be bad because they contradict natural law.

From these five exemplars, we can identify three basic principles of moral naturalism: (1) A permanent, moral order exists within the natural; therefore, moral values are real and objective elements of human nature. (2) Human beings share a common nature, and morality involves the perfecting of certain inherent human characteristics, which requires obedience to natural law. (3) Reason is the distinctive capacity of human nature and gives us the ability to discern the good.

4.3 CONTEMPORARY ADVOCATES OF NATURALISM

The contemporary intellectual world includes many forms and subtle variations of moral naturalism. Natural Law Theory remains dominant in Roman Catholic theology and in the work of philosophers influenced by Catholic doctrine. For example, Alasdair MacIntyre (b. 1929), whose work in moral theory is rich and influential, has worked to revive a form of Aristotelian ethics centered on virtues. These virtues, as he argues in *Dependent Rational Animals*, are grounded in our biology. We are rational *animals*, he asserts, and we must accept the conditions that represent our continuity with other animals. In particular, MacIntyre emphasizes our vulnerability and our dependence on others as generating moral virtues.[8]

Indeed, many ethicists who combine a focus on virtues or traits of character and adopt a naturalistic and perfectionist stance do so without making teleological assumptions about the cosmos. This means that, in their view, one need not assume a transcendent purpose to value the perfection of innate human potential. Philippa Foot (1920–2010) and Rosalind Hursthouse (b. 1973) both draw on the concept of *natural goodness*.[9] They note that a healthy or flourishing state is relative to the type of organism a creature is; it requires the effective interaction of all the parts of the organism, and of the organism with its environment. We may learn from simple observation when a plant or animal is thriving and what conditions assist or disable that healthy state. Clearly, for animals, it involves experiences of pleasure, freedom from pain, the exercise of capabilities natural to the organism, and, for social animals, positive contributions to its group. These form a ground from which morality can arise.

Another version of ethical naturalism is found in the provocative account given by sociobiologist E.O. Wilson in his Pulitzer Prize-winning book, *On Human Nature*:

> The first dilemma, in a word, is that we have no particular place to go. The species lacks any goal external to its own biological nature....

> The danger implicit in the first dilemma is the rapid dissolution of transcendental goals toward which societies can organize their energies....

> The second dilemma ... is the choice that must be made among the ethical premises inherent in man's biological nature.

Note that Wilson affirms human (biological) nature as the only source of morality. But our biological nature includes conflicting tendencies and so gives ambiguous guidance. We must choose: thus "Human nature is not just the array of outcomes attained in existing societies. It is also the potential array that might be achieved through conscious design by future societies."[10]

4.4 IMPLICATIONS AND CRITICISMS OF NATURALISM AND NATURAL LAW

Critics of moral naturalism and natural law theory have been quite thorough. My plan is to examine challenges to the foundations of the theory in this section; later sections will include additional criticisms. I may sometimes suggest a line of response; and I will merely note here that, interestingly, some of the criticisms contradict each other.

1. *Classic moral naturalism presumes that there is purposefulness in nature*, that the cosmos is teleological, moving toward specific normative ends or goods. It is a view generally rejected by contemporary science, which is mechanistic, using cause-effect mechanisms and chance events to explain natural processes. The universe has no *telos*, no inherent and intentional goal. This has been orthodoxy since the seventeenth century when the giants of the Age of Science—Galileo Galilei (1564–1642), René Descartes (1598–1650), Robert Boyle (1627–91), and others—rejected the long-dominant Aristotelian worldview. Incompatibility with scientific assumptions explains much of why moral naturalism, especially natural law, has been seen as a discarded theory, and why many contemporary advocates do not invoke teleology. But it is difficult to reject teleology and yet retain moral naturalism; the hazard is that one is either left with sophisticated *descriptive* accounts only, not norms or moral laws; or, one has smuggled in a normative teleology without announcement. Given evolutionary biology, when we say that "the moth has camouflage coloring in order to hide from predators," we know we are using a shorthand expression. No moth had this intention; it is not a feature developed *on purpose*. It is the result of random variation and selection based on natural advantage. The appearance of intricate teleology is the result of millions of accidents.

There are, however, a few notable philosophers who refuse to explain away the striking purposiveness of living things: Thomas Nagel (b. 1937), for example, has subtitled a recent book, *Why the Materialist Neo-Darwinian Conception of Nature Is Almost Certainly False*. He does not endorse either the view that the universe is intelligently designed or the straightforward teleology of Aristotle, but he argues that the inability of science to explain the origin of life with physical and chemical laws, along with its inability to explain consciousness and intention as a property of matter, "suggest that principles of a different kind are also at work in the history of nature, principles of the growth of order that are in their logical form teleological rather than mechanistic."[11]

2. *There is, in fact, no human nature*—or so goes the criticism. What is needed to make a robust moral naturalism goes beyond shared membership in the same biological species by genotype; it requires that all human beings possess a common cluster of distinctive capacities, a shared set of purposes, and innate valuing of the same intrinsic goods. But that is just what we do *not* possess, according to many philosophers, psychologists, and social scientists.

The American philosopher Richard Rorty—he who advised an ironic outlook concerning moral values (Chapter 3)—asserted, "There is nothing deep inside each of us, no common human nature, no built-in human solidarity to use a moral reference point. There is nothing to people except what has been socialized into them."[12] He did, however, allow that we share the ability to feel pain—but then, so do all other animals. Evolutionary psychologists would point out that we humans share other genetically-enabled features and capacities as well: sensory systems, emotionality and certain basic emotional responses, a brain with a large prefrontal cortex that permits planning and symbolic reasoning, among others. And Donald Brown's list of cultural universals (Chapter 3) also seems to imply a common core of human experience. Whether these are sufficient for the requisite concept of human nature is debatable. Nonetheless, there are currently many thinkers who believe that substantive, normative ethical principles can be derived from preferences and responses that are hardwired in the human brain.[13]

3. *Those who advocate moral naturalism necessarily elevate certain aspects of human nature they find positive and reject those they find negative.* It may be part of human nature to be jealous, aggressive, or spiteful, for example, but moralists discount those traits or seek to repress them. Epicurus, for example, finds pleasure to be intrinsically good, and he values reason because it is of practical use in achieving the pure and mild pleasures he sought. But it also means that some natural human tendencies or capacities—the tendency to seek immediate gratification or the capacity to lie, for example—may be harmful or evil despite their naturalness. A normative concept or criterion must then be employed to select which natural capacities are relevant. Mencius was quite explicit about this in the passage quoted above. Aristotle saw two natural vices for every virtue; he also claimed that if moral virtues were not internalized through practice by a certain age, they could never be achieved. If we humans are both naturally selfish and naturally compassionate, on what basis do we decide it is morally right to elevate the latter and suppress the former? This careful picking of natural traits, many of which are identified as potentials to be perfected, suggests that some moral standard other than human nature is being used to make the choices. Perhaps this selective approach masks what is actually cultural or subjective as natural.

4. *What is natural is a given, a starting point; it does not dictate the normative.* One important capacity of humanity is that we may respond to what is natural in many ways. Our intellect, our experience, and our civilization may inform our considered choices. This seems to be Wilson's point

in wanting us to confront fateful choices about which genetic traits to nurture in our society. Even if jealousy is natural, as evolutionary biologists claim, we can choose whether to cultivate or suppress that emotion and the behavior that often accompanies it. In the classic film, *The African Queen*, there is this interchange between the prim young woman, Rose Sayer, and the gin-guzzling captain of the *Queen*, Charlie Allnut:

> *Charlie Allnut*: "What are you being so mean for, Miss? A man takes a drop too much once in a while, it's only human nature."
>
> *Rose Sayer*: "Nature, Mr. Allnut, is what we are put in this world to rise above."

When we decide to "rise above" our nature, we employ some independent basis for our moral judgments. We need not limit what we might become to what we are. We should not deny our agency, our capacity to act and to change the world, to turn "what is" into "what must be."

4.5 UNNATURAL PRACTICES

Although moral naturalists acknowledge that human nature may contain negative characteristics and aspire to perfect positive ones, many have also recognized the possibility of our acting *contrary to nature*. They have labeled some contrary-to-nature acts and practices *unnatural* and judged them to be particularly abhorrent. They often carry a connotation of perversion and a response of disgust. Those who practice them are termed *degenerate*, which is defined as "having lost the physical, mental, or moral qualities considered normal and desirable." Across the world, many such acts have often been criminalized and labeled "crimes against nature"—some being too vile to be named in the law, yet apparently common enough to require a criminal statute.

Labeling practices "unnatural" has been used to deny, exclude, prohibit and shame. Many sexual practices have been condemned as unnatural, including masturbation, oral and anal sex, sexual fetishes, homosexual sex, sex with multiple partners, pedophilia, bestiality, sadism and masochism, sex with the dead, and so on. As we saw in the opening case for this chapter, *polygamy* (which is a general term for a marriage with multiple partners) has been called unnatural. There is, however, an interesting sexual asymmetry: *polygyny* (which is the practice of a man's openly marrying multiple women) has been treated as unnatural, but less severely so than *polyandry* (which is the practice of a woman's openly marrying multiple men). Apparently "unnaturalness" admits of degrees.

What might be meant by calling an act "unnatural"? What aspect of its meaning might convey moral condemnation? Reviewing alternative meanings is illuminating and might shed further light on what is meant by "natural" as well.[14]

(1) "Unnatural" might refer to something that is statistically rare or abnormal. If this is the intended meaning, it should carry no negative connotation. Playing the E-flat Monstre ophicleide—a huge, antique, brass instrument—is a rare skill, but that doesn't make it morally wrong. And I am not sure we would want to call it unnatural. This interpretation would not apply to some of the sex acts that have been condemned as unnatural, since they are quite common.

(2) "Unnatural" might refer to something that is not seen in other animals, especially primates. This assertion was sometimes heard regarding homosexuality. But in fact, homosexual preference *is* found among other animals. Here too, the claim is false regarding the facts of certain targeted practices; and even if it were true, it is difficult to see why that would provide a moral justification for its being wrong. Moreover, it is an odd move to resort to animal behavior to establish moral norms for human nature; it seems to contradict the focus on human nature.

(3) It is unnatural if it does not proceed from innate desires. The idea is that learned behavior, socially constructed behavior, is not natural. This is a tricky claim. Is using language natural to humans? One *learns* to use a *particular* language. But, as Epicurus pointed out, there are desires— say, for a special cheese or fine wine—that are clearly not innate. This claim has been used as a charge against homosexuals: "being gay is a lifestyle choice"—and so rebuke and "rehabilitation" programs follow. Many responded that homosexuals are "born that way," that being gay is an inescapable natural orientation. From our earlier critique, we might conclude that neither claim proves the rightness or wrongness of homosexual acts: something is not right or wrong just because it is chosen *or* because it is natural. Something that is learned may not be considered natural, but that does not imply that it is *un*natural.

(4) It is unnatural if it violates or frustrates natural functioning. This notion, based on Aristotle's concept of a natural purpose or *telos* for everything, has played a significant role in Roman Catholic doctrine and the lives of the faithful. Every organ in the body has a function; according to this doctrine, it is permissible to aid that function, but not to violate or frustrate it. Eye glasses and hearing aids are fine, since they aid our eyes to see and our ears to hear; condoms and other contraceptive devices

are wrong, however, because they frustrate the purpose of the sexual organs, which is reproduction. This sort of judgment inevitably leads to complex and confusing policies as it intersects with other doctrines: Catholicism, for example, condemns contraceptive devices which frustrate the "natural purposes" of the organs of reproduction; yet sleeping masks and earplugs, which frustrate the purposes of eyes and ears, are not of concern. The fundamental meaning of *perversion*, however, is to alter or deflect something from its original purpose in such a way as to violate or corrupt that purpose.

(5) It is unnatural if it is disgusting. Disgust is a visceral emotional response that expresses our repulsion at certain substances, objects, or sensations; it is associated with a fear of contamination through contact or ingestion. It may relate to a simple sensation, such as touching something slimy, or to an act or idea. Though it is a natural response, the things that elicit it and the threshold that triggers it, are subjective. There is a very large range of the disgusting that may provide an informative index of social acceptance of acts and ideas. Many people once found interracial sex—or even interracial kissing—disgusting. Many still find homosexual sex, even kissing, disgusting. These percentages have dwindled, along with those who are disgusted by masturbation or oral sex. By contrast, the percentage who are disgusted by eating red meat has climbed dramatically. My point is that disgust at various acts and practices tends to follow rather than determine moral judgments. It is true, however, that a visceral response can continue long after one has intellectually decided the condemnation was in error.[15]

In the Bountiful case, it is interesting that the court's decision was based on harm and not on the question of the "unnaturalness" of polygyny, although the concept is embedded in the law. But this negative concept of ethical naturalism is problematic: under some of the above interpretations, ironically, saintly conduct and supererogatory acts are unnatural!

4.6 NATURAL RIGHTS

In the eighteenth century, moral naturalism added another dimension: the doctrine of **natural rights**. Perhaps the most famous articulation of this thesis is the ringing opening to the Declaration of Independence penned by Thomas Jefferson (1743–1826): "We hold these truths to be self-evident, that all men are created equal, that they are endowed by their Creator with certain unalienable Rights, that among these are Life, Liberty and the pursuit of Happinesse." These human rights[16] are inalienable, meaning that they are inherent in human nature and cannot be taken or given away. The truth that we have such rights is evident to any rational person who considers the nature of a human being; for Jefferson, it is a matter of direct apprehension, not in need of proof.

In Jefferson's language, such rights are our shared endowment created by God. Today, many advocates of natural rights avoid the claim of divine endowment, finding instead that the value of human nature is itself sufficient ground. In 1948, the recently-formed United Nations adopted the *Universal Declaration of Human Rights*, which has since become the most-translated document in the world. The first "Whereas" clause of the Preamble states: "Recognition of the inherent dignity and of the equal and inalienable rights of all members of the human family is the foundation of freedom, justice and peace in the world." Notice that this affirmation moves from a recognition of inherent properties of human nature to their implications for moral (and legal) conduct. Such rights, it is claimed, are *natural* rights because they are derived from human nature; they are *human* rights because they are possessed by and apply to all human beings, and thus they are *universal* rights whether they are officially protected as *legal* rights or not.

What is a right? Rights are entitlements, and philosophers commonly recognize two sorts. The first are entitlements to specific sorts of actions, to the exercise of certain capacities. They are called *negative rights* because the entitling of one individual enjoins all other individuals not to interfere with such actions or exercise. Thus, negative rights create a protected sphere of freedom in which individuals are free to act. The rights to life and liberty, for example, enjoin others not to detain, abduct, enslave, or kill any being possessing such rights. The second sort are entitlements to the acquisition or possession of specific goods, services, or advantages. These are called *positive rights* because their ascription obligates others to provide these things. The right to an education is a positive right, obligating governments to provide schooling.

Both types of rights raise questions of boundaries, since no right is absolute. Negative rights may be infringed or violated for good reasons: the right to free expression may be restricted to prevent slander and incitement to violence; and even the right to life may be overridden by the need for self-defense against an attacker. In the ruling concerning Winston Blackmore and the Bountiful community, the court decided that the right to freely practice a religion could be encroached when the practice caused significant harm to individuals or violated their individual rights. In these matters, there is overlap between the moral questions and the law, largely focused on the priority of rights. With positive rights, however, the boundary question is two-part: (1) what agency or individuals have the rightful responsibility to provide the good, service, or advantage? and (2) what is the quality, quantity, or limit of the entitlement? These questions have, for example, been the core of the debate regarding the universal right to health care in the United States.

The *Universal Declaration of Human Rights* attempts to answer these questions regarding the right to education in Article 26, which is worth quoting in full:

> (1) Everyone has the right to education. Education shall be free, at least in the elementary and fundamental stages. Elementary education shall be compulsory. Technical and professional education shall be made generally available and higher education shall be equally accessible to all on the basis of merit.
> (2) Education shall be directed to the full development of the human personality and to the strengthening of respect for human rights and fundamental freedoms. It shall promote understanding, tolerance and friendship among all nations, racial or religious groups, and shall further the activities of the United Nations for the maintenance of peace.
> (3) Parents have a prior right to choose the kind of education that shall be given to their children.[17]

For the right to education, it seems obvious that the relevant provider is government, because basic education must be "free"; and an attempt is made to address the rightful quantity and quality of education to be provided. In other cases of positive rights, however, the obligated party may be unclear. Who is obligated to provide whatever is entitled by the right to clean drinking water, or the right to employment of one's choice, or "the right to a standard of living adequate for the health and well-being [of oneself and one's family], including food, clothing, housing and medical care and necessary social services...."?[18]

4.7 THE CRITIQUE OF NATURAL RIGHTS

The oldest objection to this concept is strong: *natural law and natural rights are fictions; only positive law and legal rights have authority.* How can human rights exist *by nature*? We can say that they are God-given, but that takes us down the road to theism and Divine Command. We can say that they are endorsed by many cultures, but that grounds them in culture. Jefferson said they were "self-evident." That provoked a response from the British philosopher, Jeremy Bentham (1748–1832). In a propagandistic pamphlet that argued against the *Declaration of Independence*, Bentham wrote:

> They [the signers of the Declaration] are about "to *assume*," as
> they tell us, "*among the powers of the earth, that equal and sepa-
> rate station to which*"—they have lately discovered—"the *laws
> of Nature, and of Nature's God entitle them.*" What difference
> these acute legislators suppose between the laws of *Nature* and
> of *Nature's God*, is more than I can take upon me to determine, or
> even to guess. If to what they now demand they were entitled by
> any law of God, they had only to produce that law, and all contro-
> versy was at an end. Instead of this, what do they produce? What
> they call sell-evident truths.[19]

This foreshadowed Bentham's later, more famous comment: "*Natural rights* is simple nonsense: natural and imprescriptible rights, rhetorical nonsense,—nonsense upon stilts."[20] Not that Bentham disvalued *legal* rights: for him, rights are "the fruits of the law, and of the law alone. There are no rights without law—no rights contrary to the law—no rights anterior to the law."[21] Bentham believed strongly that the concept of natural rights promoted instability and anarchy. People start claiming all sorts of rights and violations, none of which have legal standing, leading to chaos and rebellion. (Recently, "incels"—a group of young men who are "involuntary celibate"—have claimed they have a positive natural right to sex, which is a human good, and are disgruntled that women are not providing it.)

Yet despite Bentham's vociferous warnings and the philosophically shaky foundations for natural rights, no other concept, no other political tool, has been as effective to this very moment in securing social reform and legal protections. Advances in access and protections for women, racial minorities, employees, prisoners, children, those with physical disabilities, gays and lesbians, the transgendered, patients, immigrants and refugees— all have been promoted around the world through the concept of natural rights that *should* receive legal status. The same rights-talk is being used in campaigns to improve the treatment of animals. In these campaigns, we speak of "recognizing" the right to *X*, as though it preexisted, rather than "creating" the right. Rights-talk is politically potent for moral reform.

A world without human rights seems a dangerous prospect, so we continue to pursue its justification. Some philosophers seek to ground rights in human agency. Alan Gewirth (1912–2004) argued that we cannot live a human life without agency, our ability to act; this in turn requires that we must respect the conditions of agency—natural rights—in ourselves and, for rational consistency, in others as well.[22] James Griffin (b. 1933) has also proposed a moral conception of natural rights that is rooted in the autonomy of human agency. Griffin asserts that natural rights secure the key component of autonomy: our capacity to develop and pursue conceptions of a worthwhile life, which is the source of human dignity and of highest value.[23] These are promising lines of defense, and I will return to the discussion of rights in Chapter 7.

4.8 HUMAN CAPABILITIES

In recent years, a novel approach to the moral implications of human nature has been proposed by the Nobel Prize-winning economist/philosopher Amartya Sen (b. 1933) and developed by philosopher Martha Nussbaum (b. 1947).[24] It is known as "the capabilities approach" and is derived from the concept of human well-being and its requirements. Freedom to pursue well-being is of central moral importance. This pursuit has a fundamental requirement: our need to use human capabilities to do and to achieve what we have reason to value. One's freedom consists in the power to exercise certain specific capabilities.

The ability to move about freely and travel without restriction is such a capability; but note that it is not only factors like physical disability or governmental restrictions that constrain this capability, but also such conditions as the lack of transportation systems and poverty. Since the focus is on welfare and what is valued, rather than on specific notions of human perfection, Nussbaum's approach may accommodate a wide range of human diversity in values. This means that our "universal human nature" is constituted by the capabilities that freedom requires in the practical pursuit of whatever is valued; it is not a specific list of what should be valued universally.

While this approach is promising, it remains "an approach" not a mature theory; its advocates resist a tighter theoretical formulation, and the list of required capabilities varies among proponents. Currently, there is significant work to be done in developing further its moral implications. But this approach grasps yet another concern with ethical naturalism: giving a central place to human nature entails a focus on our core similarities; but the thicker we make our concept of things human share, the more are we likely to obscure or ignore human differences. Naturalism seems to give little attention to difference (except for the charge of unnaturalism); it certainly does not see difference or diversity as a source of moral value.

4.9 HUMANITY AND MORALITY

Grounding morality in human nature carries the implication that human beings have a special moral status. Indeed, we are, so far as we know, the only creatures who have moral agency and the moral responsibility it entails. While we may recognize the moral standing of animals, it is we who ascribe it. As human beings, we own a dignity and natural rights that may be violated but never removed from us. This view of morality is, one might say, *anthropocentric* (= human-centered) or *species-centered*. Though we extend moral consideration to non-humans, morality is of, by, and for human beings.

The implications are significant. We are privileged within the natural order. *Our* well-being is supreme. We judge the good as the *human* good. Insofar as we might imagine extending morality beyond the human, we nonetheless apply our species-centered moral judgments. Thus, the very conception of morality is *humane*. When, for example, we wonder whether any rights should someday be extended to androids or robots, or to chimps and dogs, we approach the judgment using criteria we have developed, criteria that recognize their human-like traits and capacities. And, again, *we* would make the judgment to extend them. On this view, if humanity were to disappear, moral value—all good and bad—would disappear as well.

But suppose we were one day to engage a race of aliens: would we expect our morality to transcend humanity? Wouldn't a morality derived from human nature apply only to the human species? And what if, either by technological progress or close encounter, we were to confront creatures whose intelligence and skills were well above ours: would we then bow to their superiority? Are beings with a superior nature—and therefore a superior morality—impossible?

Genetic manipulation is becoming easier, more precise, and more informed by genome analysis. Human beings clearly face the possibility not just of genetic therapy, but also of genetic design and enhancement. If our ethics is based on human nature, how will that help us decide what sort of nature we should give to the humans of the future? Can we, without self-contradiction, as E.O. Wilson implies, apply our morality to the issues of human enhancement? Are we able to judge the morality of transhumanism, the intentional creation of beings that are better than the humanity that has walked the earth in recent millennia?

These questions are not merely speculative; they are conceptual. They force us to consider the range and limits of morality (especially a morality based on human nature), to examine our commitment to humanity *as it is* as opposed to the process and possibility of "perfecting" our human nature or transcending it.

Conversely, if we take an anthropocentric ethics to represent a kind of subjective bias, we might attempt to gain a larger, less parochial grounding. Perhaps we could ground our morality in Nature, not just human nature. We could ascribe moral value to the ecosystem, recognize the moral standing of all species, undertake a moral relationship with the ecosystem, in which we cautiously assess even the most precious human purposes and projects for their ecological impact. But this movement could be more radical than an environmental ethics in which we honor special human responsibilities for the environment and its creatures. It could involve the relinquishment of the "special moral status" of human beings. From such an eco-centric perspective, human expansion may be an infestation. Yet, as transformative as eco-centric ethics might be, would not its expanded moral horizons still be the horizons of human experience?

QUESTIONS FOR DISCUSSION

1 In the Canadian polygamy case, what "harm to women and children" may result from the practice? What harm to society at large? (Remember this was a ruling about polygamy in general, not just about issues peculiar to the Bountiful community.)

2 Incest is a practice widely considered "unnatural" and morally wrong. Suppose it was limited to consenting adults who practiced safe sex, would the practice still be morally wrong? Why or why not?

3 According to the *Universal Declaration of Human Rights*, "Men and women of full age, without any limitation due to race, nationality or religion, have the right to marry and to found a family ... Marriage shall be entered into only with the free and full consent of the intending spouses" (Article 16). On what basis can you justify this right? What could you say to convince parents whose culture allowed forced marriages that it would violate their daughter's moral rights to force her into marriage (like Shafilea Ahmed, Chapter 3)?

4 Does the fact that a creature can feel pain, can suffer, confer any rights? If not, why not? If so, which ones and why?

5 At what point, if ever, should we grant rights to robots? When they demand them? An influential answer is whenever they can pass the Turing Test, which is named for the pioneer computer scientist and logician, Alan Turing (1912–54). Essentially, the test is to see whether normal people engaging in conversations with a robot—without seeing it—could consistently be unsure as to whether they were speaking to a human or a robot. Is this test an example of species-centered ethics? What does a non-anthropocentric ethic involve?

QUESTIONS FOR PERSONAL REFLECTION

1 Is this sound advice: "Never engage or participate in an act you find disgusting"?

2 How would you describe what is involved in "human flourishing"?

3 Review Martha Nussbaum's "core capabilities" as listed on *Wikipedia*. Do all seem necessary for the "flourishing" life you just described? Would you add any to her list?

SUGGESTED SOURCES

Aristotle. *Nicomachean Ethics.* Robert C. Bartlett and Susan D. Collins, trans. (Chicago: U of Chicago P, 2012).

Curry, Patrick. *Ecological Ethics*, 2nd ed. (Cambridge: Polity P, 2011).

Finnis, John. *Natural Law and Natural Rights* (Oxford: Oxford UP, 2011).

Foot, Philippa. *Natural Goodness* (Oxford: Clarendon P, 2001).

Lenman, James. "Moral Naturalism," in *The Stanford Encyclopedia of Philosophy*: http://plato.stanford.edu/entries/naturalism-moral/ (accessed May 2016).

Nuccetelli, Susana, and Gary Seay, eds. *Ethical Naturalism: Current Debates* (Cambridge: Cambridge UP, 2013).

Nussbaum, Martha C. *Creating Capabilities: The Human Development Approach* (Cambridge, MA: Belknap/Harvard UP, 2011).

Witte Jr., John. *The Western Case for Monogamy over Polygamy* (Cambridge: Cambridge UP, 2015).

NOTES

1   The mainstream Mormon Church won a ruling forcing the Blackmore Group to eliminate "Latter Day Saints" from their name. Blackmore then founded "The Church of Jesus Christ (Original Doctrine), Inc." Bountiful was, however, denied the status of a religion for tax purposes by yet another court ruling.

2   Epicurus, *Letter to Menoeceus*, in *Greek and Roman Philosophy after Aristotle*, Jason L. Saunders, ed. (New York: Free P, 1966, 1994), 51.

3   Ibid.

4   The practice of giving the name "Epicurean" to restaurants with rich cuisine shows how public misunderstanding of Epicurus' actual views distorted the connotations of his name—a problem he mentioned in the passage quoted.

5   Mencius, *Mencius: An Online Teaching Translation*, trans. Robert Eno. (Version L0, May 16) VI.A.6, 109: http://www.indiana.edu/~p374/Mengzi.pdf (accessed May 2016).

6   Cicero, *De Re Publica*, III, xxii.

7   Thomas Aquinas, *Summa Theologiae*. *Prima Secundae*, trans. Fr. Laurence Shapcote (Lander, WY: The Aquinas Institute for the Study of Sacred Doctrine, 2012), I–II, q.94, a.2, ad 3; p. 229–30.

8   Alasdair MacIntyre, *Dependent Rational Animals* (Chicago: Open Court, 1999).

9   See Philippa Foot, *Natural Goodness* (Oxford: Clarendon P, 2001); and Rosalind Hursthouse, *On Virtue Ethics* (Oxford: Clarendon P, 1999).

10   Edward O. Wilson, *On Human Nature* (Cambridge, MA: Harvard UP, 1978); inset quotations from pp. 3 and 5; this quotation from p. 203.

11   Thomas Nagel, *Mind & Cosmos: Why the Materialist Neo-Darwinian Conception of Nature Is Almost Certainly False* (Oxford: Oxford UP, 2012), 7.

12   Richard Rorty, *Contingency, Irony, Solidarity* (Cambridge: Cambridge UP, 1989), 175.

13   See, e.g., Richard Joyce, *The Evolution of Morality* (Cambridge, MA: MIT P, 2006); or Christopher Boehm, *Moral Origins: The Evolution of Virtue, Altruism, and Shame* (New York: Basic Books, 2012).

14   This list of alternative meanings is based on: John Corvino, "Why Shouldn't Tommy and Jim Have Sex?" in *Same Sex: Debating the Ethics, Science, and Culture of Homosexuality* (Lanham, MD: Rowman & Littlefield, 1997).

15 For a discussion of the relation between disgust and moral judgment, see Daniel Kelly, *Yuck!: The Nature and Moral Significance of Disgust* (Cambridge, MA: MIT P, 2011).

16 I shall presume, with the United States Supreme Court, that Jefferson ultimately meant "all men" to include women and human beings of all races and ethnic backgrounds—or at least that it is the logical implication of the larger principles of the document and of the Constitution that followed.

17 *The Universal Declaration of Human Rights*, Article 26; available at: http://www.un.org/en/universal-declaration-human-rights/ (accessed July 2018).

18 Ibid., Article 25.

19 George III enlisted the services of the propagandist John Lind in writing a pamphlet, "An Answer to the Declaration of the American Congress," which was printed in London and so widely distributed that it ran through several editions in 1776 alone. The concluding summary essay, "Short Review of the Declaration," by an anonymous author, was nearly certainly written by Jeremy Bentham, who was rooming with John Lind. The quotation is from the first edition, pages 119–20. Italics in the original. The facsimile text is available at: https://archive.org/details/cihm_20519 (accessed July 2018).

20 Jeremy Bentham, *Anarchical Fallacies; being an examination of the Declaration of Rights issued during the French Revolution*; in *The Works of Jeremy Bentham*, ed. John Bowring, vol. 2, 501 (1843; New York: Russell & Russell, 1962; facsimile reproduced by the Liberty Fund), available at: http://oll.libertyfund.org/titles/bentham-the-works-of-jeremy-bentham-vol-2 (accessed July 2018).

21 Jeremy Bentham, *Pannomial Fragments*, Chapter 3; in *The Works of Jeremy Bentham*, ed. John Bowring, vol. 3 (1843; New York: Russell & Russell, 1962; reprinted by the Liberty Fund), available at: http://oll.libertyfund.org/titles/bentham-the-works-of-jeremy-bentham-vol-3 (accessed July 2018).

22 Alan Gewirth, *Human Rights: Essays on Justification and Application* (Chicago: U of Chicago P, 1982).

23 James P. Griffin, *On Human Rights* (Oxford: Oxford UP, 2008).

24 Though the capabilities approach has been developed in many published works, Sen's and Nussbaum's fullest presentations to date are, respectively, in Amartya Sen, *Development as Freedom* (Oxford: Oxford UP, 1999) and Martha C. Nussbaum, *Creating Capabilities: The Human Development Approach* (Cambridge, MA: Belknap/Harvard UP, 2011).

CHAPTER FIVE
Egoism

On April 24, 2013, Rana Plaza—a busy nine-story commercial structure that housed shops, banks, businesses, and a garment factory—collapsed in Bangladesh. The death toll would eventually climb to 1,100.

Didar Hossain, a young man who worked nearby, rushed past police to help save victims, which he did despite the danger. On the second day, he discovered a little girl, alive, but with her hand caught in the rubble. He tried for five hours to extricate her. Realizing with horror that she could not be removed without amputating her hand, he left her to find a doctor.

The one doctor he could find in the crowd outside refused, saying he had no interest in entering such a death trap. Instead, he handed Didar a knife and some anesthetic and said, "Good luck!" Didar returned to the girl, and while they both screamed and cried, performed the amputation, tied her wound, and carried her out.

In the end, Didar Hossain pulled 34 people out of the rubble, having to perform two other amputations in the process. When he visited the girl in the hospital, he first apologized for having to remove her hand.[1]

5.1 OUR NATURAL SELF-INTEREST

Many thinkers who have scanned human nature have been most impressed by our egoism, our concern for our own well-being. They conclude that the dominant motivation of human beings is the protection and promotion of our own individual self-interest. For example, Thomas Hobbes (1588–1679), in *Leviathan*, his monumental work that launched modern political philosophy, claimed that "every man is presumed to do all things in order to his own benefit."[2] Hobbes rejected Aristotelian teleology and the notion that there is a highest good for humans inherent in our nature. He found instead that we are by nature selfish, competitive, fearful, and anti-social; and we use reason only to serve our passions and desires.

I want to unfold two claims made by Hobbes and others of similar views. Both are claims about human nature.

1. The first claim concerns our motivation. The view expressed is more extreme than the notion that we often act in self-interest, or even that self-interest is our dominant concern. The claim is that *all* humans are *always* motivated *only* by *self-interest*. We might, in fact, distinguish two separate elements in this claim: (a) that all human motives are always and everywhere reducible to *one* basic motive (which is termed a *monistic* theory

of motivation); and (b) that this universal basic motive is the promotion of individual self-interest.

2. The second is the claim that, given our nature and the laws of science, *we cannot do otherwise*. Our self-interested motive is "hard-wired"; it is inescapable human nature.

Taken together, these claims comprise a theory of human behavior called **psychological egoism**. It is a descriptive theory: it purports to state what, in fact, motivates people. It commands great force, because it combines reductive simplicity with the widest, universal range of explanatory coverage; it attempts to use just one motive to explain all human behavior. But it also alleges it presents psychologically necessary facts, not just happenstance. This drive for self-interest is innate; it is who we are as individual human beings. In other words, it is our nature; we simply cannot behave in any other way.

Those who accept this theory often go further by specifying just what is meant by "self-interest." The most reductive view is that it simply means we are motivated to gain pleasure and avoid pain—and nothing else. Although we will shortly consider other interpretations, we begin with the hedonistic view because of its initial simplicity.

A century after Hobbes, Jeremy Bentham (who had ridiculed natural rights) opened his 1780 work, *An Introduction to the Principles of Morals and Legislation*, with these dramatic words about human nature:

> Nature has placed mankind under the governance of two foreign masters, *pain* and *pleasure*. It is for them alone to point out what we ought to do, as well as to determine what we shall do. On the one hand the standard of right and wrong, on the other the chain of causes and effects, are fastened to their throne. They govern us in all we do, in all we say, in all we think: every effort we can make to throw off our subjection, will serve but to demonstrate and confirm it. In words a man may pretend to abjure their empire: but in reality, he will remain subject to it all the while.[3]

For Bentham, Nature rules: pleasure and pain are our "masters" and we are "fastened to their throne." He does seem to allow us a certain capacity to distance ourselves: he calls them "*foreign* masters"; he says that we may try to "throw off our subjection" and do otherwise (say, act unselfishly and not for pleasure—though what could motivate us is not clear); and he allows that we may be moved to "pretend to abjure their empire" (by seeming to act on other considerations). But none of this works for us in the end: we are still shackled to seeking pleasure and dodging pain.

Although psychological egoism is a descriptive theory of human motivation, we must give it careful attention because, if true, it has enormously significant implications for our normative study: it would shut down all further inquiry in philosophical ethics. There is a venerable principle in ethics: *ought* implies *can*. It means that we cannot prescribe the impossible. It would be meaningless to say, "Everyone ought to have a deep knowledge of the *specific* interests of every other person," since we finite humans simply cannot do that. Psychological egoism says that our only motivation is necessarily self-interest. If this is true, any proposal for moral action to be other than self-interested would be doomed; we simply *could not* behave otherwise. Any talk of behaving differently would be wishful fantasy at best, a reach into what is impossible in this world. Thus, the theory of psychological egoism represents a serious challenge to philosophical ethics.

5.2 PSYCHOLOGICAL EGOISM: A CRITIQUE

Theories gain explanatory power when they can show that many apparently different phenomena are actually forms of the same thing and subject to a single law. This is, to reiterate, the attraction of psychological egoism: it reduces the confusing complexity of human motivation to just one: self-interest. It also has the air of cut-to-the-truth realism: people may seem or claim to act for disinterested or high-minded purposes, but in fact they are masking their promotion of their own good. It denies the possibility of **altruism**, which is selfless concern for the well-being of others, because *self*-interested action is the only sort of which humans are capable. In the end, each of us cares only about ourselves. *But is this true?*

Are we all really so tightly focused on advancing our own good? Just look around: people engage in all sorts of acts and practices that are *harmful* to their own well-being—things that ruin their health, spoil their relationships, diminish their finances, and risk their lives. But egoists will reply by sharpening their position, drawing a distinction between one's *genuine* self-interest and one's *perceived* self-interest. Their claim is that people always act according to what they *believe* at the moment to be in their self-interest (whether it is *actually* in their interest or not). It is not part of the theory that people are always smart or make no mistakes.

That clarification does not resolve the issue, however. People often do things they *know* are not in their self-interest: the smoker says, "I know I should quit, but I want a cigarette"; the drinker says, "I have a big test tomorrow morning and I know I'll regret it, but I'll take one more shot."

To this point, egoists may offer different replies. They may claim that such statements are hypocritical utterances that do not reflect true beliefs—the smoker and the drinker don't really believe they need to quit—though that involves claiming to know the thoughts of others better than they do themselves. Or, egoists may claim that "perceived self-interest" merely means getting what you want for yourself at the time, which is what the weak-willed smoker and drinker are doing—though that move involves a significant and dubious shift from the concepts of *interest* and *well-being* to the concepts of *want* and *desire*.

Setting aside these arguments, one might also object from another angle that psychological egoism actually violates the facts of human behavior. However one accommodates cases of self-harm, it seems obvious—and morally uplifting—that acts intended to benefit *others* often occur. People do act altruistically, without regard for their own interests. Think of Didar Hossain, who repeatedly risked his life and undertook emotionally painful tasks to rescue trapped strangers. And what of the mother who risks death to save her child, or the soldier who leaps on a grenade to save comrades, or the German who risked all in the Third Reich to shelter a Jew? But it is not only the striking cases of heroes and saints that show altruism. Ordinary people do sometimes act with selfless care: we make sacrifices for loved ones, give charitable gestures, extend kindnesses, and volunteer for causes. Holding a door open for somebody following you is a (very tiny) unselfish act. Altruism is not even rare. Still, we elevate the more extreme cases of doing good for others because the significant self-sacrifice involved seems to remove the possibility of other motives.

To that argument, psychological egoists have offered different replies.

1. One egoist reply is to claim that the apparent selflessness in such actions is superficial; the real motivation of such acts is to achieve a perceived benefit for oneself, usually some intangible but valued benefit, such as a saintly or heroic reputation, honor and glory, or a bolstered sense of one's own virtue. If this unpleasant assertion of self-centeredness flattens all moral action and dishonors those who act in such "noble" ways, so be it. It is an unavoidable reality, according to the egoist.

2. Many egoists would add hedonism to their claim: even heroes and saints are indeed acting out of self-interest, more specifically by seeking to obtain pleasure—the pleasure they get from accomplishing those deeds and from the admiration it brings. Even if such acts involve pain and suffering, endurance, or humiliation, the actions are not forced and are aimed ultimately at pleasure. The egoist may, if pressed, reinterpret "pleasure" as "satisfaction of desire"—but the self-interest argument remains.

3. The egoist may claim that self-deception rather than hypocrisy is at work in such actions. It is possible to *believe* one is acting for the interest of others when actually one is busy pursuing one's self-interest. Even such self-deception serves our self-interest, since it allows us to keep a nobler view of ourselves.

All these arguments involve the claim that *all actions are motivated by a self-interest that is often hidden*, even from the agent. There are critical counterarguments to each of the egoists' arguments. Let us take them up in order of the claims listed.

1. Certainly there are cases in which actions that benefit others are done out of self-interest. A donor gives a large gift to obtain recognition and praise—intangible benefits, but a result that is desired and valued. Perhaps there are even times when someone becomes a hero to gain glory and praise. But this view of human motivation seems to require a calculating mindset, an incessantly tactical state of mind; in contrast, many selfless acts seem impulsive, done without the time or deliberation that a self-interested agent would require. And, for the cunningly self-interested, such a heroic act would entail complicated calculations: there is significant risk or pain or loss involved as well as potential gain. Does the soldier leaping on the grenade really think through the possible benefit to reputation and *therefore decide* to act?

2. The definitive critique of the pleasure argument was made by Joseph Butler (1692–1752), a bishop in the Anglican Church, in a set of sermons preached at Rolls Chapel, London, in the 1720s.[4] Though they appear in sermons, his arguments are persuasive because of their conceptual precision and analytical rigor. Butler recognizes that people's motives are complex, sometimes opaque, sometimes self-deceived. Nonetheless, the egoist's claim that everyone always seeks self-satisfaction or pleasure by accomplishing their intent is trivial and empty. The real issue is *what* they intend and *why*. He thought it obvious that people may intend things that express benevolence and so engage in action aimed at the well-being of others, though we may also intend things that express concern for our own well-being. Both may lead to pleasure or satisfaction, but conflating them misses the point.[5]

Imagine a playboy who goes clubbing looking for pleasure (his aim) and happily finds it; compare him with someone like Mother Teresa, who is portrayed as one who went out each day to help the sick and destitute unfortunates of Calcutta (her aim) and also found pleasure in doing so. It is, in short, the *aim* that represents our motivational target, not the hedonic or emotional *byproduct* that results. It is one thing to act with pleasure as your aim; quite another to act for an altruistic aim and find pleasure in your success. A piece of evidence that supports this point is that it is their particular aims that matter to the playboy and the nun. If the nun were simply seeking pleasure as her aim, one might easily convince her to forswear her demanding benevolence and go clubbing.

Moreover, it is problematic to equate pleasure with the satisfaction of one's desires. No doubt, we do experience pleasure from desire satisfaction; but ready-to-hand counterexamples show that the two are conceptually distinct and may not occur together. Addictions, with their compellingly intense desires, often give little pleasure when the need is satisfied. Conversely, I may find pleasure in a song I hear on the radio, although I had no desire to hear it and tuned in serendipitously. In fact, sometimes one can take pleasure in anticipating or even delaying the satisfaction of desire. Here is the famous Winnie-the-Pooh on the pleasure of anticipation: "'Well,' said Pooh, 'what I like best—' and then he had to stop and think. Because although Eating Honey *was* a very good thing to do, there was a moment just before you began to eat it which was better than when you were, but he didn't know what it was called."[6] This "giving" and "taking" and "finding" of pleasure indicate that it is not necessarily a matter of motive or desire satisfaction.

3. Ah, but these "altruists" are deeply self-deceived, says the egoist. Yes, they have different tastes in pleasure, different sources of satisfaction; but they do not know their true motives, which are hidden from them. Self-deception is the result of unconscious motives. Thus, it seems the last refuge of psychological egoism is the unconscious: *whatever* we may say or think, our *unconscious* motivation is our pleasure or self-satisfaction. Even Didar Hossain was actually driven to rescue others by unconscious motives of self-interest. With this appeal to the unconscious, we are silenced and our debate appears to be at an impasse.

There are, however, two counterarguments. The first is that the psychological egoist has now defended a monistic theory of motivation by excluding any possible evidence to the contrary. It is an *untestable* theory in principle, and therefore *unfalsifiable*. This is like claiming there are gremlins in the forest and, when challenged, adding that they are invisible, incorporeal, undetectable gremlins who leave no traces. Such theories, which discount all possible evidence to the contrary, are always dubious. The second counter is that, once we resort to unconscious motivation, we open the door to other equally defensible—and similarly empty—theories. For example, I could claim that all people are actually motivated not for pleasure or self-satisfaction, but for sleep. You say we are hungry and desire to eat, but I say we are unconsciously seeking the lethargy that comes with a full stomach. You say we desire the pleasure of sex, but I say it is not pleasure we seek: it is the lovely drowsiness or sleep that follows sex. You say, "But we want to awaken, feeling good and charged with energy." I say, "Yes, and what do we do? We immediately engage in all sorts of things that will tire us." I say we are self-deceived. Unconsciously, we all seek sleep. It is a silly theory, of course, but a parallel to the theory of unconscious self-interest or pleasure motivation—equally plausible and equally vacuous.

5.3 THE SELF AND *HOMO ECONOMICUS*

Despite this philosophical critique, the conception of the self that is embedded in egoism has been enormously influential. It portrays a self that is continually engaged in social transactions, negotiating benefits and harms. In the nineteenth century, as the field of economics emerged from ethical theory and applied mathematics, this conception was established as the basis for modeling human behavior in the marketplace.[7] For classical economists, we are *Homo economicus*: self-interested, satisfaction-seeking, rational, labor-averse agents whose actions and choices consistently reflect these qualities. When we engage in exchanges with others in the marketplace, we seek to maximize our benefits (whatever we desire); we calculate risks, costs, and benefits rationally; and we seek *efficiency* in our transactions. And everyone we exchange with behaves in the same way. Our self-interest is identified with whatever we desire. While the satisfaction of desires may be pleasurable, economists have preferred the general term *utility*.

The Scottish philosopher Adam Smith (1723–90) was a founder of economic theory. In perhaps the most famous passage of his classic treatise, known familiarly as *The Wealth of Nations*, Smith wrote:

> Whoever offers to another a bargain of any kind, proposes to do this. Give me that which I want, and you shall have this which you want, is the meaning of every such offer; and it is in this manner that we obtain from one another the far greater part of those good offices which we stand in need of. It is not from the benevolence of the butcher, the brewer, or the baker that we expect our dinner, but from their regard to their own interest.[8]

We would be misguided to expect altruism or benevolence in the marketplace. If Paulo is buying a car, he naturally wants to get the lowest price with little trouble and low risk; if Paula is the seller, she naturally wants the highest price she can get with little trouble and low risk. Both want the best deal for themselves, the greatest utility. Everyone is a self-interested consumer of goods, services, and experiences. Moreover, the market value of goods is not intrinsic to them; it is determined by what people are willing to pay or exchange for them. Classical economists do acknowledge that some goods are intangible: people are willing to pay for prestige, for example. But even those are objects of self-interested transactions.

Classical economic theory proceeded to research on the assumption that this model of the self is accurate. But this conception has proved defective on at least three grounds: (1) actual human beings do not behave in the way the model predicts; (2) it describes the "consumer self" and ignores the self that has commitments and projects; and (3) it fails to capture the "transformative self." I will explain each in turn.

1. When economists called *Homo economicus* "rational," they meant only that he adjusts means to ends and is consistent in his choices and preferences; they did not intend the term as an evaluation of the desires or ends he had.[9] But there is now ample empirical evidence that human beings display cognitive biases that regularly yield *inconsistencies*; that we also occasionally make choices to benefit others (altruistic choices); and that we are more motivationally complex creatures than this *Homo economicus* model, even when we enter the marketplace. Recognition of such evidence has recently inspired the field of behavioral or experimental economics, which is devoted to giving a more accurate, empirical account of our economic behavior.[10]

2. The conception of the self as consumer, however one construes the goods we "consume," does not capture our engagement in projects that matter to us. The answer to the question "What's in it for me?" might be that it advances a project or cause to which I am committed. Such projects can range so broadly that they can carry us beyond even a stretched and strained conception of self-interest. These are the sorts of projects that are often described as engaging in "a cause that is larger than yourself or anyone alone." (Strictly speaking, for the classical economist, unless we engage in these projects for our own self-interest, we are acting irrationally.)

3. The transactional model of the self—whether construed in the pleasure-driven, satisfaction-of-desire, or cost-benefit version—fails to capture exchanges that are designed to *transform* the self and its desires. A college education is a good example. The typical story about the value of a college education is based on a cost-benefit model of decisions and the egoist's model of the self: how much additional income or other benefit will result from the investment in tuition and other expenses, minus opportunity costs incurred by the time spent in college? Notice the hidden assumption

that the agent is a constant, a fixed point; that all transactions are about satisfying the agent's desires, whatever they currently may be. But an education is about transforming the person, which may result in altering, refining, or expanding one's desires. One may seek self-improvement or self-actualization, as well as self-satisfaction; transformation of the self as well as consumption of goods.

5.4 EVIDENCE AND ALTRUISM

Revealing that humans have inherent cognitive biases that scuttle the rationality of our decisions; that individuals are not only consumers but often participants in larger projects; that individuals invest in transformative as well as transactional exchanges—these revelations have challenged the model of *Homo economicus* and provoked major revisions in the discipline of economics. But they do not provide direct or decisive support for claims of altruism. Evidence regarding altruism has, however, appeared in other areas of research.

To some thinkers, psychological egoism seemed to be confirmed by the evolutionary theory of Charles Darwin (1809–82), or at least by its "survival of the fittest" image, a term coined by the evolutionary enthusiast, Herbert Spencer (1820–1903). This easy association is, however, misguided. Darwin's account of competition and adaptation applied to *species* not *individuals*. It did not foreclose the possibility that acts of individual altruism might be an advantage to the species. Indeed, research in several fields has converged on the view that reciprocity, cooperation, trust, and a sense of fairness are evolved behaviors that have been crucial to the development of primate social organization. We could not have our complex society without patterns of conduct that show regard for others, and these patterns are now deeply embedded in our nature.[11] Though we can be selfish and self-interested, we also can and do act on behalf of others. At minimum, human nature tilts toward altruistic behavior as a consequence of our living together.

In the 1980s, the social psychologist Daniel Batson (b. 1943) advanced a hypothesis: if someone feels empathy for another person, she may act altruistically, helping the other without regard for what she can gain for herself. Batson and others developed research protocols to test his empathy–altruism hypothesis. After decades of studies, although there are still doubters, the consensus of researchers is that empirical evidence offers strong support for the claim that empathic concern for someone in need generates altruistic motivation to ameliorate that need.[12]

As a result of both philosophical critique and scientific research, psychological egoism is largely a discredited and discarded theory today. That is an important conclusion both for our understanding of human nature and for the possibility of philosophical ethics. Were it true, there would be little use to call any act "morally right." Were we, as Bentham says, "fastened" to a single sort of motivation, calling it "right" would merely put a moral halo on what is unavoidable.

5.5 ETHICAL EGOISM

Adam Smith thought the natural and rational self-interest of all individuals in free exchanges had a surprising outcome: it produced the good for all. The transformation of individual self-interest into social good is a mysterious process for which Smith introduced a metaphor that became famous: *the Invisible Hand.*[13] It is as though an "an invisible hand" blends our consistent pursuit of our own interests into a serendipitous macro-phenomenon, which is the good for all. Whether one has faith or doubts regarding this alleged effect of free markets, as students of moral philosophy, we should note that it matters whether one's moral aim is self-interest, from which the social good is a happy by-product; or whether our aim is primarily the social good, and self-interest is merely a means to achieve it or perhaps a component of it. Only the former stance represents genuine egoism. I will have more to say below about this claim that egoism is a means to the common good. First, however, we must examine the view that egoism is our moral duty.

Ethical egoism is a normative theory that asserts it is *morally right* to act in such a way as to promote one's self-interest. Typically, it has its foundation in naturalism, justifying this claim by referring to human nature. But ethical egoism does not need to embrace the monistic motivational rigidity of psychological egoism. According to ethical egoism:

"*X* is right" = "*X* maximizes the good for oneself."

Notice that this formulation sharpens the advice to "promote your self-interest." It identifies self-interest with obtaining "the good"; and instead of merely "promoting," it imposes a moral injunction to *maximize* the good—to obtain as much good as one possibly can. This generic formulation becomes more specific with the supplementary theory of what counts as "the good."

Ethical egoism was advocated by the controversial novelist and thinker, Ayn Rand (1905–82). A Russian-born anti-Communist and immigrant to America, Rand championed "the virtue of selfishness."[14] She called her philosophy "objectivism," asserting that securing one's own well-being and happiness is the sole moral purpose of one's life, that self-sacrifice and altruism are evil because they disvalue one's own life, and that the good is achieved through reason and creative productivity. What is the good? Rand says that our innate "pleasure-pain mechanism" serves as a guidance system for our values,[15] though it guides us to independent and varying goods. She strongly affirms individual rights, and rejects the idea that the needs or desires of another should ever impose any obligations or constrain one's own freedom.

Do not assume that ethical egoism licenses everyone's whims. Egoists like Rand acknowledge that people may have desires and make choices that undermine their well-being. That is why they typically emphasize reason in choosing one's actions. But for Rand, reason is to be used to identify our genuine self-interest and the most efficient means to achieve it—not to give consideration to the interests of others. For her, one who engages in altruistic acts is not just misguided; he or she is *immoral*. To risk oneself as Didar Hossain did to save others is morally wrong, according to ethical egoism.

As a descriptive theory, psychological egoism was focused on human *motivation*; ethical egoism is sometimes given a similarly "intentionalist" interpretation, calling it morally right to have a self-interested intent. Most accounts of ethical egoism demand more than intent, however; they focus on *results* or *consequences*. **Consequentialist theories** hold that the rightness or wrongness of an action or practice is determined solely by its consequences.[16] For the egoist, what determines whether an act is right is simply whether the outcome results in the maximal good for the agent; the means are only of concern in relation to the results they produce.

Consequentialist theories are contrasted with deontological theories (recall Chapter 2), which hold that we have morally binding duties or ethical principles that govern what is right and wrong. A consequentialist rejects the notion that we should follow duties or principles whenever they do not produce good effects in the world; it is the goodness of outcomes that govern. And yet the moral directive to maximize the good itself becomes our moral obligation, our one guiding principle.

No one, of course, can be certain of future events. For the moral agent, who must make decisions based on available information, consequentialism enjoins her to act according to the *reasonable expectations* of consequences that will result. This involves more than having a self-interested intent: for the egoist, it means I must carefully consider what actions I may reasonably expect to maximize the good for me. That's the best I can do; indeed, it is what I am *obligated* to do. The outcome may prove my action wrong, but I should not be blamed if that result could not have reasonably been foreseen.

The tendency to ground the ethical in the psychological is starkly displayed in Bentham's quotation above, when he says: "Nature has placed mankind under the governance of two foreign masters, pain and pleasure. It is for them alone to point out *what we ought to do*, as well as to determine what we shall do. On the one hand *the standard of right and wrong*, on the other the chain of causes and effects, are fastened to their throne."[17] It is not simply that we are in fact constrained by our nature; it is that this nature is normative and provides moral requirements. Part of the attraction of ethical egoism is it puts no theoretical or practical strain between what we naturally do and what we ought to do.

5.6 TESTING EGOISM AS A MORAL THEORY

When we turn to evaluate ethical egoism, we quickly find additional attractions. Clearly, an attractive element is what we might call the egoist's singular moral principle: the moral obligation to value one's own life and well-being. On the one hand, one's circle of moral concern is encouragingly small: it's limited to oneself. My moral life is all about me. On the other hand, the concern for self-interest, built on an affirmation of self-worth, might well include the moral duty to develop one's potential, as well as the obligation to take care of oneself and maximize the good for oneself. It is a starkly simple theory, and it seems to unify the various spheres of our lives: whether we are interacting with family and friends or professional colleagues or vendors in the marketplace, we should seek to maximize our self-interest.

But when one elevates egoism to a moral theory, problems arise—in the first instance, doubts about its coherence. Remember, a theory of normative morality (even cultural relativism) is proposed as applicable to all moral agents; to advocate it is to urge that everyone adopt it. Moral prescriptions are in that sense *universalizable*. But suppose I am an ethical egoist, what am I advocating, exactly? Is it that: (a) every person should act to maximize his or her self-interest—even when their actions harm me; or (b) I should seek to maximize my self-interest and everybody else should also act to promote *my* self-interest; or perhaps (c) I should act in my own self-interest and everyone else is irrelevant? The problem with option (a) is that it is self-contradictory to advocate actions that maximize my self-interest and actions that will violate my self-interest. The issue with (b) is that it advocates egoism for (only) oneself and a directed *altruism* for others, without a defensible reason for such exceptionalism. It violates both the universalizability criterion and the principle of equal treatment where there is no relevant difference. Drawing an unjustified moral difference between oneself and others is arbitrary, not rational. The difficulty with (c) is that it describes an attitude, not a genuine moral theory; and again, it arbitrarily treats oneself as exceptional.

See how this plays out when we look at the phenomenon of giving moral advice. Suppose the egoist's sister says she is in a serious moral dilemma and asks, "Brother, what should I do?" Should the egoistic brother (a) contradict his moral beliefs and say, "Do X" even though he knows X will have a negative impact on him? Should the brother (b) calculate the likely consequences and say "Do Y" because he knows Y will benefit him—whether Y would help or harm his sister? Or should he (c) say, "I am just concerned about myself, Sis; I have no interest in your problems unless they affect me." The last two responses would eliminate or pervert the practice of giving moral advice—let alone what they would do to sibling relationships. Only the first seems to preserve genuine advice-giving, but at the cost of self-contradiction. Unless these issues can be resolved, ethical egoism seems incoherent or implausible.

In addition, ethical egoism presents bizarre characterizations of several ethical practices. Personal sacrifice would, of course, be morally wrong; so would actions fitting common interpretations of "saintly" behavior. Moral sentiments like compassion and remorse seem to be pointless distractions. Regarding the story of the collapse of Rana Plaza, the egoist would say that it was the doctor who refused to enter the ruins who did the morally right thing; Didar Hossain's actions were morally wrong. The only sort of hero that would receive moral endorsement is the one who cunningly survives against all odds, or the creative genius of heroically forceful self-expression, such as the artistic genius who struggles to create a masterpiece, or the ruthless business person who triumphs over fierce competitors.

Could the ideal of justice have any relevance? Justice would seem to be of narrow, instrumental concern, perhaps interpreted as assuring only a basic civic order and individual rights in the relentless pursuit of self-interest. But it seems to be a weak concept of rights that is valid only for its service to self-interests. Bentham, remember, rejected the concept of rights; he thought rights are merely a fancy way of constraining our actions in advance, of preventing people from doing what would produce the best consequences. I suppose that the committed advocate of ethical egoism might claim that all these implications for moral concepts are not faults, but iconoclasms that are affirmed as corollaries to the theory—in other words, intentional, revolutionary improvements to traditional moral theory. But that stretches credulity.

The effective moral agent, for the egoist, is an always-alert and punctilious calculator of costs and benefits. Emotions play no relevant role in morality. Guilt, for example, seems useless; greed may be good. Moral virtues seem to be reduced to prudence, cunning, self-awareness, and keen skills of practical intelligence, though it may be that persuasiveness and deception are useful at times as well. And perhaps most damning is that ethical egoism would seem to condone acts and practices that are commonly seen as morally repulsive—even require them in certain situations. The cases that have introduced our earlier chapters involve murder, polygamy, and sexual abuse, among other acts. So long as these acts were in the self-interest of the murderer, polygamist, and abuser, they would be morally good—in fact, obligatory if, in the situation, they maximized the agent's pleasure or self-interest. With this implication, egoism seems to be an anti-ethical theory, not a theory of moral conduct. To call it a moral theory would require the rejection of many aspects of what it means to take "the moral point of view" (Chapter 1). The world constructed by the egoist is as Hobbes famously said, "A war of every man against every man." It is a world in which each of us is focused only on getting for ourselves as many benefits, as much good as we can; other people are mere means to that end or competitors.

5.7 ENLIGHTENED SELF-INTEREST

Perhaps I have presented too raw an interpretation of egoism thus far, as though egoists were not just single-minded, but simple-minded. Surely ethical egoism, with its emphasis on reasoning, could promote an *enlightened* self-interest. How might an egoist "enlighten" the conception of self-interest beyond crude maximization of self-satisfaction? There are at least three or four ways.

1. The egoist might move from preoccupation with immediate consequences to longer-term implications, thus extending the temporal horizon for moral accountability. We all learn early that momentary pleasures can sometimes lead to pain. Plus, learning to defer gratification is a sign of maturation; we can learn to manage our natural tendency to discount the future, to rate a payoff now more highly than the same or better payoff

next week. In making this shift, the egoist becomes more concerned with self-interest *in the long run*, not just the benefits received in the short run or as an immediate result. This does, however, present a problem for the egoist—actually, for any consequentialist: how long is the long run and how is one to balance the near-term effects with longer term effects? As the economist John Maynard Keynes (1883–1946) famously observed, "In the long run we are all dead."[18]

2. One might develop and enrich the conception of the good beyond pleasure and the satisfaction of desire. Also, one might reject a monistic theory of value in favor of a *pluralistic* theory, which says that we recognize more than one thing as good, things that are fundamentally different from each other. The nature of the value or values one seeks to maximize can also make a significant difference in the impact of self-interest. Some things we might value, like beach-front property, are scarce. Some goods, that is, such as status or power, are achieved only in relation to others' not having them. (These create what is called a "zero-sum game" in which gain requires loss, and the total amount of available good never changes.) Many goods, however, like knowledge and the appreciation of beauty, are freely available and achieving them is open to individual efforts and interest. And a few goods, like peace and justice, benefit everyone. Our pursuit and achievement of these different sorts of goods has different effects upon others who share our conception. Let me explain.

Suppose we sort various conceptions of the good into three types based on how one's pursuit and achievement of the good affects others who also value it.

- For Type I, one's achievement of the good diminishes or eliminates the chance that others can obtain it. Pursuit of the good is a zero-sum game: if I gobble up beach-front property, there is less available for others. If I gain the status of top dog in some hierarchy; no one else can share it.
- Type II goods are those for which one's achievement of the good has no direct effect on the chances of others for a similar success. My gaining knowledge or experiencing the beauty of nature or art has no direct effect on your chances to gain or experience the same.
- With Type III goods, however, the achievement by any one person *increases* the likelihood or even assures that others will gain the good as well. If a statesman achieves peace, it is a gain for all who value it. The same is true of social justice and environmental health.

These values construct different social relationships. Adopting Type I values construct a world in which others are my competitors; I can only succeed if others fail. Pursuing Type II values does not affect others directly; it seems to leave social relationships open: other people may be irrelevant or quite important. For example, my gaining knowledge depends on others, from writers and scientists to teachers and technicians. And I cannot experience the beauty of music or painting without musicians or artists. But others may also hinder my pursuit—as when crucial knowledge is withheld from me or when my raucous neighbor disturbs my serenity. Finally, with Type III values, since everyone benefits from the success of anyone, there is an inherent bond with others and a communal good.[19]

Though an ethical egoist may recognize goods of any of three types, there would be a kind of oddity in an egoist whose value was of Type III: "I want to maximize social justice (or world peace or environmental health) *for me.*" And yet Hobbes will argue that we set up a government to maintain the peace for selfish reasons—though everyone benefits. Benefits to others, however, remain incidental and irrelevant to an assessment of the consequences. The larger point here is that enlightened self-interest may involve changes in one's conception of the good and that may alter the impact of egoistic conduct on others.

3. A related shift involves one's understanding of the role of others and their welfare in the achievement and security of one's own well-being. The more I see my own welfare entangled with the welfare of others, even dependent upon it, the less "raw" are my egoistic decisions. Homeowners know that the market value of their house depends in part upon the quality of the neighborhood. Businesses make charitable contributions not only to gild their reputation as a successful enterprise, but also to support the community in which their employees live and work. Hard-nosed egoists may constantly ask themselves, "What am I getting out this?" or "What's in it for me?" Nonetheless, when combined with a concern for long-term interests and more complex goods, the realm of self-interest and maximal benefits becomes much wider. Life for the egoist becomes more complicated.

These three moves certainly soften the impact of egoism; but while they serve to make the agent a more sophisticated, more astute egoist, they do not remove its problems. Some of these are rooted not in the concept of interests or the way they are pursued, but in the concept of the self. That may suggest a potential fourth move: one may expand the sense of self. One's moral obligation, then, is to maximize the good for one's family, one's loved ones, one's kin—or some even larger group that claims one's identity. This removes the ugly implication that the egoist must act selfishly even when so acting would harm one's children or spouse or friend. The biological phenomenon of kin selection seems to offer a naturalistic grounding for this expansion: kin selection is an evolved strategy that favors the survival and reproduction of an organism's genetic relatives, even at the cost of diminishing the individual's own chance of survival or reproduction. It is as though the sense of self is expanded to include one's genetic relations. Kin selection is often seen as an evolutionary origin of genuinely altruistic behavior, and it may indeed be a bridge between altruism and a modest notion of the common good. Nonetheless, it seems unlikely that an egoist's sense of self could be stretched so far as to include future generations or even most people now on earth—let alone strangers crushed in the rubble of a collapsed building.

QUESTIONS FOR DISCUSSION

1   How would psychological egoism explain the actions of Didar Hossain and the doctor who remained a spectator? Can Hossain's actions be explained as an "enlightened" form of self-interest?

2   Plato tells the story of the Ring of Gyges in the *Republic* (359a–360d). In this myth, an ancestor of Gyges, a shepherd, discovers a magical ring that enables the wearer to become invisible simply by turning it. Knowing he cannot be discovered, the man ultimately seduces the queen, murders the king, and claims the throne for himself. Plato asks us to consider: what would we do, if we had no fear of being identified, caught, or punished? Is it only such social fears that restrain our basest desires?

3   Explain the difference between maximizing *pleasure*, maximizing the *satisfaction of desires*, and maximizing *self-interest*.

4   Discuss this claim: "If you compare two people—a doctor who spends her vacation as a war-zone volunteer for Doctors Without Borders, and a guy who spends his week drinking beer and watching pornography—they are both satisfying their desires; and when they do that, they are both just pursuing their own self-interest."

5   Give examples of the consequentialist problem of balancing short- and long-term effects.

6   Consider this case: Carla wants very much to attend college; she has high hopes for a professional career. Sadly, her mother has become disabled, requires care, and is otherwise alone. Carla wants to do what is right. From a moral point of view, what should she do and why—postpone her plans and care for her mother, or try to arrange for others to be the care-givers? Does she have a *moral* obligation to herself?

7   What practical difference does it make whether an egoist applies "raw" self-interest or "enlightened" self-interest?

QUESTIONS FOR PERSONAL REFLECTION

1   How do you respond to the claim that "your highest moral purpose is your own well-being"? Are there other purposes that seem "higher"?

2   When you think about the things you value, where do they fall within the typology given in section 5.7?

3   How can you tell whether someone's actions are genuinely altruistic or are the motivated by enlightened self-interest? What indicators or evidence might you use?

SUGGESTED SOURCES

Batson, C. Daniel. *The Altruism Question: Toward a Social-Psychological Answer* (1991; New York: Psychology P, 2014).

Bloomfield, Paul, ed. *Morality and Self-Interest* (Oxford: Oxford UP, 2007).

Butler, Joseph. *Five Sermons* (Indianapolis, IN: Hackett, 1983).

Joyce, Richard. *The Evolution of Morality* (Cambridge, MA: MIT P, 2007).

Mansbridge, Jane J., ed. *Beyond Self-Interest* (Chicago: U of Chicago P, 1990).

Peterson, Martin. *The Dimensions of Consequentialism: Ethics, Equality and Risk* (Cambridge: Cambridge UP, 2015).

Shaver, Robert. "Egoism," in *The Stanford Encyclopedia of Philosophy*: http://plato.stanford.edu/entries/egoism/ (accessed July 2018).

NOTES

1   The collapse of Rana Plaza was a major disaster covered globally by the media. Didar Hossain's story in particular was a widely reported one. See, e.g., "Bangladesh Rescuer: 'I Cut Off Limbs to Save Lives,'" *BBC: Asia*, May 3, 2013: http://www.bbc.com/news/world-asia-22384529 (accessed June 2016).

2   Thomas Hobbes, *Leviathan*; G.A.J. Rogers and Karl Shuhmann, eds.; 2 vols. (1651; London: Continuum, 2005) 2: 1.15, 125.

3   Jeremy Bentham, *An Introduction to the Principles of Morals and Legislation* (1789; New York: Hafner, 1948), 1–2.

4   Joseph Butler, *Fifteen Sermons Preached at the Rolls Chapel* (1726), especially Sermons XI and XII.

5   Butler distinguishes between *self-love* and *selfishness*. Self-love is "regard to our own Interest, Happiness, and private Good." There is nothing wrong with self-love; indeed, we should pursue our long-term well-being. Selfishness, however, is the disregard of others, and is quite apart from self-love. It is a confusion to equate selfish acts with acts of self-love or altruism on the basis that satisfaction or pleasure results from all of them.

6   A.A. Milne, *The House at Pooh Corner*, Ch. 10.

7   For both a brief account of the emergence of economics and the groundbreaking discussion of the critique in this section, see Amartya Sen, *On Ethics and Economics* (Oxford: Oxford UP, 1999).

8   Adam Smith, *An Inquiry into the Nature and Causes of the Wealth of Nations* (1776), I.2.

9   Sometimes, they included "self-interested" in the very definition of "rational" as well, though this risks vicious circularity.

10 The 2017 Nobel Prize for Economics was awarded to Richard Thaler for his pioneering work in developing the foundations of behavior economics. A popular book that documents examples of our deviations from rational decision making is Dan Ariely, *Predictably Irrational* (New York: HarperCollins, 2008).

11 On the role of role of reciprocity, cooperation, and trust among primates, see Frans de Waal, Stephen Macedo, and Josiah Ober, *Primates and Philosophers: How Morality Evolved*, 5th ed. (Princeton, NJ: Princeton UP, 2009); and Christopher Boehm, *Moral Origins: The Evolution of Virtue, Altruism, and Shame* (New York: Basic Books, 2012). On their role specifically in human behavior, see e.g., Richard Joyce, *The Evolution of Morality* (Cambridge, MA: MIT P, 2007).

12 The empathy–altruism hypothesis was presented in C.D. Batson and B. Leonard (1987), "Prosocial Motivation: Is It Ever Truly Altruistic?" in *Advances in Experimental Social Psychology*, 20, 65–122. For the assessment of research, see C. Daniel Batson, David A. Lishner, and Eric L. Stocks, "The Empathy–Altruism Hypothesis," and related articles in *The Oxford Handbook of Prosocial Behavior*, edited by David A. Schroeder and William G. Graziano (Oxford: Oxford UP, 2015).

13 The term has probably become more significant than Smith intended: he used it only three times in all his writings. His earliest use of the term, in *The History of Astronomy*, referred to superstitious accounts of the gods' manipulation of astronomical phenomena. In *The Theory of Moral Sentiments*, he uses it to describe the way in which unintentional benefits may result for the poor from the greedy consumption of the rich. In *The Wealth of Nations*, he never refers to "*the* invisible hand," but rather "*an* invisible hand."

14 Ayn Rand, *The Virtue of Selfishness* (New York: Signet Books, 1964).

15 Ibid., 18.

16 Because consequentialist theories focus on the end or purpose, they are sometimes also called *teleological* theories (from the Greek word, *telos*, meaning "end, purpose, or goal").

17 I have italicized the normative language for emphasis.

18 John Maynard Keynes, *A Tract on Monetary Reform* (London: Macmillan, 1923), 80.

19 I have detailed and applied this typology more fully in Daniel R. DeNicola, "A Typology of Conceptions of the Good," *Personalist (The)* 59:1 (January 1978): 38–46.

CHAPTER SIX

Utilitarianism

Project Prevention is a non-profit organization that pays drug-addicted women $300 cash in exchange for sterilization or long-term birth-control.[1] It was formed in 1997 by Barbara Harris, who had adopted four of the eight children of a California addict. Her group claims to promote a social good. Children born to drug addicts are often neglected or abused; others are stillborn, have genetic or developmental defects, or are born addicted and suffer through withdrawal. Nearly all who survive require special care—at a public cost of billions of dollars a year in the US alone.

Beyond increasing public awareness of the problem, "Project Prevention seeks to reduce the burden of this social problem on taxpayers, trim down social worker caseloads, and alleviate from our clients the burden of having children that will potentially be taken away." Moreover, "Unlike incarceration, Project Prevention is extremely cost effective and does not punish the participants." As of mid-2018, over 7,000 women have been paid to be sterilized or given long-term birth control implants and over 280 men received vasectomies; these are addicts who earlier produced a total of about 6,000 living children who are in foster care or are waiting adoption.

The addict may use the cash for anything, including getting another fix. Indeed, the Project has used such slogans as "Don't let pregnancy get in the way of your crack habit."[2] The group does offer referrals to treatment programs, but does not fund them. Critics claim the Project has no concern for the addicts, and that it targets minorities and the poor. But although the proportion of Black "clients" is roughly twice that of the general population, the largest group (about 60%) is White. Some argue that addicts are incapable of making such a life-altering decision rationally; given their addiction, a cash incentive is seductive at best, coercive at worst. Others claim that our right to reproduce should not be bargained away, just as we should not sell ourselves—or be seduced—into slavery.

Ms. Harris is quoted as saying, "We don't allow dogs to breed ... We neuter them. We try to keep them from having unwanted puppies, and yet these women are literally having litters of children." Yet she has also said: "Some people are so into the women and their rights to get pregnant that they seem to forget about the rights of the kids. They act like these children don't matter. People need to realize these women don't want to have babies that are taken away from them."[3]

But Mary Barr, a spokesperson for the National Advocates for Pregnant Women in the US, says "Today I'm a successful woman with a house and family ... But I used to be homeless and addicted to crack cocaine ... My children are happy and healthy. My daughter has just started studying at college to be a doctor, on a full scholarship. If Project Prevention had got to me, she wouldn't exist."[4]

6.1 THE RIGHT AND THE GOOD

Utilitarianism, the focus of this chapter, is the name for a cluster of closely related ethical theories that embody a distinctive way of thinking about moral issues and public policy. We may preview aspects of utilitarian thinking in the operations of Project Prevention: the aim to promote a social good, concern for the welfare of children, the balancing of costs and benefits, and the single-minded focus on results. In this morally provocative case, the foundation claims the social good is achieved largely by preventing harm: it works to reduce the social and financial burden of unwanted and often afflicted children born to drug addicts, to prevent the miserable lives such children are likely to have, to discourage the practice of repeated abortions, and so on. The incentive payment for sterilization is modest, so the total financial cost is comparatively small, and the addicts receive money, not punishment; rehabilitation efforts would cost much more—and they are seldom successful. The addicts are happy to receive the cash. Yes, they might use the money for another fix; but that would likely have occurred by other means anyway, and it is greatly outweighed by the benefits. Moral critics may raise doubts about whether the women are in a proper state to make such a decision, whether such an incentive is coercive, whether reproductive rights should be traded, whether the program targets minorities or disrespects women—but their doubts and ethical scruples only serve to restrain us from doing what is needed to prevent harm and make the world a better place. So says the utilitarian.

Utilitarianism, like ethical egoism, is a type of consequentialism. Consequentialist moral theories, as we have seen, focus on the outcomes of actions and practices, emphasize instrumental reasoning (the selection of efficient means for given ends), and enjoin us to produce the most good. The development of economics and the spread of economic models have made this cost–benefit orientation commonplace in our age. As a result, for us it is difficult to recapture just how breathtakingly radical this way of thinking was when utilitarianism was promulgated in nineteenth-century Britain by Jeremy Bentham, James Mill (1773–1836), and his son John Stuart Mill.[5] An account of the intellectual history of this period in Britain is well beyond our scope; here I can only mention a few motifs that such an account would include: the spread of democratic and republican models, the promotion of social reform through legislation, debates over slavery and the slave trade, the awakening of the women's suffrage movement, earnest charity, the global extension of colonialism during the long reign of Queen Victoria, the rise of the social sciences, and faith in the possibility of social progress. Utilitarianism is deeply embedded in all these, being both a reflection of them and an impetus for them. Most radical theories are striking in what they reject and in the simplicity of what they propose. In practice, the apparent simplicity usually gives way to knotty complexities, and theorists need to reclaim and rehabilitate some of what was first rejected. All this is true for utilitarianism. Let us begin with its striking simplicity.

One of the problems of moral theory is the relationship between the right and the good, between what ethics requires of us and the prospect of gain or loss of the things we value. We have seen the tension that can arise: Abraham's Divine Command ethics required him to sacrifice his son, whom he loved. Firmness in the right (righteousness) overrode concern for any human desire or common good, or claimed righteousness itself to be the only good. Consequentialist theories, by contrast, assert a simple, straightforward connection: *what is right is to secure what is good.*

Instead of contending with Ten Commandments, ancient and contested sacred texts, varying cultural norms, multiple and conflicting natural rights, or other such complexities, consequentialism offers morality a single principle, a master key that can always and everywhere unlock any moral dilemma: *maximize the good.* There is no need to prioritize principles or resolve their conflicts when there is only one valid principle. The principle that we are morally obligated to promote the good is the **Principle of Utility.**

Moreover, ethical theories that make what is right a matter of following age-old rules or commands or human rights impose a kind of harness or restraint on human action. (This is why Bentham opposed the concept of natural rights.) They are the moralizing weight of the past. Such rules keep us in line, but they do not improve the world. They are not progressive. Utilitarianism says in effect, "Throw off the harness of stultifying morality! Remove the shackles of prior constraints! Look to the future and consider how what you do might make a difference. Morality is not a weight; it is a force. Think about what will actually improve lives and make the world a better place—for that is the true purpose of morality!"

For example, inherited morality, fossilized in Victorian law, may state that marriage is a life-long sacred union, a contract bound by oaths; that wives cannot own property or divorce their husbands; that the marriage must continue even when the relationship is emotionally empty or abusive. Such a morality enforces misery and improves nothing. The utilitarian instead directs the moral force toward acts and practices that would make life better. This attention to outcomes or results gives ethics an empirical cast; the moral agent needs to know about causes and effects, and to adjust efforts in accord with actual experience.

To summarize: consequentialism is radical in that: (1) it reduces morality to a single master principle; (2) it directly links right action to the maximization of the good; (3) it looks to the future and downplays the binding moral status of rules, codes, rights, and precedent; and (4) it calibrates actions by experience, by the outcomes achieved, the differences made.

6.2 FROM EGOISM TO UTILITARIANISM

Although consequentialism has only one master principle, the maximization of the good, it requires two specifications or subsidiary principles. They answer two important questions: "*What* is the good?" and "*Whose* good is to be maximized?"

The philosophical study of value is called **axiology**. In ethics, it focuses on the nature of the good (in aesthetics, it includes the study of beauty). Utilitarians are united in the view that *utility* is the good. But this generic term masks subtle differences among them. Early utilitarians, like many egoists, embraced the view that *pleasure* is the good. John Stuart Mill, as we shall see, subtly shifts this concept of utility further, preferring *happiness* as the good, though it consists in pleasures. Others prefer the *satisfaction of desire*, and economists have tended to use the term *welfare* synonymously. Later utilitarians often prefer the term *well-being*.

The second question—"Consequences for whom?"—is a way of asking, "Who counts, who matters, when one considers the costs and benefits of an act or practice?" The answer lays down a *distributive principle*; it determines the normative way to distribute the good (and any collateral harm). An ethical egoist counts only herself; her welfare alone matters in determining what is right. Hobbes, as we saw, professed that model. Bentham's keen interest in social reform drew him to a different distributive principle: especially in public issues, he claimed that one should seek the greatest good *for the greatest number*. This formulation is now known as the defining doctrine of **utilitarianism**. When an act maximizes the good, producing the best possible total consequences for the greatest number, we call that act **optimific**. For a utilitarian, only the optimific act is the morally right act, the action we should take; any other action would be wrong.

Although Bentham elaborates his views and Mill modifies them significantly, it is prudent to begin with the vanilla version of utilitarianism that they share:

"*X* is right" = "*X* produces the greatest good for the greatest number," or

"*X* is right" = "*X* is the optimific act."

Even this basic formulation displays many attractive aspects, including those that made it radical: (1) the simplicity of a single principle that harmonizes the right and the good; (2) the focus on the future and objective results; and (3) the move from morality as constraints on action to morality as a goad for betterment. But there are more. (4) Utilitarianism entails agent impartiality. Egoism, as I noted, entails an unwarranted partiality: the egoist counts; others do not. But when one considers "the greatest number," each individual counts as one, including the agent. Another distinguished utilitarian, Henry Sidgwick (1838–1900), put the point this way: "The good of any one individual is of no more importance, from the point of view (if I may say so) of the Universe, than the good of any other."[6] (5) This impartiality is also **egalitarian**, since it not only rejects discrimination among individuals, it implies that *all individuals matter*; all are capable and worthy of experiencing the good. (6) Indeed, given the usual theories of value it embraces, it may actually expand the moral community: *any creature that can suffer (that is, experience pain or harm, as well as pleasure) has moral standing*, and their suffering must be registered as a negative effect of action. The capacity to suffer, wrote Bentham, should mark "an insuperable line" in how we treat all creatures. An early champion of the moral standing of animals, Bentham asserted: "The question is not, *Can they reason?* nor, *Can they talk?* but, *Can they suffer?*"[7] Finally, (7) the theory offers a hope and guide for the formation of public policy and the resolution of ethical conflicts. It directs our moral energies away from prior commitments, individual differences, and personal prejudices toward participation in the construction of the collective good, the betterment of our world.

6.3 BENTHAM'S CALCULUS

Jeremy Bentham was an English social reformer and philosopher who took a law degree but never practiced, preferring instead to direct his considerable energy to projects for the public good. A child prodigy, Bentham's brilliance was edged with eccentricity: for example, before he died at age 84, he had made extensive preparations for his body's dissection and its preservation and display as an "auto-icon."[8] As we have seen,

Bentham was a hedonist and enemy of natural rights. His most important philosophical statements were presented in his influential 1789 work, *An Introduction to the Principles of Morals and Legislation*, which sets forth his ethical system. Blessed with family wealth, Bentham pursued wide-ranging research on topics such as prison design (he designed the "panopticon"[9]) and penal code reform, electoral reform, economic theory and fiscal practice, humane treatment of animals, and refrigeration processes. In a posthumously published essay, he argued for the liberalization of laws regarding homosexuality.

The ringing simplicity of Bentham's "greatest good for the greatest number" principle quickly encountered complexities. If our only moral task is to maximize the good, which is pleasure, we need some way to quantify and measure the pleasure and pain produced, both for a single individual and for a group.[10] Indeed, the measurement must be precise enough to compare the pleasures and pains of alternative actions, so that one might identify the optimific act. And the measurement must assign negative weight, not neutrality, to pain. One must subtract the harm done from the good achieved to get the *net benefit*.

Since the process of measurement implies a unit of measurement, Bentham used the term *hedon* for a unit of pleasure and *dolor* for a unit of pain. He cleverly developed a "hedonic calculus" based on these units. He proposed to consider several aspects of pleasure:

1. *Intensity*—how strong is the pleasure (or pain)?
2. *Duration*—how long will the pleasure (or pain) last?
3. *Certainty*—how probable is it that one will experience the pleasure (or pain)?
4. *Propinquity*—how long would one have to wait for the pleasure (or pain)?
5. *Fecundity*—how likely is it that the pleasure (or pain) will breed other pleasures (or pains)?
6. *Purity*—how unlikely is it that the pleasure will lead to pains (or the pain to pleasures)?

To incorporate "the greatest number," he added the distributive criterion:

7. *Extent*—how many people will experience pleasure (or pain) as a result?

Bentham proposed a basic moral decision procedure: (1) specify the alternative actions; (2) for each action, using the seven criteria, compute the total *hedons* and subtract the *dolors* to calculate the net pleasure; (3) identify and do the optimific act, that is, the one that produces the greatest net pleasure.

It may be easy to imagine using this "calculus" in a rough-and-ready way to make decisions. For example, Emily decides whether the pleasure of yet one more drink is worth the hangover that is likely to follow. Tyrone decides whether the pain of paying for a swimming pool will be worth the pleasure that he and his family will have. But this procedure is not really a calculus; it lacks crucial aspects. (1) Bentham never really stated just what a single *hedon* or *dolor* is, nor did he explain an adequate technique for measuring them. Clearly, he intended a subjective measure, because he discussed factors that affect individual differences in experiencing pain and pleasure; and he focused on actual pleasure and pain, not an ideal calculation. But he gave us no way of determining just how many *hedons* Emily's next drink would be, nor how many *dolors* she could expect for her hangover. These terms are merely names for units of pleasure and pain, not definitions. This is both a theoretical and a practical problem. (2) Bentham did not specify how the six factors affecting pleasure are to be weighed in relation to each other. How much low-grade, long-lasting pleasure equals an intense but brief pleasure? How should we compare a mild pleasure that is certain to be enjoyed tonight with an intense pleasure that is less certain and perhaps a month away? And with regard to pain, is it, so to speak, better to pull the Band-Aid off slowly with some pain, or to snatch it off rapidly but with intense pain? (3) Bentham's formulation requires two basic maximizations: the greatest pleasure and the greatest number. But these two are independent, of course; they do not automatically increase in parallel. How should one weigh extent against pleasure? That is, how are we to choose between a policy that would give a high number of net hedons to a few individuals and a policy that would give a few net hedons to a very large number of people? Bentham does not stipulate an answer.

Think just how complicated it would be to apply Bentham's calculus to the Project Prevention operation. Besides the pleasures and pains of everyone affected, one has the additional problem of considering the impact on "possible individuals"—infants who will never be born as a result of their program.

The details of quantifying and measuring subjective states became the work of later psychologists; the details of a calculus of utility were left to later economists. But the vision of Bentham's utilitarianism was clear if not precise: actions, policies, and practices should be aimed at producing the greatest net good for the greatest number.

6.4 JOHN STUART MILL

One of Bentham's closest friends was James Mill, a Scottish philosopher, historian, and public intellectual. When Mill's wife delivered their first child, a boy named John Stuart, Bentham became his godfather. Mill declared that he would bring up this child to be a great advocate for utilitarianism, and his plan was shockingly successful. It helped that the boy was a genius." But the education was rigorous: young Mill was homeschooled under the demanding and restrictive tutelage of his father. The results were astounding: he began Greek at the age of three; at eight, he learned Latin. The list of works he had read by age thirteen is enormous, most in the original languages. He would become one of the most influential philosophers of liberalism. But this intensive academic training unsurprisingly took its toll. As Mill famously recounts in his *Autobiography*, when he was twenty, he suffered a breakdown so severe that he contemplated suicide. Yet he reasoned his way out of his depression: believing his emotional development was stunted, he began reading Romantic poetry—taking doses of poetry as though it was medicine—until he gradually recovered. He became a staunch advocate of freedom and happiness.

His later biography is as fascinating as his early years. He was employed by the East India Company for thirty-five years, rising in the ranks to become responsible for all official correspondence with India—though he never once visited the country. He fell in love with a married woman, Harriet Taylor, a relationship that scandalized Victorian England, though they eventually married. Harriet was a brilliant thinker and writer who undoubtedly contributed to Mill's work. Mill authored the greatest defense of personal freedom ever penned: *On Liberty*. An opponent of slavery, he wrote "On the Negro Question" in 1850 as a rebuttal to a racist essay by the Scottish intellectual Thomas Carlyle. He was elected to Parliament, where in 1867 he introduced the first legislation to grant women suffrage. It failed. But in 1869, Mill wrote *The Subjection of Women*, a sustained argument for the equality of women. On these and many other social issues, Mill is a subtle yet forceful thinker, a progressive who seems to read "the right side of history." His life and work comprise an exemplary utilitarian program.

6.5 QUALITATIVE HEDONISM

Mill first presented his classic account in a series of articles in *Fraser's Magazine for Town and Country* in 1861. They were reprinted in 1863 as a single text simply called *Utilitarianism*, and it has become a canonical text in ethical theory. By the time it appeared, the doctrine of utilitarianism was both influential and controversial, and Mill wrote his essay to explain and defend the doctrine. It may be read as a set of defensive and persuasive responses to fourteen objections to the theory (unnumbered in Mill's text, but I have paraphrased them in **Figure 2**). He considers each of the objections in turn, following an introductory chapter in which he sets forth the problem to be addressed and his purpose.[12] In the course of his argument, Mill presents and refines Bentham's "**greatest happiness principle**" (a version of the Principle of Utility that names happiness as the good), extending his account, discussing its implications, and portraying the quality of life the utilitarian seeks.

The first objection—utilitarianism rejects pleasure (Obj. 1)—Mill dismisses as an "ignorant blunder." The second, however—the claim that it is base to reduce the human good to sensual pleasure (Obj. 2)—inspires a response that introduces a significant and controversial amendment to the theory. While Bentham had acknowledged different sources of pleasure, Mill claims that "some *kinds* of pleasure are more desirable and valuable than others." This view is now called *qualitative hedonism*. According to Mill, there is a hierarchy of pleasures in which "mental pleasures," for example, are better, worthier, than sensual pleasures. Human beings require and prefer pleasures that employ "their higher faculties." Mill writes:

> Few human creatures would consent to be changed into any of the lower animals, for a promise of the fullest allowance of a beast's pleasures; no intelligent person would consent to be a fool, no instructed person would be an ignoramus, no person of feeling and conscience would be selfish and base, even though they should be persuaded that the fool, the dunce, or the rascal is better satisfied with his lot than they are with theirs. They would not resign what they possess more than he for the most complete satisfaction of all the desires which they have in common with him.... It is better to be a human being dissatisfied than a pig satisfied; better to be Socrates dissatisfied than a fool satisfied. And if the fool, or the pig, are of a different opinion, it is because they only know their own side of the question. The other party to the comparison knows both sides.[13]

There are three critical points to make about this remarkable explication. (1) One might initially think that Mill's qualitative distinctions are reducible to Bentham's quantitative criteria, so there is nothing really

FIGURE 2   MILL'S *UTILITARIANISM*

A SUMMARY OF ARGUMENTS CONSIDERED

Objections to Utilitarianism

Chapter 2

Obj. 1. Utilitarianism is opposed to pleasure.

Obj. 2. Utilitarians suppose that life has no higher end than pleasure—a base doctrine "worthy only of swine."

Obj. 3. Happiness cannot be the rational purpose of human life and action because: (a) it is unattainable; (b) we are not entitled to happiness; and (c) we can do without happiness.

Obj. 4. The utilitarian standard is beyond the reach of human beings: it is expecting too much of people to require that they shall always act to promote the general interests of society.

Obj. 5. Utilitarianism makes people "cold and unsympathizing"; it "chills their moral feelings."

Obj. 6. Utilitarianism is a godless doctrine.

Obj. 7. Utilitarianism replaces principled morality with expediency.

Obj. 8. Utilitarianism is impossible to practice because there is not sufficient time, prior to acting, to calculate and weigh the possible effects of several possible actions on the general happiness.

Obj. 9. People who practice utilitarianism will tend to make an exception for themselves.

Chapter 3

Obj. 10. Utilitarianism has no natural sanction, no natural basis for its binding force, its obligations, or its motives.

Chapter 4

Obj. 11. There is no proof of the Principle of Utility.

Obj. 12. Virtue is not regarded as a good by utilitarians.

Obj. 13. A virtuous person acts without any thought of the pleasure he or she will receive in fulfilling obligations; at the very least, increasing pleasures is not always the overriding motive of a virtuous person.

Chapter 5

Obj. 14. Utilitarianism cannot account for justice, because justice is opposed to the expedient; justice is giving people what they deserve—not what will make them happy.

new here. Perhaps mental pleasures produce more hedons than sensual pleasures because they are more enduring, fecund, and pure, for example. Although Mill accepts that argument, he goes further in this passage: having the *capacity* for such pleasures is a good in itself. Indeed, it seems to be a higher good than actual experiences of lower pleasures. Note that Mill does *not* say "It is better to be a human being *satisfied* than a pig satisfied"; he says "It is better to be a human being *dissatisfied* than a pig satisfied." If some pains are better than some pleasures, then a new criterion has been introduced, a factor that makes qualitative distinctions among pleasures and pains. Pleasure is not the only good; perhaps it is not even what ultimately governs the good. As the political philosopher Michael Sandel (b. 1953) has observed, "Mill saves utilitarianism from the charge that it reduces everything to a crude calculus of pleasure and pain, but only by invoking a moral ideal of human dignity and personality independent of utility itself."[14]

(2) This view that pleasures, experiences, or activities form a hierarchy of worthiness has been an influential tenet of Western culture since Plato. It is largely based on such a doctrine that we have decided it is better to teach physics or history in high school than billiards or basket-weaving. But how are we to determine which of two pleasures or activities is the higher or better? Mill proposes a superficially simple test: ask people who are competent and experienced in both. If we are wondering whether, say, rugby or poetry is the better activity, it will not help to ask people who are fanatics for either rugby or poetry; rather, we must ask people who are expert at *both* rugby and poetry. Only they are in a position to make a valid comparison. Mill says, "The judgment of those who are qualified by knowledge of both, or, if they differ, that of the majority among them, must be admitted as final."[15]

Some philosophers deny that any justification for such hierarchical distinctions can be found. While there may be a basis to discriminate good rugby play from bad, superior poems from inferior ones, these skeptics argue there is no basis to judge poetry superior to rugby, or vice versa.[16] These distinctions of low and high activities are largely a matter of personal prejudice, they say. In any event, most philosophers regard Mill's test as a surprisingly silly proposal. (Imagine trying to assemble the focus group of those rare individuals who are expert in both rugby and poetry.) Nonetheless, Mill believes that judging the quality of a pleasure to be gained from an activity requires knowledge and direct experience of it, and he seems to believe also that people will naturally converge in their judgments. So, although such judgments are subjective, they will naturally form a consensus—and that is the only sort of test that is possible.

(3) The third point: a hint of circularity is present in Mill's notion that we are to consult people who are "susceptible to both classes of pleasures" and defer to their judgments. But how could we identify individuals with such a susceptibility or capability except by the actual judgments they make? If someone familiar with both prefers rock-and-roll to opera, we can always say she simply doesn't appreciate the good of opera, she is not really susceptible to its pleasures. It seems we must accept the judgments of experts, but can know them to be expert only by their judgments.

Mill's shift to qualitative hedonism is reflected in his preference for *happiness* as the good, though he retains its foundation in *pleasures*. The concept of happiness he advocated is "not a life of rapture; but moments of such, in an existence made up of few and transitory pains, many and various pleasures, with a decided predominance of the active over the passive, and having as the foundation of the whole, not to expect more from life than it is capable of bestowing."[17] In Mill's discussion, the concept of happiness slides from a specific feeling to a broader, vaguer, more inclusive concept of the positive quality of an enjoyed, flourishing life. But the concept is not empty of meaning, nor is this range of meaning illegitimate. Though Mill characterizes a life of happiness, he does not imagine that individuals will find happiness in exactly the same activities or experiences. Some people love music; others love adventures in nature; others develop a passion for chess. But these are sources of their happiness—ultimately components of a happy life—and Mill's liberalism would never intentionally impose a notion of happiness that restricted personal freedom. He believed we can acknowledge these important individual differences while still giving a substantive, general characterization of happiness as the ultimate desire of all.

6.6 THE PROOF OF UTILITY

But is there any proof of the Principle of Utility (Obj. 11)? Is it possible to prove that happiness—whatever the details may be—is the good? Although Mill acknowledged that "ultimate ends do not admit of proof," he does offer the only sort of proof of which the Principle of Utility is "susceptible." He asserts:

> "The only proof capable of being given that an object is visible, is
> that people actually see it. The only proof that a sound is audible, is

that people hear it.... In like manner, I apprehend, the sole evidence it is possible to produce that anything is desirable, is that people do actually desire it ... No reason can be given why the general happiness is desirable, except that each person ... desires his own happiness. [Thus,] we have not only all the proof which the case admits of, but all which it is possible to require, that happiness is a good: that each person's happiness is a good to that person, and the general happiness, therefore, a good to the aggregate of all persons."[18]

But Mill recognizes that the Principle of Utility requires more: it is not enough to prove that happiness is *a* good; we need proof that it is *the* good, the only good. Is it true that happiness is the *only* thing people ultimately desire? Although individuals may variously value music or adventure or virtue for itself, they desire it as a component of their happiness. Of course, Mill is aware that people may desire things that leave them unhappy, and some souls may in fact choose a wretched life, but he believes these choices are not rationally intelligible. Such choices can only be explained by interpreting them as an irrational, misguided, or perverted attempt to secure happiness.

Years later, the English philosopher G.E. Moore (1873–1958) objected to this "proof" as linguistic sleight of hand. Moore noted that "visible" means *capable of being seen*; "audible" means *capable of being heard*—but "desirable," as Mill is using the term, does not mean *capable of being desired*; it means *worthy of being desired*. Visible things and audible sounds are not necessarily *worthy* of being seen or heard. The analogy is false.

But Mill may have been *asserting* ethical naturalism: his point may simply be that moral values are grounded in human nature, and that it is human nature to desire happiness. Thus, what is worth desiring will be a function of what humans by nature desire. His larger point is that genuinely rational action always aims at the good as it is perceived; and happiness is, by human nature, what all such action seeks—therefore happiness is the good, the only good, or the all-embracing good.

One can easily understand the problem of proof that Mill faces: it is the problem of proving intrinsic value. Imagine this scenario: a mother getting ready to leave her house, patiently responding to the persistent "why?" questions of her young daughter. "Why are you leaving now?" *To catch the bus.* "Why are you taking the bus?" *To get to work.* "Why are you going to work?" *To earn money.* "Why do you want money?" *So that I can pay for our rent and clothes and our toys and all the things we want and need.* "Why do you have to do all that?" *So we'll all be happy.* "Why

MORAL PHILOSOPHY: A CONTEMPORARY INTRODUCTION

do you want to be happy?"—and at this point she stops. *Because it's good to be happy*. All of those intermediate steps—the bus, work, the money—they are means to an end. They have value, but it is **extrinsic value**. Their value is drawn from something extrinsic to them. When better means to the same end appear, their value is diminished: if the mother buys a car, she may no longer value the bus as much. But the end of this chain, happiness, has **intrinsic value**. It is good for its own sake, and is not selected as a means to something else. We can prove extrinsic value by showing it is an efficient means to a given end. But there is no proof outside itself for something's intrinsic value. Its value is recognized; it is self-justifying, not justified by its usefulness in obtaining something else.[19]

6.7 FROM ACTS TO RULES

The utilitarian understands that when a moral agent is faced with a choice, the actual consequences are never a certainty; and the further into the future we consider our actions' effects, the less certain we are of them. Therefore, the agent's calculation is to be made in terms of *reasonable expectations as to outcomes*. Certainly, an agent can be blamed for miscalculating, for ignoring relevant considerations, or for basing an action on unreasonable prospects. But although some would insist on a review of eventual actual consequences to evaluate the act, everyone would expect the agent only to do what would reasonably be judged optimific given the best information at the time.

Still, one might argue that utilitarianism seems to require so much of moral agents as to be impossible to comply in practice. First, there are the issues of attention and time. It seems to require continual calculation, because any act is wrong if there is an alternative that would have more utility. But often there is not sufficient time to weigh possible effects on the general happiness of innumerable possible actions (Obj. 8). It requires a vigorous and perceptive moral imagination to frame all of one's alternatives. In addition, utilitarianism seems to be unreasonably demanding. It sets the *highest* and best possible action—always doing the utmost to promote the greatest good—as the *minimum* standard for moral behavior (Obj. 4). This is simply beyond the reach of human beings. Since one has a duty to do the optimific act, there is no possibility of going beyond duty for extraordinary good; that is, supererogation is eliminated. Moreover, there is no respite from the demands of morality, since a good utilitarian, it seems, should calculate every action, indeed every possible action, *at every moment*.

Utilitarianism puts the agent in an unmanageable predicament. Imagine that Cynthia has $1,000 in the bank. She may be going about her business, not thinking about her savings—but, as a utilitarian, she should be. Should she keep the money there to let her savings grow? Or should she pay a debt with it? Or should she spend it for something that would bring her joy? Or perhaps she should divide it among ten needy friends? Should she lend it to someone in need? Or should she send it to any one of a hundred charities—maybe disaster relief or sponsorship of children? Which of these would be the optimific act producing the greatest good for the greatest number? All this calculation is so exhausting as to be impossible; yet anything less than the optimific act would be wrong— and Cynthia was not thinking she faced an ethical decision at all. But she should also be thinking of the good she could do with her car or by acting as a helpful volunteer instead of using her savings. This swirling sense of possibilities for promoting happiness would fill her waking moments—in fact, she should also consider how much good she could do if she reduced her sleeping hours. A diligent utilitarian, it seems, is likely to experience both moral and physical (and perhaps financial) exhaustion.[20]

Furthermore, a utilitarian moral agent must face this predicament without any fixed ethical principles, beyond the injunction to promote the greatest good. She has no moral standard for choosing the means to an end; indeed, no means are prohibited; the expedient action is taken to be the right action (Obj. 7). Justice, for example, normally a powerful moral ideal, does not serve as a moral touchstone; it is waved in favor of expediency (Obj. 14). Consider these cases:

A. The sheriff knows that a murder was committed by an unknown assailant who quickly left the country, and there is no chance to apprehend him. But there is a dangerous man, a local man, innocent of this murder, but tied to other killings. The sheriff plants evidence that implicates this man and finally leads to his imprisonment. He reasons that it promotes the social good, calming the fears of citizens by "solving" a murder, and protecting the public by putting a dangerous and otherwise guilty criminal behind bars.

B. Members of an isolated commune determine that the optimific arrangement would require that one of them become a slave to the others. They correctly calculate that, although the negative costs to the slave would be significant, they would be outweighed by the good enjoyed by others. They decide to determine who will be the slave by having the least specialized team members draw lots.

Even if the greatest happiness is in fact produced in both cases, one might ask, "But what about justice?" Is it just to frame a man for a crime he didn't commit or to enslave someone at random for the benefits to others? Or is justice, like natural rights, a nonsensical restraint on doing the most good?

In part, these and similar objections and scenarios arise because of the focus on actions. What I called the vanilla version of the theory, its purest version, is known as **act utilitarianism**. Recall that it asserts:

"X is the right act" = "X is the optimific act"

Mill gradually pulls away from this straightforward act utilitarianism. He moves toward what is now called **rule utilitarianism**.[21] This is a more complex form of the theory, which asserts:

"X is the right act" = "X is prescribed by one of a set of rules, which, if followed, would produce the greatest good for the greatest number"

The relevant calculation of maximal utility thus shifts from individual acts to rules or principles. Under rule utilitarianism, the situation of the moral agent becomes more manageable: one is not faced with evaluating all possible actions at every moment; instead, one follows rules that have been tested for on-the-whole utility-production. Mill's answer to the "insufficient time" objection (Obj. 7) is that "there has been ample time, namely, the whole past duration of the human species." The received rules we have learned are continually tested in human experience, however. As Mill says, "The corollaries from the principle of utility, like the precepts of every practical art, admit of indefinite improvement, and in a progressive state of the human mind, their improvement is perpetually going on."[22]

As to justice, which Mill regards as "the only real difficulty in the utilitarian theory of morality," he claims "Justice is a name for certain moral requirements, which, regarded collectively, stand higher in the scale of social utility, and are therefore of more paramount obligation, than any others."[23] This talk of "corollaries," "precepts," and "requirements" suggests a recognition of moral principles, yet Mill seems to claim that, although an agent may start from a stock of moral rules and apply available moral principles in reasoning, nevertheless, in the end the decision comes down to the utility of individual acts. He says:

> "Particular cases may occur in which some other social duty is so important, as to overrule any one of the general maxims of justice. Thus, to save a life, it may not only be allowable but a duty to steal or take by force the necessary food or medicine, or to kidnap and compel to officiate the only qualified medical practitioner. In such cases ... we usually say, not that justice must give way to some other moral principle, but that what is just in ordinary cases is, by reason of that other principle, not just in the particular case. By this useful accommodation of language ... we are saved from the necessity of maintaining that there can be laudable injustice.... It has always been evident that all cases of justice are also cases of expediency."[24]

Nonetheless, it seems that Mill has introduced another hierarchy: apparently there is a "scale of social utility" in which some requirements stand lower while others, like justice, stand higher; and the higher carry greater moral obligation. The explication of Mill's system seems to require three types or tiers of rules or principles: (1) Basic are the ethical rules we learn from common experience, like *Don't kill or inflict pain needlessly*, or *Don't lie, cheat, or steal*. These are tested, morally useful rules. But sometimes they may conflict. (2) To resolve such situations, we need rules about rules; that is, we need principles that prioritize the rules: *Life is more important than property*, or *Justice outweighs the benefits gained by enslavement*. But even these cannot resolve every moral situation one may encounter. (3) When no rule applies, we turn to the master rule (sometimes called "the remainder rule"), which is act utilitarianism: *Do what you reasonably expect to produce the greatest good for the greatest number*.

There is an important and complex issue that hides in Mill's discussion. If one claims that each and every morally right act must maximize utility, even acts involving justice or other moral principles, rules are at best a shorthand guide to what is right. Rules have no special status and rule utilitarianism is then fully reducible to act utilitarianism. Perpetual background calculation of individual acts is still required. But if it is the rules that have a utility independent of individual acts, if we turn to calculating the utility of individual acts only when our tiers of rules fail to resolve a problematic situation, then act utilitarianism is only a failsafe, a last resort. Rule utilitarianism is not then reducible to a straightforward act utilitarianism. But this entails that we may find ourselves in situations in which we are obliged to follow a rule that has great utility, despite the fact that in our current situation, it is not optimific. It suggests that following judicious rules may do more good over the long haul than trying to do the most good in each and every situation. But how then can we test and assure the utility of a rule? To put the critical question simply: when it is pressed to the extreme, must rule utilitarianism either transform into a deontological theory or collapse into act utilitarianism?

Project Prevention, our opening case, runs on rule utilitarianism: it has general policies—a $300 stipend paid in cash, traded for sterilization, only offered to addicts, and so on—which are justified, it claims, by their utility. These policies work for the greater good. But one could imagine a case that fit all the policies, but in which the prospects were not good. In such a situation, one would ask: is it better to follow the policies which have high utility (rule utilitarianism), or to resort to a case-by-case judgment (act utilitarianism)?

The interpretation of rule utilitarianism and the status of moral rules remain controversial to this day—even among committed advocates. Some have proposed that it is best to apply the test of utility to practices rather than rules or acts. We would therefore test the practice of slavery for the production of the greatest good for the greatest number, not a particular case or rule; the practice of paying addicts for sterilization, rather than a particular exchange. This has predictably been called *practice utilitarianism*. And most of the same questions of interpretation raised with rule utilitarianism would apply to this form as well.

6.8 THE ADEQUACY AND IMPACT OF UTILITARIANISM

The previous discussion has identified problems with utilitarianism that challenge its adequacy as a moral theory—at least according to some critics. These include the ambiguity of key concepts, the practical tasks for moral agency, a level of expectation so demanding it leaves no room for supererogation, and the contested status of moral rules and principles.

Beyond these issues internal to the theory, many critics have pointed out that this approach gives no place to moral sentiments or emotions. The moral agent is, much like Mill himself in his early years, a dispassionate, rational calculator. Even in Mill's day, the doctrine was thought to be "cold and unsympathizing" (Obj. 5). Contributing to this assessment is a related issue: the flat impartiality of the calculations. Normal human beings develop strong emotional ties, close relations, with family and friends, but utilitarians take no count of these relationships. Since each and every person counts as one, I have no reason to privilege the goodness for my children or my spouse or parents over those of distant people unknown to me. Indeed, it would be wrong for me to be more concerned about my daughter than a stranger, to choose her goodness over theirs. But partiality to ourselves and those we love, along with the emotions connected to care and compassion, are deeply embedded aspects of moral life.

What this criticism reveals is that the natural home of utilitarian thinking is the domain of ethical social policy—issues such as health care and criminal punishment. It fits well the considerations of military policy, the corporate boardroom, and the legislature. Its concern for the greatest good is directed toward the greatest number of individuals, but these are individuals abstracted to a number, without consideration of their individuality, without any nod to special relationships among them.

Utilitarian theory does appear to harmonize all dimension of one's life (though with the austerity noted above), giving us one principle by which to act in all situations. But some critics have argued the utilitarianism may enjoin a person to violate their integrity. Imagine this case:

> Josh, an employee of an American corporation working in the Middle East is kidnapped by terrorists and brought to a camp where about twenty-five men, women, and children are captive. He learns that these prisoners will soon be executed by their captors, their murders to be publicized to stoke fear and recruit others willing to kill. Josh, an unexpected American hostage, is a prize and will not be killed, but will be traded for weapons. But he is given a choice: he will be given a gun, and if he will select and kill one of the prisoners, all the others will be spared and released; if he declines, they will all be executed as planned. The prisoners overhear this bargain and besiege him to accept the bargain.[25]

The act of highest utility is clear: Josh is morally obligated to choose and kill a prisoner. Critics like Bernard Williams (1929–2003), claim that utilitarian calculation may, as in this situation, compel us to abandon our most cherished beliefs and principles, to destroy our integrity. In dire cases such as this, someone else (the terrorist captor) has structured a situation into which a moral agent (Josh) is thrust, disrupting the agent's own projects and plans, values and choices. It is another (malevolent) agent that has established the architecture of choices, not Josh. Utilitarians may argue that "integrity" is being used as a name for a set of principles that are held without regard to consequences. A true utilitarian finds the decision simple (though serious) and feels no loss of integrity in saving many lives by taking one—just as Mill says we experience no loss of justice when theft or kidnap is necessary to save a life. But surely this is not just "another problem solved." We would find something wrong with Josh if that were his response. There is little doubt that a strictly utilitarian approach would sometimes require us to ignore traditional moral touchstones.

The British philosopher and Nobel laureate, Bertrand Russell, was the godson of John Stuart Mill. He wrote an essay in the 1920s called "The Harm that Good Men Do," in which he said, "A hundred years ago there lived a philosopher named Jeremy Bentham, who was universally recognised to be a very wicked man.... I ... discovered what was the really serious charge against him. It was no less than this: that he defined a 'good' man as a man who does good." Mill himself described Bentham as "the great subversive." These quotations relish the utilitarian's posture as one who rejects the constraints of received, authoritative morality in favor of empirical results, or reasonable expectations of them. For Russell, much of the harm done in the world was done by people who claimed to be acting in accord with morality, but were heedless of the actual consequences of their actions.

Enlightenment liberalism represents, in part, a rejection of any morality that is directed toward virtuous fitness for a life after death in favor of personal fulfillment and social progress in this life. Resisting the egoistic preoccupation that may accompany the individualism of the Enlightenment, utilitarianism reaches outward to society and forward to the future and our descendants. One of its attractions to me is the ethical vividness it imparts to the consequences of our actions for future generations. There is, though, little guidance from utilitarian theorists regarding the timeframe we are to use in considering consequences. Consider a policy for the fossil fuel industry that benefits those now alive, saving jobs and reducing costs, while ignoring climate change and resource depletion problems for future generations. Does it have more "visible" utility than one that addresses climate change but requires hardships now? This issue of near versus far term, of those now alive versus future generations is a matter of the purview of our moral interest, and it is a problem for all forms of consequentialism (as we saw with egoism and its "enlightened" varieties). Concern with this life, rather than a life after death, can too often truncate to a concern only with the here and now or the near future.

QUESTIONS FOR DISCUSSION

1   Is Project Prevention doing morally good work? (Reviewing the material cited in notes 1–3 may be helpful in reaching a considered judgment.)

2   Bentham lists "propinquity" (nearness in time) as one of the measures of pleasure, presumably valuing an immediate pleasure more than one in the future. Psychologists have demonstrated our natural tendency to do this, but they call it "discounting the future" and consider it a cognitive bias—a minor but predictable irrationality. Yet "deferred gratification" is also considered a mark of maturity. Is it valid to discount future rewards? (Remember the issue is not uncertainty—Bentham lists certainty as a separate criterion.) Would propinquity remove concern for future generations?

3   Explain why is it "better to be a human being dissatisfied than a pig satisfied"? If Mill has smuggled in a good other than pleasure, what is it?

4   Refute this claim: Watching or playing rugby and reading or writing poetry are equally worthwhile activities, and so are poker and physics.

5   "Utilitarians cannot protect the rights of individuals." Explain why this claim is plausible. Do you agree with it, or can a sophisticated utilitarian give an adequate reply?

6   A familiar case for utilitarian analysis is this: Would you torture a terrorist to discover the location of a bomb set to detonate within hours? But what if the terrorist, the one who placed the bomb, was a thirteen-year-old?

7   Explain why act utilitarianism makes supererogation impossible.

8   Lifeboat cannibalism: After a devastating gale, a crew of men endured nearly three dreadful weeks in a 13-foot lifeboat. They debated drawing lots for a sacrificial victim, some noting that it would be better for one to die so the others could have a chance to survive. Some pointed out they had wives and families at home; others were single. The next day, however, the cabin boy, Parker, fell into a coma. Taking matters into his own hands, a man named Dudley said a prayer and then killed Parker with a knife. The remaining men then drank his blood and ate his flesh. They thus survived for several days more when a ship was sighted and rescued them. Did Dudley do the right thing? [This is the case of *Regina vs. Dudley and Stephens* (1884), a famous British case.]

QUESTIONS FOR PERSONAL REFLECTION

1 Mill claims that due to the psychology of association, means to the end of happiness can, over time, become components of happiness itself: if playing tennis makes me happy, it can become true that a happy life for me must include tennis. What are the components of a happy life for you?

2 Consider this claim: "There is not one moral principle, however compelling, that could not properly be overridden or violated in certain circumstances."

SUGGESTED SOURCES

The primary sources for this chapter are: Jeremy Bentham, *An Introduction to the Principles of Morals and Legislation*; and John Stuart Mill, *Utilitarianism*.

Eggleston, Ben, and Dale E. Miller, eds. *The Cambridge Companion to Utilitarianism* (Cambridge: Cambridge UP, 2014).

Sandel, Michael J. *Justice: What's the Right Thing to Do?* (New York: Farrar, Straus, and Giroux, 2009), Chapter 2, "The Greatest Happiness Principle: Utilitarianism."

Scheffler, Samuel. *The Rejection of Consequentialism: A Philosophical Investigation of the Considerations Underlying Rival Moral Conceptions*, 2nd ed. (Oxford: Clarendon P, 1984).

Sidgwick, Henry. *The Methods of Ethics*, 7th ed. (1874; Indianapolis, IN: Hackett, 1981).

Singer, Peter. *The Most Good You Can Do: How Effective Altruism Is Changing Ideas About Living Ethically* (New Haven, CT: Yale UP, 2016).

Smart, J.J.C., and Peter Singer, eds. *Utilitarianism: For and Against* (Cambridge: Cambridge UP, 1973).

NOTES

1 Unless given special citation, the facts, figures, and quotations in this case are drawn from the Project Prevention website: http://projectprevention.org/ (accessed July 2018).

2 Jon Swaine, "Drug addict sterilised for cash—but can Barbara Harris save our babies?" *The Daily Telegraph*. October 19, 2010: http://www.telegraph.co.uk/news/health/8071664/Drug-addict-sterilised-for-cash-but-can-Barbara-Harris-save-our-babies.html (accessed July 2018).

3   See the discussion of the evolution of Ms. Harris's comments on Wikipedia at: https://en.wikipedia.org/wiki/Project_Prevention (accessed July 2018).

4   Quoted in Swaine, "Drug addict sterilised for cash."

5   For a history of utilitarianism, see Bart Shulz, *The Happiness Philosophers: The Lives and Works of the Great Utilitarians* (Princeton: Princeton UP, 2017).

6   Henry Sidgwick, *The Methods of Ethics* (1907), Book III, Chapter xiii.4, 382.

7   Jeremy Bentham, *An Introduction to the Principles of Morals and Legislation*, Chapter XVII, Section 1.iv, n. 122.

8   Images of the auto-icon abound on the Internet, but University College London has developed a high-resolution, rotating image of it at http://www.ucl.ac.uk/Bentham-Project/who/autoicon/Virtual_Auto_Icon.

9   The panopticon is a design for a prison that has cells arranged in a circle around a well or tower, from which guards could observe all prisoners at all times.

10 This requirement and the assumption that it can be achieved is given the technical term *aggregationism*.

11 His name is regularly found on lists of individuals with startlingly high IQs.

12 I cannot discuss every one of these objections and rebuttals, but my discussion includes a brief examination of many of them.

13 Mill, *Utilitarianism*, Chapter 2.

14 Michael J. Sandel, *Justice: What's the Right Thing to Do?* (New York: Farrar, Straus, and Giroux, 2009), 56.

15 Mill, *Utilitarianism*, Chapter 2.

16 For example, see Oliver Letwin, *Ethics, Emotion and the Unity of the Self* (New York: Routledge, 2010), Chapter 2, "High Activities and Low Activities."

17 Mill, *Utilitarianism*, Chapter 2.

18 Ibid., Chapter 4.

19 We might imagine an eccentric person for whom riding the bus was an intrinsically wonderful experience, not a means to get anywhere in particular. But then the same problem of proof would apply to bus riding as an end-in-itself.

20 I will return to this problem of the demands of morality in Chapter 14.

21 This is evident especially in his response to the objections about the impossible predicament of moral agency, and in his treatment of justice, to which he devotes a lengthy final chapter.

22 Ibid., Chapter 2.

23 Ibid., Chapter 5.

24 Ibid.

25 I have adapted this case from one developed by Bernard Williams in "A Critique of Utilitarianism"; in *Utilitarianism: For and Against*, ed. J.J.C. Smart and Bernard Williams (Cambridge: Cambridge UP, 1973), 98–99.

CHAPTER SEVEN
Kantianism

Carmen decided to apply for a prestigious fellowship from a private foundation to help cover her tuition. She uploaded her essay and filled out the long, online application accurately—except that she indicated she was a citizen of the United States, when she knew all too well that she was an undocumented immigrant, a "Dreamer" brought to the US as a toddler by her parents. She had lived nearly two decades in the US, worked at various retail jobs, was a licensed driver, and thought of herself as American in every way. She knew she'd put a false answer in the blank, she did not, however, realize that US citizenship was a condition of eligibility.

Carmen's academic advisor, Professor Stevens had promised to give her a superior reference, and soon the foundation sent her a reference form. She was asked to provide a confidential evaluation of Carmen's scholarship and character. That part was easy to complete, because Carmen was a star in both respects. But the concluding instructions asked the advisor to check the correctness of the information Carmen provided and to state whether the advisor knew of "any reason why this applicant should not be considered for this fellowship."

Professor Stevens was surprised to see that Carmen had claimed citizenship; she knew that Carmen was undocumented. Rereading the materials, she discovered that citizenship was a condition of eligibility for the fellowship. What to say? She wavered between checking the "No" box and filling in the blank labeled "Yes (please explain)." She disliked making a false affirmation. But citizenship seemed irrelevant to the award—Carmen had native fluency in English. She was the ideal candidate in every other respect—plus financial support was required if she was to continue her studies. And if her status became known, Professor Stevens thought, she could always say she was unaware of Carmen's status or that she'd not read the materials carefully. Besides, the grant would be made directly to Carmen, so the university was not implicated. And Carmen's essay was excellent.

But in the end, what she wrote on the form was: "Yes. I must report that Carmen does not hold US citizenship as required for the fellowship—though she has lived in this country virtually all her life." Though no reasons were given, Carmen did not receive the fellowship.

7.1 PREVIEW

Immanuel Kant (1724–1804) is widely regarded as the central figure in modern philosophy and one of the most important philosophers in history. He is also one of the most challenging.

Kant rarely left his hometown of Königsberg, Prussia (now Kaliningrad, Russia), where his disciplined habits earned a mythic reputation. His parents were Pietists, followers of a Lutheran movement that emphasized piety and Christian principles in daily life. He grew from a talented student to a respected professor at the University of Königsberg. Kant, like Jeremy Bentham, was a bachelor who loved conversation with friends, but his philosophical work was always foremost in his attention. He undertook large-scale philosophical projects for which he completed monumental texts. The primary example is his three great "critiques" that systematically explicate the capacity, effects, and limits of human reason: *Critique of Pure Reason* (1781), *Critique of Practical Reason* (1788), and *Critique of Judgment* (1790). Kant argues that the human mind structures experience and we cannot know "things-in-themselves," that reason is the foundation of morality, and that aesthetics derives from our capacity for disinterested judgment.

Kant's major works on ethics are: *Groundwork of the Metaphysics of Morals* (1785), the *Critique of Practical Reason* (1788), and the *Metaphysics of Morals* (1797).[1] In these works and his lectures on ethics (published from student notes), Kant's deepest concern is the concept of moral agency: what it means, what it requires, to be a moral agent. He sought to secure morality and our capacity for moral action from being absorbed by either religion or science. Religion may usurp our agency through its demand to yield our will to divine authority; science may brusquely deny our agency through determinism, which reduces rational conduct to caused behavior. Within the space he preserves for morality, Kant develops a deontological ethical theory that unites reason and the will, elevates duty, and vigorously opposes consequentialism.

7.2 GOOD WILL

According to consequentialism, whatever is good is found in states of affairs. A good will, therefore, is simply one that aims at producing the best states of affairs. According to Kant, however, that interpretation misplaces what is of moral value. Kant writes:

> A good will is not good because of what it effects or accomplishes—because of its fitness for attaining some proposed end: it is good through its willing alone—that is, good in itself.... [I]f by its utmost effort it still accomplishes nothing, and only good will is left (not, admittedly, as a mere wish, but as the straining of every means so far as they are in our control); even then it would still shine like a jewel for its own sake as something which has full value in itself.[2]

For Kant, it is the will that has intrinsic value, and the will alone. In fact, Kant announces:

> It is impossible to conceive anything at all in the world, or even out of it, which can be taken as good without qualification, except a *good will*. Intelligence, wit, judgment, and any other *talents* of the mind we may care to name, or courage, resolution, and constancy of purpose, as qualities of *temperament*, are without doubt good and desirable in many respects; but they can also be extremely bad and hurtful when the will is not good ... It is exactly the same with *gifts of fortune*. Power, wealth, honor, even health and that complete well-being and contentment with one's state which goes by the name of '*happiness*' produce boldness, and as a consequence often over-boldness as well, unless a good will is present.... [A] good will seems to constitute the indispensable condition of our very worthiness to be happy.[3]

We could easily imagine a supervillain with intelligence and power, or a courageous fighter for a brutal regime. Having these qualities would only make the villainy worse. Even happiness is not good without qualification. In contrast to Mill's view, Kant claims that happiness is not a good in itself: the happiness of a dictator or retired mobster, for example, would not be good because they would be unworthy of it. What makes happiness good is the good will that deserves it. Indeed, these and all other such qualities become good only when associated with a good will.

One might, however, question whether a good will is truly "good without qualification." Are good intentions sufficient? Does morality simply require that we "mean well"? Don't good intentions require moral understanding in order to manifest their goodness? After all, an ignorant person who means well can do a lot of unintentional harm. But, we should also keep in mind that Kant's conception of a good will is something stronger than a mere wish for good, as is revealed in his "straining of every means" phrase. Besides, there does seem to be something morally valuable in a good will alone. Imagine this scenario: two people try to rescue a child in a burning car; one is killed when the car explodes, but the other is able to extract the child to safety seconds before. The two willed the same thing: the rescue of the child. Doesn't their good will make them equally praiseworthy from a moral perspective, even though only one of their efforts resulted in the good outcome of a life saved?

Moreover, the absence of a good will seems to alter the character of an act. Imagine an elderly man who needs help carrying groceries. He is helped by a young woman of good will who carries the groceries three blocks from the store into his apartment kitchen, rejecting a small reward for his help. Now imagine the same scenario, the same result, except the young woman's intention was to see whether there might be anything worth stealing in the apartment. Our moral judgment of what she did is changed by her motive: she lacked a good will.

We may doubt whether Kant has proven his claim that a good will is the *only* conceivable thing that is good without qualification, and we may question whether a good will is *sufficient* for moral action; but perhaps it is *necessary* for a morally good act. We need to know more about the meaning of a "good will."

7.3 DUTY AND IMPERATIVES

A life without morality would be a life in which we are ruled by our urges and desires, our sentiments and emotions—our "natural inclinations"—as they arise. Although we are subject to our inclinations, as mature human beings we are also capable of rationality and morality; that is, we are capable not only of doing what we want, but also of doing what is right. Our will may be directed in many ways, but a good will is directed toward what is right. Through our capacity to reason, we can identify right action, which gives us moral obligations. Kant uses the term *duty* for that which we are morally obliged to do. Because he believes morality is about doing one's duty without regard to consequences, his position, like that of Divine Command Theory (Chapter 2), is *deontological*.

Simply doing one's duty, however, is not sufficient. Kant distinguishes acting *in accord with duty* and acting *from duty*. We can grasp the difference with a comparison case: Paula and Denise both attend a school with an honor code; they take an oath not to violate academic integrity. Neither one ever cheats. Paula is inclined to cheat, but she refrains out of concern for being caught. She is acting *in accord with* her duty. Denise, also inclined to cheat, believes cheating is wrong and refrains from it because it is right to do so. She is acting *from* duty. Kant would find Denise, but not Paula, to be acting morally—even though Paula doesn't cheat.

We can now characterize more fully what Kant means by a **good will**: it is the will to do what is right *because it is right*, and not because of any desire or emotion or benefit. Indeed, Kant believes that an action has moral value *only* when it is done *from duty*. He admits, however, this can be difficult to ascertain in practice. Suppose I have a duty to serve as a juror when called, and—unlike many people—I enjoy the role of a juror. So, when I receive my summons, I eagerly anticipate the possibility of a juicy trial, and I also believe it is my duty to serve. Am I acting from duty? Our motives are not always singular or transparent to ourselves or others. A good way to test our motives, a litmus test for a good will, can be found in situations in which our duty and our inclinations conflict. Suppose instead that the weight of being a juror in a serious case makes me anxious; I know it will trouble my sleep; and the call for service is at a time that is personally inconvenient. But although I could petition the court with a falsified excuse, I believe it is my duty to serve, and so I accept. Such acts, done for the right reason alone, reveal clearly the good will of the agent. They would, Kant says, "shine like a jewel," echoing Shakespeare's judgment: "So shines a good deed in a weary world."[4]

Because we are human beings, buffeted by various inclinations, our obligations appear to us as imperatives. We discern what is right, and it has for us an imperative force: "X is right" becomes "Do X." Some obligations constitute what Kant calls *perfect duties*: these are duties that must be met in specific ways and admit of no exceptions. The obligations to repay a loan and to avoid lying are perfect duties. But Kant also recognizes moral obligations for which the dutiful act may vary widely depending upon our situation, our role, and our capacities. These he calls *imperfect duties*. Our moral obligations to be charitable and to develop our talents are imperfect duties, because they do not require specific actions. What charities we support and what talents we should develop are left for the agent to decide.

Moreover, imperatives may vary with circumstances and purposes. Take the imperative "Get a good night's sleep." That sort of instruction has an implicit condition: it might be "*If you want to win tomorrow*, then get a good night's sleep." (You can imagine many other plausible "if" clauses.) Note that the imperative applies only when one accepts the "if" condition. If you don't care about winning, then a good night's sleep may not be relevant. Kant calls such *if-then* instructions **hypothetical imperatives**. The supreme principle of morality, by contrast, would be an imperative that applied *categorically*, that would direct moral agents regardless of their circumstances, roles, relationships, purposes, or desires. This would be a **categorical imperative**. Is there such an imperative?

Reason requires that any valid moral imperative or judgment be equally applicable to every relevantly identical situation. This means that if X is right for Susan under condition C, then X is also right for Tom, Dick, and Henrietta and anyone else under condition C. This requirement, you will recall, is called *universalizability*. Justification is an exercise in reasoning, and, according to Kant, a moral imperative is justified if it is valid for *all* rational beings. If an imperative was valid for a moral agent *regardless* of circumstances, then it would be valid for any and all moral agents. Thus, a supreme moral principle must be universalizable. It cannot be an imperative such as "Thou shalt not kill," because there may be circumstances in which killing may be justified, such as self-defense, protection of an innocent, or warfare. The Golden Rule—"Do unto others as you would have others do unto you"—has a superficial universalizability, but it also fails as stated because it appears to be grounded in wants or desires. The only moral imperative that does meet these tests is the requirement of universalizability itself. Because it is the only such principle, we capitalize it as *The Categorical Imperative*. Its key idea is that all moral agents, whatever their circumstances, should act only on principles that are universalizable. If particular desires or circumstances are not relevant, then the only necessary imperative a fully rational agent must follow is to act as a rational agent. The supreme principle of morality is, therefore, an extension of rationality. Acting morally is a special way of acting rationally. We might summarize this as:

> "*X* is right" = "*X* complies with the Categorical Imperative and *X* is enacted with a good will (that is, from duty)."

7.4 THE CATEGORICAL IMPERATIVE

Phrasing this insight as an instruction, Kant formulates the Categorical Imperative:

> *Act only on that maxim which you can at the same time will that it should become a universal law.*

This imperative may seem abstract and lacking in content, but Kant provides examples of its impact and alternative formulations to unpack its meaning. It prescribes a decision-procedure to test the morality of our actions. Consider first one of Kant's illustrative cases:

> [A man] finds himself driven to borrowing money because of need. He well knows that he will not be able to pay it back; but he sees that he will get no loan unless he gives a firm promise to pay it back within a fixed time. He is inclined to make such a promise; but he still has enough conscience to ask "Is it not unlawful and contrary to duty to get out of difficulties in this way?"[5]

The first step in Kant's decision-procedure concerns a "maxim," by which he simply means "a rule of conduct." First, we must: (1) *Formulate the act in question as a maxim.* In this case, the maxim would be: "Whenever I believe myself short of money, I will borrow money by promising to pay it back, though I know that this will never be done." A more general formulation is: "Whenever I have a need, I will make a false promise to gain what I need." The next step is easy: (2) *Universalize the maxim.* The maxim becomes: "Whenever *any person* is short of money, he or she may borrow money with a promise to pay it back, knowing all the while this will never be done." Or, "*Anyone* will make a false promise to gain what they need." The third step may seem a bit mysterious: (3) *Will the universalized maxim.* One attempts now to will a world in which everyone makes false promises to gain what they need. Kant implies that this willing may prove impossible—at least without contradiction. But we must try by taking the universalization seriously, thinking through its implications, and accomplishing the fourth step. (4) *Examine for consistency the state of affairs that would be produced by the willed, universalized maxim.* If there is inconsistency, the act in question is morally wrong; if there is no inconsistency, the act is morally permissible. In Kant's case of false promises, we find an inconsistency. Imagine a world in which everyone makes lying promises whenever it is convenient. The whole purpose of making a promise is to bind future action, and if everyone does not feel bound, false promises will become commonplace, and the entire practice of making promises will be devalued and disappear. It is as though Kant asks, "What if everyone did that?" But, beware! This is the part that is often misunderstood: what makes the act wrong is not the bad outcome that would result if everyone made false promises; it is not a matter of the consequences at all. It is that the man in this case is willing a world in which he can both make a promise and yet promises would no longer be made. *That* is the fatal inconsistency. It is impossible, or irrational, to will both simultaneously. Such irrationality cannot be moral.

This procedure has several noteworthy aspects, beginning with the looseness of the very first step. (1) The maxim on which one intends to act is not obvious. Even for Kant's false promising example, I stated a more specific and more general version of the maxim, and both are plausible. Formulating a maxim is not as straightforward as Kant implies: it involves framing the nature of the act; it requires moral imagination, self-awareness, and a sense of moral relevance. In this case, one must recognize the act as lying or a false promise to gain money, not as simply a clever strategy to increase one's own happiness. How should we frame Carmen's conduct in the scenario that opens this chapter (though she may have had no maxim in mind)? Alternative formulations of maxims often express deep ethical conflicts: Is abortion the exercise of a woman's right to choose and to control her own body, or is it murder of an innocent—what is the proper maxim? Moreover, a person who acts spontaneously—pulling a child from a burning car, for example—does not likely have a moral maxim in mind at all. The hero is left to reconstruct possible motives after the fact.

(2) The universalization requirement serves to eliminate the temptation to treat one's own case as special. Reason requires that different treatment is justified only by relevant differences. Making an exception of oneself is irrational, and it is a source of much immorality. Universalization engenders a form of impartiality. I stand equal with all other human beings when I invoke the question, "What if everyone did that?" And if it is permissible for me to act in a certain way, then anyone else may act the same way in similar circumstances.

(3) As Kant has given this initial formulation of the Categorical Imperative, it would determine whether an act is wrong; presumably, if the act passes the test, it is morally permissible (not wrong). Kant puts the weight on the test of whether one can will the maxim and its universalized form consistently. Thus, evil agents with evil purposes cannot consistently will the maxims of their evil acts; an evil will is irrational. Critics note, however, even if the test filters out immoral maxims, maxims unrelated to morality may pass this test. "Put your left shoe on first" is perfectly consistent with willing "Everyone should always put the left shoe on first." This suggests that the procedure does not capture or determine the property that makes an act a moral act.

The force of these points is to question whether Kant's formal principle contains sufficient moral substance. A test that merely rules out what is morally wrong does not lead us toward what is morally right. Merely refraining from doing which is wrong is not all that is required to do one's duty. Furthermore, is rational action, the consistent willing of universalized maxims, sufficient to distinguish even between what is wrong and what is morally permissible? Of course, Kant also stipulates a good will. And Kant has much more to tell us about the Categorical Imperative, as he unfolds alternative ways of understanding this supreme principle.

7.5 ALTERNATIVE FORMULATIONS OF THE CATEGORICAL IMPERATIVE

Kant derives three additional formulations of the Categorical Imperative, each of which articulates a set of implications and deepens our understanding of the conditions of moral agency. The formulations are these:

> Principle of Nature: *Act as if the maxim of your action were to become through your will a universal law of nature.*

> Principle of Humanity: *Act in such a way that you treat humanity, whether in your own person or in the person of any other, never simply as a means, but always at the same time as an end.*

> The Principle of Autonomy: *Act as though your will, and that of any rational being, is through its maxims at the same time making universal law.*

In these formulations, Kant enriches the concept of universalizability. The point of the Principle of Nature is to consider the implications if your action were truly woven deeply into our human nature. The Principle of Humanity requires that we treat people as ends-in-themselves, as rational, moral agents. It enjoins us not to use people, not to treat them simply as a means to our own ends. For example, Kant's false promiser treats the lender merely as a means to his own end: obtaining needed money. He doesn't consider or care about the effects of his lie or the way he treats the lender. Of course, there are times when we need to have someone serve as a means to our end: Kayla needs a letter of recommendation for her graduate school application; her academic advisor is a means to her end. Fred needs a plumber to fix his sink, and so he finds one who serves his purpose. But Kant says we shouldn't treat people as a means *only*; even while they serve as means, we should also treat them as an end-in-themselves. But what does that involve? This principle requires that we treat people with respect, as beings of intrinsic worth. Only rational, moral agents—only *persons*—can be ends-in-themselves. This principle is sometimes called *Respect for Persons*. When we interact with others, we should remember that they are persons, having values and purposes just as we do. When we use people as a means only, we disrespect them by denying their essential humanity, their personhood.

The Principle of Autonomy reveals the double-sided nature of moral action: moral agents are subject to the moral law, but in acting rationally and autonomously they are in effect making laws for all other rational agents. As a moral agent, you are bound to act according to the moral law. And when you determine the right action, you are in effect saying this is also the right action for *any* moral person in this situation. Moral agents possess **autonomy**, which is a condition of a free will; this is contrasted with **heteronomy**, which refers to a will determined by inclinations, by causes or principles other than the moral law.

Kant also offers an expanded version of this principle that interprets the community of rational agents as a *Kingdom of Ends*. In this ideal kingdom, everyone is king and all are also subjects. In an elevated and memorable passage, Kant writes:

> In the kingdom of ends everything has either a *price* or a *dignity*. Anything with a price can be replaced by something else as its equivalent, whereas anything that is above all price and therefore admits of no equivalent has a dignity.... Now morality is the only condition under which a rational being can be an end in himself; for only through this is it possible to be a law-making member in the kingdom of ends. Therefore morality, and humanity so far as it is capable of morality, is the only thing which has dignity.... *Autonomy is therefore the ground of the dignity of human nature and of every rational nature.*[6]

We now see that a moral agent is not only one who has good will, who seeks to do what is right for the right reason, and follows the moral law as determined through the Categorical Imperative. It is essentially a *person*: a rational creature, a being with free will and autonomy, who possesses dignity and is worthy of respect, who respects all other persons as having these same characteristics, and who is both subject and king in regard to the moral law.

Although Kant develops a complex metaphysical structure to support this claim, one might wonder whether he can prove or provide evidence for his claims that we are such creatures—free, autonomous, rational, having a dignity beyond all price. The short answer—but not his final response—is "no." It is not that Kant hasn't found a proof; it is rather that no such explanation or proof is technically possible. One cannot verify or prove scientifically such features of moral agency. It is therefore impossible to prove that humans are moral agents as he has described them.

Is that the end—after the hard climb up the steep and rocky face of Kant's mountain from the good will, through the Categorical Imperative and its various formulations, to the thinner air of autonomous moral agency, to reach the top and find only that there is not even proof that we are moral creatures? No, we need to go a little further to reach the peak, what Kant calls "the extreme limit of all moral inquiry." It is this: although he cannot prove that this whole complex of assertions is true, he has proved that *if we are to have any morality, we must assume it to be true.*

FIGURE 3	KANT'S *GROUNDWORK OF THE METAPHYSICS OF MORALS (Grundlegung zur Metaphysik der Sitten)*

AN OUTLINE

Preface

The traditional divisions of philosophy as logic, physics, and ethics.

The distinction between *a priori ethics* (from reason alone) and *a posteriori ethics* (empirical ethics).

The aim and method of the *Groundwork*.

Chapter 1

The concept of the good will as unqualifiedly good.

The motive of duty and its appearance as an imperative.

Reverence for the moral law.

Chapter 2

A typology of imperatives, including hypothetical and categorical.

The identification of the unique Categorical Imperative as the supreme principle of morality.

The Alternative Formulations:
    The Principle of Nature, with four illustrations.
    The Principle of Humanity, or Respect for Persons as ends-in-themselves.
    The Principle of Autonomy—contrasted with heteronomy and expanded to the Kingdom of Ends.

Chapter 3

Freedom as necessary for autonomy and rational agency.

Freedom and Autonomy as requiring "two standpoints": the distinction between the sensible and the intelligible (phenomenal and noumenal).

How a Categorical Imperative is possible.

The inability to know the Intelligible world or to explain freedom: the extreme limit of moral inquiry.

Nevertheless, the necessary presumption required for any morality.

Kant has structured what he calls a **transcendental argument**. It takes this form: assuming *X*, what conditions are necessary for *X* to be possible? It proceeds by unearthing necessary presuppositions. In this case, Kant has asked, "What are the necessary presuppositions of any morality?" or "What conditions make moral agency possible?" Thus, Kant claims to have shown that morality requires agents with an integrated set of characteristics including free will and autonomy. One's rationality is even presupposed by the question "Why should I be rational (or moral)?"—which is, after all, a request for sound reasons. It implicitly acknowledges the compelling force reasons would have.

Kant believes that this conception of autonomous moral agency deflects the threat of dissolving the will of the individual into the will of God, and it reflects Enlightenment values in ascribing autonomy (and dignity) to all persons. It also deflects the threat of a scientific determinism that would eliminate the normative force of morality, reducing all free will choices to inevitable behavior. (I have summarized Kant's presentation in the *Groundwork* in **Figure 3**.)

7.6 THE IMPORT OF KANTIAN ETHICS

The view from the peak of Kantian ethics seems quite beautiful. The highest good is virtue. Though we do not always do the right thing, we humans are capable of rationality and morality. We each have all the glorious attributes of a moral person. With our autonomy, free will, and inherent dignity, we are endowed with moral rights. We can grasp the ideal of the Kingdom of Ends as a community of mutual respect in which each person is sovereign and all are united in their good will and reverence for the moral law. This is possible because our individual differences—race, gender, physical ability, talent, and so on—are not morally relevant. Our backgrounds, our identities and individuality—these are part of our physical identity. But as moral agents, as persons, we are the same, possess the same rights, and deserve the same respect. In his later works, Kant adds elements to this vision that are hinted at in his titles: *Religion within the Limits of Reason Alone* (1793) and *The Republic of Perpetual Peace* (1795). The latter was an explicit source for the Charter of the United Nations, including the Statute of the International Court of Justice (1945). Kant's moral vision informed the *Universal Declaration of Human Rights* (UDHR) adopted by the UN General Assembly in 1948, which has since been translated into over 500 languages and dialects and become an international standard and tool for political critique and reform.

Yet I must also report that Kant believed in racial inequality and laid conceptual groundwork for racism. Some claim he "created" the concept of race, but that is a bit misleading—though he certainly established its currency. In a 1775 essay titled "Of the Different Human Races," Kant gave what is generally regarded as the first attempt to make a scientific distinction between *species* and *race*. He identified four races: White, Negro, Hun (Mongol or Kalmuck), and Hindu (or Hindustani). Though he thought all human beings descended from a common line, he perceived clear-cut racial differences. While he surmised that racial differences were due to environmental factors over time, they were not insignificant. Skin color was a prominent criterion of classification. But, most appallingly, Kant claims that racial differences include not only physical but psychological, intellectual, and moral differences. These, predictably, form a hierarchy of races with Whites at the top. These racist sentiments contradict Kant's moral theory, in which our individual, phenomenal differences are not morally relevant—unless, that is, we take Kant to mean that certain non-White humans (Negroes and Native Americans, especially) are so deficient in capacities as to fail to be moral persons, lacking in the characteristics required for moral agency.

How are we to absorb such startling and disappointing beliefs? Are his racist views a regrettable lapse from his elevated universalism? Or is there a consistent racism embedded in his larger moral theory? Is there evidence that Kant later changed his mind as he worked through his universal moral philosophy—despite authoring several pieces that express these views? These are hotly contested issues among scholars today. However one comes to terms with this jarring aspect of Kant's writings, it should remind us that he was ultimately a man of his times; that all philosophy is written from a biographical and cultural context; and that Kant's brilliance and moral insight were hobbled by his narrowly Prussian experience. And, of course, one may embrace major aspects of Kantian moral theory without embracing his racism.

In stressing the deontological position that we should do what is right because it is right, Kant knows that this demands that we must do our duty regardless of consequences, must follow our ethical principles even when it costs us dearly. This is what it means to have *integrity*—a harmony and consistency among all the various spheres of our lives. The honor code of the US Air Force Academy, culminating in the duty "to do the right thing despite pressure or temptations to the contrary," is intended to apply to all aspects of the cadet's life, to assure the integrity of the individuals who graduate to become officers. Notwithstanding the value of the virtue of integrity, it is not good without qualification; to be admirable, the principles it reflects must be morally valid. Otherwise, doing one's duty regardless of effect can degenerate into a robotic fanaticism.

One might wonder whether the Kingdom of Ends is a happy place. Kant believes we can be assured of "a peculiar kind of contentment—contentment in fulfilling a purpose which in turn is determined by reason alone, even if this fulfillment should often involve interferences with the purposes of inclinations."[7] This is a way of saying that virtue is the good—and its own reward. Fortunately, happiness sometimes comes to moral persons. But, although good people will always deserve to be happy, the necessary "interference" with our inclinations means that they will often be unhappy, having to act against their desires and hopes and with real cost. Bad things do happen to good people. Although Kant can be dismissive of happiness, he does recognize that it would be just for good people to be happy; and if perfect justice would require good people to be rewarded with happiness, happiness must certainly have some positive value. This perceived injustice in the universe—that the good may suffer while the wicked may be happy—troubled Kant. Late in his life, he argued, perhaps conceded, that perfect justice must presuppose an afterlife in which the good are rewarded and the wicked are punished (Chapter 2).

But he steadfastly affirms that justice also obliges us to punish wrong-doers in this life. For Kant, punishment is an aspect of respect for persons. We must draw a clear line between a wrong-doer who is sick and one who is guilty. When we treat people as though their actions are a result of sickness, we absolve them of responsibility, we deny that they acted autonomously, and we refuse their reasoning and diminish their personhood. Punishment is the reverse: it is a legal act that holds the person responsible, acknowledges their status as an autonomous agent, engages their reasoning, and ascribes guilt to their act. Kant was, in fact, a defender of capital punishment, arguing that it retained respect for the moral agency of a criminal who commits an act that is particularly heinous.[8] Justice requires that "whoever has committed murder, must die." It is in the Kantian spirit that we think justice is not satisfied if a prisoner is accidentally killed on the way to his execution. Gruesome as it sounds, we want the prisoner to be awake, fed, and fully aware of the execution and its reasons. It must be formal: the deliberate and considered taking of the life of a moral person in full possession of his capacities.

7.7 CRITIQUE OF KANTIAN ETHICAL THEORY

In this section, I will discuss five criticisms of Kantian ethics and point to attempts to rebut them or to amend his theory.

1. Many philosophers reject the conceptions of libertarian free will and autonomy that Kant's theory requires. They argue from **determinism**, the view that every event is the effect of antecedent causes produced in accord with natural laws; thus, the state of the world at any moment (given the

laws of nature) determines everything that happens thereafter. At least initially, determinism undermines all moral theories that presuppose we can make choices among genuine possibilities, since it asserts that only one future is possible from any given present. But the doctrine is especially challenging for the Kantian's model of moral agency. What sort of event could a freely-willed, autonomous decision to act be? Take Carmen's impulsive act to claim citizenship and her advisor's considered decision to report her undocumented status. If both acts are either predetermined and so neither person could have done anything else, or if they are uncaused, random events, neither possibility presents the autonomous, rational act Kant requires for a free will. What Kantians need to supply—and indeed many have rallied to the task—is a coherent model of free will, which for Kant requires an act based on the recognition of reasons, not caused by physical or psychological or neural states. A free choice would need to be neither a random spasm nor the necessary outcome of one's prior state. Although Kant acknowledged that no one can prove we have such moral agency, he asserts that we must postulate it if we are to have any morality—but this still requires the conception to be coherent.

Whatever one thinks of the free will issue, many wrong-doers (and most of the really horrible wrong-doers) are today recognized as acting from psychological compulsion, not freely. Thus, the scope of responsibility may be much narrower than Kant supposed. Further exploration of the great metaphysical issue of free will is not possible here, though I must mark its importance. Other critiques, however, focus on the content of the morality Kant developed, and I turn now to examine some of the most significant.

2. Kant believes that some duties, such as the duty not to lie, are absolute in that they *admit of no exceptions*. Lying is a triple-play of disrespect: it disrespects the person you try to deceive, it disrespects your own person, and it disrespects the truth. Lying is manipulation through deception, which abandons reason and denies autonomy, resorting to treating the others as a means only. Again, thinking of the opening scenario: not only is Carmen's falsehood wrong, it is wrong for Professor Stevens even to entertain the reasons that might lead to a false affirmation. Lying for the greater good, lying to protect—all lies are wrong. Suppose, says the familiar counterexample, that during the Nazi regime, you hide a Jewish neighbor in your basement and a Gestapo officer knocks on your door and demands, "Is there a Jew in this building?" Though Kant would hope to avoid a direct answer, if pressed, he asserts, you must tell the truth. The same would be true in this scenario: another door, another knock, but now it's a crazed-looking man with a large gun demanding to know the way to

the playground on which your child is playing. You might try to deflect him from his apparent intention, but you must not lie, says Kant. For many of us, this truth-telling requirement is not only rigid, it is morally wrong.

Though this is an example of a particularly harsh injunction, it is indicative of a general criticism: Kantianism cannot, or rather does not, deal with exceptions. Kant seemed to think that universalizability requires an absolutism that rejects exceptions, but that is dubious. It is true that he allows flexibility of response when it comes to imperfect duties. In the case of my duty to be charitable, I may respond in various ways that suit my circumstances and preferences—but even here, that flexibility of response is not granting an exception from the duty itself. It is also true that in the matter of lying, Kant was concerned with moral responsibility. He believed that, if one remains responsible only for the truth, one bears no responsibility for what others do with the information, good or evil; but if one lies, one carries the responsibility for whatever happens as a result. Still, it is as though Kant is unduly concerned to avoid blame. Thus, if you act with good will, reason astutely, tell the truth, and so on, your moral responsibility is fully met, and you need not be concerned about what flows from such actions, nor should you be blamed for it. The upshot of this viewpoint is that the keeping of one's own virtue intact by single-mindedly doing one's duty may result not only in one's own unhappiness, but in widespread damage and harm to innocent people. The root of the "no-exceptions" problem is in Kant's insistence on a single, supreme moral principle, which means that all duties are essentially forms of the same duty. By contrast, William D. Ross (1877–1971) advocated a *pluralistic* deontological theory, one which recognized at least seven contingent duties, such as beneficence, self-improvement, justice, and others.[9] Though he calls these *prima facie* duties—duties "at first glance"—he describes them as real duties that depend for their application upon circumstances. They may, unfortunately, conflict. We might imagine approaching the lying cases as a conflict of two duties: truth-telling and protection of life. Ross resists putting such duties into a hierarchy of relative priority and asserts that a moral assessment of the particular situation is required to resolve such conflicts of principles. Nevertheless, he might agree that protection of life generally outweighs truth-telling. Of course, reliance on one's intuitions to resolve such conflicts would not suit Kant; he expects rationality to harmonize as well as universalize our reasons.

3. An incisive criticism is that Kant's account gives no positive place for our emotions; worse, he construes the emotions as among the unruly inclinations we must discipline by reasoning. He seems to uphold the view that emotions are passions that come over us and thwart our autonomy.

Irrational and fickle forces that they are, they are not morally reliable—even when they propel us to do what is right. This is a benighted view, picked apart by philosophers and rejected by contemporary science. Emotions have a cognitive function: they help us understand the world; they are not opposed to reason; they reflect and reveal our values; indeed, they play a crucial role in decision-making and in moral life. Compassion, indignation, remorse, admiration, and other moral emotions are not only natural features of human experience; they shape the will and motivate moral action. Disvalue such emotions and morality becomes desiccated and distorted. (Chapter 10 will consider the role of emotions in morality.)

4. Kantianism seems to reject the concept of supererogation. Supererogatory acts are morally good acts that *go beyond duty*, such as doing a great favor, granting mercy, or helping a stranger at a level beyond what is normally expected. But Kant claims that an action has moral value only if it is done from duty. For him, supererogatory acts are impossible—there is no moral value beyond what is required by duty. But this seems to rule out the highest, most revered moral actions of human experience—the actions that characterize saints and heroes.

Consider the parable of the Good Samaritan:

> A man was going down from Jerusalem to Jericho, when he was attacked by robbers. They stripped him of his clothes, beat him and went away, leaving him half dead ... [A] Samaritan, as he traveled, came where the man was; and when he saw him, he took pity on him. He went to him and bandaged his wounds, pouring on oil and wine. Then he put the man on his own donkey, brought him to an inn and took care of him. The next day he took out two denarii and gave them to the innkeeper. "Look after him," he said, "and when I return, I will reimburse you for any extra expense you may have."[10]

The astounding goodness of the Samaritan lies in the fact that he does so much more for the injured man than would normally be expected; he acts beyond what is required of a moral agent. Kant would seem to deny the moral value of his actions. One response by Kantians might be to claim that the Samaritan did not go beyond duty: his actions are universalizable and in fact required of any rational moral agent. This would certainly set a high bar, and it goes well beyond Kant's own focus on identifying actions that are morally wrong. And it also deprives the act of one of its most revered moral aspects: it was *not* required; it was *freely given*—a kind of moral gift. This is a key feature of supererogatory acts—mercy, for example, is not required, but rather bestowed out of moral generosity. As

Shakespeare's Portia says, "The quality of mercy is not strained; / It drop-peth as the gentle rain from heaven / Upon the place beneath."[11] It would be ironic indeed to rule out such inspiring acts as having no moral value.

5. Kant has argued that morality is a form of rationality dependent upon freedom and autonomy, which conveys rights and dignity. In emphasizing respect for persons, universal rights, and dignity, Kant both extends and limits the community of moral considerability to moral agents. He writes:

> The fact that the human being can have the representation 'I' raises him infinitely above all the other beings on earth. By this he is a person.... that is, a being altogether different in rank and dignity from things, such as irrational animals, with which one may deal and dispose at one's discretion.[12]

Animals are not members of the Kingdom of Ends, not entitled to respect. Among the responses one might make is that Kant has a "speciesist" ethic. But that is not strictly accurate, for Kant includes only *persons* as moral agents; this means that any genetic humans who are not moral agents are not persons. Embryos, pre-rational children, the senile or uncon-scious, and the mentally defective have a shadowy and precarious place in Kant's moral consideration; they are not moral agents. Their moral standing seems to depend on their potential or their history as persons. On the other hand, Kant would extend *personhood* to any rational aliens or androids who could apprehend the moral law and act with free will.

If morality is grounded in human exceptionalism, based on a set of special features that give moral stature to humans, then it becomes difficult to honor the continuity of living creatures, to recognize the moral stand-ing of animals. Christine Korsgaard (b. 1952), a contemporary philosopher who advocates a modified Kantianism, argues that humans are indeed morally special. We reflect on our desires, seek reasons for action, and we decide whether to treat our desires as reasons for acting or whether to follow a rule. The "problem of normativity," the identification of what is right, is uniquely a human problem.

Today, there are distinguished philosophers such as Korsgaard, who, moved by the profound moral insights of Kant, work to rehabili-tate his theory by addressing the concerns presented here and others. The Neo-Kantians, as they are called, retain a deontological framework and value respect for persons, universalizability, justice, and universal rights; they admire the right act for the right reason done without regard to personal cost. They hold with the claim that some acts are wrong (or right) no matter the increase in happiness or general welfare that results.

But they may tweak the interpretation of these concepts, acknowledge the role of moral emotions, and modify or reject other aspects of Kant's thought. For example, Marcia Baron (b. 1955) has argued that the critiques regarding Kant's elimination of supererogatory acts, over-emphasis on duty, and a passive view of emotions are misguided or exaggerated, based on a more comprehensive and sensitive review of Kant's works, including his non-ethical writings.[13] More radically, Korsgaard has recently argued that we should acknowledge non-human animals as ends-in-themselves.[14] She claims that treating persons as ends-in-themselves means acknowledging that they have their own ends, their own values, things which they consider good or bad; and similarly, non-human animals are also creatures for which things can be good or bad. They too have the experience of valuing.

We are now at the halfway point in this exploration of moral philosophy. Before proceeding with our exploration of additional theories, it seems wise to pause for taking stock. In particular, it will be helpful to compare and contrast Kantianism and utilitarianism, the most influential forms of deontology and consequentialism among philosophers. This will help sharpen the understanding of both approaches and prepare for the quite different sorts of theories that will occupy the second half. A brief Interlude for this purpose follows.

QUESTIONS FOR DISCUSSION

1　Give some examples contrasting *acting in accord with duty* and *acting from duty*.

2　Consider the story that opens this chapter. Does it matter that Carmen didn't realize citizenship was a condition of eligibility for the fellowship? Did Professor Stevens do the right thing? Was her promise to write "a superior reference" relevant? Are there situations in which if everyone involved does the right thing, the result will be unfair?

3　People frequently misrepresent themselves on dating websites— how is that different from what Carmen did? How might a deontologist "soften" Kant's strict prohibition against lying? How would a utilitarian evaluate Professor Stevens's action?

4　What is your moral evaluation regarding the case of two people attempting to rescue a child from a burning car? Would a utilitarian say that only the successful rescuer did the morally correct act— since only that act was optimific? Is Kant correct that a good will does not need good consequences to have moral value?

5 Give some examples of using a person as a means to an end only. How would your examples need to change if the people were to be treated also as ends-in-themselves?

6 One of Kant's illustrations of the Categorical Imperative involves suicide. He asks if we could universalize the maxim that I will "shorten my life if its continuance threatens more evil than it promises pleasure." He concludes that because this question is "asked out of self-love," its universalization would be inconsistent. In short, he claims that we would be seeking both to further life and to destroy it. What do *you* think of this argument? Is there, *contra* Kant, a maxim of rational suicide that could consistently be universalized?

7 Kant argues that we each have duties to ourselves, including the duty to develop our talents and the duty not to incapacitate ourselves so that we can't carry out our duties. He asserts that masturbation is vile (worse than suicide!) because it involves treating oneself only as a means to an end, not as a person of dignity—and therefore violates the duty of self-respect. But how is it possible to have a duty to oneself? Having a duty usually implies that others have a right to claim it from you. Can you have a claim against yourself?[15]

8 Can an act be both morally right and irrational? What would be an example?

9 Evaluate Kant's claim that punishment treats perpetrators as moral persons, while treating them as sick or damaged by their experiences denies their moral agency.

QUESTIONS FOR PERSONAL REFLECTION

1 Have you misrepresented yourself? How can we distinguish between the "non-serious" cases and the "serious" ones?

2 How would you explain and justify the idea of human dignity?

3 What do you think of the claim that lying is "a triple play of disrespect"—disrespecting the victim, oneself, and the truth?

SUGGESTED SOURCES

The primary source for this chapter is Immanuel Kant's *Groundwork of the Metaphysics of Morals* (*Grundlegung zur Metaphysik der Sitten*).

Alexander, Larry, and Michael Moore. "Deontological Ethics," *The Stanford Encyclopedia of Philosophy* (2016) https://plato.stanford.edu/entries/ethics-deontological/.

Baron, Marcia W. *Kantian Ethics Almost without Apology* (Ithaca, NY: Cornell UP, 1999).

Korsgaard, Christine. *Creating the Kingdom of Ends* (Cambridge: Cambridge UP, 1996).

O'Neill, Onora. *Acting on Principle: An Essay on Kantian Ethics*, 2nd ed. (Cambridge: Cambridge UP, 2014).

Wolff, Robert Paul. *The Autonomy of Reason: A Commentary on Kant's* Groundwork of the Metaphysics of Morals (New York: Harper Torchbooks, 1975).

NOTES

1   The German titles are: *Grundlegung zur Metaphysik der Sitten, Kritik der praktischen Vernunft,* and *Metaphysik der Sitten.*

2   *Groundwork,* Chapter 1. I have used the translation of H.J. Paton, modified with Americanized spellings.

3   Ibid.

4   William Shakespeare, *The Merchant of Venice*, Act V, Scene 1. The line is quoted by Willy Wonka in the film, *Willy Wonka and the Chocolate Factory*, when Charlie returns his pilfered candy for no foreseen gain—the right act for the right reason and quite against his inclinations.

5   *Groundwork,* Chapter 2.

6   Ibid.

7   Ibid., Chapter 1.

8   *Metaphysics of Morals,* Part I, contains Kant's views on crime and punishment.

9   See W.D. Ross, *The Right and the Good*, ed. Philip Stratton-Lake (1930; New York: Oxford UP, 2002); and *Foundations of Ethics: The Gifford Lectures Delivered at the University of Aberdeen, 1935–6.* (Oxford: Clarendon P, 1939).

10   Luke 10: 30, 33–35 (NIV). This biblical parable is (in the Latin Vulgate version) the source of the word "supererogation."

11   William Shakespeare, *The Merchant of Venice*, Act IV, Scene I.

12   Immanuel Kant, *Lectures on Anthropology*, Akademie-Textausgabe, Berlin. 7: 127; quoted by Lori Gruen in "The Moral Status of Animals," *Stanford Encyclopedia of Philosophy* (Sept. 13, 2010 ed.).

13   Marcia W. Baron, *Kantian Ethics Almost without Apology* (Ithaca, NY: Cornell UP, 1995).

14 Christine Korsgaard, *Fellow Creatures: Our Obligations to the Other Animals* (Oxford: Oxford UP, 2018).

15 See, e.g., Marcus G. Singer, "On Duties to Oneself," *Ethics* 69, No. 3 (April 1959): 202–05.

Interlude: Principled Ethics

Kantianism and utilitarianism have been the dominant competing ethical theories for over a century. At least superficially, they share important features. Both exemplify what I would call "principled" ethics. This is the view that doing the right thing is a matter of following the proper principle(s): if one obtains the right moral principle(s), they can serve as keys that can unlock any moral dilemma. Both Kantianism and utilitarianism attempt the ultimate in simplicity by enshrining one principle as supreme—the Categorical Imperative and the Greatest Happiness Principle, respectively—and the rest is extrapolation, interpretation, and application. The supreme principle is a master key, the only key one ever requires.

Both these principles oblige the moral agent to consider the larger moral community in acting: Kant requires universalizability and regard for the Kingdom of Ends; utilitarians require each one to count as one and to consider the well-being and suffering of all conscious beings. These visions are, in this aspect, egalitarian. Yet there is a notable difference in their criteria for moral standing, however, resulting in moral communities with differing membership.

Both theories emphasize the role of reason in morality, but they also part ways on this point. For Kant, morality is simply the practical application of rationality; it is because we are rational agents that we are capable of moral action—or so we must necessarily assume (as his transcendental argument concludes). Kant argues that a supreme ethical principle, and the Categorical Imperative in particular, must be derived *a priori*, that is, by reasoning alone. The utilitarians claim to derive the good from human experience. They use reason as a calculative faculty, to compute expected outcomes and efficiently arrange means to ends. Moral education—the production of moral agents by moral agents—would require the development of full autonomy and rationality (in different modes), and would rule out straightforward indoctrination.

Kant's moral vision is relatively "internal," focusing on one's motives and a good will, reverence for the moral law, and the psychological struggle for duty to overcome inclinations. Bentham and Mill have a moral vision that is relatively "external," looking to outcomes in the world. Yes, they are interested in moral psychology, but primarily as it is implicated in obtaining maximal results. Kant sees it as the contrast between autonomy and heteronomy; utilitarians would see it as the contrast between a morality of self-righteousness and one of social improvement. One might be tempted to observe that each theory focuses on a different aspect of morality: Kant is interested in the agent's will and the form of the act; utilitarians are interested in the consequences of the act. This is true, but both present what they believe to be the full picture of moral assessment. Kant rejects the relevance of consequences like pleasure or happiness; utilitarians make all moral judgments from results. While utilitarians find the good in valued mental states, Kant sees virtue (righteousness) itself as the good.

For Kant, all moral agents are equal in dignity and their individual differences are not morally relevant. For utilitarians, *Homo economicus* is the classic model for all moral agents—though people differ widely in their desires and in their interests. One's moral worth, one's status as moral agent or patient, are not dependent upon intelligence, personal appearance, social rank, gender, race (though the latter two were often circumvented in practice), religion, or any other individual difference. Under both theories, moral agents take a disinterested perspective, deciding not so much "what I should do" but "what one should do." They make no claim to special privilege or partiality and suppress or largely ignore their own emotions. Strong feelings may cloud objective judgment. In a sense, their models of the moral agent and the philosopher of morals coincide.

Supererogation appears not to exist as a category of moral action in either system. Since Kant holds that the moral worth of an act derives solely from its dutifulness, to act without a sense of moral obligation is of no moral value; alternatively, it would be erroneous to believe such an act was one's duty and required by moral law. For the utilitarians, doing the most good *is* obligatory, so going beyond such a duty is logically impossible. Yet it seems unlikely that Kantians would intend to disvalue such actions or that utilitarians would intend to require sainthood of us all.

Both these visions of moral life make individual freedom a primary value—a reflection of their Enlightenment origins. Some critics argue, however, that freedom alone does not offer a substantive answer to the question "How should I live?" (Free to do what?) It is the case that Kant's discussion seems more centered on what one should *not* do, and—other than providing illustrative cases—his positive advice is mostly adverbial: act with respect for others, act rationally, act from duty, and so on. Among utilitarians, however, John Stuart Mill in particular does discuss the good life substantively.[1] To become more precisely prescriptive (the opposite of excessive abstraction) would at some point risk imposing a repressive uniformity.

Deontology celebrates the dignity and righteousness of living up to moral principles that arise from fundamental values. Consequentialism celebrates the possibilities of human agency to create happier lives and to improve the world. In their Kantian and utilitarian forms, these two visions have largely shaped modern morality.

Nonetheless, both theories seem to lack something crucial to our moral relationships. The problem was articulated nicely by Michael Stocker (b. 1940) in an influential article titled, "The Schizophrenia of Modern Ethical Theories."[2] The moral "schizophrenia" he diagnoses is a disjunction between one's motives and one's reasons or justifications. Stocker charges: "It is not possible for moral people, that is, people who would achieve what is valuable, to act on these ethical theories, to let them comprise their motives. People who do let them comprise their motives will, for that reason, have a life seriously lacking in what is valuable." Among his illustrations is this Kantian scenario:

> Suppose you are in a hospital, recovering from a long illness. You are very bored and restless and at loose ends when Smith comes in … You are now convinced more than ever that he is a fine fellow and a real friend—taking so much time to cheer you up, traveling all the way across town, and so on. You are so effusive with your praise and thanks that he protests that he always tries to do what he thinks is his duty, what he thinks will be best. You at first think he is engaging in a polite form of self-deprecation, relieving the moral burden. But the more you two speak, the more clear it becomes that he was telling the literal truth: that it is not essentially because of you that he came to see you, not because you are friends, but because he thought it was his duty.[3]

And if Smith were not a Kantian but a utilitarian, you would feel the same. Smith would say something like, "Well, I considered all the good I might produce today, and coming to see you turned out to be optimific. If going to the dentist or something else had netted more good, I wouldn't have been here." As Stocker says, "Surely there is something lacking here." We would like Smith's visit to reflect his sincere affections, felt emotions, personal relationships and commitments. The reason he gives—adherence to an ethical theory—seems extrinsic in some way, a cold adherence to rules. A moral response should be genuine for the agent; it should come from "deeper" sources within the person.

This haunting critique not only suggests the need for ethical theory to embrace our emotional and relational aspects, it also puts the question of whether any ethic of principles can avoid this problem. When we adopt a principle to govern our actions and then proceed to act on it, are we not accepting a policy-driven life, one in which the principle is "put on" like a harness, suppressing the very wellsprings of moral action?

We will examine four theories that attempt to address this critique in Chapters 9–12. But first, we turn to an approach that embraces both rationality and autonomy, but sees morality as a matter of mutual agreement.

NOTES

1   See Mill's response to Obj. 3 in *Utilitarianism*, Chapter 2.

2   Michael Stocker, "The Schizophrenia of Modern Ethical Theories," *Journal of Philosophy* 73, no. 14 (Aug. 12, 1976): 453–66.

3   Ibid., 462.

CHAPTER EIGHT
Contractarianism

The homeowners who live in Oak Woods, concerned to protect the value of their property, informally agree to replace their subdivision's aging entryway and repair its crumbling walls. The project will be expensive, but after their homeowner's association agreed on a design and cost, everyone voluntarily contributed—except Trent.

It's not about the money. Trent certainly can afford his share. It is rather, a lifelong pattern of conduct—even he isn't sure whether it's a game or a matter of principle. When he was an undergraduate, he preferred to sneak into concerts and clubs, rather than buying a ticket or paying a cover charge. He shared an apartment with three people, but managed to leave the cleaning to them. When he studied abroad, he encountered a public transportation system that expected all riders to have a ticket but conducted only random checks (with steep fines for violations).

Trent enjoyed literally being a "free rider"—the term used for a person who benefits from a collective project without contributing a fair share. Dodging the conductors, he made it a sport to ride the buses and trams without buying a ticket.

Trent now argues that he should not be obligated to do something simply because other people get together for their own interests and create a good that also benefits him. He didn't urge people to fix up the subdivision entryway or walls—though he admits he likes what they've done and is happy that his property value is secure. When pressed, he also admits that, although he needed blood some time ago after an automobile accident—he has never considered giving blood. Trent asserts that he made no promises in these matters, that he is doing nothing illegal or immoral, and that he's only being smart in reducing needless personal costs.

8.1 THE MORAL AND THE LEGAL

The moral and the legal are distinct but overlapping spheres. In Chapter 1, I distinguished them in order to focus sharply on the nature of morality. (Traffic rules are matters of law, not of morality, for example.) But they do have a deep relationship, and it will be helpful to remind ourselves of their connection. Both morality and the law are systems that tell us what to do and what not to do: they produce imperatives. The law is an aspect of the public or political; it prescribes the structure and procedures of governance. By contrast, morality may seem naturally more personal or private, and yet important moral concerns give content to the law. Laws against murder, rape, theft, fraud and other crimes are rooted in our collective sense of their immorality. These two systems are not isolated: they share modes of thought, views of human nature, and they are continually interacting.

The law can sometimes overreach. Moral concerns that are not widely shared can result in intrusive laws—for example, laws against certain consensual sex acts. But a new moral consensus can result in laws that forbid a previously accepted practice—dueling, for example, changed from an honor-bound ritual to a crime.[1] Of course, laws may be enacted that violate rights and are unjust—for example, laws against interracial marriage. People of moral conscience may protest laws they deem to be unjust. These two forms of social management, moral and legal, are continually evolving, adapting, and responding; and their relationship is subtle and fluid.

The last two chapters have discussed especially clear examples of the connection between moral theory and governance. Utilitarianism, as we have seen, is a moral theory that sought to shape the aims and methods of social policy and governance. The law is among the most powerful of social institutions to protect and promote public welfare. The utilitarian progressives saw government as an agent for public good; they viewed the elimination of slavery and child labor, prison reform, women's suffrage, and expanded education as moral causes that required enlightened legislation. Immanuel Kant's moral theory and his ideal of a "republic of perpetual peace" later helped form the first durable instrument of international justice: *The United Nations Universal Declaration of Human Rights*. Both approaches view ethical principles as grounding and motivating governance, morality as the very foundation of polity.

In this chapter, we examine a type of theory that is explicitly directed to both spheres and promises their unity: contractarianism. Its political form is ancient and is known as **Social Contract Theory**, which holds that the legitimacy of government derives from the consent of the governed. The form it gives to moral theory is called *contractualism*, which holds that morality derives from social agreement. Both forms rely on two key concepts: *contract* and *consent*. After an analysis of those concepts, we will examine three versions of the social contract, followed by the theory of contractualism.

8.2 CONTRACTS AND CONSENT

There are moments when a mere utterance creates a fact: "You are now united in marriage." To be effective, such statements (they are called *performatives* by philosophers) have to be uttered by the proper person under specific conditions. The "uniting in marriage" statement, for example, won't create the fact of marriage unless it is made by an appropriate official speaking to two persons of legal age who hold a marriage license. In most jurisdictions, those being married must be acting of their own free will and not be simultaneously married to someone else. Often, important performatives that have social implications—taking an oath, apologizing, being baptized, awarding a degree or an honor—require a procedure or ritual. After they have been "performed," the world is different: new moral and legal facts have been created.

Promises are performatives: when I make a promise, I create a moral obligation. Sometimes, promises are verbal and informal: "I promise I won't be late tonight." But we have developed more formal, explicit, and specific ways of promising—often stated and preserved in writing—called *contracts*. A contract is a promise of a *quid pro quo*—a benefit or advantage to be given in return for something. It represents an agreement between two parties, a mutual promise, to carry out an exchange: the singer agrees to perform at a specific time and place and the sponsor agrees to pay her fee for the performance. The signing of a contract is a performative that creates new moral and legal rights and obligations. Today, many contracts are likely to be elaborated with conditions and contingences addressed in minute detail. For the contract to be valid, however, certain conditions must be met: the signing must be voluntary, not coerced; the parties must be of legal age and of sound mind; both parties must act in good faith (without fraud or deception); and the stipulations must not violate any law, if the contract is to be legally enforceable.

The commitments expressed in a contract further cooperation, reduce risk and uncertainty in transacting with others, and expand trust (especially when backed up by enforcement or penalties for default). The contract is a quintessential embodiment of Enlightenment liberal thought: it is an instrument of practical reason that promotes the intents and purposes of the contracting parties, who, as individuals of free will, may consent to exchanges they deem fair.

The obligations one incurs under a contract are self-imposed. They arise from one's consenting to the stipulations of the contract. Without consent, there is no valid contract. Giving consent, like making a promise, is also a performative: it confirms agreement, assent, approval, or permission. Fundamentally, it is a declaration of one's will, and therefore must be made under appropriate conditions—it must be free and not coerced or produced by external causes; it must reflect a mental state that is sound, sober, and rational; it must be given in awareness of all pertinent facts; and it must be the will of a responsible individual (not a minor or an individual of diminished capacity, and not an individual without the authority to consent to the matter at hand).[2] Consent is always directed to a specific object: one does not simply consent, one consents *to some particular thing*. And the object of consent normally arises externally, not from one's own mind, but from a received request or proposal. This differentiates consent from other declarations of the will, such as giving orders or writing a last will and testament, in which there is no received proposal, no consent. Rather, a consent permits others, who have made a request or proposal, to move ahead cooperatively, by receiving (outward) confirmation of one's (inner) will. In many ways, the concept of consent reflects a Kantian concern with agency, autonomy, and the direction of the will.

In explicating these aspects of consent, I may wrongly suggest that the process is always formal, involving documents, witnesses, and signatures. In most cases, things are much more informal and subtle. In some contexts, all that is required for consent is an "OK," or even a nod of the head. Even silence can be construed as consent in some situations—though that may be risky in others, and flatly unacceptable in matters such as consent for medical procedures, electronic bank payments, and sexual relations. Failure to say "no" is no longer considered to be giving consent to sexual relations, for example; in such contexts, an affirmation of consent is generally required: "Yes, it's OK." (And it requires that such consent be freely given by a partner who is of age and in a competent mental state.) An agreement, such as a contract, implies mutual consent, the two parties "being of one mind" regarding its conditions.

A lack of consent or contract leaves the parties without permission or formal obligation. The unwilling homeowner, Trent, in the case that opens this chapter, refuses to cooperate because he has signed no contract that requires him to do so. He would assert that he never agreed to the actions that others are asking him to do.

8.3 SOCIAL CONTRACT THEORY

During the period given the name "Middle Ages," it seemed that divine providence ordained natural laws, established the social and moral order, and anointed kings and popes to rule. As European thought developed, however, governance was understood to be a human creation, something that could be altered or created anew by human action. This insight was energizing, spawning parliaments and legislation, reforms and revolutions. Immediately, the pressing question became: *If government is not ordained by God, what is the source of its legitimacy, its authority?* An apt model for the creation of legitimate constraints and expectations was ready-to-hand in the commercial concepts of contract and consent. A ringing response to the question, breathtaking in its implications, is that government gets its authority from the consent of the governed; it is citizen consent that legitimates government. We, the governed, have consented to a social contract under which our government operates. Known as Social Contract Theory, this view led to philosophical debates about the purposes of government, the provisions of the social contract, and the nature of consent; correlatively, it generated a practical emphasis on political documents—laws, charters, declarations, contracts, and constitutions.

The idea of a social contract has several elements. First, theorists present an account of the "**state of nature**." This is a description of the period prior to civil society; that is, before any government is established. Dilating upon a view of human nature, the theorist portrays life with others as it would be without laws, without authorities or cooperative institutions, without political structures. Second, the theorist offers an account of the motivations that inevitably lead the individuals in the state of nature to sit down together to establish a political order, to negotiate a political contract. This element answers the question, "Why do we need government?" As a contract, it would represent individual consent, mutual agreement, and binding assurances. Third, there is a statement of the provisions of the agreement or pact, the Social Contract itself. This is sometimes further divided into two contractual steps: (a) the pact of union (*pactum unionis*) which transforms the individuals into a deliberative civil society; and (b) the agreement instituting a form of government (*pactum subjectionis*) that is the product of their deliberations. Finally, an account of social life under the agreed regime is usually included, occasionally addressing specific problems that may arise, such as punishment for crimes or the possibility of replacing a failed regime.

Taken as history, social contract theory is absurd. The state of nature is dubious anthropology, and there is not and never was a pact or contract agreed to by all humans. But this sequence of events is not intended to be historical (though some passages in social contract texts might suggest that). To understand social contract theory, it is best to understand the state of nature not as an anthropological account of early human history, but as a logical construct or philosophical thought-experiment.[3] It is a way of thinking about what life would be like if there were no government. It functions as a rational reconstruction or idealization, an illuminating scenario that provides philosophical insights—from which we are to draw conclusions *as if* the sequence from state of nature to polity were real.

Two of the most famous social contract theorists are English philosophers we have met earlier: Thomas Hobbes and John Locke. We met Hobbes as a hedonistic egoist (Chapter 5) and Locke as an advocate of religious tolerance (Chapter 2). These different "first impressions" are, we shall see, consonant with a deeper knowledge of their views.

Thomas Hobbes was born prematurely on April 5, 1588, when his mother was frightened by hearing of the approach of the Spanish Armada. He later remarked that his mother had "brought forth twins—myself and fear." As many have noted, fear seems to have been Hobbes's lifelong companion, and it is the key passion in his political theory. When the English Civil War began, he prided himself, a Royalist, on being "the first that fled" to Paris. Years later, scorned for his unpopular and subversive ideas, he escaped Paris to return to Restoration England. Despite his fears, Hobbes lived to the age of 91—double the life expectancy in 1679. He had been a child prodigy: at 14 years of age, he translated Euripides play *Medea* from the Greek into Latin iambics.[4] He would produce a number of translations of Classical works during his life. His monumental work, *Leviathan*, presents his moral and political theory. It is a bold attempt to establish a political philosophy on a sound, empirical human psychology—a psychology that was, in fact, extrapolated from the science of mechanics.

Hobbes believed that human beings are creatures pushed about by two forces: *desire*, which attracts; and *aversion*, which repels. Pleasure is the good, but the desire for power is our dominant appetite. Our dominant aversion is the fear of death. All humans, he observed, have a basic instinct for self-preservation, and it is possessed by all equally. So broad is its relevance that this instinct entitles each individual to do all things necessary for self-preservation—including self-defense and the right to suppress or subdue others or take their goods to save oneself. But it is obvious that if everyone possesses the right to all things, it comes to nothing except mutual destruction. This is what Hobbes conceives the state of nature to be: a clash of desires, aversions, and natural entitlements that leaves everyone insecure. He writes:

> Nature hath made men so equal in the faculties of the body and
> mind, as that, though there be found one man sometimes mani-
> festly stronger in body or of quicker mind than another, yet when
> all is reckoned together the difference between man and man is not
> so considerable as that one man can thereupon claim to himself
> any benefit to which another may not pretend as well as he. For,
> as to the strength of body, the weakest has strength enough to kill

the strongest, either by secret machination or by confederacy with others that are in the same danger with himself ...

Hereby it is manifest that, during the time men live without a common power to keep them all in awe, they are in that condition which is called war, and such a war as is of every man against every man ...

In such condition there is no place for industry, because the fruit thereof is uncertain, and consequently no culture of the earth, no navigation nor use of the commodities that may be imported by sea, no commodious building, no instruments of moving and removing such things as require much force, no knowledge of the face of the earth; no account of time, no arts, no letters, no society, and, which is worst of all, continual fear and danger of violent death, and the life of man solitary, poor, nasty, brutish, and short.[5]

Even egoists, given desire and fear, will sit down to negotiate a peace. It is in their self-interest to do so. Hobbes believes there can be no civilization without an agreement to establish order. And there is no trustworthy agreement without a power to enforce it. That power must be indivisible and unrestricted. In such circumstances, preferring tyranny to anarchy, individuals will consent to empower a single sovereign, an absolute authority with legislative, executive, and judicial power in one. They will retain no right to property, no right to rebel against a cruel sovereign; they retain only their right to self-preservation. All else is given up to gain safety. The obligation to obey will dissolve only if the sovereign loses power, particularly the power to secure the people collectively. The sovereign is not a party to the contract; he is simply appointed to keep the peace and how he does it is his business.

John Locke, a physician as well as a philosopher, came from Puritan stock. He was fortunate among political philosophers in that his work was published just as those who shared his views came to power. His sympathies were with Parliament, not King James II, and Locke became known as the apostle of the Glorious Revolution of 1688. He epitomizes the early liberalism that arose in England and Holland; grounded in common sense, Locke will sacrifice logical consistency to avoid extremism. His *Second Treatise of Government* was inspiration and guide to those who founded the American republic.

Locke's view of the state of nature seems much more positive than Hobbes's, and it rests on a sunnier view of humanity. For Locke, the state of nature is for humans "a state of perfect freedom to order their actions and dispose of their possessions and persons as they think fit, within the bounds of the law of nature." It is "a state of perfect equality, wherein all the power and jurisdiction is reciprocal, no one having more than another." It is not, he assures us, "a state of license." We are rational creatures, and reason—embodied in natural law—teaches us that our equality means no one "should harm another in his life, health, liberty, or possessions."[6] Being creatures of God, we do not possess the right to commit suicide. Yet there are certain "inconveniences" that compel us into a social contract. These include the possibility of violence (indeed, the least difference is liable to end in conflict), especially since individuals have the right to interpret laws, including proper punishment, and conflicts of property ownership will arise.

Locke's acknowledgment that conflict is possible or likely, and his use of a more restrictive definition of "war" ("a sedate, settled design upon another man's life"), result in a state of nature that is not as different from Hobbes's vision as first appears. Although both believe that natural law applies in the state of nature, Hobbes sees only the right of survival. Locke, however, affirms not only self-preservation, but the right to property, the duty of non-maleficence (not to harm others), and the right to punish those who harm you.

According to Locke, the contractors will instinctively agree that even anarchy is better than tyranny, because there is real terror in submitting oneself to the arbitrary will of an all-powerful authority. For Locke, a government is given a trust—not a contract that gives a government rights. The government is to serve the people in securing their individual lives, rights, and property. It operates through a separation of powers with implicit checks and balances. The ultimate power is in the people, who may rightfully rebel any time the government betrays its trust. Locke appears willing to endure a tyranny of the majority (since he provides for no minority protections) rather than face the arbitrariness of absolutism.

The central problem of liberal political philosophy might be posed this way: *How can the moral autonomy of the individual be made compatible with the legitimate authority of the state?* The model of an implicit social contract attempts to resolve this question by featuring the act of consent. Entering a contract requires the autonomy of the individual contractors; it is their willful creation of the state that legitimizes its power over those who so consented. Though Hobbes and Locke both use this model, they begin with different assumptions and arrive at very different political conclusions. (I have condensed their views for comparison in **Figure 4**.)

FIGURE 4   HOBBES and LOCKE: SOME COMPARISONS

Thomas Hobbes (1588–1679)	John Locke (1632–1704)
Royalist—sympathies with the king.	Whig—sympathies with Parliament and middle class.
Rationalist in method, usually.	Empiricist in method, usually.
"Good" is merely the name given to that which one desires. Pleasure and self-interest shape desire.	"Good" refers to those self-evident values revealed and imparted by God.
State of nature is a state of war. "War" means not only actual conflict, but the willingness to resort to conflict.	State of nature is a state of "peace." War is a "sedate, settled design upon another man's life."
Assumes all would consent to the pact of union.	The pact of union is binding on only those who consent.
In the contract situation, it is self-evident that tyranny is better than anarchy.	In the contract situation, it is agreed that anarchy is better than tyranny.
Individuals enter the contract out of their need for security and fear of death.	Individuals enter the contract in order to protect their right to property.
A pact of subjection is signed, binding on all except the sovereign.	No pact of subjection; rather, a trust is bestowed on government, giving it no real rights.
The commonwealth is highly centralized, having unlimited powers to insure the security of the people, taken collectively.	The commonwealth is highly decentralized, having a deputation to protect the rights of the people, taken individually.
Power is indivisible and absolute.	Separation of powers, with implicit checks and balances.
Ultimate power resides in the sovereign.	Ultimate power in the people of the contract.
There is no right to rebellion; however, the obligation to obey dissolves if the sovereign loses the ability to insure security.	Right to rebellion any time the government: (a) acts contrary to natural law; (b) acts against the trust of the people; and (c) has irresolvable disagreements among its separate powers.
The social contract institutes the tyranny of one person.	The social contract institutes the apparent tyranny of the majority.

8.4 JOHN RAWLS AND THE JUST STATE

The most influential text in political philosophy in the twentieth century was written by John Rawls[7] and titled simply, *A Theory of Justice*. In this work, Rawls develops an elaborate version of the social contract. Whereas Hobbes is concerned with security and Locke is focused on protecting rights, Rawls is concerned with justice. He asks not only what gives the state legitimacy, but what makes the state just. In the first sentences of this magisterial text, Rawls declares, "Justice is the first virtue of social institutions, as truth is of systems of thought. A theory however elegant and economical must be rejected or revised if it is untrue; likewise, laws and institutions no matter how efficient and well-arranged must be reformed or abolished if they are unjust." Thus, for Rawls, those consenting to create a government will work to construct one that is, above all else, just. Justice is a key aspect of legitimacy.

Justice is a normative concept that is concerned with the distribution of rights, advantages, and goods (*distributive justice*); punishments (*retributive justice*); and reparations (*restorative justice*). The basic principles on which a state is structured concern distributive justice; they will be embodied in the constitution that results from a social contract. For many thinkers, justice should be understood as a normative *pattern* of distribution: a society is just if people receive what they deserve according to their individual merit, for example, or according to their effort, or according to their need. Rawls rejects such a "pattern" approach and instead draws upon an element of social contract theory: the importance of procedure. He develops a "pure procedural" theory of justice. According to Rawls, *if the decision-making procedure is fair, then whatever is decided is just.*

An analogy may help. If a group is playing poker for money, what is a just distribution of the money at the end of the game? A pattern theory might say that the results would be just if the best player got the most money (merit) or if the player who was desperate for money got the most (need). The Rawlsian view is that, *so long as the game was fair*, however the chips fall and the money is distributed would be just. Justice is what results from a fair procedure.

Rawls replaces the state of nature concept with what he calls the **Original Position**—though it plays a similar role. We are to imagine that the people in the Original Position are choosing the basic principles on which their society will be organized. They possess the usual characteristics assumed in social contract theory: they are rational, self-interested, autonomous, and of equal stature in terms of voting. But, in order to assure fairness, Rawls imagines that they make their choice behind a **Veil of Ignorance**. It is as though they suffered severe amnesia: they do not know their identity—not their gender or race or occupation or position in society. They know they must have values, plans, aspirations—but they have no clue as to what those are. When they choose the principles of their society and the veil is lifted, they will discover their place in the world. Rawls says, "The fairest rules are those to which everyone would agree if they did not know how much power they would have."

Rawls restricts his conditions of fairness to the choice of basic principles. To see the impact of this idea, however, imagine this scenario: the city sanitation works are on strike, garbage has been piling up for weeks creating a health hazard, and the mayor finally decides she personally must negotiate directly with the union representatives. What difference in the negotiations might there be if they were behind a veil of ignorance? What if they did not know, when the veil was lifted, who among them would be mayor and who the garbage truck drivers?

Behind the veil of ignorance, under conditions of fairness and alert to many possible principles, the individuals would, Rawls claims, choose two principles for their governance:

> 1. Each person is to have an equal right to the most extensive basic liberty compatible with a similar liberty for others.

> 2. Social and economic inequalities are to be arranged so that: (a) they are to be of the greatest benefit to the least-advantaged members of society ... and (b) offices and positions must be open to everyone under conditions of fair equality of opportunity.[8]

If we did not know our identity, these principles would assure us of equality of rights, an optimal range of freedom, equal access and opportunity. And if, when the veil is lifted, I find I have the lowest position in the social order, I would know that the worst would be as good as it could be. The justice of these principles, remember, is derived from the fair conditions under which they are chosen.

The position we occupy in society is not a simple matter of our choice. Each of us is born with a specific genetic endowment, the child of individual parents, at a certain time and place and socio-economic position in society. We did not choose any of these "given" aspects of our identity. They are ours as an outcome of the "Natural Lottery." We are launched into life from different starting points, with unequal advantages and disadvantages. For Rawls, this constitutes an inherent unfairness that should be addressed through our social structures; ironically, the veil of ignorance reveals its problematic import. But natural inequality is not a special moral issue for Hobbes or for Locke, whose contractors know their identity and place in the world. Many thinkers go further, asserting that, although it is true that individuals do not *deserve* their natural advantages and disadvantages—their talents and limitations, their parents and their genetic defects—they are *entitled* to them and to everything that flows from them.[9] For them, the most advantaged owes nothing to the least advantaged. Privilege does not, in their view, create obligation.

8.5 MORALITY BY CONTRACT

To this point, we have examined contractarian responses to the central question of political philosophy. Social contract theory embodies and applies conceptions of human nature, choice theory, and principles of morality. It is possible, however, to formulate a contract-based theory of morality itself—a position that has come to be called **contractualism**. Contractualism holds that:

"*X* is right" = "*X* is stipulated in the moral contract," and

"*X* is wrong" = "*X* is in violation of the moral contract."

The content of the normative theory, exactly what things are right or wrong, will depend on the provisions of the contract. In some versions of contractualism, we can only affirm what is morally *permissible* or not under the contract, not what is right. As with social contract theory, we must reconstruct a performative event that is not historical, but rather a thought-experiment in which specific conditions and assumptions allow us to deduce consensual outcomes.

An influential version of contractualism is articulated by contemporary philosopher T.M. Scanlon (b. 1940) in a book titled *What We Owe to Each Other*.[10] In his account, the moral contract involves "mutual recognition" of the inestimable value of each other as moral agents, beings who distinctively have the capacity to assess reasons and justifications for actions. For Scanlon, the moral contract is more concerned with *wrongness* than with *rightness*—indeed, in his account, the term "good" merely means "not wrong." (Note that I have throughout employed the term *permissible* for "not wrong.") For Scanlon, an act that is morally wrong is one that is unjustifiable. Whereas Hobbes and Locke seek to secure and expand self-interest through a bargain with others, Scanlon seeks conditions in which each person can pursue interests and engage in actions that are justifiable to others. Whereas social contract theorists, including Rawls, seek a contract or principles everyone would *agree to*, Scanlon's more minimal contractualism seeks principles no one could *reasonably reject*. He says, "An act is wrong if its performance under the circumstances would be disallowed by any set of principles for the general regulation of behavior that no one could reasonably reject as a basis for informed, unforced, general agreement."[11]

Scanlon believes that acts like killing and stealing are to be condemned unless they are undertaken with a rationale that is reasonably justifiable to others. He also gives particular attention to various ways we can go wrong through creating expectations in others: false promising and lying (both Kantian concerns) are obvious, but so are the broader cases of letting others form reasonable but false expectations of what we will do, or misleading others about our intentions. These latter cases are subtler, because they need not involve outright promising or lying.

The alert reader can detect elements of Kantianism in both Rawls's and Scanlon's views. For Scanlon, however, it is not so much Kant's Categorical Imperative in either its initial formulation or the Principle of Nature that is fundamental, but rather his Principle of Humanity and the Kingdom of Ends—the mutual respect of equal, morally capable persons. Duty or obligation—what we owe to each other—thus is grounded in recognition and respect, first and foremost. Moral reasoning is here focused on explanation and justification for actions and policies; it is not the *a priori* reasoning of logical consistency. Thus, it is possible, as some critics have noted, to interpret Scanlon as offering an attempt to perfect Kantian theory.

What we owe each other, contrary to the position taken by free-riding Trent, is not a matter of explicit consent or written agreement; but rather of what would not be rejected by reasonable people. It would be grounded in the recognition of others as of inestimable value in themselves.

There are, you may have noticed, tensions between the versions of contractualism that emphasize the self-interest to be gained from the contract (such as Hobbes's), and those that emphasize the compelling rationality and social good of the contract (such as Rawls's or Scanlon's). For the former, it is relevant that there are always individuals who cannot benefit us in personal ways. To reveal this relevance, let's look at the business of health insurance. When we buy health insurance, we consent to pay a premium for various sorts of medical reimbursements as the need arises. We are members of a pool of insured people who have consented to similar arrangements. It is nearly certain that, in any given period, some will benefit more than others—the healthy will help offset the costs of the sickly. Thus, not everyone's membership in the cohort benefits us. But the least advantaged, the sickliest, are not freeloading—that would entail medical fraud. The attraction of insurance is to share the risk of illness or injury; that is implied in the contract.

The different versions of contract theory might therefore identify different ranges of individuals as included among the "equal" contractors. If all contracts were motivated only by immediate or direct personal gain, why would I contract with someone who cannot benefit me? Are all individuals eligible to buy into this health insurance? The egoistic agent wants a direct, personal benefit from any contract, including the social contract: "Why should a single, sixty-year-old man pay for insurance that covers maternity expenses?" "And why should he have to pay taxes that support local schools?" We might as well ask, "Why should I have to pay taxes to fund roads I won't drive on, or programs I don't support, or the salaries of politicians I don't like." Such questions reject public goods as relevant benefits from the social contract.

Earlier I noted the varying goals for the contract: security, protection of property, social justice, and the establishment of moral expectations are among the goals of the theories we have considered. They also differ as to the nature and extent of the rights one has under the contract. But each theory seeks what any valid contract can produce: *open commitment to a shared set of expectations*. With an explicit social or moral contract, we know what we owe and what is owed to us. We should comply and expect compliance. Contract-based theories also establish a limit to what morality can demand of us, and we can reasonably expect only a certain amount of self-sacrifice from others.

Before turning to a critique, I want to draw together some of the advantages of contractualism. Not least among these is the view that moral rules are merely those principles that rational people would accept in order to pursue their interests while enjoying social harmony. "Why should we be moral?" The answer is: because we would, under proper conditions, agree to it. Moreover, the contract model does, as I noted earlier, entail individual rationality, autonomy, freedom of will, and consent—and thereby recognizes our moral agency. We would agree to moral precepts because we rationally understand their benefits for us; but being human, we follow those precepts because the rules are enforced—there is a price for immorality. We expect others to live up to the provisions of the contract—those who breach the contract, including those who freeload, are punished or chastised. Free-riders like Trent violate the contract: they do not pay what we all owe to each other. In this view, it is wrong to take advantage of others by relying on their ethical behavior, using it to open a space in which one can get away with unethical, selfish behavior. Thus, moral obligations seem reasonable without resorting to Reason in the formal, Kantian sense.

8.6 CRITIQUE OF CONTRACTUALISM

It is now time to critique this vision in which our moral and political principles are the stipulations and reasonable implications of hypothetical contracts.

1. The blunt observation that these theories are based on a historical fiction, a contract event that never happened, is not, by itself, an astute critique. Many theories, even scientific theories, are based on postulated entities, idealizations that do not exist—frictionless surfaces, infinite trials, ideal observers, for example. Besides, these fictional contracts are carefully constructed thought-experiments from which reasoned conclusions can be drawn. But their fictive nature does raise a concern: we never actually give our consent to the agreement we are supposed to honor; and consent, like any performative, requires a performance. In reply, contract theorists usually revert to the concept of *implicit consent*: we have implicitly consented to the social or moral contract.

Implicit consent, however, is a problematic concept—not fatal to the theories, perhaps, but certainly in need of elaboration. Consent seems to be an act that must be deliberate, an exercise of will, a performative that requires the explicitness of a sign, an utterance, a signature. How can it be implicit? I said earlier that silence sometimes indicates consent, but that hardly seems sufficient in the case of the social or moral contract—theories in which the act of consent is the origin of the social or moral order.

Does just growing up in a state imply that one has consented to its embedded principles—assuming one could unambiguously identify them? Socrates, in Plato's *Crito*, refused to escape his imprisonment on the grounds that to break the laws of the city-state that had nurtured him like a parent would be unjust.[12] He had, he argues, implicitly consented to the laws of Athens by accepting the benefits they provided him as he grew from youth to maturity. But aren't we all formed by a culture before we are really equipped to consider rejecting it? Immigrants and refugees who desire to live permanently in a new state are asked formally to consent to its principles. But what is the act of consent for those who are born in that state? Does it take a specific act of early rejection to avoid implicit consent? *Can one reject the social contract?* And what of the moral contract?

Does everyone, including Trent, just by becoming an adult human being, give implicit consent to the moral contract?

The contractualist might reply that all this is making the act of consent too formal. The notion of implicit consent only means that living as social, rational persons necessarily presumes consent to certain basic principles—in much the same way that playing chess or baseball presumes we have agreed to the rules of the game, whether we have explicitly agreed to them or not. But it is when we encounter those who follow different rules and divergent expectations, or when one wishes to alter or reject the rules or expectations, that explicitness is required.

2. Some critics have said that limiting moral action to the requirements of a contract rules out supererogation. I believe that is a mistaken conclusion. Supererogatory acts, by definition, cannot be contractually obligated. In fact, setting contractual limits to moral duties *opens* the possibility for supererogation—good deeds that are not required of us. Such acts must be contractually permissible—that is, they must not be precluded by contract. This is possible, however, only if one recognizes that the moral sphere, the range of morally good, is broader than what is contractually required. Many thinkers have observed that a good society requires more than contract compliance; it relies on forms of good conduct that are ultimately unenforceable. Lord John Fletcher Moulton (1844–1921), British jurist and mathematician, went further: "The greatness of a nation, its true civilization, is measured by the extent of its obedience to the unenforceable."

3. In my presentation of the theories, I skirted the question of who is included within the moral contract, who is entitled to shape the pact of union. This issue of contractual inclusiveness has been raised by philosopher Martha Nussbaum, among others. In *Frontiers of Justice*, Nussbaum identified problems regarding three groups excluded or marginalized from social contract theories (including also the sophisticated version elaborated by John Rawls).[13] The first group is humans with disabilities. Many, especially those with mental impairments, may not meet the various criteria for being contractors, yet they should have moral standing; and in any event, it is not likely that their interests are comprehended with the contract. Second, the restriction to species membership means that animals cannot be included in the moral contract. They cannot apprehend the meaning of principles or give formal consent, and no basis is provided for their being moral patients. They are placed outside the moral order. Third, the social contract creates a political union or nation state, a polity of contractors to whom the provisions apply; but that leaves unattended the question of how such states are to interact with each other. Rawls's

account of justice, for example, is designed to create a just society, but it requires amendment to address issues of international relations and problems of global justice.[14] Contract theory either places these groups as outside the moral sphere or requires amendments or a different approach to address their interests. Nussbaum advances her capabilities approach (Chapter 4) as one that may address these three issues better than the model of a social contract. She extends justice to the otherwise excluded by honoring basic entitlements, the capabilities required to live "a decent and dignified life."

One might also ask whether future generations of humans are excluded. They cannot consent either, though one might attempt to apply the concept of implicit consent to them as well. This would be odd, though, because we would then have obligations to people who could not have reciprocal obligations to us. Plus, the concept of non-existent (or not-yet-existing) individuals giving implicit consent is a metaphysical tangle. If we were to claim that future individuals are "pre-committed" even before they exist, we would inch closer to Kant's abstract ideal of the Kingdom of Ends. In a Rawlsian approach, however, we might add the stipulation that those behind the Veil of Ignorance do not know what time, what generation, into which they'll be born—and thus extend the range of their consent into the future.

4. There is a larger theoretical point, a paradox, raised by this issue of excluded groups. On the one hand, it is clearly a moral act, a decision with enormous moral implications, to choose what groups or individuals have seats at the contract table, since it is that group that determines those who deserve moral consideration. On the other hand, according to contractualism, morality comes into being (only) by contract. This is the reason most accounts of contractualism imagine a natural need or drive, without a moral sanction, as the motivation for contract. And yet moral sanction is needed even in the first stage, the *pactum unionis* or pact of union—the sitting down to make a contract—and not only in the second stage in which the provisions are determined.

5. A contract is an artifact of reason and will, not of sentiment. There is no regard for emotions as moral phenomena. Yes, emotions (as with Hobbes's fear) may serve as stimulus for agreement and compliance with the contract. And emotions may provide problems to be anticipated in the social contract (Rawls, for example, addresses the civic problems that envy of the more advantaged may generate). But positive moral emotions, such as compassion, love, and hope, cannot be produced by contract; and the theory provides no affirmation of one's emotional life. This omission is a defect: while the contract model may work for the social order and

the wide sphere of moral interactions, it makes awkward the attempt to apply it to our lives with family and friends. (More about this contrast will be taken up in the next chapter.)

6. Two problems arise from cases of non-compliance. Normally, if a contract is violated by others, one is freed from its obligations. If the contracted singer does not show up to perform, the sponsor is released from the obligation to pay her. Of course, the singer may then have new obligations or penalties. But is it the case that we are liberated from our moral obligations if others behave immorally? Are we ever freed from our moral obligations? Do free-riders like Trent absolve the rest of us from our normal duties to the group?

The second issue is that under contractualism it may be difficult to distinguish between outright violations and moral dissent or reform. Are the scoundrel and the moral reformer both simply in breach of contract? How could one ascribe a higher purpose to those who dissent or seek reform if morality is nothing deeper than whatever was originally contracted? Can the social or moral contract be amended? How that might happen is our next topic.

8.7 DISSENT, VIOLATION, AND REFORM

Those social contract theories that allow for civil disobedience have a partial answer to the question of the difference between a simple violation and dissent or attempts at reform. The key is that dissent and reform proceed from a sense of injustice, from a sense that morality requires something different. Moral dissent is described in a series of stages of progressive seriousness and disaffection.

How may one respond to a law or practice perceived to be unjust? The first response is to pursue available legal channels for changing the situation—writing letters, phoning legislators, organizing publicity campaigns, for example. If these steps are earnestly pursued without result, one could move to *civil resistance*, acts of protest that appeal to the public and symbolically address the target of injustice. These acts are nonviolent and normally lawful. They may include vigils, demonstrations, marches, sit-ins and occupations, petitions, boycotts, divestments, and other group actions.

If even these steps fail to correct a serious injustice, one faces the hard choice of whether to disobey the law, for the next step is **civil disobedience**. Under most interpretations, civil disobedience is a deliberate act that: (a) is intended to urge the elimination of an unjust law or practice;

(b) ritually violates the law in question, a symbolically related law, or a relatively minor statute; (c) appeals to the public's sense of justice; (d) rejects the specific law or practice, but not the values or legitimacy of the whole system of laws—and therefore is committed with a willingness to accept appropriate punishment for the illegal action. Philosophers and activists debate whether the act must also (e) be nonviolent—though there is general agreement that violence is not essential, not the inherent purpose of civil disobedience. We can see in this progression the evolution of the Independence Movement in India, led by Gandhi, and the Civil Rights Movement in the United States, led by Martin Luther King and others. There is, of course, a final and more extreme step—but it is undertaken only when one loses confidence in the values and practices of the whole system of laws. That is *civil rebellion*, organized violence that attempts a revolution.

If civil disobedience is to have moral value in contractarianism, it must be provided for in the contract; the conditions under which it is permitted must have careful definition. But all these moral actions, triggered by perceived injustice and of increasing seriousness, apply to the *social* contract and the resulting governance. How could they apply to the *moral* contract? Is it even possible that the moral contract could harbor an injustice—that it could ever be morally right to resist or disobey a moral principle?

Perhaps we do need to "renegotiate the moral contract" periodically, as our collective sense of morality evolves. It took centuries to establish a moral consensus against slavery, though the practice continues despite antislavery laws. In World War II, Dwight Eisenhower commissioned a group known as the Monuments Men (though it included women), who were charged with saving as many of the cultural artifacts of Europe as possible during combat. They were tasked with locating, identifying, preserving, and eventually returning millions of artworks and other artifacts stolen by the Nazis. Their work affirmed a new moral principle: *the spoils of war do not belong to the victor*. Does the moral contract include such specific provisions or does it address only more fundamental moral principles—respect, justification, autonomy, etc.? Contractualism affirms that morality is created by agreement. But perhaps any moral contract is simply an attempt to articulate prior (pre-contract) relations of morality.

QUESTIONS FOR DISCUSSION

1 Trent may be a jerk and an unpleasant neighbor, but is his behavior morally wrong? Is he wrong to claim that we are not obligated to contribute to any group effort that benefits us?

2 Consent is a fraught issue in sexual relations. There has been a recent shift from inferring a partner's consent from an absence of "no," to a requirement for a clear "yes." Below is a typical university policy. Discuss the ways in which such a policy addresses subtle issues of consent. How important is the shift to an "only yes means yes" policy?

    Sexual activity requires consent, which is defined as positive, unambiguous, and voluntary agreement to engage in specific sexual activity throughout a sexual encounter. Only "yes" means "yes"—it cannot be inferred from the lack of a "no." Consent to some sexual acts does not constitute consent to others, nor does past consent to a given act constitute present or future consent. Consent must be ongoing throughout a sexual encounter and can be revoked at any time. Consent cannot be obtained by threat, coercion, or force. Consent cannot be obtained from someone who is asleep or otherwise mentally or physically incapacitated. Sexual relations without consent is sexual assault.

3 Which is the more important goal of governance: peaceful order (Hobbes), protection of rights and property (Locke), or justice (Rawls)? What are the implications of this choice for life under these social contracts.

4 Explain the implications for Rawls's two principles of justice.

5 Rawls is said to work "in the Kantian tradition." Compare Kant's Kingdom of Ends with Rawls's original position, in which individuals choose behind a veil of ignorance.

6 What do we owe to each other—not because of particular relationships or roles, but just as fellow human beings? Do we owe anything? Do those born with advantages have special obligations to those with disadvantages?

7 How can we distinguish a moral dissident engaged in civil disobedience from someone who simply violates the laws?

8 By what means do societies enforce the *moral* contract?

QUESTIONS FOR PERSONAL REFLECTION

1 How do you respond when someone behaves like Trent during a cooperative project you're fully engaged in? How should we deal with a free rider?

2 Post-apocalyptic worlds are popular now in literature and cinema. Many seem like a reversion to a state of nature. Does Hobbes's account apply more frequently than Locke's in these fictions?

3 Have you engaged in conduct that fits the account of civil resistance or civil disobedience? Can you identify those aspects of your experience that match the description?

SUGGESTED SOURCES

The primary sources for this chapter are Hobbes's *Leviathan*; Locke's *Second Treatise of Government*; Rawls's *A Theory of Justice*; and Scanlon's *What We Owe to Each Other*.

Ashford, Elizabeth, and Tim Mulgan, "Contractualism" *Stanford Encyclopedia of Philosophy* 2012, https://plato.stanford.edu/entries/contractualism/.

Gauthier, David. *Morals by Agreement* (Oxford: Clarendon P, 1987).

Lovett, Frank. *Rawls's 'A Theory of Justice': A Reader's Guide* (New York: Bloomsbury, 2011).

Morris, Christopher W., ed. *The Social Contract Theorists: Critical Essays on Hobbes, Locke, and Rousseau* (Lanham, MD: Rowman and Littlefield, 1999).

Nussbaum, Martha C. *Frontiers of Justice: Disability, Nationality, Species Membership* (Cambridge, MA: Belknap Press of Harvard UP, 2006).

Southwood, Nicholas. *Contractualism and the Foundations of Morality*, reprint ed. (Oxford: Oxford UP, 2014).

Springborg, Rebecca. *The Cambridge Companion to Hobbes's Leviathan* (Cambridge: Cambridge UP, 2007).

NOTES

1 The example of dueling is discussed in Kwame Anthony Appiah, *The Honor Code: How Moral Revolutions Happen* (New York: W.W. Norton, 2011).

2 One may, of course, create a contract while having no intention of complying with its terms; but the contract nevertheless makes compliance obligatory.

3 We might take a comparable idea from geometry. Every circle may be regarded as if it had been constructed by moving a point about another point at a fixed distance in a single plane—though it may not have been constructed in that way at all. The deductions one may be led to by this "as if" construal remain valid even if the circle were actually constructed by a different method.

4   He had his follies, however. Overestimating his skill in geometry, he claimed to have discovered how to square the circle. On this matter, he became embroiled in a prolonged controversy with an Oxford professor of geometry, making quite an ass of himself.

5   Thomas Hobbes, *Leviathan*, Part I, Chapter XIII.

6   All quotations are from John Locke, *The Second Treatise of Government*, Chapter 2.

7   It was he who advanced the concept of reflective equilibrium as the goal of philosophical ethics—see Chapter 1. John Rawls, *A Theory of Justice* (Cambridge, MA: Harvard UP, 1971; 2nd revised edition, 1999).

8   Ibid. (1971), 302; rev. ed., 53. For simplicity of exposition, I have omitted the phrase "consistent with the just savings principle." That principle sets forth the main duty we owe to our successors: the saving of sufficient material capital to maintain just institutions over time. This is Rawls's amendment to deal with future generations, an issue taken up later in this chapter.

9   For example, Robert Nozick, *Anarchy, State, and Utopia* (New York: Basic Books, 1974).

10 T.M. Scanlon, *What We Owe to Each Other* (Cambridge, MA: Belknap Press of Harvard UP, 1998), 153.

11 Ibid., 153.

12 Plato, *Crito*, 48c–54e.

13 Martha C. Nussbaum, *Frontiers of Justice: Disability, Nationality, Species Membership* (Cambridge, MA: Belknap Press of Harvard UP, 2006).

14 Rawls recognized this concern and attempted to address it in several later works, including *The Law of Peoples* (Cambridge, MA: Harvard UP, 1999).

CHAPTER NINE
Virtue Ethics

That Charles Van Doren (b. 1926) would become a brilliant intellectual and academic surprised no one. His father was a Pulitzer Prize-winning poet and literary critic; his uncle had also won a Pulitzer for his writing; and his mother was a noted novelist. Charles studied Great Books at St. Johns College, turned to astrophysics for his Master's degree, and then earned a doctorate in English. Both graduate degrees were from Columbia University, where he was soon appointed to the faculty. He had become an articulate, handsome man, who spoke persuasively about the importance of reading and the power of great books. He developed a reputation for high-mindedness and integrity.

In the mid-1950s, a producer of the very popular quiz show, *Twenty-One*, approached Van Doren (who didn't even own a TV set) to be a contestant on the show. The idea of the courtly and telegenic public intellectual testing his knowledge was, no doubt, attractive. On *Twenty-One*, two contestants would enter "isolation booths," unable to see each other or the audience, but only to hear the host when the microphone was opened. The host then put complex questions to the contestants whose answers would add or subtract points depending on correctness, aiming to reach 21. Van Doren agreed to be a contestant in 1957. On the show, he established a winning streak that earned him $129,000 (a boon worth over a million dollars today)—and became enormously popular.

Soon, allegations of cheating in TV quiz shows surfaced. They became the focus of several inquiries, including one by Congress. Van Doren initially dismissed the accusations, yet he went into hiding to avoid testifying. But in 1959, he appeared before a congressional committee and admitted that he was given both questions and answers before each show. He claimed he asked to go on without that help but was coaxed into deception by the producer, who said that this practice was common in the entertainment business, that his success would inspire his huge audience to read and to engage the life of the mind—and that he wasn't likely to defeat the current champion otherwise. Van Doren later said he knew this rationale wasn't true, but he wanted to believe it.

Van Doren opened his testimony with these words: "I would give almost anything I have to reverse the course of my life in the last three years." He explained: "There was one way out which I had, of course, often considered, and that was simply to tell the truth. But, as long as I was trying to protect only myself and my own reputation, and, as I thought, the faith people had in me, I could not believe that was possible. But I was coming closer and closer to a true understanding of my position. I was beginning to realize what I should have known before, that the truth is always the best way, indeed it is the only way, to promote and protect faith." He had become the leading figure in a national scandal that nearly doomed the TV quiz show genre. He resigned his position at Columbia in disgrace.[1]

9.1 MORAL THEORY AND HUMAN RELATIONSHIPS

We commonly describe human relationships in terms of "closeness." It is a spatial term we use metaphorically to refer to degrees of intimacy and affection. We might imagine our relationships ordered along a continuum by degrees of closeness: on one end, typically, would be parents and siblings, children, "close" friends, partners and spouses; somewhere in the middle would likely be teachers and coaches, more distant relatives, neighbors, classmates, and acquaintances; and at the other end would be strangers, citizens—unnamed people at the concert, the family who just passed you in their car, anonymous folk shown in televised images of a distant natural disaster. Call the first end the *personal*; call the second, the *public*. It seems clear that the two major approaches to moral theory we have examined so far, deontology and consequentialism, are oriented toward public or civic relationships. The natural arena for the distinctive concepts and concerns of these theories is the relationship between one moral agent and others—conceived as abstract, fungible (that is, interchangeable) beings.

Think about these concepts: *rights, respect, tolerance, contracts, impartiality*. They are all concepts best applied to civic relationships, to our interactions with fellow citizens, the public, passersby, or strangers. Awkwardness arises when they are imported into contexts of close, personal relationships: we end up with spouses who tolerate each other, pre-nuptial agreements between engaged lovers, family members invoking their rights, and treating one's child with an indifferent equality to others. Something about the quality and value of "closeness" seems to be broken or lost when such things occur. Concepts suited to one context (the public) seem to be misapplied in another context (the personal) with unpleasant results. Yet our close relationships are normally suffused with moral concern and should surely be embraced by our ethical theorizing. What seems to be missing from these theories is attention to those moral concepts and concerns that have their natural home in the intimate end of the continuum, such as *character, commitments, affection*, and *care* for those in close relation. This may be the root of the "moral schizophrenia" that troubled Stocker (see the Interlude)—after all, it was a friend who came to the hospital bedside, not just a generic moral agent. (**Figure 5** presents a summary of this continuum of human relationships with its contrasting ideas.)

Closeness involves intimacy. By intimacy, I mean *a quality of human relationships that results from mutual self-disclosure over time*. This deeper, disclosed understanding of a person is normally accompanied by affection

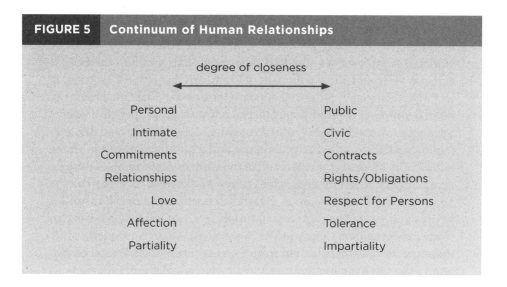

FIGURE 5   Continuum of Human Relationships

degree of closeness

Personal	Public
Intimate	Civic
Commitments	Contracts
Relationships	Rights/Obligations
Love	Respect for Persons
Affection	Tolerance
Partiality	Impartiality

and a desire to nurture and further the well-being of that person. And it also informs our interactions and positions us to know the interests and needs of the person. None of these qualities typically accompany our relationships with strangers. We do not know them, and consequently even well-intentioned kindnesses toward strangers may be misdirected. To avoid ethical mistakes, a good will needs moral understanding—understanding that includes individuality.

In the next four chapters, we will examine moral theories that arise from or give attention to elements of the personal side of the continuum. In this chapter, we will examine an approach that focuses on *character*—a central concern in the infamous Van Doren case.

9.2 CHARACTER: AN ETHIC OF VIRTUES AND VICES

Deontologists are rule-centered and focus on duty (however derived); consequentialists are outcomes-centered and focus on welfare (or other interpretations of the good). But there is also a third major approach to moral theory: **virtue ethics**. Advocates of virtue ethics are agent-centered and focus on the virtues and vices that define character. Deontology and consequentialism take the central question of ethics to be: *What should I do?* That is: *What is the morally right thing to do?* Virtues ethics elevates a different question: *What sort of person should I be?* That is: *What is a morally good person?*

This focus on character is not new—it is ancient. In the West, it emerges in Classical Greece and produces sophisticated theories, of which the works of Aristotle (384–324 BCE) are most influential. In the East, it emerges even earlier in the thought of Confucius (551–479 BCE). It was, in fact, the dominant approach to ethics in Europe until the Enlightenment, when deontology and utilitarianism became ascendant. In 1958, however, Elizabeth Anscombe (1919–2001) wrote an article that signaled dissatisfaction with the state of ethical theory and a budding interest in virtue ethics.[2] The interest truly bloomed in the work of Alasdair MacIntyre (b. 1929), beginning in 1981 with *After Virtue*.[3] All these advocates of virtue ethics analyze moral character in terms of positive and negative traits— virtues and vices. Their interest naturally leads to a strong concern for character formation. Compared to deontologists and consequentialists, therefore, virtue ethicists tend to give greater attention to moral education, to the sort of upbringing that nurtures virtue and prevents or restrains vice; they also tend to give more importance to the emotional dimensions of morality and the ethical dimensions of friendship and other personal relationships; and, speaking broadly, they generally take more interest in the psychology of moral agency.

A **virtue** is a positive, settled trait or disposition of one's character; a **vice** is a negative trait. Honesty, courage, and generosity are examples of commonly recognized moral virtues; dishonesty, cowardice, and stinginess are familiar vices. While they are "settled" or embedded in one's character, many theorists recognize that they are dispositional—they are tendencies or dispositions to act in certain ways. An honest person may have a lapse, but it would then be "uncharacteristic." Some theorists would, however, emphasize that a genuinely honest person would act honestly even under strained circumstances. (When a lapse is "out of character" or uncharacteristic is thus a fine point—witness the Van Doren case.) Moreover, if a person has a particular virtue, say generosity, it means that she acts generously in a natural and unstrained way; her generosity is habitual. Indeed, we might think of virtues and vices as habits of conduct. This has two implications: (1) habits of conduct are learned and ascribed by repetition, not acquired simply by insight, reading, or attending lectures; and (2) habits may be acquired by deliberate practice, but they become unselfconscious; they are repeated without thinking. This suggests a process in which outward form is gradually internalized as "second nature." Though virtues and vices are developed within the personal relationships of one's formative years, they may ultimately have an impact in the public sphere since they are displayed and tested in one's civic relationships.

Virtue ethics points us to role models, exemplars who embody moral virtues and vices. Accounts of real and fictional moral heroes and the injunction to emulate them, and also cautionary tales of those who were undone by vices—these are frequent elements of moral education, sometimes called "character development," in a virtues approach. The stories often focus on a particular virtue or vice: "The Little Dutch Boy," whose steadfastness held back the sea; David's courage in battling Goliath; George Washington's honesty at the fabled cherry tree; the persistence of "The Little Engine That Could," or the deceit of Aesop's "Boy Who Cried Wolf." It is rarer to have an idealization of a person who is fully virtuous, that is, who displays all moral virtues (without vices). Moral theorists need such a paragon, however, and Confucius, Aristotle, and other theorists celebrate such a figure in their writings. The virtuous person is the idealized standard of moral action. For virtue ethics:

"X is right" = "X is what a virtuous person would do."

This approach must therefore identify the virtues and explain their interaction if we are to recognize them or emulate them.

9.3 CONFUCIAN ETHICS

Confucius, known in China as Kongzi ("Master Kong"), taught that the ethical life was a well-ordered life.[4] Ideally, the order to be achieved in one's person was reciprocal with the well-ordered state—and both reflected the natural order of the cosmos. The goal was a kind of balance or harmony that optimized human relationships. Only a virtuous person could embody such moral balance. Moral training—the acquisition of virtue—begins in the nest of the extended family, which Confucius understands as multi-generational. The relations of child to parent, to siblings, to grandparents, to earlier ancestors, to other relatives—and *vice versa*—are the venues for virtue. Unless one acquires such personal virtues, one cannot later be virtuous in public and professional life. For Confucius, the moral life is seamless: there are no tensions between public and private virtues. Morality arises from the personal and is extended into the political relationships and roles.

Confucius identified "Five Constant Virtues" which define the good person. (1) First and most important is *Ren* (or *Jen*), the virtue of compassion, expressed in benevolence and charity. It is the quality that gives us our humanity and is dearer than life itself. In this virtue we take the perspective of the other person and act according to the principle of "What you do not wish for yourself, do not do to anyone else." (2) *Li* is the distinctive Confucian virtue of propriety. It is the quality of conducting oneself with courtesy, with the grace of socially appropriate behavior. For Confucius, the sphere of politeness and good manners lies within the larger sphere of the ethical and mirrors it. (3) *Yi* is the virtue of uprightness, self-control, and righteousness. This virtue concerns oneself, one's deportment and fortitude, one's personal integrity as expressed in rational action and prudent decisions. *Yi* is illustrated in the stories of Bao Zheng, a judge who firmly resisted pressure from corrupt government officials and became a symbol of justice. It is achieved by following *Zhongyong*—the way of the Golden Mean—behaving with neither excess nor deficiency, but with an "unswerving pivot" that assures balance and harmony. (4) *Zhi* is wisdom, a deeply intuitive sense of right and wrong, of justice and injustice. (5) *Xin* is fidelity, the virtue of honest dealings, good faith transactions, in which one's actions match one's words. It implies unison of mind and conduct, forthright speech, and authenticity and integrity of personality.

These virtues blend to make what Confucius calls *Chun-tzu*, literally "the lord's son," but figuratively, the ideal or superior person. Such a person is the ethical paragon. "It is true of the really great man [person] that every move he [or she] makes becomes an example for generations."[5]

9.4 ARISTOTLE AND OUR *SUMMUM BONUM*

Almost two centuries later and half a world away, Aristotle developed and taught an ethical theory that included many elements found in Confucianism: the notion that moral development reflects the natural order; that it is essentially a matter of self-cultivation, of acquiring certain virtues; that these are first learned within the family, practiced and perfected, and ultimately displayed in public life; that morality supports and requires a good community and sound laws; and that virtue requires avoiding excess or deficiency.

Aristotle's view (as we saw in Chapter 4) is that the universe and everything within it has a *telos*—a purpose, goal, or culmination. This means that everything, including human beings, can be fully understood only as *teleological*, as having a natural, normative purpose. Ethics prescribes the requirements for the actualization of the highest and best aspects of our human nature; it is a call to be fully human. This is, you will recall, a form of *moral perfectionism*, in which the good life requires the perfection of certain traits of human nature, the actualization of human potentials.

Moral motivation arises from the idea that there is an unattained but attainable self that one ought to strive to reach.

The tract called *Nicomachean Ethics*[6] is an extended search for the highest human good, the *summum bonum*—the best life open to us and an analysis of that life. You may also recall that Aristotle identifies our highest good as *eudaimonia*, a term usually translated as "happiness"—though I think "flourishing" is a better translation, since Aristotle assures us he does not mean an emotion or a state of mind, but rather an activity that is done "with excellence."

The Greek term for "virtue" or "excellence" is **aretē**. The concept may be applied not only to humans, but even to objects like knives: an excellent knife may have the virtues of a sharp blade, a grip that fits the hand, good balance, a purpose-designed shape, strong construction, and so on. *Aretē* thus refers to a quality or feature of a thing that is conducive to fulfilling that thing's *telos*. Human virtues are those qualities of character that conduce to our *eudaimonia*, our flourishing; our vices are those qualities that thwart or diminish it. When Aristotle describes *eudaimonia* as an activity pursued "with excellence," he means "with virtue," with *aretē*.

It is easier to understand these ideas if we start with an obviously purposeful activity, rather than the whole of human life. Let's take tennis. The game has a purpose or *telos*, which is to win by a higher score against an opponent in a game defined by certain rules. We can, of course, get on the tennis court just to have fun or to get exercise or to show off a new outfit—but such motives do not reflect the distinctive purpose of tennis. Tennis players are better or worse at the game; that is, they have strengths or excellences (such as good eye-hand coordination and a strong backhand) and weaknesses or liabilities (slow reflexes and weak wrists). Those qualities that are conducive to winning might be called the virtues of tennis; those that reduce the chance of winning are its vices. Moreover, the highest good in tennis is not found in the state of being an excellent tennis player; it is in the activity of actually playing tennis and playing with excellence.

Unless we understand the *telos*, we cannot identify the relevant virtues and vices. Aristotle believed that our highest good (our purpose) will be found in our distinctive capacity of rationality. We are capable of being sophisticated reasoners. We may use our reason to determine what we should do and to make other practical judgments. This capacity is called practical reason (*praxis*) and, when we reason with excellence, **practical wisdom** (*phronesis*). In the roles of judge, war commander, or executive, one pursues a life of practical reason; but reasoning about practical matters is of course required of all of us. Also, we may use reason to explain and understand the world, to seek the truth and contemplate meaning. That capacity is called theoretical reason (*theoria*) and, when done with excellence, theoretical wisdom (*sophia*). A life of theoretical wisdom is pursued by philosophers and scientists. Aristotle's teacher, Plato, had imagined a figure who embodied a life of both theoretical and practical wisdom—the Philosopher-King—but Aristotle seems less confident that such "lives" can be fully combined.

After considering both in some detail, Aristotle concludes that the life of theoretical reason is better. He summarizes his reasons in this passage:

> The activity of the intellect, which is contemplative, seems both
> to be superior in worth and to aim at no end beyond itself, and to
> have its pleasure proper to itself ..., and [since] the self-sufficiency,
> leisureliness, unweariedness ..., and all the other attributes ascribed
> to the blessed man are evidently those connected with this activity,
> it follows that this will be the complete happiness of man, if it be
> allowed a complete term of life.[7]

There is a "but" to this judgment, however: "But such a life would be too high for man; for it is not in so far as he is a man that he will live so, but in so far as something divine is present in him." We simply cannot sustain such a life of pure intellectual activity. We are human: we must eat and drink and sleep and move about; we need warmth and companionship; to contemplate, we require peace and security. In other words, we need the outcomes that only practical reason and productive work can bring. Food must be grown, shelter built, and peace kept. But high-energy Aristotle doesn't let us abandon the highest good. *We must keep in mind that the ultimate purpose of the activities of practical reason is to create and sustain the conditions for theoretical reason.* "We must not follow those who advise us, being men, to think of human things, and, being mortal, of mortal things, but must, so far as we can, make ourselves immortal, and strain every nerve to live in accordance with the best thing in us; for even if it be small in bulk, much more does it in power and worth surpass everything."[8] And this is why "happiness" may be a misleading translation of *eudaimonia*: a moral perfectionist need not believe that one can actually attain a perfect life or way of living; rather, one must persist in the active attempt to actualize that life or way of living. This sort of flourishing cannot be judged on the basis of a single act or even a period of years; according to Aristotle, this judgment requires the purview of a whole life.

9.5 ARISTOTELIAN VIRTUES

There are intellectual virtues associated with the life of contemplation, but it is the virtues associated with matters of practical reason—the moral virtues—that concern us here. Though it seems all too easy to acquire vices, virtues must be acquired through practice, and the practice must start when we are young, before our character is fully formed. If we are to acquire courage, for example, we must begin by acting *as though we were* courageous. At first, it is a kind of pretense, but after we have purposefully "pretended to be" courageous in many actions, acting courageously becomes habitual, and we gradually come to own courage as a trait.

Aristotle offers three sorts of help for us in this process in determining what virtue requires. First, Aristotle notes that *a virtue is a mean between an excess and a deficiency.*[9] Courage, for example, is a mean between foolhardiness (an excess) and cowardice (a deficiency). For Aristotle, the "mean" is not a mathematical midpoint, but rather the "just right" amount, an amount that is appropriate to the person and the situation. A virtue is not a knack; it requires insight and moral understanding. Practical reason is required—and also developed—to discern the mean, the virtuous act. Second, we can apply self-knowledge. In the beginning, as we try to match the mean, we are likely to err. If we are alert to our natural tendency to lean toward one vice or its opposite, however, we can self-correct for our bias. So, if I know I tend toward recklessness and bravado or toward fearfulness and timidity, I should try to compensate by adjusting my personal calibration of the appropriate, courageous action. Third, we can emulate persons recognized for their courage: it can inspire and guide us to ask what such a person would do. The role models of literature and history can be powerful in this regard, as can living exemplars of courage.

Aristotle discusses courage, generosity, truthfulness, and even magnificence, among other virtues, but he considers "the crown of the virtues" to be *pride (megalopsychia)*—the justified pride of the magnanimous, or "great-souled," man. This is the virtue that lies between vanity and humility. It is embodied in the person who is worthy of great things, who is high-minded and of noble spirit. But elements of Aristotle's detailed portrait are likely to make us cringe: "He is free of speech because he is contemptuous, and he is given to telling the truth, except when he speaks in irony to the vulgar." "Nor is he given to admiration; for nothing to him is great." And "He is one who will possess beautiful and profitless things rather than profitable and useful ones; for this is more proper to a character that suffices to itself." And some aspects seem irrelevantly trivial:

"A slow step is thought proper to the proud man, a deep voice, and a level utterance."[10]

Our emotions reflect our values. They are functions of our virtues and vices for Aristotle, so our emotional life is an aspect of our ethical life. The principle of seeking the mean, the appropriate, applies to emotions as well. Our emotions are subject to moral evaluation: "Anybody can become angry ... that is easy, but to be angry with the right person and to the right degree and at the right time and for the right purpose, and in the right way—that is not within everybody's power and is not easy."[11] What *is* easy is to get it wrong.

The flourishing life Aristotle envisioned is a life with friends—friends who recognize virtue in each other. Though he celebrated self-sufficiency, he also wrote, "Without friends, no one would want to live, even if he had all other goods."[12] Flourishing is also a life of leisure—by which he means that quality of time in which we can do things for their own sake, not because we are paid to do them. Yet Aristotle is also a realist: he knows that having a flourishing life, actualizing our best selves, can be helped or hindered by external factors. It is easier to be good, he thought, if we came from good stock, had a family and friends, enjoyed good health, possessed a reasonable amount of wealth, were good-looking, and had good luck. These things do not by themselves give us a virtuous soul, but they can support it; and their lack can be an obstacle. We cannot achieve *eudaimonia*, however virtuous we may be, if we have a debilitating illness, live in dire poverty, are rejected as unattractive, or die young from an accident. Human good is not a matter of the inner purity of soul or a good will; it is an outward matter of how we live. Aristotle reminds us that we are rational beings who pursue happiness, wisdom, and self-sufficiency—but who are ultimately at the mercy of chance and luck.

9.6 MACINTYRE AND THE REVIVAL OF VIRTUE ETHICS

In *After Virtue*, Alasdair MacIntyre claims that the ethical theories that emerged from the Enlightenment—including utilitarianism and Kantianism—were doomed to fail. When Enlightenment thinkers rejected Aristotle's teleological approach in science in favor of mechanism, they rejected it in ethics as well. Regrettably, this left ethical theory cut off from its essential content: the shared common purpose or end to which ethics directs us. Moreover, he claims, the emphasis on individualism belies the communal nature of morality, and it tends to degenerate into subjectivism. Moral judgments end up being no more than the venting of emotions, which is a morally bankrupt result. MacIntyre therefore advocates the revival of an Aristotelian ethical framework and a refocusing on the importance of virtues.

MacIntyre frames his theory in terms of *practices*. His rather complex definition follows and should be read carefully:

> By a practice I ... mean any coherent and complex form of socially established cooperative human activity through which goods internal to that form of activity are realized in the course of trying to achieve those standards of excellence which are appropriate to, and partially definitive of, that form of activity, with the result that human powers to achieve excellence, and human conceptions of the ends and goods involved, are systematically extended.[13]

So, chess and basketball, farming and sculpting, scientific experimentation and dentistry—all are examples of practices. Each practice has a distinct good that cannot be experienced except by actual engagement in the practice over time. The only way to comprehend and experience the good that is intrinsic to chess is to become a player. A virtue is a property or ability that is conducive to realizing the ends of the practice; a vice debilitates the achievement of the good. What is a virtue in one practice may be irrelevant or even a vice in another: for example, being fleet of foot is a virtue in basketball, but it is irrelevant to dentistry; and the careful deliberateness of a good chess player may be a liability in basketball. Practices normally have rules or principles or traditions that establish the ways one may pursue the goal (*telos*), and that also distinguish various roles, such as the coach and various playing positions in basketball, or the dentist, oral surgeon, orthodontist, dental hygienist, and patient, in dentistry.

To reach the level of *moral* virtues, however, one has to imagine an overarching practice of practices, a practice of citizenry, of being human. For all people—or at least all people in a society or culture—to have a shared *telos*, there needs to be a common practice they share, one which defines the traits conducive to its intrinsic good. It is as though the individuals with their utilitarian preferences, the autonomous agents in Kant's Kingdom of Ends, or the consenting parties of contractualism, were instead to become teammates, pursuing a shared goal and coordinating their activities under a set of common values.

The renewed emphasis on the communal context of ethics, the focus on virtues and vices, and the revival of teleological conceptions has shaped a huge literature since the 1980s. These works include comprehensive accounts, critiques, and analyses of specific virtues and vices. Even *epistemology* (the theory of knowledge) has seen the development of a virtues approach, in which knowledge and understanding are the aims; attention is turned toward the capacities and qualities that aid in the achievement of knowledge, including virtues such as curiosity and intellectual humility, and epistemic vices like gullibility and willful ignorance.

9.7 A COMMENTARY ON VIRTUE ETHICS

Any fully elaborated theory of virtues ethics has three basic tasks: it must (1) articulate a shared human *telos* sufficiently compelling to provide moral motivation; (2) identify the virtues and describe their dynamics; and (3) present an account of moral education, of how virtues are acquired and vices suppressed. These basic requirements harbor complications, and the questions they raise straddle the boundary between the conceptual (philosophical) and the empirical (psychological). Let's briefly examine each.

1. **The *Telos*.** What is the *telos* or aim that is the purpose of human life, that defines shared values and virtues, and that supplies moral motivation? For Confucius, it is a harmonious life; for Aristotle, it is *eudaimonia*, a self-actualizing form of happiness. For MacIntyre, it may be a flourishing communal practice. Do we share values or a common purpose today? The individualism of Enlightenment theories presumes only that we have our own interests and purposes; what we share is reason, a thinly-defined human nature, and principles of transactions. Interestingly, both Confucius and Aristotle required a unifying force beyond nature: Confucius believed human morality was tied to the divine order of *dao*; in Aristotle's thought, everything in the cosmos is sustained and drawn toward actualization by the Unmoved Mover. These concepts are not providential or personal gods, but they are transcendent and unifying conceptions. What conception of a unifying *telos* is plausible for our secular, pluralistic world?

2. **The Economy of Virtues.** *How many moral virtues (and vices) are there and what are they?* Confucius identified the five I named, though each one seems to be a cluster of traits. Aristotle selects important virtues for discussion, but does not number them or provide a full roster. Today's Boy Scouts repeat a list of twelve: "A Scout is trustworthy, loyal, helpful, friendly, courteous, kind, obedient, cheerful, thrifty, brave, clean, and reverent."[14] Today's Girl Scouts seek to be "a go-getter, innovator, risk-taker, and leader" (G.I.R.L.).[15]

How do the various virtues (and vices) relate to each other conceptually and developmentally? This leads us to a plethora of questions about the dynamics of being virtuous. Are moral virtues individuated in a tidy way? Do they stand alone: that is, can I be fully honest without being courageous, for example? Or do they form an economy or ecology of virtues in which they interact or depend upon each other? Are some more logically or psychologically basic than others or more important morally? Are some virtues a subset or component of others? Must the virtues be acquired in a particular order? (And nearly all these questions can also be asked of the vices.) We might use a simple image: are virtues like crayons in a box, usable independently? If so, how many crayons are there and which ones make a full set? And are some basic, like red, yellow, and blue, while others are derivative, like orange and periwinkle? Or are they like threads that form a pattern that is one's character?

What blend transforms us from having distinct virtues to a unified virtue? What or who is the idealized person of virtue—the inspirational paragon to be emulated? Confucius speaks of the Sage who combines all the Constant Virtues in harmonious relations; Aristotle celebrates the *phronimos*, the person of practical wisdom, and it is practical reason that blends the traits. These figures embody the roster of virtues, yet their personality is unified and wholehearted. They have a kind of authenticity or integrity that reflects the singularity of virtue, not a collection of separate virtues.

3. **Moral Education.** *What is the process by which virtues are acquired and vices suppressed or eliminated?* This is ultimately a question of the psychology of moral development and the pedagogy of moral education. Both Confucius and Aristotle suggest that starting young within the context of family life is important if not essential. Some rules may guide us (such as the Principle of the Mean), and we may strive to be like the strikingly virtuous paragons. But, for Aristotle, long practice is required for internalization. "We become just by performing just action, temperate by performing temperate actions, courageous by performing courageous action."[16] This process involves emotional development as well; it is not simply a matter of developing theoretical or calculative reasoning skills. Although virtues theorists focus on the character of individuals, they usually stress the role of the community both in nurturing the development of virtues and in serving as the arena in which virtues and vices are tested and displayed. Both Confucius and Aristotle doubted that good character could be developed without a good community.

As Rosalind Hursthouse (b. 1943) has observed, Aristotle's thought has an aspect that is especially realistic: "he never forgets the fact that we were all once children." She rightly takes this to be an attractive and advantageous facet of virtue ethics. When we read other theories, we get "the impression that we, the intelligent adult readers addressed, sprang fully formed from our father's brow. That children form part of the furniture of the world occasionally comes up in passing ... but the utterly basic fact that we were once as they are, and that whatever we are now is continuous with how we were then, is completely ignored."[17]

These three components are required for theoretical completeness. This point is not meant as criticism, though specific responses or proposals for each of the three may generate a critique. There are, however, critical points that represent direct challenges to the approach of virtue ethics, and it is to them that we now turn.

9.8 CHALLENGES TO VIRTUE ETHICS

Five challenges will be presented here. With each one, the stakes for a successful virtue ethics rise as the implications deepen. We begin with a challenge to its adequacy.

1. *Can virtue ethics account for moral reform?* If the human *telos* remains constant, and if morality is a practice governed by traditions, what sort of change could be sanctioned? MacIntyre would reply that the traditions that shape practices are open, evolving traditions, always in dialogue about the intrinsic goods and methods of the practice. But if goods are intrinsic to practices, and if moral reform involves changing practices, what is the source of its goodness? Is it actually overturning one practice for another? Are there wholly new moral virtues to be introduced? Of our list of virtues and vices changes, are we to interpret that as a deepened understanding of a permanent list, or as a response to new conditions of human flourishing? At best, it seems that the role for moral reform is limited or problematic. To use a simple analogy: baseball, for example, can introduce a new rule or two, innovative equipment and uniforms, advanced technology for replays, but it cannot embrace becoming football or some other sport that is not within the tradition, the practice, of baseball.

2. *Is virtue ethics a throwback or can it be made contemporary?* The virtues approach to morality is historically found in close-knit societies that have largely been sexist, racist, xenophobic, and focused on honor. It reflects aspects of tribalism. Both Confucius and Aristotle assumed that talk of virtue was directed to men, not to women or all human beings. (For Aristotle, a woman's *telos* was determined by her anatomy: the gestation and nurturance of children.) Even the English word *virtue* is related to virile, meaning "manly," and both are ultimately derived from the Latin

word, *vir*, meaning "man." The heroic warrior is an early influential ideal, though the statesman, the sage, and the gentleman became competing models as civilization became more urbanized. But all are male in origin and stereotypically masculine. Moreover, both ancient China and Classical Greece were cultures built on slavery. Aristotle defended slavery, indeed he gave us the argument that slavery is in the interest of the slave—although he was minimally reformist in urging that not everyone captured in war should be enslaved, but only those who were "slaves by nature." MacIntyre has argued against individualism and the idea of an autonomous self, placing all in subservience to the goals of society. His moral vision often seems reactionary, more suitable for a theocracy than for a liberal democracy.

At its best, the world of Classical Athens elevated four traits known now as "the pagan virtues": temperance, courage, wisdom, and justice. Medieval Christianity added and enshrined the three "Christian virtues" of faith, hope, and charity. The challenge this historical context raises is to find a contemporary expression of virtues ethics that fits the world we live in. What virtues are called forth in the context of an open, egalitarian, globalized society? Are not racism, sexism, and xenophobia among our list of vices?

This challenge is being taken up by contemporary virtues theorists. Hursthouse, for example, would keep some virtues identified by Aristotle, such as courage—though with a different characterization—but would add others, such as compassion. Judith Shklar (1928–92) waded into this issue by exploring a list of five "ordinary vices": cruelty, hypocrisy, snobbery, betrayal, and misanthropy. In *Technology and the Virtues*, Shannon Vallor (b. 1971) attempts to discern the virtues needed to flourish in the future.[18] No effective answer to this challenge is possible, of course, unless we share a common purpose, our *telos*, as human beings. Articulating that shared purpose for a pluralistic and inclusive world remains the first and fundamental task of virtues ethics.

3. *Does virtue ethics offer adequate moral guidance?* When reading the literature of deontological and utilitarian ethics, one can get the impression that our lives are just one moral dilemma after another, and that moral theory is about resolving such dilemmas. Virtue ethics reminds us that morality is connected to character, a personal way of being in the world; virtue gives texture to daily life and is manifested in conduct. Of course, we do face moral decisions, perhaps some of enormous importance. Does an ethic of virtue provide sufficient guidance for determining what we should do in such situations? Maybe it would guide us if the question were, "Should I cheat on a quiz show?" But for someone facing a complex

moral choice—abortion, euthanasia, a response to blackmail—it is hardly helpful to say, "Do what a virtuous person would do." It is perhaps slightly more informative to cite a specific role model: Christians advocate asking "What would Jesus do?"—but an answer is not obvious when facing moral questions that didn't arise in Jesus' world, questions such as "Should screening of human embryos be used to eliminate genetic diseases?" What virtue is useful for that choice? And which virtue is called for in a situation in which values collide? Should the person secretly hiding a Jewish neighbor be honest or compassionate in responding to the Nazi soldier's question: "Is there a Jew in this house?" Hursthouse argues that trying to do what a virtuous person would do does give substantial direction in many decision-making situations; that its ambiguity is no worse than is found in applying utilitarianism or Kantianism; and that some tragic moral dilemmas have no "correct" or "right" outcome.[19] Nevertheless, this concern does pose a challenge to the adequacy of virtue ethics as a normative moral theory.

4. *Are virtues and vices always context-dependent?* A third challenge concerns the identification of virtues and vices. Take the virtue of loyalty: the trait of unwavering support for or allegiance to a person, a group, an institution, a cause, or an ideal. It is opposed to fickleness and betrayal. But one can be loyal to a virtuous friend or to a villainous criminal, to a noble or a hateful organization. Is being loyal a virtue regardless of its object? Or does its moral value depend upon the worthiness of the object of one's loyalty? Can loyalty be a bad thing, a vice, if it is "misplaced" loyalty? The same might be asked about courage. Does the daring terrorist at least possess the virtue of courage—or is it not a virtue when displayed in such an act, for such a cause? Might there be moral vices that become virtuous in certain situations? Lisa Tessman (b. 1966) has identified "burdened virtues"—virtues that are required to survive under conditions of oppression, but which do long-term moral damage to their bearer's well-being.[20] Can we, in short, identify traits as moral virtues independent of their objects and the contexts in which they are exercised? If not, we must be using a criterion of moral goodness that is independent of the traits; it is something else that makes loyalty a virtue when it is toward a good friend, not the loyalty itself. Of course, one could claim that it isn't loyalty at all when the object is bad, or that no terrorist could be courageous, or that no true virtue could damage one's well-being—but that also builds moral worth from some other source than the trait. This point is rather like raising Kant's question about whether something is good without qualification: are loyalty, courage, honesty, perseverance, and so on good *without qualification?*

There are, I think, two directions for a reply that would not abandon the virtue-vice distinction. (A) The virtues theorist might claim the moral goodness of these traits is, in part, a function of their interaction: moral traits form an ecology, and they become distorted when taken in isolation. The misguided loyalist and the courageous terrorist simply lack other key virtues. (B) There is a supreme, governing quality that integrates the moral virtues—something like the role Aristotle gave to practical wisdom (*phronesis*). Like the conductor of an orchestra of traits, practical wisdom (or something similar) brings forth the goodness of each virtue and integrates them in a deft and artful way. In sum, this challenge puts a burden on the second task: the need to explicate the dynamics of virtue-vice interaction.

5. *Does character exist?* An objection that, if true, would be fatal to virtues ethics is the claim that *character* and *virtues* and *vices* simply do not exist, at least not in the way virtues ethics requires. Virtues ethics assumes that character and its traits are relatively stable qualities, established early, either from genetics or early inculcation. The objectors, however, say that individuals behave in different ways depending upon context: there are no settled traits. They cite empirical evidence from psychological studies and experimental philosophy (the latter is a new method in which philosophical intuitions about human nature are tested in surveys and experimental situations). Take honesty, for instance: a variety of experiments suggest that nearly everyone (90 per cent in frequently cited studies) will cheat on a task if the circumstances are right—and then a high percentage will lie about it. As the playwright Terence said, "I am human, and nothing human is alien to me."[21] How we act, what we do, who we are morally depends on moral luck, the vicissitudes of our experience. Perhaps Charles Van Doren is Everyman who, unfortunately, had bad moral luck. Or take compassion: Experimenters have claimed that the likelihood that someone will engage in a modestly altruistic act (like alerting a stranger they had dropped something or giving change to a street person) is increased if the smell of baking bread is in the air.[22] A morally irrelevant, chance factor seems to influence moral behavior. The upshot of this research is that our conduct is not defined by fixed traits, and also that our disposition to moral behavior is affected by irrelevant factors and moral luck. No one has a fixed character, the researchers claim, and we are capable of acting in more ways than we would like to believe.[23]

These conclusions are challenging, but they claim great significance from meager results. Some philosophers are impressed; others do not find them convincing and question the validity of the experiments or claims that are drawn from the results. (For example, a concern might be that experimenters cannot test the same situation with the same person for behavioral comparison, so we don't know whether the smell of a bakery *changed* the behavior of each person; we know only that the percentage of altruistic acts is higher with the ambient aroma.) Still other philosophers are developing context-sensitive accounts of traits, arguing that one can still meaningfully refer to a person's character without implying that it will be manifested under any condition or circumstance.[24] This does seem to square with common sense: we commonly may say that a friend is talkative, even though he says little when he is ill; another friend is quiet and reserved, though too much to drink one night made her loudly talkative. Though one wonders what conditions or how many "uncharacteristic" actions it takes in order to determine that an ascribed virtue is just not present? How should one decide whether Charles Van Doren is an honest man whose cheating and lying were exceptional, or whether instead he is a dishonest man with the vices of cheating and lying, and a thin veneer of honesty?

9.9 THE VIRTUES OF VIRTUE ETHICS

Virtue ethics is a communitarian theory, rooted in history, psychology, sociology, and perhaps anthropology. The contemporary versions can appear nostalgic for ancient or even tribal societies in which individual guidance and character derived from a shared sense of cosmic and moral order. They decry the loss of a shared purpose, and they reject the cacophony of modern moral concepts that have accrued from various eras and circumstances—ideas that are incoherent in combination today. They offer a deconstruction of contemporary morality—some critics have opined that virtue ethics is better at diagnosis and critique than it is at cure. But this approach has numerous attractions:

1. Virtue ethics incorporates deserved attention to personal relationships and the emotional dimension of life. Our emotions reveal our values, which are key elements of our character. In this line of thought, morality is neither a bounded compartment of certain decisions and actions, nor is it a set of imperatives and rules that moral agents must accept. It is the pervasive call and guide to our best selves, to a flourishing life together.

2. A special place is also given to saints and heroes—and villains. A coherent account of supererogatory acts is possible: they are virtuous acts, excellent in their desires and reasoning, extraordinary in their goodness or in the conditions under which they were performed. My earlier case of the men who tried to save a child in a burning car is about virtuous men; both the one who succeeded and the one who failed displayed

courage and compassion in a quick response under life-threatening conditions. Both were virtuous and heroic. But depravity and villainy can also be accounted for in terms of traits. The attention to vices directs philosophical consideration to such traits as cruelty and weakness of will, faults that bedevil an ethic that focuses only on principles.

3. In addition, a virtues approach promises to heal the alleged "schizophrenia" of ethical theories. Remember again the friend visiting you in the hospital? When the guest comes to see you, under this theory, he may not be simply following an adopted principle of conduct; he may well be acting out of something deeper in his character: care, friendship, kindness, or compassion. Our acts are, in a literal sense, *characterized* morally.

4. The focus on virtue offers an integration of the various spheres of our lives—personal, professional, and public. Moral integrity is both a composite of the virtues and a virtue itself. But this advantage requires a principle or capacity for the ultimate blending of individual virtues. And virtue theorists disagree about whether private and public virtues are the same or require each other. Can one be a virtuous public servant but have a scandalous private life? Or can one be a morally admirable parent, but also a ruthless and corrupt executive?[25] Confucius and Aristotle, like most virtue theorists, deny this bifurcation and aspire to link the personal and the political spheres.

5. Finally, in virtue ethics, the moral agent is situated and individual, not abstract nor generalized. In contrast to Kant's view, our individuality, our personalities, are morally relevant—as are our community and the particular relationships we have within it. It places enormous weight on the process of moral education. Character education involves the acceptance of moral practice and its traditions, the emulation of paragons, the trials and errors of long practice to act *as if* we possessed the virtues, the gradual internalization of community standards, and the development of skills of practical reason. Though she is always aided by reason, the virtuous person's virtue is habitual or natural—and her acts are not self-consciously calculated to protect her virtues. Virtues theory interprets free-will or voluntary action as action that flows from character, not action that follows a freely adopted principle or rule.

QUESTIONS FOR DISCUSSION

1 Given the brief account of the quiz show scandal, how would you assess the moral character of Charles Van Doren? You may wish to supplement this account with some of the historical materials listed in endnote 1.

2 Your author claims that whenever, in our personal relationships, we reach for concepts like contracts or rights or tolerance, it means that the quality of that relationship is "broken." Do you agree—or are there times when the moral concepts from the political or public sphere are appropriately applied in healthy personal relationships?

3 What similarities or commonalities can you cite in the moral visions of Confucius and Aristotle?

4 What are the most important virtues for contemporary society? What are the most damaging vices in our society? (Remember to keep the list to traits of character.)

5 How does living in poverty, having a debilitating illness, or feeling unattractive by cultural standards make it more difficult to be a good person?

6 Is a suicide bomber who genuinely believes in the cause a courageous person?

7 Can one have honesty without courage, or compassion without generosity?

8 Other moral theories speak of virtues: Divine Command Theory has its piety and faith; utilitarianism, its marketplace virtues; Kant, his good will; etc. How is their treatment of virtues different from that given in virtue ethics?

QUESTIONS FOR PERSONAL REFLECTION

1 How would you describe your own character in terms of virtues and vices?

2 Is there an individual you try to emulate because that person seems to have "practical wisdom"? Has our current preoccupation with celebrities undercut the admiration for moral heroes?

3 Under what circumstances should (and would) you break your loyalty to your family members or close friends?

SUGGESTED SOURCES

The primary sources for this chapter are the Confucian *Analects* and *Liki* (also known in English as *The Record of Rites*) and Aristotle's *Nicomachean Ethics*.

Casey, John. *Pagan Virtue: An Essay in Ethics* (Oxford: Clarendon Press of Oxford UP, 1991).

Crisp, Roger, and Michael Slote, eds. *Virtue Ethics* (Oxford: Oxford UP, 1997).

Hursthouse, Rosalind. *On Virtue Ethics* (Oxford: Oxford UP, 1999).

MacIntyre, Alasdair. *After Virtue*, 3rd ed. (1981; Notre Dame, IN: U of Notre Dame P, 2007).

Russell, Daniel C. *Cambridge Companion to Virtue Ethics* (Cambridge: Cambridge UP, 2013).

Sanford, Jonathan J. *Before Virtue: Assessing Contemporary Virtue Ethics* (Washington, DC: Catholic U of America P, 2015).

Shklar, Judith N. *Ordinary Vices* (Cambridge, MA: Belknap Press of Harvard UP, 1985).

NOTES

1 Charles Van Doren's testimony may be found online at the History Matters website: http://historymatters.gmu.edu/d/6566/. Numerous books and a movie, *Quiz Show*, have recounted the scandal.

2 G.E.M. Anscombe, "Modern Moral Philosophy," *Philosophy* 33 (1958), 1–19.

3 Alasdair MacIntyre, *After Virtue: A Study in Moral Theory*, 1st ed. (1981); (3rd ed., Notre Dame, IN: Notre Dame UP, 2007).

4 Confucius has a role in Chinese culture that is often compared to that of Socrates in Western culture. The major works of Confucian thought have contested authorship. In much the same way that scholars search for the "historical Socrates" in the writings of Plato and others, other scholars seek the "real Confucius" in the works that are elaborated or paraphrased by others. The works of special concern here include the *Analects* and *Liki*.

5 Originally from *Liki*, Chapter 31; reprinted in *The Wisdom of Confucius*, ed. Lin Yutang (New York: Modern Library, 1938), 129–30.

6 It is probably dedicated to Aristotle's only son, Nicomachus, or perhaps to his father, who had the same name.

7 *Nicomachean Ethics*, 1177b18–25.

8 Ibid., 1777b31–35.

9 Note that this implies there are twice as many vices as there are virtues.

10 Ibid., 1123a35–1125a17 provides the full description.

11 Ibid., 1109a26–28. This passage in this, its widely quoted form, is slightly paraphrased and omits Aristotle's mention of the trait of generosity and wise spending.

12 Ibid., 1155a5.

13 Alasdair MacIntyre, *After Virtue*, 175.

14 The Scout Law, Boy Scouts of America, https://www.scouting.org/discover/faq/question10/ (accessed July 2018).

15 Girl Scouts, G.I.R.L. program, http://blog.girlscouts.org/2018/03/girl-scout-week-how-to-be-girl-every-day.html (accessed July 2018).

16 Aristotle, *Nicomachean Ethics*, 1103b1–3.

17 Rosalind Hursthouse, *On Virtue Ethics* (Oxford: Oxford UP, 1999), 14.

18 See: Hursthouse, ibid.; Judith N. Shklar, *Ordinary Vices* (Cambridge, MA: Belknap Press of Harvard UP, 1984); and Shannon Vallor, *Technology and the Virtues* (Oxford: Oxford UP, 2016).

19 Hursthouse, ibid.

20 Lisa Tessman, *Burdened Virtues: Virtue Ethics for Liberatory Struggles* (Oxford: Oxford UP, 2005).

21 Terence, *Heauton Timorumenos* (*The Self-Tormentor*).

22 For a supportive discussion of these sorts of experiments, see: Kwame Anthony Appiah, *Experiments in Ethics* (Cambridge, MA: Harvard UP, 2008).

23 For a challenge to the role of character in moral behavior see: John Doris, *Lack of Character: Personality and Moral Behavior* (Cambridge: Cambridge UP, 2005).

24 An example is Candace L. Upton, *Situational Traits of Character: Dispositional Foundations and Implications for Moral Psychology and Friendship* (Lanham, MD: Roman & Littlefield, 2009).

25 For a rich, sociological, and historical treatment of these questions see: Richard Sennett, *The Fall of Public Man*, 40th anniversary ed. (1977; New York: Norton, 2017).

CHAPTER TEN
Emotions and Moral Sentiment Theory

Marie had always been a "tomboy," a girl who loved the outdoors and sports. Her mother was always urging her to "dress up" a little and to "use some makeup." In high school, she went out with boys, but was usually bored. It was in college, where she realized, with reluctance, that she was actually attracted to women. She rejected and hid those feelings for a while, but she couldn't deny she was growing close to her friend, Yuki. One evening, in a spirit of exploration, their relationship became sexual. They became a couple.

Marie knew she loved Yuki, and after two affectionate months together, she decided she must come out to her family. It wasn't about a lifestyle; it was about a special relationship. She thought about bringing Yuki home for Thanksgiving holiday, but decided that would only make things more difficult. She had to do this alone.

Thanksgiving in Marie's family involved her brother, and her grandmother, as well as her parents. As they took turns saying what they were thankful for, Marie said she was thankful for her friend, Yuki. When her mother asked who Yuki was, Marie said "she's my special friend, my serious girlfriend." Her mother said, "What do you mean, Marie? Are you a ... lesbian?" And she began to cry. Marie was silent.

Her father was angry and couldn't even look at her. Her grandmother muttered, "That's disgusting." Her brother quietly said he known it all along and felt relieved. Marie couldn't say more. She realized she had twinges of guilt and shame, but she simply could not deny her love for Yuki. When her father finally spoke, he said he didn't feel thankful for his daughter, and she would not be welcomed home at Christmas.

10.1 THE NATURE OF EMOTION

Emotionality is part of our humanity. No one doubts the potential power of emotions like joy and love, jealousy and grief. Whether this power is a good thing, however, is a question of historic resonance. One view, epitomized in the writings of the ancient Stoics, is that our emotions are passionate states, "storms in the soul," that come over us and cause us to lose control. Our passions are the natural enemy of our reason, and we need self-control to banish them or keep them chained in our psychic cellar. Echoes of this view are heard in Kant's grouping the emotions with our desires as "inclinations" that must be governed by reason. (Ironically, this oppositional interpretation is shared by some who celebrate passion.

For many Romantics, reason is cold, calculating, and deadly; passion is warm, spontaneous, and alive.) The contrasting view is that emotions are not experiences that "overcome" us from the outside as though we were mugged; rather, they are affects that reflect and shape our values and our personal "take" on our situation. Emotions are complex experiences with both physical and mental dimensions; they have an evaluative or judgmental aspect. Our emotionality is actually allied with our rationality, and life without emotion would not be a good life or even a human life.

The two views are encapsulated in two well-known characters from different incarnations of the *Star Trek* series: Spock and Data. Spock embodies the Vulcan philosophy that a devotion to logic is the only way to prevail against the debilitating sickness that is emotion. Data, on the other hand, is an android whose computational intellect is startling, but who believes he lacks something of immense value, something that humans possess: emotion. One can easily cite cases to support either view: Shakespeare's Othello is a man undone, driven to murder, by irrational jealousy; but righteous indignation—an emotional response to injustice—has energized many heroes of reform movements for the rights of oppressed groups.

Contemporary research (in philosophy, psychology, and the social sciences) supports the second view: emotions are complex, cognitive phenomena related to perception, memory, imagination, judgment, and reasoning, and having both mental and physiological aspects that display a subjective evaluation of their objects. What is the evidence that emotions are cognitive? (1) They have an evaluative aspect, and evaluations or judgments are cognitive activities. Thus, anger—which may flush the face, raise the voice and blood pressure, and alter one's posture—also displays the subjective judgment that someone has committed an affront, a reprehensible act, and should be held to account.[1] (2) Our emotions are sometimes justified or unjustified. Mary says, defensively, "You have no reason to feel jealous." Tyrone says, "My worry about where you were was justified." A mother says, "You should feel grateful for what you have." (3) Facts alter our emotions. Sara's fear of a spider dissipates when she discovers that it's plastic. (4) We make reasonable inferences from someone's emotions to their beliefs or values. From the obvious grief that Lee is feeling over his grandmother's death, I reasonably infer that he loved or admired her, that he valued her life. (5) We often judge someone's rationality, even their sanity, by the appropriateness of their emotions. Indeed, the complete lack of emotion may indicate mental pathology.

There is a normativity implied in this cognitive view; that is, some instances of emotion are better than others: Othello's emotions went awry; the civil rights heroes' indignation was good. I believe there are three distinguishable modes of emotive normativity. (1) We might aim at what popular psychologists call *emotional intelligence*—having a high "EQ." This involves understanding one's own emotions and the emotions of others, behaving with sensitivity to others, and displaying emotions in ways that are appropriate for the social context. We would avoid obtuseness, insensitivity, brutishness, or naïveté. (2) Our aim might be therapeutic: that is, we might seek *emotional health*. The focus would then be on mental stability, emotional balance and resiliency, satisfaction or joy in living, along with the release from disturbing and dysfunctional emotions and pathologies. (3) Or, we might aim at *moral emotionality*. We would view emotions, not in terms of personal effectiveness or mental health, but in ethical or moral terms. "Good" emotions would somehow be connected to being a good person, doing what is right, or living a morally good life.

Aristotle captured the normativity of emotion in the passage cited in the last chapter, in which he speaks of virtue as including being "angry with the right person and to the right degree and at the right time and for the right purpose, and in the right way." Aristotle may be combining all three normative aims, but the intriguing question of whether these three aims ultimately converge—so that emotional intelligence is both morally sound and mentally good—is beyond our scope. In this chapter, we will focus on the ways in which our emotions bear on morality, and also ways in which morality evaluates or shapes our emotions.

10.2 EMOTIONALITY AND MORALITY

There is a set of emotion-types that are intrinsically moral; they embody moral judgments. Some of these moral emotions are directed inward toward oneself: among these are negative emotions such as *guilt, shame*, and *remorse*; and positive emotions, such as *pride*. Others are moral emotions directed outward, toward others: among these are negative emotions such as *indignation* and *contempt*; and positive emotions such as *compassion* or *admiration*. Not all emotion-types fit this category: *embarrassment* and *annoyance*, for example, seem to be focused on matters that do not rise to the level of the moral. But many other emotion-types, such as *anger, jealousy, hope*, and *joy*, may acquire a moral tinge depending upon their objects, the context, and the actions they motivate. Nearly all emotion-types may themselves become the objects of moral judgments: "Her hatred is wrong," "His jealousy is reprehensible," or "They were disrespected and are right to be angry." But the following is not a moral judgment: "She is wrong to be embarrassed about that; it wasn't her fault." It expresses a different sense of "wrong"—a kind of mistake. There are a few negative emotion-types that seem to be inherently morally wrong, or at least to require a special effort of moral justification: for example, *envy*, *spite*, and what the Germans call *Schadenfreude*—feeling pleasure at another's pain, joy at the misfortune of others.

Emotions may motivate us; they are a crucial link between our moral understanding and moral action. Compassion may motivate kindness or charity—or even supererogatory acts, as in the tale of the Good Samaritan. Indignation may spur us to right an injustice. In Stocker's case of the principled hospital visitor, the schizophrenic disconnect he describes occurs in part because it seems that the visitor's emotions are not engaged. The visit is motivated by duty or by cold calculation, not by affection, or even compassion. This observation suggests that the moral worth of some actions derives not from acting from duty, but from acting from certain emotions or sentiments. Emotions are the natural human products of valuing or caring: our emotions reveal what we care about, what matters to us; and what matters, in turn, generates our emotions. Some would say that emotions are not only natural, they are essential, even fundamental, to morality. Consider all the emotions in our introductory case: Marie's mixed feelings of love, guilt, and shame; her mother's surprise and sadness; her father's anger; her grandmother's disgust and contempt; her brother's relief—all embody judgments that reveal values.

10.3 MORAL SENTIMENT THEORY

Our moral judgments are rooted in our emotions, not in reason; reason only serves as a lens through which we view and reflect on our emotions—this is the central claim of **moral sentiment theory**. It evolved in the writings of three eighteenth-century leaders of the Scottish Enlightenment:[2] Francis Hutcheson (1694–1746), David Hume (1711–76), and Adam Smith (1723–90), whom we met in Chapter 5, each developed a version of the theory.

Hutcheson, influenced by the thought of Anthony Ashley-Cooper, known as Lord Shaftesbury (1671–1713), held that human beings make ethical judgments using an innate, God-given capacity he called *moral sense*. It functions in tandem with our innate self-love and concern for the welfare of others, and gives us pleasure at whatever affirms and promotes them. This is not sensuous pleasure, but a morally-tinged pleasure, a feeling of approval. And, conversely, we experience a negative feeling, a disapproval, at whatever denies or acts against those concerns. All our moral evaluations are made through this moral sense. The emotions of disapproval or approval do not by themselves justify our judgments; rather, they represent our moral valuing.

Though Hutcheson's is an early form of moral sentiment theory, it does contain important features that are found in the later, more elaborated versions. First, emotions represent moral values; moral thinking is essentially reflection on our emotions. The feelings of approval and disapproval are especially important and are linked to judgments of right and wrong. These feelings are spontaneous and unconstructed: reason can justify or even alter these sentiments, but it never precedes their evaluation. These emotions may be evaluations of oneself or of others or of states of affairs. In addition, though the theory acknowledges self-love, it also elevates benevolent feelings toward others; and in claiming the importance and innateness of these feelings, the theory rejects egoism. Finally, the theory gives attention to moral psychology, to the mental processes involved in moral apprehension, evaluation, and motivation.

Although the terms are sometimes used synonymously, I might offer a distinction between *emotion* and *sentiment*. We can use "emotion" to indicate emotion-types, like fear and hope, but we also use the term to indicate an emotional experience—which is the usage that concerns us now. In that sense, an emotion is *an occurrent event*; it is a temporally bounded episode: "I was sad yesterday morning," or "I had a pang of envy when I saw her." By contrast, a sentiment is a *disposition*, a tendency to feel or have a specific emotion in regard to a particular object. As such a disposition may last much longer than an emotion. On the occasion of their golden wedding anniversary, a couple may affirm, "We've been in love for fifty years." That doesn't mean they felt the emotion of love continuously for half a century. They may have argued and been occasionally disappointed or unhappy, but they retained the disposition or tendency to experience feelings of love. This terminological distinction only develops, however, after the great flowering of moral sentiment theory. Indeed, the word "emotion" was rare in the eighteenth century; "passion" was the word preferred, and it was often used interchangeably with "sentiment" and "feeling."[3]

10.4 DAVID HUME'S MORAL THEORY

As a young man, David Hume was devout. Born near Edinburgh to Calvinist parents, he grew up in the Church of Scotland and regularly attended local services. His father died just after his second birthday, and he was raised by his mother alone. She knew he was a precocious boy, so when his older brother left to study at the University of Edinburgh, young David—just 10 or 11 years old—went with him. His family wanted him to study law; he did try law, but he found it "nauseous." He was drawn instead to classics and to philosophy. Despite this keen interest, he disliked the strictures of formal academic life and thought he could learn as much by reading on his own; so, he left the university at about age 15 without earning a degree. As he pursued his independent study, he began to question his religious beliefs. Searching anxiously for arguments to bolster his faith, he collected and analyzed proofs for God's existence—along with arguments for atheism. In the end, Hume emerged a skeptic on matters of religion. His beliefs, later articulated in what clergymen called the "dangerous propositions" of his writings, would cost him the chance for a professorship at two different universities. Instead, he made a career as a writer, chiefly of philosophy and history, always arousing controversy. And though he never married, Hume was a flirtatious and witty guest at many a dinner party.

Hume's moral philosophy is set forth mainly in Book 3 of *A Treatise of Human Nature* (1739–40), which he began writing at age 23, and in *An Enquiry Concerning the Principles of Morals* (1751). He opened his discussion in the *Treatise* with the observation that there is a logical gap between facts and values, and moral theories cannot derive their moral judgments from facts. (This is known as the *Fact-Value Dichotomy*; its implications will be discussed more fully in Chapter 13.) When we give our moral approval or disapproval of an act or a practice, we are not making a rational judgment based on empirical facts or on conceptual relations (using reason alone). Even with murder, Hume asserts, "examine it in all lights, and see if you can find that matter of fact, or real existence, which you call *vice*."[4] Upon careful reflection, we will discover that all we rest such judgments on is our own feelings of approval or disapproval. The claim that "*X* is right" or "*X* is wrong" is not a rational judgment: our moral approval or disapproval is an *emotional response*. All our motivations lie in our passions. As Hume controversially stated it: "reason is, and ought only to be the slave of the passions."[5]

Hume draws on Hutcheson's concept of an innate moral sense, the notion that human beings have a faculty of *moral* perception. To explain the workings of this faculty, Hume identifies the three roles of moral agent, moral receiver or patient, and moral spectator. Suppose that Samantha (the agent) serves food to Bob, a homeless person (the receiver), in a soup kitchen. According to Hume, Samantha is acting out of a virtue such as benevolence or charity. Bob will experience pleasant feelings, both from the food and from the act. Janet, who observes this act (the spectator), will perceive Bob's response and will sympathetically experience those pleasant feelings along with Bob. Now for the critical point: Janet's sympathetic feelings *constitute* her moral approval of Samantha's benevolent act. Negative sympathetic feelings would constitute disapproval. Of course, in most cases, we do not actually witness the acts we judge, but we can read or hear about them, and we may imagine the receiver's feelings in these cases. At times, we are both actor and spectator, approving or disapproving of our own actions. What we judge may be an action or a practice or, even more basically, a character trait—what Hume calls a "quality of mind." When we approve, we may feel pride, esteem, or admiration; blame and guilt are emotions of disapproval.

In some respects, Hume retains a virtues ethic. But he interprets virtues and vices as dispositions to have certain moral emotions that serve to motivate our actions. Moral approval is the spectator's positive sentiment elicited by the observed actor's tendency to have certain moral sentiments. This means that when, for instance, Alisha judges Xavier to be kind and feels approval, or when she judges Andrea to be mean and feels disapproval, her feelings are aroused by observing Xavier's and Andrea's dispositions to act and talk in certain quite different ways. Hume divides virtues and vices into those that are "artificial," by which he means they involve moral emotions that arise from cultural invention, social practice, or adopted rules; and those that are "natural," which arise from inborn responses of pleasure and pain. Hume classifies justice, honesty, chastity, patriotism, and modesty, among others, as "artificial" (though he gives eccentric interpretations for some of these traits); benevolence, gratitude, friendship, and wit are among his list of "natural" virtues.

Hume used the word "utility" to refer to the useful consequences of an agent's actions—these also generated the pleasant (or unpleasant) feelings the receiver would experience. His use of the term—especially in the *Enquiry*—led others to refer to his theory as a "theory of utility." The term stuck, and this aspect of his work inspired Jeremy Bentham and later "utilitarians." (We'll return to Hume a bit later.)

10.5 ADAM SMITH ON SYMPATHY AND MORAL JUDGMENT

Adam Smith was another Scottish philosopher who never knew his father—he had died while Adam was still in his mother's womb. He also would never marry. Smith entered Glasgow College at the age of 13, where he was an admiring student of Francis Hutcheson. He later studied at Balliol College of Oxford University, though he was not pleased with his professors there—in part because he was reprimanded for reading Hume. Nonetheless, Smith himself became a professor—first as Professor of Logic, then as Professor of Moral Philosophy, at Glasgow University. He published *The Theory of Moral Sentiments* in 1759, and it quickly became so popular that students from other countries came to Glasgow to study with him. Despite this renown, he left his university post to become a private tutor and travel. In 1776, he released his second major work, *An Inquiry into the Nature and Causes of the Wealth of Nations*—usually shorted to the *Wealth of Nations*. It is considered the first great work of modern economics, a classic that launched a new discipline and helped create the concept of *Homo economicus* (Chapter 5). But there is little doubt that Smith, contrary to his later reputation, is more philosopher than economist. At least superficially, there are tensions between Smith's moral and economic visions, but we will concentrate on his moral theory.

Smith asserts that human beings are by nature sympathetic. He says: "How selfish soever man may be supposed, there are evidently some principles in his nature, which interest him in the fortune of others, and render their happiness necessary to him, though he derives nothing from it except the pleasure of seeing it."[6] We naturally have pity for those in misery, sorrow for the sorrowful, and are buoyant with those who are joyful. Not only the virtuous, but "the greatest ruffian, the most hardened violator of the laws of society, is not altogether without" such sympathy. This is the fundamental capacity of morality; in Smith's story, all moral judgment and ethical behavior rest upon our innate ability to sympathize with the sentiments of others.

If the process of sympathizing seems intuitively simple, it is quite complex in Smith's presentation. Careful analysis is required because the concept does so much work in his theory. By "sympathy," Smith does not mean "pity" or any other particular emotion or sentiment. Nor does he mean "benevolence," "altruism," or other positive attitudes toward others. Neither does he intend either the projection of one's own feelings into another or the vicarious experience of the *actual* feelings of another. Smith pointedly acknowledges that "we have no immediate experience of what other men feel." To explain sympathy, Smith introduces a second innate, morally relevant capacity: imagination. It is worth quoting his account at length:

> As we have no immediate experience of what other men feel, we
> can form no idea of the manner in which they are affected, but
> by conceiving what we ourselves should feel in the like situation.
> Though our brother is upon the rack, as long as we ourselves are at
> our ease, our senses will never inform us of what he suffers. They

never did, and never can, carry us beyond our own person, and it is
by the imagination only that we can form any conception of what
are his sensations. Neither can that faculty help us to this any other
way, than by representing to us what would be our own, if we were
in his case. It is the impressions of our own senses only, not those
of his, which our imaginations copy. By the imagination we place
ourselves in his situation, we conceive ourselves enduring all the
same torments, we enter as it were into his body, and become in
some measure the same person with him, and thence form some
idea of his sensations, and even feel something which, though
weaker in degree, is not altogether unlike them.[7]

Precisely what we do feel may be different in intensity or even be a different emotion-type altogether: besides pain, "our brother" may be a lout
and feel anger and spite, whereas we find ourselves flushed with embarrassment and regret for his conduct.

Smith further observes that we possess an innate, affective desire: the
desire for "fellow-feeling." We naturally take pleasure, says Smith, in "shar-
ing" feelings; we are distressed when our feelings vary from others'. Each
of us is Actor, doing and feeling; and Spectator, observing and responding
to others.[8] When as Spectator we discover that our sentiment coincides
with that of an observed Actor, we experience fellow-feeling; we warmly
approve and judge her sentiment "just and proper, and suitable to [its]
objects." When our sentiments are dissonant, however, we disapprove,
finding her feeling and what flows from it unjustified.

Fortunately, there are forces that work to bring our sentiments into the
harmony we naturally prefer. There are social conventions that limit the
range of socially acceptable emotional expression. Realizing that other
people will not share the intensity of one's own feelings, yet desiring
fellow-feeling and concord, one "can only hope to obtain this by lower-
ing his passion to that pitch, in which the spectators are capable of going
along with him." That is, we naturally temper or "flatten" our emotional
expression. Thus, observer and observed each make adjustments to
approach a congruence of sentiments.

The process of "sympathizing" works something like this:

1. Someone (the Spectator) sees someone else (the Actor)
   showing direct or indirect signs of an emotion.
2. From contextual clues and personal experience, the Spectator
   interprets the situation of the Actor, the emotion-generating
   circumstances.

3. The Spectator imagines him- or herself in the situation of the Actor.
4. As a result, the Spectator experiences his or her own emotion—the feeling he or she would have in such a situation.
5. The Spectator compares the felt emotion with that of the Actor.
6. If the emotions coincide, the Spectator experiences a pleasant fellow-feeling tinged with approval—and judges the Actor's feeling to be just and appropriate. If the sentiments are quite different, the Spectator will feel discomfort, disapprove of the Actor's response, and judge it to be unjust and inappropriate.

It is significant that Smith traces morality neither to reason nor to our ability to apprehend and apply principles, but rather to a natural capacity for emotional bonds between people. Unlike his teacher Hutcheson, however, Smith discerns no specifically moral emotion and no moral sense. Second, sympathy inevitably ends in judgment—approval or condemnation. But what exactly is being judged? Primarily, it is the actor's emotion, though not in isolation; the spectator judges the emotion's appropriateness comparatively and in relation to the interpreted context of the actor, along with any implied motive to act. But the judgment is not the outcome of deliberation; rather, it seems to be the cognitive content of a second-order emotion: the spectator's emotion of approval or disapproval devolving from the perceived harmony or disharmony of sentiments. Smith would interpret the responses of Marie's family at Thanksgiving as so many spectators attempting to "sympathize" with Marie's love and finding they themselves would have quite different feelings—and hence, they have emotions of disapproval.

10.6 SMITH'S IMPARTIAL SPECTATOR

Smith claims that observing and judging others characterize only the first stage of moral development. The primary perspective is that of spectator; yet, from early on, we also experience the reciprocal viewpoint, that of being observed and judged. Our natural desire for fellow-feeling spawns a desire for approval or praise, probably first sought from our parents, but generally from all with whom we interact. As Smith's story of moral development unfolds, both perspectives, the judge and the judged, are crucial.

The second plateau of moral development involves what Smith terms "self-approbation and self-disapprobation." We learn to judge ourselves from judging others and being judged, applying the same sympathetic procedure. But in order to sympathize with ourselves, we must open up some sort of psychic distance within us. Smith says:

> We can never survey our own sentiments and motives, we can never form any judgment concerning them; unless we remove ourselves, as it were, from our own natural station, and endeavor to view them at a certain distance from us. But we can do this in no other way than by endeavoring to view them with the eyes of other people, or as other people are likely to view them.[9]

The "people we live with" thus provide a "mirror" with which we can reflect on our actions and imagine their approval or disapproval. This is complex, for it requires that I know my own heart, imagine specific others sympathizing with me, imagine their resulting judgment, and react to that imagined judgment. Smith is quite explicit about this psychic distance and its necessity:

> When I endeavor to examine my own conduct ... I divide myself, as it were, into two persons: and that I, the examiner and judge, represent a different character from that other I, the person whose conduct is examined and judged of. The first is the spectator, whose sentiments with regard to my own conduct I endeavor to enter into, by placing myself in his situation, and by considering how it would appear to me, when seen from that particular point of view. The second is the agent, the person whom I properly call myself, and of whose conduct, under the character of the spectator, I was endeavoring to form some opinion.[10]

We thus have a second significant task for imagination in moral development: this mental self-bifurcation is made possible by imagining other sympathetic spectators. Smith implies that self-knowledge is made possible by self-consciousness, which is achieved by imagining the judgments of others. Although the self is not entirely a social construct—there is a human nature, which includes sympathy, imagination, and the desire for approval—for Smith, the self is forged in social interaction, on which self-knowledge and moral development are entirely dependent. Moreover, moral rules arise as abstracted generalizations of the judgments of spectators; they are emergent, empirically-based prescriptions. As he says, a moral rule is developed "by finding from experience, that all actions of a certain kind, or circumstanced in a certain manner, are approved or disapproved of."[11]

The actual experience of being observed and judged has led to one's imagining spectatorial responses to our actions. To judge the propriety of one's own sentiments, motives, and actions, one must scrutinize them as though they were someone else's. This leads directly to the next stage of moral development: if we are judged, we desire to be judged fairly, independently, impartially, free from prejudice and special interest; therefore, we will imagine a best judge, an *Impartial Spectator*. This is a significant move: instead of imaginatively consulting familiar spectators, historical paragons of virtue, or oneself, we realize that to obtain an optimal judgment, we must imagine the sympathy of an impartial spectator. (Remarkably, this concept of impartiality seems transparent to Smith; at least, he must not think that the Impartial Spectator needs elaborate theoretical construction, for he provides none. He seems to think of it as a common-sense notion.) For Smith,

> "X is right" = "X would excite an emotion of approval in an Impartial Spectator."

The imagined Impartial Spectator becomes internalized as a *conscience*, to be consulted as our moral guide. Knowing the Impartial Spectator's judgments provides moral guidance that ultimately supersedes the judgments of parents, peers, or imagined spectators. Conscience is not construed as the voice of one's deepest feelings, nor is it a superego or insistent memory of parental sanctions. Instead, it is a representative of a spectator, distinct from and impartial to oneself, yet lodged within, internalized as "the man within the breast." Through this device, Smith provides a sense of impartiality and rational consistency in moral judgments, yet the process of moral evaluation remains one of sympathy and emotional experience. He has attempted to synthesize a working objectivity out of the subjectivity of moral experience, and moved us from seeking *approval* to seeking *virtue*, from actions that are praised to those that are praiseworthy.

Perhaps Marie's twinges of guilt and shame at her announcement arose from her imagining how others were judging her. She judged herself as well, of course, and affirmed her affection for Yuki. No doubt she would yearn for a fair and impartial judge, if she must be judged. And there are indications in the narrative that she may indeed have internalized such a perspective as her conscience.

10.7 THE CASE OF DISGUST

The popular social psychologist Jonathan Haidt (b. 1963) has developed a form of moral sentiment theory in which he traces our moral beliefs as arising from basic emotions. Haidt believes that we engage in reasoning largely to find evidence and affirmation for our initial feelings (a claim resonant with Hume's position). As in most contemporary theories, our natural capacities for emotionality and empathy, our "moral sense," is analyzed as an outcome of evolution, not God-given (as with Hutcheson).

One basic, universal, human emotion is disgust. Haidt and other contemporary researchers believe that disgust is a protective response originally evolved to prevent the ingestion of harmful things. Contamination through the mouth ("gustatory" contamination), or even by touch, is prevented by our revulsion against "dis-gusting" things. The smell of organic decay, sliminess, bodily fluids and waste, for example, are likely to provoke our disgust. But as this emotion developed and broadened with social evolution, it gained a moral tone. Thus, we may be disgusted by incest; Marie's grandmother was disgusted by lesbianism. Haidt has actually produced a "disgust scale" and claims to show that social conservatives have a lower disgust threshold (that is, they find more things more disgusting) than social progressives.

Martha C. Nussbaum and others have noted the moral perception that disgust may represent, the ways that immoral actions disgust a moral agent. When you are disgusted by someone's racist remark or inappropriate touch, your feeling indicates a moral perception that what the person is doing is wrong. But Nussbaum has also cautioned against using our unconsidered disgust response as moral judgment.[12] After all, racists are disgusted by interracial sex; homosexual relationships disgust homophobes; Nazis were disgusted at Jewishness. Moral disgust can be misguided. It is a "raw" response; it needs to be processed by reasoning and other emotions. Fortunately, our sense of what is disgusting can change as we grow—or else we might not now eat the foods we found "yucky" in childhood, and some of us might not have sex at all. Though our emotions are primary, they can be altered by reasoning, by observing others, and especially by familiarizing experiences.

10.8 COMMENTARY AND CRITIQUE

The key elements of Moral Sentiment theory are: (1) a view of emotion as moral perception; (2) a second-order emotion of approval or disapproval that constitutes our moral evaluations; (3) a capacity for understanding and being affected by the emotions of others—called "**sympathy**" in the eighteenth century; and (4) for most theorists, a process or device such as rational reflection by which one's emotions are subjected to normative criteria. Without this last element, the theory leaves us in subjectivism.

Although the term "sympathy" etymologically suggests "feeling together"—having the same emotion—it is misleading for us, because we primarily use the term to mean "a feeling of pity or sorrow for someone else's misfortunes." "Sympathy cards" extend condolences to grieving friends. But the word "empathy" was coined only in 1908 and so was not known to the Scottish *literati* of the eighteenth century. If we define **empathy** as "the capacity to have another person's emotions"—literally to feel *their* pain—that is not what Hume or Smith have in mind. But often it is defined more broadly as "the capacity to understand and be affected by the feelings of another," and that gets us closer to their meaning. What they describe is an *imaginative simulation* in which one tries to put oneself in the situation of another. Thus, *moral imagination* is crucial. One who lacks these two capacities is amoral, a sociopath.

For these "sentimental" theories, the moral agent is not an abstract reasoner, but a social creature, an engaged and sensitive actor. As we all go about our lives observing and being observed, and we are alert to and shaped by the perceptions others have of us. Smith frames this as a kind of moral theater, with actors and spectators. Moral sentiment theory thus connects the inner aspects of emotion with the outer social interactions of daily life.

For these theories, moral education is (to borrow the title of Gustave Flaubert's great 1869 novel) *L'Éducation sentimentale*—a "sentimental education," an education of the emotions. It requires an enlargement of our moral imagination; a refinement of our moral understanding; the reach for proper, impartial judgments; and the internalization of this perspective—that is, the development of a morally robust conscience. We can quicken and enlarge our moral imagination through travel, through literature (and today, cinema)—through any activity that helps extend the reach of our emotional understanding. Emotional intelligence would seem to be greatly helpful as well, as would emotional health. All of this reveals the view of morality as a matter of empathy in interpersonal relations—not of duties or principles or projects.

There are criticisms to consider, of course:

1. A frequent criticism is that moral sentiment theory is really a theory of moral psychology, but offers little as a philosophical theory of ethics. No doubt, the works of Hutcheson, Hume, and Smith present provocative

accounts of moral development and the psychology of moral judgment. But each of their works also contains both a metaethical theory and a theory of normative ethics, and Smith is especially clear and expansive in his presentation. I believe it is difficult for philosophers who prize reason to accept Hume's view that passions are prior to reason and govern them—particularly if they also retain the view that emotions are simply inclinations or disruptions to reason. Hume's assertion places emotion in opposition to reason, it is true, but he clearly believed emotions had cognitive content and conveyed perceptions. As our understanding of the cognitive aspects of emotions has deepened, we are beginning to appreciate the ways in which rationality and emotionality are complementary, not contradictory, capacities. These findings enrich the accounts one can give of the emotive basis of morality. These insights have led to a new wave of theories that base morality on emotional experience or empathy.[13]

2. A related criticism is that moral sentiment theory reduces moral judgments to outbursts of emotion and thereby eliminates the possibility of serious moral debate.[14] Instead of real deliberation, we merely vent our feelings at each other. There is a trenchant response to this critique: it is based on a misinterpretation. As with the previous critique, it assumes that emotions have no cognitive content; on the contrary, moral sentiment theory affirms that morality rests on emotions that embody moral perceptions and judgments. For example, Hume's account says that our moral judgments are *constituted* by our emotions of approval and disapproval—they are not simply expressions or outbursts of emotion. Your emotion of disgust at a racist remark says something about the remark; you are not simply venting your feeling. Moreover, emotions respond to moral perceptions; they have a cognitive aspect in informing us about whatever we judge: our anger indicates a perceived slight or insult; envy indicates we desire something possessed by someone else; and disgust reveals an almost physical revulsion and rejection. While these judgments are subjective, our moral sense is a capacity humans share, and thus there are basic emotional responses that we naturally share.

3. A more concerning critique is that moral sentiment theory provides little guidance to moral agents. It accepts our emotions as definitive and has nothing to offer to decide cases of conflict or uncertainty. Let's evaluate this critique by considering an especially hard case: abortion.

Suppose two people are debating the morality of abortion. If they are sincere, they are not—according to moral sentiment theory—merely emoting at each other. Rather, their debate reflects different judgments, that is, differing emotions that arise in them when reflecting on the practice of abortion—one of approval, one of disapproval. But the theory does take us beyond this description. It also suggests that the most helpful debate would be for the disputants to empathize with each other and with women who face an unwanted pregnancy. They should imagine the desperation and devastation of a girl pregnant and too young, or one who has been impregnated by rape; and they should also imagine the deep religious revulsion to the termination of an innocent human life. Thus, the theory directs us away from abstract cases and pre-packaged principles to an empathic connection with individuals in specific situations. In our opening scenario, of all the people at the table, it seems to be Marie's brother who imagines the courage and pain and release it must require of his sister to come out and face such harsh judgments. But, as Marie herself experiences, uncertainty and mixed emotions may remain. Whether that is a problem with the theory or a realistic assessment of moral life is debatable.

4. It may be argued that moral sentiment theory wrongly diminishes the role of reasoning in moral action. Conflicts and deliberation with others might be understood as the dissonance of different emotional responses, but does that interpretation work for situations in which we ourselves try to determine the right thing to do? Is this really just a matter of having "mixed emotions"? At least sometimes, at least some people, when faced with a difficult decision, do try to reason their way to what is right—examining their motives, thinking through the likely impact of their choices, trying out explanations for actions, applying principles. Is all of this a kind of self-deception?

"No," Hume and Smith would reply. We must reflect, we need to reason our way through a complex moral situation. But we start from and end with our moral emotions. How we reason about moral choices and the relevance of such reasoning is, as we shall see, a central issue of the next chapter.

5. But in the end, the critic says, empathy is limited. Perhaps the optimistic view of moral imagination I have espoused ignores real limits to the range of our understanding; perhaps there is a subjective barrier to empathic emotional experience. This is expressed by a person who says, "You can't possibly understand me, because you are not a Q"—where "Q" refers to a cultural, racial, religious, class, gender, or other group or role with which the person identifies. "Men cannot understand the abortion issue, because they are not women." "White people cannot understand what it is to be a Black person." "You can't understand what it is to be a parent unless you have children." What can we say to such a shut down? Hume and Smith did acknowledge cultural barriers; they were inattentive to gender barriers. Well, it is true we cannot feel someone else's pain. We can't experience another person's consciousness. But having

CHAPTER TEN: EMOTIONS AND MORAL SENTIMENT THEORY   213

some understanding of a person and his situation may help us know better what *we* would feel in such a situation. We cannot presume we fully understand, of course; that would be arrogant. Successful empathy requires both understanding and imagination—and it seems these are indeed limited for each of us. Distance and difference add difficulty. But the pronouncement of such an absolute and irremovable barrier to any understanding shuts down communication and forestalls the important, obligatory effort of empathy and moral imagination.

QUESTIONS FOR DISCUSSION

1 The coming-out story that opens this chapter describes a cauldron of emotions. Explain how these various emotions represent moral judgments. Do you think our moral evaluations are at bottom moral responses?

2 When is getting angry morally bad and when is it morally good? Some claim that anger is always an infantile response; that better, more constructive approaches always exist. Do you agree?

3 Describe a situation in which you are asked to justify your emotion—your fear or your guilty feeling. How would you go about it? Can you have an obligation to feel a certain emotion—for example, are you obligated to feel grateful when you receive a great gift?

4 Consider the emotion for which we use the German word, *Schadenfreude*—feeling pleasure or satisfaction in someone else's pain. Is that emotion always morally wrong? What about taking pleasure in seeing a reckless driver stopped by police for a violation? Should we feel good when wrongdoers are justly punished?

5 What are the pitfalls in Smith's account of moral sympathizing? What is your response to Smith's concept of an idealized Impartial Spectator who is internalized as our conscience? Can an Observer be both sympathetic (have emotions) and impartial?

6 Former President Obama was once criticized for identifying empathy as a crucial quality in a nominee for the Supreme Court. Is the quality of empathy important in a judge? Can empathy be a liability—can it "go too far"?

7 How do you respond when someone says "You can't possibly understand me (or us)" because you don't have a certain identity or experience? Do we have an obligation to try to understand each other—even in the face of such claims?

QUESTIONS FOR PERSONAL REFLECTION

1 Have you ever sensed that you didn't feel the way you were supposed to feel? Did you reflect on what this meant, what it said about your "take" on the situation?

2 How has your personal sense of what is disgusting changed? Are there things that you once thought disgusting but now don't? Is there anything you once accepted but now find disgusting?

3 Smith thinks we feel judged, sometimes unfairly, and so want a fair and understanding judge. Are there situations in which you have felt seriously misjudged, misunderstood?

SUGGESTED SOURCES

The primary sources for this chapter are David Hume's *A Treatise of Human Nature* (Book 3) (1739), and *An Enquiry Concerning the Principles of Morals* (1751); and Adam Smith's *The Theory of Moral Sentiments* (1759).

Baier, Annette C. *A Progress of Sentiment: Reflections on Hume's Treatise* (Cambridge, MA: Harvard UP, 1991).

Broadie, Alexander. *The Cambridge Companion to the Scottish Enlightenment* (Cambridge: Cambridge UP, 2003).

Griswold Jr., Charles L. *Adam Smith and the Virtues of the Enlightenment* (Cambridge: Cambridge UP, 1999).

Haidt, Jonathan. *The Righteous Mind: Why Good People Are Divided by Politics and Religion* (New York: Vintage, 2013).

Krause, Sharon R. *Civil Passions: Moral Sentiment and Democratic Deliberation* (Princeton, NJ: Princeton UP, 2008).

Nichols, Shaun. *Sentimental Rules: On the Natural Foundations of Moral Judgment* (Oxford: Oxford UP, 2007).

Nussbaum, Martha C. *Hiding from Humanity: Disgust, Shame, and the Law* (Princeton, NJ: Princeton UP, 2008).

Prinz, Jesse. *The Emotional Construction of Morals* (Oxford: Oxford UP, 2009).

Rasmussen, Dennis C. *The Infidel and the Professor: David Hume, Adam Smith, and the Friendship that Shaped Modern Thought* (Princeton: Princeton UP, 2017).

NOTES

1   It is interesting that the Stoics held a cognitive view of emotion; but they believed the judgments involved were typically misjudgments, errors of extending the will beyond our ability to control events.

2   The illumination of the Enlightenment began somewhat later in Scotland than on the European continent.

3   Sometimes the word "sentimentalism" is used to refer to moral sentiment theory, but that technical term can confuse a contemporary reader who associates the term with an inclination to unbridled, easy, and shallow emotions.

4   David Hume, *A Treatise of Human Nature*, 3.1.1.

5   Ibid., 2.3.3.

6   Adam Smith, *The Theory of Moral Sentiments*, I.1.1.

7   Ibid., I.1.2.

8   Note that Smith has combined the perspectives of Hume's agent and receiver into an actor who acts and feels. The three roles in Hume are reduced to two in Smith.

9   Ibid., III.1.2.

10   Ibid., III.1.6.

11   Ibid., III.4.8.

12   See Martha C. Nussbaum, *Hiding from Humanity: Disgust, Shame, and the Law* (Princeton, NJ: Princeton UP, 2008); and, for example, Daniel Kelly, *Yuck!: The Nature and Moral Significance of Disgust* (Cambridge, MA: MIT P, 1997; and William Ian Miller, *The Anatomy of Disgust* (Cambridge, MA: Harvard UP, 1998).

13   See, for example: Simon Blackburn, *Ruling Passions: A Theory of Practical Reasoning* (Oxford: Oxford UP, 2000); Shaun Nichols, *Sentimental Rules: On the Natural Foundations of Moral Judgment* (Oxford: Oxford UP, 2007); and Jesse Prinz, *The Emotional Construction of Morals* (Oxford: Oxford UP, 2009).

14   In Chapter 13, I will discuss a metaethical theory, emotivism, that affirms this view of moral judgments.

CHAPTER ELEVEN

Care Ethics and the Feminist Standpoint

I n Europe, a woman was near death from a special kind of cancer. There was one drug that the doctors thought might save her. It was a form of radium that a druggist in the same town had recently discovered. The drug was expensive to make, but the druggist was charging ten times what the drug cost him to make. He paid $400 for the radium and charged $4,000 for a small dose of the drug. The sick woman's husband, Heinz, went to everyone he knew to borrow the money and tried every legal means, but he could only get together about $2,000, which is half of what it cost. He told the druggist that his wife was dying, and asked him to sell it cheaper or let him pay later. But the druggist said, "No, I discovered the drug and I'm going to make money from it." So, having tried every legal means, Heinz gets desperate and considers breaking into the man's store to steal the drug for his wife.[1]

11.1 STAGES OF MORAL REASONING

The story of Heinz was developed by the American psychologist Lawrence Kohlberg (1927–87) for use in his research on moral development. Kohlberg was interested to discover how people reason about moral matters, and his method was to present a set of moral dilemmas—scenarios like that of Heinz—and ask the subjects what they would do and why. In order to unearth their reasoning, he would ask penetrating follow-up questions. In the Heinz case, for example, he would ask these questions (in this order), each followed by "*Why or why not?*"

1. *Should Heinz steal the drug? (Why or why not? Etc.)*
2. *Is it actually right or wrong for him to steal the drug?*
3. *Does Heinz have a duty or obligation to steal the drug?*
4. *If Heinz doesn't love his wife, should he steal the drug for her? Does it make a difference in what Heinz should do whether or not he loves his wife?*
5. *Suppose the person dying is not his wife but a stranger. Should Heinz steal the drug for the stranger?*
6. *Suppose it's a pet animal he loves. Should Heinz steal to save the pet animal?*

7. *Is it important for people to do everything they can to save another's life?*
8. *It is against the law for Heinz to steal. Does that make it morally wrong?*
9. *In general, should people try to do everything they can to obey the law? How does this apply to what Heinz should do?*
10. *In thinking back over the dilemma, what would you say is the most responsible thing for Heinz to do?*

The lengthy interviews drew out thoughtful responses, which were coded accorded to the types of reasons that were given—*not* to the main

FIGURE 6	Kohlberg's Stages of Moral Reasoning

Premoral Level

Stage 1	Pain Avoidance and Obedience	Making moral decisions solely on the basis of self-interest. Disobeying rules if one can avoid being caught.
Stage 2	Instrumental, Relativist, Exchange of Favors	Recognizing that others have needs, but making satisfaction of one's own needs a higher priority. Cooperating and exchanging with others from self-interested motives.

Conventional Level

Stage 3	Good boy/Good girl	Making decisions on the basis of what pleases others. Striving to maintain a concordance of personal relations. Seeking approval.
Stage 4	Law and Order (Most adults stop here.)	Looking to social norms, conventions, and laws to determine what is right. Thinking of rules as inflexible, unchangeable. Respecting authority.

Principled Level

Stage 5	Social Contract	Recognizing that rules/laws are social agreements that can be changed when necessary. Using considered personal values or conscience as a test for rules and laws.
Stage 6	Universal Ethical Principles	Bases moral decisions on autonomously adopted ethical principles that are universal and consistent. Such principles transcend specific rules and laws.

questions, but to the *why or why not* questions. After years of research, including cross-cultural interviews, Kohlberg discerned what he claimed to be a universal pattern of moral development: our moral reasoning matures by passing through distinct stages that are invariant. We cannot skip a stage, though we can stop at a stage lower than the highest. He organized these as three levels, each with two stages of increasing "adequacy" and sophistication. Summarized in **Figure 6**, these stages show progress from bald self-interest and pain avoidance to reflective, principled moral reasoning. (You might note a broad similarity between Kohlberg's empirical findings and the stages described by Adam Smith—especially the advance from conforming to others' judgments to internalizing one's own sense of what is right.)

Much as one would view the development of a person's ability to speak, Kohlberg took his results to describe the development of a person's capacity for moral reasoning—though with normative implications. There seemed to be implications for moral education, ways to encourage the natural development process. And there were implied evaluations of moral theories: Kant is likely to "score higher" than the hedonistic egoist. His research was widely influential. It seemed that there is a universal morality embedded in natural human development.

But there was a provocative anomaly in the data: significantly fewer women reached the "principled level"—most got no higher than Stage 3 or 4, the "conventional level." Was this the harmful byproduct of sexist socialization? Why this "arrested development"—surely females were not less capable of principled morality?

11.2 DIFFERENT VOICES: FROM GILLIGAN TO KITTAY

One of Kohlberg's graduate students, Carol Gilligan (b. 1936), detected another possibility: gender bias in the formation of the stage concepts. For practical reasons—the availability of large and compliant populations of research subjects—Kohlberg's original research that established the stages was limited to males: the military, prison populations, male university students. Gilligan believed this had produced a conceptual structure with a gender bias. She critiqued Kohlberg's stage structure as male-based and unreflectively generalized to women.

In 1982, she authored *In a Different Voice: Psychological Theory and Women's Development*, a book that argued men and women tend to speak with "different voices" on moral matters; they reason with different ethical concerns.[2] The masculine voice is "logical and individualistic," reasoning with abstract principles, tending to be concerned about rights and justice, given to focus on decision making in puzzling, difficult dilemmas. By contrast, the feminine voice is more concerned about taking care of people, protecting important personal relationships, and attending to human needs. Gilligan claimed that Kohlberg's highest stage of principled reason, like historical ethical theory, represents "the voice of the father" and a concern for justice; what it lacks, what it fails to capture, is "the voice of the mother" and a concern for care and love.

Though these differences reflect strong, innate dispositions in men and women, they are, Gilligan acknowledged, stereotypical. She professed the possibility of combining care and justice or uniting these perspectives as the ultimate goal of moral development, though she offered no solution; and the book was received as a feminist manifesto. In her later work, however, she attributed these male-female differences to the effects of enculturation and social structures, not to genetic differences. But Gilligan was a developmental psychologist, not a philosopher; thus, the task of formulating the ethics of care as a moral theory was taken up by others.

Nel Noddings (b. 1929), an American philosopher of education, developed the theory in a 1984 book called *Caring: A Feminine Approach to Ethics and Moral Education*. Drawing on a maternal perspective (she herself mothered ten children), Noddings said that caring relationships are fundamental to human life. In such a relationship, there are two parties: the *one-caring* and the *cared-for*. The one-caring is "engrossed" in the well-being of the cared-for, nurturing and protecting, and setting aside her selfish desires and interests. True caring is on the terms and in the interests of the cared-for; it is neither a projection of one's own expectations, nor is it a means of control. The cared-for should respond to the efforts of the one-caring, but not necessarily in a mirrored reciprocal caring—a response of reciprocated care is not guaranteed. This is not the relationship of atomistic, independent, and equal individuals; it is not contractual. Rather, it is an asymmetrical relationship between unequal and dependent individuals. One cannot care in this way for distant strangers, nor can caring be generated by a sense of duty. It requires what is popularly called "quality time."

Caring is a capacity, a feeling or emotion, a motive, a trait, the primal moral virtue, and a quality of action. It is also a basic human good:

> The relation of natural caring ... [is] the human condition that we, consciously or unconsciously, perceive as "good." It is that condition toward which we long and strive, and it is our longing for caring—to be in that special relation—that provides the motivation

for us to be moral. We want to be moral in order to remain in the
caring relation and to enhance the ideal of ourselves as one-caring.[3]

Caring is not, however, an ethical principle. Indeed, Noddings rejects
principled ethics as "ambiguous and unstable," producing self-righteousness and divisiveness. Whenever a principle is upheld, there is implied
its exception and, too often, principles function to separate us from each
other. Moreover, she rejects the requirement of universalizability for ethical conduct. Instead, she focuses not on judgments or particular acts,
but on "how we meet the other morally," and—reflecting her "feminine"
approach—she wants to "preserve the uniqueness of our human encounters." Wishing to "escape relativism," however, she affirms, "The caring
attitude, that attitude which expresses our earliest memories of being
cared for and our growing store of memories of both caring and being
cared for, is universally accessible."[4]

Natural caring begins early and is awakened by affection or love—for
parents, siblings, friends—or even a pet or fictional character. It calls us to
understand the perspective of the other, the cared-for. We are roused to
nurture, "to reduce the pain, to fill the need, to actualize the dream." We
are moved to act on the behalf of the cared-for, but Noddings cautions
against problematizing the act of care, against a "premature switching
to a rational-objective mode." "To care is to act not by fixed rule but by
affection and regard."[5] As care-givers we need to engage in concretization
not in abstraction. The engrossment of caring can become consuming; it
moves subtly from exhausting to demanding: the "I must" that arises in
natural caring shifts from the urgency of want to the burden of obligation. This is what Noddings calls the shift "from natural to ethical caring."

Four points of clarification are in order. (1) Noddings is forthright in
stating that she is not advocating Christian ethics: "It is not a form of
agapism. There is no command to love nor, indeed, any God to make the
commandment."[6] She rejects "the notion of universal love" as distract-
ing and unattainable in any relevant sense. This has not prevented others
from trying to connect "Love thy neighbor" with **care ethics**, however. (2)
Nevertheless, any adequate moral theory must inform interactions beyond
those of our closest caring relationships. Noddings advocates that we meet
the other morally with a "readiness to care." This attitude is an especially
important norm for those in the "helping professions": nurses, teachers,
counselors should be "ready to care" for their next patient, student, or
client. (3) Caring for oneself is important mainly to sustain one's ability to care for others. (4) Although being cared for can actually expand
one's capacity to care, the caring relation is not structurally reciprocal;

the cared-for may be naturally responsive (open to nurturance, grateful for support, and so on) or merely display just the outward signs and acts of caring (which she characterizes as a form of ethical heroism, for it is not authentic). True caring is not contingent on reciprocity.[7]

Virginia Held (b. 1929) has developed care ethics by nudging it in new directions. In her 1993 book, *Feminist Morality: Transforming Culture, Society, and Politics*,[8] she affirmed the need for ethics to focus on actual, situated selves, not abstract individuals; to balance reason and emotion, justice and care. She takes care to be the fundamental moral value, and posits "the flourishing of children and the creation of human relationships" as the paramount goal for a good society. As the subtitle of that book proclaims, Held believes this approach can not only be applied beyond personal relationships, but it can also be transformative for civic society and culture. In a later work, *The Ethics of Care: Personal, Political, and Global*, she affirms the effectively caring person as the ideal moral agent, and elevates the relation of mother and child to be the model of moral interaction. She claims that the values and practices that constitute care ethics form a needed complement to those of liberal political society: care, trust, and intimacy can supplement justice, rights, and impartiality. For Held, the approach of political liberalism is not so much wrong as it is limited and requires the corrective of personal, care ethics. When we try to treat or set policy for those who are dependent, we gain moral insight by imagining "how we would wish to be treated by those who care about us *if we were children*, rather than to imagine what we and others would choose from the even more remote and inappropriate position of the fully independent, self-sufficient, and equal rational agent."[9] Caring about others can inform the design of political institutions, transform global negotiations, and even reduce problems of incivility and violence.

Another feminist philosopher, Eva Kittay (b. 1946), analyzes the traditional roles, both personal and professional, women have had in caring for those who are dependent. Whether in mothering, nursing the sick, teaching the young, or caring for the disabled, the care of women has been essential to society and yet undervalued by that society. In both acute and permanent situations of dependency, we rely on the care of others for our welfare. She, too, claims that liberal political ideology is incomplete, because institutions and practices of care are necessary, and dependency is inevitable—for all of us as children and also when injured or ill or in old age; for many of us with disabilities, dependency is a life-long condition. In the largest sense, we are all always dependent on others. Kittay therefore proposes a third principle to supplement Rawls's two: "To each according to his or her need, from each to his or her capacity for care, and such support from social institutions as to make available resources and opportunities to those providing care."[10] Kittay demonstrates that focusing on the need and value of care illuminates the ways in which moral agency includes dependency and vulnerability—not simply self-sufficiency and autonomy. She further advances the trend of taking care ethics from the nest of close relationships outward into the public domain.

In the works of these contemporary philosophers (and others), the focal concept of "care" has multiple and overlapping meanings. It is a value, a disposition, a sentiment or affect, a virtue, a quality of relationships, a type of action or labor, a practice, and an ethic that stands in opposition to the obedience to abstract principle. As I said, Held refers to care as "clusters" of values and practices that are context-sensitive. But in all contexts, it is not a detached appreciation; rather, it entails thought and action that is other-directed and aimed at nurturance, protection, and repair. Kohlberg's exercises in reasoning about moral dilemmas cannot easily register such a point of view. In recent decades, the focus of psychological research on moral development has shifted from patterns of reasoning to moral emotions, care, and empathy.[11]

11.3 SITUATING CARE ETHICS

There is no doubt that these women have awakened and articulated "a different voice" in ethical theory. In saying that, I do not mean that they were the first feminist philosophers to address ethical concerns. But most earlier feminist philosophers, such as Mary Wollstonecraft (1759–97), who wrote *A Vindication of the Rights of a Woman* (1782), advocated the equality of women to men as intelligent, rational agents. In the mid-twentieth century, distinguished philosophers such as Hannah Arendt (1906–75) and Simone de Beauvoir (1908–86) developed a moral vision from the experience of being a woman—yet neither vision resembled care ethics.

Nor do I mean that male philosophers had never noticed the moral relevance of care—though those who gave it significance are rare. Martin Heidegger (1889–1976), an enormously influential German philosopher, in the 1920s viewed care (*Sorge*) as fundamental to being human (*Dasein* is his term for human existence).[12] For Heidegger, care is fundamental to one's being; one cannot become an authentic self without caring. It is care that brings meaning into the world. Five decades later, Milton Mayeroff (1925–79), perhaps influenced by Heidegger, wrote a book titled simply, *On Caring* (1972), in which he said:

> To care for another person, in the most significant sense, is to help him grow and actualize himself ...
>
> In the context of a man's life, caring has a way of ordering his other values and activities around it. When this order is comprehensive, because of the inclusiveness of his carings, there is a basic stability in his life; he is "in place" in the world.... Through caring for certain others, by serving them through caring, a man lives the meaning of his own life. In the sense in which a man can ever be said to be at home in the world, he is at home not through dominating, or explaining, or appreciating, but through caring and being cared for.[13]

But Heidegger never fleshed out his claims; and Mayeroff's exclusive use of masculine pronouns (though common at the time) may have marred his discussion—it has had little impact.[14]

What is distinctive about care ethics is that it has arisen from and been shaped by the experience of women, features caring as the basic moral act and relation, and aspires to reflect this faithfully in a moral theory. Sarah Ruddick (1935–2011) wrote a paper in 1980 that some see as the founding document of care ethics; she called it "Maternal Thinking" and focused tightly on the fertile example of the care of a mother for her child.[15] These five—Gilligan, Noddings, Held, Kittay, and Ruddick—have emphasized its distinctively female perspective.[16] To properly situate an ethics of care within moral theory, however, requires comparisons and clarifications—and noteworthy, but contested, distinctions.

In general, "feminine ethics" (the term originally employed by Noddings) refers to a special contribution to ethical theory that arises from the experience of women. "Feminist ethics" is a stronger term. At minimum, it affirms the special moral perspective of women and also its development into full-blown moral theory. But at this point the term becomes contested: feminist ethics may be advanced as a *supplement* to traditional moral theory, or it may be advanced as a *replacement* for traditional theory. It obviously makes a significant difference whether one claims that feminist ethics is a needed and corrective *supplement* to traditional moral theory, or whether one claims that traditional moral theories are contaminated with sexism and should be *replaced* by feminist ethics. None of the disputants is proposing that men and women should follow different moral theories, of course. And, in any event, if an ethical theory is to be viable, it must be universalizable and adoptable by men as well as women. (Indeed, Michael Slote [b. 1941] has proposed a gender-neutral theory of care ethics.[17]) Note that, under either stipulation, "feminist ethics" is a broader term than "care ethics," and the latter is but one possible variety of the former.

How does care ethics relate to moral sentiment theory? Noddings, Annette Baier (1929–2012), and others, have acknowledged similarities between Hume's moral theory and care ethics.[18] Moral sentiment theory grounds morality in our emotions; care ethics grounds morality in relations of care—but caring, at its birth, is a feeling. Both theories depend on the capacity for empathy—though advocates of care ethics emphasize the *receptive* rather than *projective* notion of empathy or affective understanding; and caring, as elaborated by feminist theorists, involves much more than empathizing. But while care ethics focuses on a particular affect as infusing all of morality, the theories of Hume and Smith envision approvals and disapprovals of a wide range of emotions. The relationship of care is not primarily one of approvals and disapprovals.

We might, however, understand care ethics as amending or refining the descriptors for our "continuum of human relationships." Gilligan and Noddings might easily be read as complaining that long-dominant ethical theories have been derived from political or public sorts of relationships—the domain of men. This judgment is explicit in Held's and Kittay's work. (In **Figure 7**, I have added the last four descriptors in each column to reflect the insights of care ethics.)

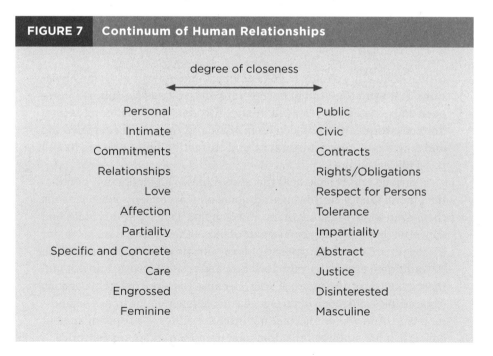

FIGURE 7	Continuum of Human Relationships

degree of closeness

Personal	Public
Intimate	Civic
Commitments	Contracts
Relationships	Rights/Obligations
Love	Respect for Persons
Affection	Tolerance
Partiality	Impartiality
Specific and Concrete	Abstract
Care	Justice
Engrossed	Disinterested
Feminine	Masculine

If one assumes an irresolvable opposition between the two relationship polarities, one might try to replace one set of concepts with the other—even though it would incur great loss. But I mentioned earlier some of the distorted relationships and stilted interpretations that result from bringing the abstract principles of public ethics into intimate relations. The other possibility is to take care ethics (personal ethics) into the public sphere. Indeed, Held, Kittay, Ruddick, and Slote have made heroic efforts toward that end; Slote, at least, has argued that, although care ethics cannot be made compatible with traditional theories, it can sustain a comprehensive and reformative view of morality on its own.[19] But the problem is that the quality of caring certainly changes if intimacy is not possible—as it is surely not, with civic relationships.

In contrast, most recent theorists, including Held and Kittay, take the view that the personal perspective supplements or complements the public perspective. Nonetheless, there is a slow but sure drive for integration. Held attempts to make the two polarities "fit together." But what would it take for a truly unified vision? As an example, suppose we saw personal values as more fundamental than public but also seek a unified view. We might then try to show how justice is an extension or projection of care. Maybe we could imagine that justice is the most caring response we can offer to people as our knowledge of them shrinks toward zero.[20]

11.4 CRITIQUE OF CARE ETHICS

Critics of an ethic of care have been quick and persistent. Some objections that were directed at earlier versions, such as Noddings's, have been addressed if not resolved by later theorists. In considering several lines of critique, we should keep in mind also that the theory is young and may require both nurturance and correction before we see its full possibilities mature.

1. Various critics have held that care ethics is an incoherent or indistinct moral theory, borrowing traditional ethical concepts when it needs them even while rejecting them, and claiming as new various ideas and concerns that have long been a part of moral theory. Some critics prefer to shelve care ethics as focusing only on motivation, requiring us to turn to traditional ethics to evaluate action and resolve issues. I do not find these criticisms to be incisive. Why? Because there are different versions of care ethics and much of the alleged incoherence stems from a composite image. And while it is true that intimate ethics is a topic of ancient concern, it has not been the dominant moral paradigm for centuries, if

ever. No doubt, the conception of *care* can vary and should be refined by any advocate. Also, there is the need to separate the reformist view that care ethics is innovative and supplementary from the view that it is comprehensive and revolutionary. Advocates of the supplementary view might embrace aspects of traditional ethics quite appropriately.

2. A more serious concern is whether the model of the moral person presented in popular versions of care ethics is overdrawn, whether the "engrossed" caring person is so other-directed as to be slavish and self-abasing. Some critics have claimed that celebrating this ideal actually encourages the oppression of women; it encourages women to find moral good in dependency, service, and self-sacrifice. It is corrosive of a care-giver's integrity. One feminist critic, Claudia Card (1940–2015), claimed that Noddings's version of care ethics "threatens to include too much, by valorizing relationships that sheerly exploit carers."[21] There are, in fact, two separable issues raised by Card: (1) *Does an ethic of care set the bar of minimal morality too high?* Is supererogatory caring even a possibility? Is moral indifference the only alternative to a full-blown, self-denying caring? (2) *Does the elevation of this sort of caring ironically valorize a morally suspect, subservient role for women?* To what extent does caring involve self-renunciation? Or is the possible response that one should also care for oneself an adequate reply?

3. Adding to this concern is the lack of attention to the *worthiness* of any potential object of care. In Noddings's theory, there is no distinction made between, for example, a woman who cares for her loving, invalid father, and a woman who cares for a crude and violently abusive husband. The attention given to the "ethics of the cared-for" is insufficient to separate these cases, and the caring person is left only with the "hope that one can learn to care and learn to be cared for." As Card has put the question: "Can an ethic of care without justice enable us adequately to resist evil?"[22] One might ask, "Is there nothing or no one that is unworthy of care—or is every living creature equally worthy of our care?" *Is not justice or some other moral ideal needed to "resist evil" and test the worthiness of the one cared-for?*

The concept of caring has been extended from its parent-child origins to adult-adult personal relationships, to human-pet relationships, and to impersonal adult-public relationships. Some extend it to causes, organizations, precious objects, places, and the environment. All are things we can "care about and for." What is required is a careful analysis of: (a) how our caring is altered by these various targets; (b) what the role of reciprocity is; and (c) how one should determine when a target is not worthy of care and continued caring would be irrational. If we are to care about everything, we certainly cannot care for everything in the same way. Some commitments of care arise naturally, but others are chosen. Does it matter morally how or what or whom we choose?

4. Most theorists recognize that the one-caring may one day cease to care. Caring creates vulnerability for the one who cares. And if, for instance, there is no reciprocal response, no "closure," in Noddings's terminology, from the cared-for; if excessive demands, weariness, conflicts, or betrayals cause a caring relationship to collapse—in such circumstances the one-caring may experience caring as a burden or an obligation, and yet persist to care heroically. But this is a rupture, a moral failure; and sadly, if the caring ceases, it takes with it an important aspect of one's humanity.

Sometimes "caring" is used in a truncated way to mean "effective caring." But surely caring or the attempt to care can go wrong. Lack of understanding, a tendency to dominance, obtuseness, overprotectiveness—all these and more can be the source of damage to relationships of care. Outright wrongdoing such as betrayal can damage a caring relationship as well. The one who cares will then seek to repair the damage.

Care that ceases, the risks of ineffective caring, and the need for repair—all are generally under-theorized in care ethics. Important progress has been made by Margaret Urban Walker (b. 1948), who has made the questions of moral repair after wrongdoing and reparations the centerpiece of her work. She is not, however, committed to care ethics, but to a broader conception of relations of responsibility.[23]

5. Another criticism concerns the liabilities that may arise from an ethic that is directed toward personal relationships, cherishes partiality, and is devoted to nurturance. The concern is not merely that no individual can have this intense sort of care for strangers; it is also that caring individuals are morally adrift when it comes to issues of social justice, equal access, human rights, and global policies. It is obvious that the awkward contexts for care ethics, the situations for which it is least prepared, are: (1) those involving relationships among strangers or civic groups, especially distant peoples; and (2) any context of dilemmas or moral practices in which caring is muted or not relevant—such as whether it is right to use torture to·extract information from terrorists, how to judge Project Prevention and its payments for sterilization of addicts, or how to set a just policy on immigration. Targets of care are not fungible; one person is not as good as any other for the one-caring.

Noddings has argued that a caring home environment is what nurtures a sense of justice, and she has accepted a place for justice to prevent partiality from leading to favoritism, to prevent personal connections from leading to prejudice, and to test larger social issues. She and others advocate a moral education which employs strategies for developing the capacity to care—and a de-emphasis on rules and principles. Other ethicists, including Held, Kittay, Ruddick, and Slote have been more assertive in claiming that it is precisely the attitude of care for others that it missing in discussions of social policy and in many dealings with strangers. Slote champions "a care ethics that takes on moral issues across-the-board," that offers "its own account of justice," and deals with "issues and concepts that have traditionally been (conceived as) the territory or purview of men."[24] The key, he believes, is to supplant the Kantian conception of individual autonomy with a relational conception.

6. Is being adept at caring sufficient to account for our all our moral obligations? One of the follow-up questions in the Heinz dilemma is "Does it make a difference in what Heinz should do whether or not he loves his wife?" No doubt, if Heinz cares for his wife, loves her, he will be more strongly inclined to do something, even something desperate, to save her life. But what if he doesn't love her anymore and the caring has ceased? Does that remove his moral responsibility for her care? Aren't there other duties with moral weight—or do we have only one supreme moral obligation: the obligation to care?

7. Finally, there is the question of what it means for ethics to be "gendered." Noddings's feminine ethics trades on stereotypes of female and male characteristics—but, in a sense, that is her point: the perspective that typifies women has been absent from theoretical ethics. The idea that gender differences might be the *source* of important moral concerns is plausible and persuasive; no one claims that each gender should have *different moral norms*, nor that care ethics applies only to women. Some critics—female and male—have, however, charged early versions of care ethics with reinforcing gender stereotypes, with portraying a single female moral vision, and therefore ignoring important differences among women and overlaps in characteristics with men. What is being charged is called **essentialism**—the belief that everything has a set of necessary and sufficient properties that make it what it is. In this case, the criticism is that care ethics assumes there is an essence, a set of properties that defines *the* female or feminine approach to ethics. In any event, the more emphasis that is given to the gender basis of the theory, the stronger is the implication of incompleteness and the need for a complementary approach.

Feminist ethics is, as I noted, a larger arena than care ethics. Walker, Card, and many others see women's experience as offering more than caring to the reform of moral philosophy.

11.5 STANDPOINT THEORY

The gender-based presentation of care ethics raises a profound question: what difference—what *moral* difference—does difference make? Gender, race, class, cultural heritage, and sexual orientation all contribute to our identity, our individuality. But what are the moral implications, if any, of our identity? Kant claimed there are none: what is morally relevant—our autonomous and rational self—is free from such particulars. That is, our differences do not affect our status as moral persons, nor are they relevant to perceiving our duties, to acting from our duty, or to the duties or rights we have. Utilitarianism acknowledges differences in our individual desires and sources of happiness, but all individuals are equal in considerability, and all are to calculate consequences using the same calculus. Traditional moral theories assume a capacity for moral understanding *shared* by human beings, and universalizability projects the application of morality to *all*. But within the last half-century or so, despite the forces of global social fusion, the belief has taken hold that aspects of our identity—especially basic aspects that we cannot choose—are significant in all spheres of experience. Difference matters. In fact, some say that the view that difference is irrelevant is a part of a particular ideology, the perspective of a privileged class—a group whose status allows them the luxury of that belief.

Standpoint theory emerged in the writings of feminist scholars in the 1970s and 1980s. A standpoint is a perspective from which we experience the world, a point of view from which we gain knowledge and interact with others. Standpoint feminists argue that gender provides a distinctive standpoint.[25] At minimum, this means that women have an understanding of the world that has been discounted and marginalized in a patriarchal society. This theory primarily has implications for the sources and objectivity of knowledge, as well as for the proper scope and direction of politics—but it indirectly has implications for moral understanding, and, hence, for morality. There are, by now, various versions of the theory, and their elements are sometimes in conflict, so a unified presentation is difficult. Let's look at some of these aspects and their ethical import.

Though one might claim that care ethics embraces a "feminine" standpoint, some contemporary advocates of standpoint theory would regard it (especially its original versions) as reflective of a male-imposed model of the feminine. Living in "a man's world," women may need a "raised consciousness" and perceptive engagement in order to articulate what is truly a woman's standpoint. Standpoint can thus be more an achievement than a given or a discovery. Some advocates trace the roots of standpoint theory to G.W.F. Hegel (1770–1831), who distinguished the perspective of slave and master; others draw explicitly on the thought of Karl Marx (1818–83) and his notion that workers have a "class consciousness" endemic to their experience of alienation and marginalization. Just as workers may have "false consciousness"—a mode of thought that prevents one from understanding the true nature of their socio-economic circumstances—so women may be blinded from their situation by patriarchal ideology. Nancy Hartsock (1943–2015) developed from these ideas the conception of standpoint as all those aspects of one's identity and individuality that affect one's knowledge, values, and modes of thought and experience. The concept thus becomes a tool of critical analysis.

Moreover, standpoint theorists usually analyze relationships, even personal and intimate relationships, in terms of power, not in terms of affect. One might see this as a quite different way of unifying the continuum of human relationships: *all* relationships are political, not merely the public or civic ones. The ethical implication seems to be an imperative to the oppressed to resist domination and loss of integrity. The notion of a neutral or objective standpoint is, according to many standpoint feminists, merely a hidden masculine hegemony (an imposed dominance). Theories that advocate objectivity, universality of viewpoint, a "God's-eye view," a "neutral perspective," or "the view from nowhere"—such theories actually embody the standpoint of the dominant (masculine) culture. There is no such objective standpoint, no "Impartial Spectator," according to these writers. Sandra Harding (b. 1935) has explained:

> Appeals to objectivity have often been used to discredit women's perceptions and feminist analyses. Consequently, many feminists have supposed that the concept and the practices it legitimates are too strong and can offer no resources for their knowledge projects. In a kind of reverse discourse, some have openly called for subjectivist voices and relativist accounts.[26]

But others, including Harding herself, have argued that it is the conception of *objectivity* that is in need of revision. Her view is that the various marginalized standpoints might contribute to a "strong objectivity"—an enriched knowledge, not mere belief, that is nevertheless socially situated.[27] This would involve more than a kind and condescending acknowledgment of "contributions" to an essentially masculine narrative; it would revise the criteria for knowledge to incorporate situated knowledge or standpoints.

11.6 RESPONSES TO STANDPOINT THEORY

Standpoint theory emerged as a theory within the social sciences, especially feminist sociology of knowledge. In much the same way that a philosophy of science is not a scientific theory, so a sociology of ethics is not an ethical theory—although it may be relevant to such theory. The arguments for, against, and within standpoint theory do, however, raise four significant concerns for moral theory that I wish to highlight.

1. The first involves the identification and individuation of a standpoint. One of the critical points raised against care ethics is likewise directed toward standpoint theory: the charge of essentialism. Early versions presumed that there is a single, distinctive women's standpoint. But then Black feminists proclaimed their own unique standpoint. As did other women of differing ethnicities. As did lesbians and gay men. This fracturing or multiplication of standpoints, each proclaiming a marginalized standpoint need not be taken as a *reductio ad absurdum* (a reduction of the position to absurdity); indeed, it may show that mainstream culture has indeed oppressed and discounted many groups—each of which has a distinctive standpoint.

Nonetheless, this approach rises or falls on our ability to individuate standpoints, to identify a unified and coherent position for such groups. Among the questions that arise are these: (a) Does the concept of a collective standpoint require us to resort to stereotypes? For some theorists, the problem is not that identity politics fails to bridge differences; it is that it masks further differences that are relevant. But when is our grouping sufficiently fine-grained? Must we end with each individual having a separate standpoint? If so, the concept has lost nearly all its explanatory and analytical power. (b) What about a woman whose working-class parents are a Latina and an African-American—does she have multiple standpoints? (This is known as the problem of *intersectionality*.) If so, how many? *Can* one have multiple standpoints? (c) Are these multiple standpoints arranged in a hierarchy? Is a Black lesbian first a lesbian, then a woman, then Black? Or do these relate in some other way?

2. The second disquieting thought is that our subjective experiences, whether clustered by class or race or gender, etc., or completely individuated, are so different that they are incommensurate; that is, our differences are so large that we can never share a common moral understanding. Can any one individual understand the standpoint of another? Must this theory necessarily collapse into subjectivism? Does standpoint theory both celebrate the subjective experience and simultaneously insert a barrier to subjective understanding? There seem to be three possible

positions: (a) our differences are ultimately not that significant morally, which is why we share human rights, for example; (b) our differences are significant in providing insight and should be welcomed as contributing to a shared and increasingly enriched moral understanding; or (c) our differences are so significant as to be ethically incommensurate, and we must make do with multiple and divergent moralities.

To me, both (a) and (c) represent *a priori* thinking. What I mean is that both declare as their starting point a position that should at best—and then, only if justified—be accepted only as an endpoint. As with all constructed barriers to empathy (see Chapter 10: "You can't possibly understand me, because you are not a Q."), they shut off discussion prior to the effort of attempting to understand, to learn from each other, which must come first.

3. A related issue is the moral role of identity. *Every* individual represents intersectionality, because we are each members of many groups. For example: Salena is a woman, a millennial, a first-generation college graduate of working-class immigrant parents, a Muslim, a member of a sorority, a resident of Pennsylvania, an American, a Democrat, a yoga teacher, and a writer—and so on and on. Each of these aspects of her identity implies membership in a group. Some she chose; others she was indelibly given. It is the unique composite of all these that form her individuality. There is, of course, a shifting hierarchy among these allegiances; psychologically, she may identify with some more than with others—though which ones may change with time and experience. Perhaps her identification as a sister in her sorority and as a Pennsylvanian will fade just as that of being Muslim and a writer will intensify. Often, a particular allegiance will intensify if it is under attack, or if one is gaining benefit from it. But having all these identities does not require that she has a splintered psyche; she doesn't need to compartmentalize her life, first "putting on one hat, then another."

What is unhealthy, *morally* unhealthy, is to reduce an individual's identity to just one aspect, one allegiance. The need to belong is powerful, but when we affirm one of our identities too strongly, we engage people as either someone like us or the Other. The others are not like us; they may be our competitors, our enemies. Similarly, when we reduce other people's complex identities to one, we dehumanize them. Salena may become simply a Muslim. Or a Democrat. Or a woman. We cease to see her as an individual person; she is reduced to being a member of one group. This reduction to our narrowest allegiances is morally dangerous: it leads to dehumanization, to oppression, to violence, even to genocide. The cure, it appears, is not to deny or suppress identity and the standpoint it carries, but to affirm our *multiple* identities and to work for a society in which each person's most prized allegiances are reflected in the emerging social order.[28]

4. Finally, I turn to the technique of analyzing all relationships in terms of power. This is a postmodern critical strategy that shines a harsh light on practices and relationships and reveals dynamics that are otherwise hidden. We find relations of dominance and oppression, for example, not only in colonial cultures or capitalist economies, but also in the classroom and in marriages. These analyses are enlightening, important, and motivating. But a concern arises when one takes this sort of analysis to be the *most* fundamental or the *only* valid form of analysis for human relationships. That assumption skews our moral understanding, for power and dominance are exercises of the will, but not of a moral will. Under such analysis, morality is a rhetorical form of social control, a social tool or weapon. We moralize, preach, inculcate, and valorize; we blame, discount, restrict, and punish—all in the name of morality. The ruling order thus uses morality to mask its domination and regulate behavior, to justify war and political purges. In this line of thought, the world is in fact an ugly and amoral political reality disguised with the make-up of morality.

In this book, we have encountered analyses that claim morality is for obedience to God, for self-interest, for a flourishing life, for the greater happiness and social progress, for the integrity of our free and rational nature, for the satisfaction of a deserved approval, for the support of those we care for, and other aims. But the dark view of this power-based analysis gives us a morality without a moral force. It defiles the quality of care, sacrifice, supererogation, and respect for others. It deflates virtue and justice. It perverts flourishing and welfare into the oppression of others. There is little doubt that moralizing can be used for control and dominance, to direct judgments and behavior. But it is a mistake to assume that all moral consideration is moralizing; it is an affront to assume that all relationships are *only* or *primarily* power relationships. That is itself a mask. It hides the care, the natural "fellow feeling," the good will, the drive for self-actualization. It dismisses our rejection and horror at moral atrocities. It denies our natural motives for moral action.

QUESTIONS FOR DISCUSSION

1 Consider the Heinz dilemma and the follow-up questions. What would be your answers to the *why or why not* questions? Can you think of responses that might fit each stage? What would Heinz do if he adopted care ethics—and how would he justify his act?

2 Explain why "Do unto others as you would have others do unto you" is not a sufficient guide for the caring as required by Noddings's care ethics.

3 What do we rightly expect from people we care for, if not reciprocity?

4 Do you think care ethics can be a comprehensive ethical theory—or must it be supplemented by ideals like justice or by other theories like utilitarianism or Kantianism? What considerations lead to your conclusion?

5 Explain why care ethics is not a special version of moral sentiment theory.

6 Refute the claim that standpoint theory is inherently divisive and erects barriers to understanding each other.

7 Redescribe a caring relationship (as described by Noddings) in terms of a power relationship.

8 What examples can you give of contemporary situations in which complex human identities are reduced to a single one? What happens in such situations when someone has conflicting allegiances?

QUESTIONS FOR PERSONAL REFLECTION

1 What is your earliest remembrance of accepting the responsibility for caring for someone or some other living thing? Was the caring "natural" or did it become burdensome?

2 List the ten aspects of your identity most important to you, the allegiances with which you most identify. Which ones are likely to change over the years? Are there any once-strong allegiances you have already left behind?

3 What aspects of your identity do you think other people emphasize?

SUGGESTED SOURCES

The primary sources for this chapter are Carol Gilligan's *In a Different Voice: Psychological Theory and Women's Development* (Cambridge, MA: Harvard UP, 1982); and Nel Noddings's *Caring: A Feminine Approach to Ethics and Moral Education* (Berkeley, CA: U of California P, 1984).

Grimshaw, Jean. "The Idea of a Female Ethic," in *A Companion to Ethics*, ed. Peter Singer (Malden, MA: Wiley-Blackwell, 1991), 491–99.

Hartsock, Nancy C.M. *The Feminist Standpoint Revisited and Other Essays* (Boulder, CO: Westview P, 1998).

Held, Virginia. *The Ethics of Care: Personal, Political, and Global* (Oxford: Oxford UP, 2007).

Held, Virginia, and Carol W. Oberbrunner, eds. *Justice and Care: Essential Readings in Feminist Ethics* (Boulder, CO: Westview P, 1995).

Kittay, Eva Feder. *Love's Labor: Essays on Women, Equality and Dependency* (New York: Routledge, 1998).

Maalouf, Amin. *In the Name of Identity: Violence and the Need to Belong* (New York: Arcade, 2001).

Slote, Michael. *The Ethics of Care and Empathy* (New York: Routledge, 2007).

NOTES

1 Quoted in Anne Colby, Lawrence Kohlberg, John Gibbs, and Marcus Lieberman, "A Longitudinal Study of Moral Development," *Monographs of the Society for Research in Child Development*, 48, no. 1–2 (1983): Form A, Appendix, 77.

2 Carol Gilligan, *In a Different Voice: Psychological Theory and Women's Development* (Cambridge, MA: Harvard UP, 1982).

3 Nel Noddings, *Caring: A Feminine Approach to Ethics and Moral Education* (Berkeley, CA: U of California P, 1984), 5.

4 Ibid.

5 Ibid., 25.

6 Ibid., 28–29.

7 As an aside: Plato makes a parallel point about erotic love, in his dialogue, *Symposium*, in which being a lover and being a beloved are explained as two quite different roles, each with its expectations, but reciprocity is not required. Plato, too, thought it was natural and also better to be a lover.

8 Virginia Held, *Feminist Morality: Transforming Culture, Society, and Politics* (Chicago, IL: U of Chicago P, 1993).

9 Virginia Held, *The Ethics of Care: Personal, Political, and Global* (Oxford: Oxford UP, 2007), 77. Italics in the original.

10 Eva Feder Kittay, *Love's Labor: Essays on Women, Equality and Dependency* (New York: Routledge, 1998), 113.

11 Because an ethic of care resists abstract formulation, I have not included the compact schema in the text. The starkest version would be: "*X* is right" = "*X* is an effectively caring act." Each version would then unpack the meaning of "effective" care.

12 Martin Heidegger, *Being and Time* (*Sein und Zeit*), trans. John Macquarrie and Edward Robinson (New York: Harper & Bros., 1962).

13 Milton Mayeroff, *On Caring* (New York: Harper & Row, 1972), 1–3.

14 Noddings cites both Heidegger and Mayeroff briefly.

15 Sarah Ruddick, "Maternal Thinking," *Feminist Studies*, v. 6 (Summer 1980), 2:342–67.

16 See, for example, Virginia Held, *Feminist Morality* and Eva Feder Kittay, *Love's Labor*; and also, Sara Ruddick, *Maternal Thinking: Toward a Politics of Peace* (Boston, MA: Beacon P, 1995).

17 Michael Slote, *The Ethics of Care and Empathy* (New York: Routledge, 2007).

18 Noddings, *Caring*; and Annette Baier, "Hume: The Woman's Moral Theorist?" in *Women and Moral Theory*, ed. Eva Feder Kittay and Diana Meyers (Lanham, MD: Rowman & Littlefield, 1987).

19 Slote, op. cit.

20 The problem with that interpretation, however, is that we often deliberately exclude familiarity and partiality to insure justice—justice is blind.

21 Claudia Card, "Caring and Evil," *Hypatia*, 5 no. 1 (Spring 1990): 105.

22 Ibid., 101.

23 See, for example: Margaret Urban Walker, *Moral Understandings: A Feminist Study in Ethics*, 2nd ed. (Oxford: Oxford UP, 2007); and *Moral Repair: Reconstructing Moral Relations after Wrongdoing* (Cambridge: Cambridge UP, 2006).

24 Michael Slote, *The Impossibility of Perfection: Aristotle, Feminism, and the Complexities of Ethics* (Oxford: Oxford UP, 2011), 98–99.

25 Prominent standpoint theorists include Nancy C.M. Hartsock, Alison M. Jaggar, Patricia Hill Collins, Sandra Harding, Sara Ruddick, Alison Wylie, and many others.

26 Sandra Harding, ed., *The Feminist Standpoint Theory Reader: Intellectual and Political Controversies* (New York: Routledge, 2004), Introduction.

27 Sandra Harding, "Rethinking Standpoint Epistemology: What Is 'Strong Objectivity'?" in Harding, ed., op. cit., 127–40.

28 The novelist and journalist, Amin Maalouf, presented a rich treatment of these issues in his book, *In the Name of Identity: Violence and the Need to Belong* (New York: Arcade, 2001). My framing of this issue is drawn from his.

CHAPTER TWELVE
Particularism and Intuitionism

A. You're standing by the side of a track when you see a runaway trolley hurtling toward you: the brakes have failed and it is out of control. Ahead on the track are five workers, who will surely be killed. You realize you're standing at a signal switch—and turning the lever will send the trolley down a side track. But there is one person working on that track, who would then be killed. Do nothing and five people will die; pull the switch and one person will die. What should you do?

B. You're standing on a bridge that crosses over a trolley line, when you see a runaway trolley hurtling toward you—the brakes have failed and it is out of control. Ahead on the track are five workers who will surely be killed. But you notice that there is a very fat man on the bridge with you, looking over at the trolley. You realize that if you push him over onto the track, he's so big he will stop the trolley before it kills the workers—but, alas, he will be killed. It is his life or the lives of five workers. Should you push him over?

12.1 FROM SCENARIOS TO MORAL EPISTEMOLOGY

It was the British philosopher, Philippa Foot (1920–2010), who sent this trolley hurtling down the tracks in 1967.[1] Her original version (which I mentioned in Chapter 1) was much a briefer account of dilemma A, and it was used incidentally, as a quick example, not as a central point of discussion—in fact, the article was about abortion.[2] Judith Jarvis Thomson (b. 1929) analyzed Foot's scenario and added dilemma B, calling the vehicle a trolley instead.[3] Neither one could have predicted that these scenarios would come to be discussed, elaborated, and used to frame other scenarios in a literature so vast it is almost a field unto itself: "trolleyology."

Their debate involved the validity of a moral principle first articulated by Thomas Aquinas and known as the **Doctrine of Double Effect**. It is often used to explain the moral permissibility of an action that does moral harm as a side effect of doing something that promotes a good. It is called "Double Effect" because the action has two effects: the good end that is intended, and the incidental harm that was foreseen but not intended. It requires that the good end be well worth the bad side-effect. Thus, the killing of one person may be morally permissible if it is necessitated to save the lives of five. (Of course, an act utilitarian would claim you are morally *obligated* to kill one to save five.) It is a contested principle—and with good reason: think of the commander who says the killing of citizens, including children, was inevitable and necessary if the enemy was to be routed. No one tried or intended to kill noncombatants; their deaths were unfortunate collateral damage. Those who object to this doctrine are often concerned about what it is used to excuse.

It might seem odd to discuss the trolley problem at this point in our journey. Although the discussion was launched by two women, the trolley cases seem to be prime examples of the sort of ethical theorizing that many feminist scholars have repudiated: focusing on the application of general principles to abstract, almost cartoonish, moral dilemmas. And the distortion increases as the problem is elaborated: Henry says, "Why don't you just yell at the workers to run for their lives." George counters, "Well, suppose all six of the workers are tied to the tracks and can't flee." The dilemma becomes even more fantastic. Where is the depth of character, the moral sentiment, the caring relationships, or the standpoint of one's identity that have been the topics of recent chapters?

That is a justifiable concern. One must acknowledge, however, that the sort of dilemma posed by the runaway trolley has morally significant analogues in the public sphere, ranging from how we should program driverless cars for just such choices to President Harry Truman's historic decision to drop two atomic bombs. But, in any event, it is a different aspect of the trolley cases that sparks interest at this point. When people are asked what they would do in Scenario A, most say they *would* pull the switch and they *should* do so. But when you ask about Scenario B, most say they *wouldn't* push the fat man, that it would be *wrong*. What is curious is why our moral intuitions about these two cases should differ. After all, in both cases, if we chose to act, we would act to save five people though one would die. Our intuitive judgments seem inconsistent—and that is troubling because rationality should result in consistent judgments. It is especially troubling for those who believe that moral judgments must ultimately and always rely on our intuition.

In this chapter, we will explore theories about how we acquire moral knowledge, theories of moral epistemology. A fundamental question is how we know we are facing an issue that is a *moral* issue or a choice that involves *ethics*—not just when we are fully alert to our moral agency and are contemplating what to do, but also when we are not thinking about morality, just being a bystander near some trolley tracks. I briefly discussed this question in Chapter 1, yet it is relevant here as well. But there is a second question: how do I know that *a particular act in this situation* is right or wrong? Knowledge informs action; moral knowledge informs moral action. But what is moral knowledge and how does one acquire it?

12.2 TAKING NOTICE

It is a crucial moment in the trolley scenarios when the bystander notices the careening trolley. The possibility of responsive action depends upon awareness. Had the bystander been oblivious to the situation, perhaps just been looking the other way, no moral dilemma, no live option to act, no burden of choice would have appeared. But the bystander did see the trolley, understood that it was out of control, saw its path and the workmen, and also noticed in both versions a way of preventing that outcome along with the harm it would do. That's a lot to take in quickly. Since the trolley case is unreal, a thought-experiment, we can say with assurance that the bystander took in everything that is relevant about the situation (unless we change the story).

In real life as well, taking notice of the situation is crucial to moral agency, though the circumstances need not be life-or-death dramatic. A man stands ready to take his overfull grocery cart through the check-out and notices that behind him in line is a pregnant woman with a small child and just two items in her cart—so he kindly lets her check out first. Or: he doesn't notice her or sees her but doesn't "see" the situation, and she waits to check out. Even if he really is a kind person, the moment is gone. But, if this is typical of him, we might say he is obtuse. In real life, the urgency is usually less than in the trolley case. We have longer to take in the situation, to notice more, and the decision is less pressured—more like the grocery check-out. Some of us act at once, "without thinking," like Didar Hossain, the Bangladeshi in Chapter 5 who rushed into the rubble to save earthquake victims. Others take time, detailing the circumstances and reviewing the options. In either case, those who act or judge have noticed enough to trigger reflection, action, or judgment. They judge or act upon their moral understanding of the situation and its options. Let us call the virtue of noticing morally relevant things *moral sensitivity*.

Individuals or groups or agencies may be morally insensitive in at least two general ways: (1) they may be callous, "hard-hearted," and uncaring about the implications of actions or policies for others;[4] or (2) they may simply be obtuse—oblivious, innocent, or ignorant of moral dimensions. Both result in a failure to engage one's moral faculties—imagination, empathy, judgment, and so on.

According to many philosophers, once one is aware of a moral situation or faces a moral choice, the proper approach is to identify the relevant moral principle and apply it to the situation. So, in the trolley dilemma, the utilitarian applies the Greatest (net) Happiness Principle to the scene and pulls the switch. The Kantian, facing the fat man on the bridge, might apply the principle of respect for persons and do nothing—because to push him over would be to use him as a means only, not as an end-in-himself. This is a standard model of moral reasoning: reach for your handy, well-honed principle; apply it to the matter at hand; and do what it requires. Principles are like keys: they unlock dilemmas. Of course, if you have just one major principle, there really are no dilemmas; there are only obscure situations which require clarification. And if you prefer to carry several principles, you need some sort of hierarchy to know which principles override which others (as we saw with Ross's *prima facie* duties in Chapter 7). Those who conceive of moral reasoning as applying principles to cases are sometimes called *generalists*. They are comfortable with abstract thought-experiments like the trolley scenarios, because the only moral knowledge that is required is whatever minimum is needed to select and apply the relevant principle.

There is an opposing view, and it is held by those known as *particularists*. In its broadest form, it rejects abstraction and claims that moral reasoning involves attending to the particulars of the situation. Aristotle, in discussing moral judgments, supports this view, when he says: "It is not easy to give a rule for how far and in what way a man may stray before he deserves blame, for the decision depends on the particular circumstances and on perception."[5] In moral philosophy, this view is called **particularism**.

Take the case of Marie's coming-out at Thanksgiving (Chapter 10): what should she have done? The particularist would say that the right action is not determined by a general principle that gets impressed like a cookie-cutter on this scene; rather it depends on many subtleties about the particular individuals and their relationships. We need not reach up for a transcendent principle; we should drill down for immanent details. In the Heinz dilemma (Chapter 11), the particularist—like many of the women Kohlberg surveyed—would want to know more about the situation before responding: more about Heinz and his wife, the illness, their relationship, the druggist, Heinz's previous efforts, and so on. And I suspect the particularist would ask for the same sort of information about the runaway trolley—who are these individuals on the trolley, on the tracks, on the bridge; and what happened to the trolley conductor? A particularist needs human faces, biographies, a more replete account of the context. She might say that what we need are not little abstract dilemmas, thumbnail sketches; we need a novel, we need their stories, if we are to have moral understanding. Imagine if the trolley case or the Heinz dilemma were turned into a richly-textured novel or film, not a brief puzzle. Our moral understanding would expand: it involves *these* individuals with *these* life situations. It would be closer to the complexities in which we actually encounter moral situations in our own lives.

Martha Nussbaum advocates particularism and the insights of literature for moral philosophy in her book, *Love's Knowledge*. She writes, "We live amid bewildering complexities. Obtuseness and refusal of vision are our besetting vices. Responsible lucidity can be wrested from that darkness only by painful, vigilant effort, the intense scrutiny of particulars. Our highest and hardest task is to make ourselves people 'on whom nothing is lost.'"[6] There is "a dialogue between perception and rule," according to Nussbaum, but perception is prior. Why are perceptions prior to principles? She advances three reasons: (1) without the ability to interpret and respond to particulars, we would not know what principles are operative in the situation at hand; (2) with only principles to guide, the well-meaning agent might still "get it all wrong" in the way the act is done; and (3) there are often elements in good action that are surprising or new and cannot be captured in an abstract principle. What we need to cultivate in moral education is moral sensitivity, the attention to particulars; and the guiding moral ideal is to become one on whom nothing is lost.

12.3 PARTICULARISM, PRINCIPLES, AND PERCEPTION

Theorists have produced a spectrum of theories that fit under the label "particularism," and the order is defined by the role given to ethical principles. The view that (a) *particulars may provide exceptions to moral rules* occupies the milder end; then comes the view that (b) *particulars might determine which principle overrides others in a given case.* (Either of those views might be used to explain why it is OK to lie to the Nazi soldier about whether one is hiding a Jew, for instance.) A stronger position is that (c) *principles are rules of thumb only*, or the view taken by Nussbaum: (d) *particulars are prior and are in dialogue with principles—they must inform and reform principles.* The most radical position is that (e) *particulars are by themselves sufficient for moral decision-making;* that is, principles have no role to play. This last is the view of Jonathan P. Dancy (b. 1946) in his book *Ethics without Principles.*[7] Dancy argues that particulars of a situation affect each other; they do not stand alone. And whether a given particular is morally positive or negative, contributing to the rightness or the wrongness of an action, can vary from one situation to another; so, our examination of moral details leads us to judgments that are holistic, that reflect the entire constellation of particulars. Such morally holistic judgments cannot be bound by prior commitment to principles. Principles are superfluous.

Particularism of this sort seems to make moral judgment similar to aesthetic judgment. Someone who is hired to transport a painting looks at it simply as an object—a valuable or fragile object, perhaps, but one that is simply an object of certain dimensions and weight and requiring protective packaging. But to look at the painting aesthetically, one must look at it carefully—scrutinize its particulars. When we observe it in this way, every detail, every aspect matters—the lines, the brush strokes, the palette and how the colors affect each other, the content, the style, the medium, etc. An element that contributes to the beauty of this painting might be dissonant in another painting. To judge any painting, we must put all this information together in a holistic way. So it is, the particularist argues, with moral situations.

If this account is valid, human beings—or more precisely, moral agents—must have a cognitive capacity of *moral perception*. When we think of perception, we think of our apprehension of the world through our senses. This includes not only properties of things, like "I see the scarf is red," or "I feel my phone is hot," but also relationships and states of affairs, like "I see Hugh is taller than Henry," and "I heard the clarinets play out of tune," or "I see we don't have a quorum." Our perceptions discern facts about the world that we might formulate as propositions, like "The scarf is red." Perceptions can compel beliefs. *But does perception yield moral knowledge?*

Many philosophers would hold that we perceive objects and descriptive facts, but they are ethically relevant only when a judgment turns on a matter of fact that is ascertainable empirically (that is through sensory, scientific observation): *Is the trolley actually on the track with five unsuspecting workers? Would the switch change the trolley's path? Is the trolley out of control?* These facts are discerned by perception; they are relevant and descriptive, but not morally normative. Scrutinizing particular facts like that—even very closely—will not compel moral judgments. As Hume proclaims, the facts do not tell us what to do.

But other philosophers hold that we can exercise *moral* perception, that we can scrutinize the particulars of a situation and gain moral knowledge directly. Robert Audi (b. 1941), for example, has argued that we can perceive moral properties, and that such perceptions ground our moral intuitions. Audi writes, "Indeed, seeing that an act or a person has a moral property may itself be a manifestation of an intuitive perceptual capacity that has considerable discriminative subtlety regarding descriptive natural properties."[8] We can, in other words, sometimes observe a situation and *see the injustice* of it, the wrong being done: yes, we perceive the facts—armored soldiers shooting into a crowd of unarmed civilians—but taken alone they are simply facts. We also perceive the *wrongness* of the act. Imagine that passersby saw us push the fat man off the bridge. They might well perceive the wrongness of our act. In Audi's view this is direct moral perception; it is different from seeing a situation *as* wrong or attempting to draw an *inference* from the facts we perceive. Similarly, we might perceive goodness or rightness—we see a kindergartener offer her cookie to a friend who's crying, or even that someone has a duty or deserves an apology.

We should notice that Audi's theory of moral perception is developed to support the concept of moral intuition. If you believe, as Audi, Dancy, G.E. Moore (1873–1958), W.D. Ross, Michael Huemer (b. 1969), and others do, that our moral judgments are ultimately intuitive judgments, you need to explain how our intuition gains moral knowledge from examining the particulars of a situation. Either moral perception or a similar capacity is required, or its cognitive function must be incorporated within the concept of intuition itself. Moral epistemology therefore requires three functions: perception of morally relevant particulars, a moral imagination (which may also require empathy) to consider possible actions and effects, and a conclusive or judgment-yielding function. Let's turn now to the theory that moral intuition is the function that forms our moral judgments.

12.4 ETHICAL INTUITIONISM

We begin with the simplest formulation of the theory:

> "*X* is right" = "*X* is in accord with one's moral intuition."

Intuitionism claims that however a moral agent may use the perception of particulars, factual input, or principles as rules-of-thumb, moral intuition determines the judgment of what is right or wrong, good or bad, obligatory or permissible. The term "intuition" refers both to (a) a cognitive, human faculty or ability and (b) a specific conclusion or judgment derived from that ability or faculty. Thus, we may speak of "using our intuition" to respond to the trolley dilemmas and also our "apparently conflicting intuitions" about the two scenarios. The simple formulation above refers to intuition as a capacity: it would be equally correct to say that intuitionism asserts:

> "*X* is wrong" = "*X* is in accord with one's moral intuition."

So, it is more precise to say:

"*X* is right" = "*X* is affirmed as right by one's moral intuition."

One might question the apparent circularity of this account: "I believe that *X* is right because I believe that X is right?" Critics also assault the validity and reliability of intuitive judgments, and some question the very existence of the "faculty" of intuition. But before we rush to criticize, however, we need to understand more fully the claims of intuitionists.

What is an *intuition*? Contemporary theorists reject the notion that an intuition is an immediate emotional reaction, a "gut response," a hunch, or a hard-wired instinct. They characterize an **intuition** as *a rational, non-inferential, evaluative cognition that is grounded by, but not deduced from, perception of particulars.* Let's unpack this. Intuitions are "evaluative cognitions" in that they involve apprehension and judgment about situations in the world—and they are affected by perceptions. They are "non-inferential" because they are not logical inferences or deductions from premises or principles that function as premises. In that respect, they are like self-evident propositions. But one should not assume that this means they are immediately obvious or "true on their face." On the contrary, determining one's moral intuition about a situation may take time and thought. But it does mean that they are not reducible to evidential facts (that's why the circularity is superficial), not susceptible of proof. Nonetheless, they are "rational" because they can be altered by reasons, by emerging and relevant factors.

Thomas Jefferson's ringing words—"We hold these truths to be self-evident, that all men are created equal, that they are endowed by their Creator with certain unalienable Rights, that among these are Life, Liberty and the pursuit of Happiness"—declared that important moral propositions have a self-evident status. One can interpret this status in several ways, giving different shades of meaning with different implications. It might mean, for example, that these truths: (a) are known with certainty; (b) require no proof; (c) are obvious, immediately understood to be true by any rational person; (d) are not inferred from other premises or principles, but are foundational in that they themselves serve as moral premises, from which moral conclusions may be drawn and decisions may be made; and/or (e) they are moral intuitions, truths known intuitively. Though all of these interpretations may be found in versions of intuitionism, most contemporary versions emphasize the last two.

Intuition may be confused with *conscience*, a concept that is largely ignored or discarded in recent moral theory. In Walt Disney's version of

Pinocchio, Jiminy Cricket was a moralist who memorably crooned "always let your conscience be your guide." He was a surrogate conscience for Pinocchio, the puppet who wanted to be "a real boy" but crucially lacked a conscience. Conscience is usually pictured as an internal sense of the rightness or wrongness of one's past or contemplated actions. Psychologists may see it as the internalization of parental, social, or other authoritative voices. Conscience is a self-reflective, self-oriented faculty, in which our "better self" speaks to us; whereas intuition may yield moral judgment (or so it is claimed) about one's own or others' actions as well as hypothetical scenarios. What they share is the "internality" of their moral guidance, a subjectivity that prevents any public inspection of a rationale for our actions.

Intuitionists do not claim—as some critics assume—that our intuition is infallible and its moral judgments certain. *All* our knowledge-yielding faculties are fallible: they may err; they function better under some external conditions than others; their accuracy may be affected by the agent's mental or physical state; they may be refined or stultified; some may lack the faculty altogether; and what they yield is affected by the input of our other faculties. Take our sensory system for taste: we may mistake nutmeg for cinnamon in the coffee; our sensitivity to spices would be better if we had just drunk water than if we had just used mouthwash; our sense of taste would be sharper if we were alert and healthy as opposed to sick and drugged; we may, through experience and training, develop a sophisticated palate, or ruin our palate through smoking; a person may completely lack the sense of taste, because of genetic defect, disease, or accident; and our ability to taste is heavily influenced by our sense of smell, so much so that it is often difficult to differentiate the two sources. Moreover, all our cognitive systems benefit from a rich imagination and are hampered by a lack of imagination: we must draw on our knowledge and imagination as to what spices *might* be in the coffee we are tasting. And, of course, our imagination can mislead us—influencing what we think we sense. Our moral intuition is no exception to these liabilities. A sociopath may lack moral intuition altogether; but it is also possible to have one's moral perception numbed or improved in sensibility. Our intuition works best when we are in good mental shape, when we have a rich moral imagination, when we are unbiased, and when we have reflective time and can scrutinize the particulars of the situation. The trolley scenarios are especially problematic for intuitionists because so few particulars are provided, the imaginative possibilities are constrained (we're given only two possibilities)—and in a real situation, we would have so little time for moral consideration. Even so, we do have intuitions about these dilemmas (assuming we take them seriously).

If one has different intuitions about the two scenarios—*yes* to the switch in A, but *no* to pushing the fat man in B—is it evidence for inconsistency or unreliability? Not necessarily. It may point to morally relevant differences in the cases despite the "equal" result in lives lost. Perhaps the second scenario narrows the gap involved in the Doctrine of Double Effect: perhaps, in short, pushing the fat man appears more like an act of intentional killing than the foreseen "collateral damage" that would follow one's intentionally throwing the switch—even if the results are the same.

12.5 CRITIQUE AND REBUTTAL

No one doubts that information is relevant to moral judgments. An objection to particularism, however, is that "scrutinizing the particulars" appears to be an endless task: there are infinite particulars in any situation, and it may be difficult to estimate the moral relevance of others not yet surveyed. Moreover, scrutinizing seems to work in the opposite direction from reaching a conclusion. The sort of exhaustion that might come from this injunction is vividly portrayed in the short story, "Funes the Memorious," by Jorge Luis Borges. Ireneo Funes had been knocked unconscious, and "when he came to again, the present was so rich, so clear, that it was almost unbearable." His apprehension of particulars was amazing: "With one quick look, you and I see three wineglasses on a table; Funes perceived every grape that had been pressed into the wine and all the stalks and tendrils of its vineyard." The liability of such remarkable perceptiveness was, however, debilitating and ultimately fatal. "Funes ... was virtually incapable of general, Platonic ideas ... His own face in the mirror, his own hands, surprised him every time he saw them ... He was the solitary, lucid spectator of a multiform, momentaneous, and almost unbearably precise world." According to the narrator, Funes wasn't very good at thinking, because "To think is to ignore (or forget) differences, to generalize, to abstract. In the teeming world of Ireneo Funes there was nothing but particulars—and they were virtually *immediate* particulars."[9]

As piercing as this objection is, it can be removed by two additions to particularism: (1) the theory must define—or at least envision—a reasonable stopping point from which further scrutiny is not morally relevant and the agent's task of perception is ended; and (2) particularism is—to put it crudely—an input theory and must be coupled with a theory of moral output that yields knowledge, judgment, and moral action. In general, particularists adopt ethical intuitionism, which is why they are presented and critiqued together here. We turn, therefore, to objections to ethical intuitionism.

1. The first concerns the reliability of moral intuitions. Our knowledge-gathering may never be infallible, but any faculty or system that claims to yield truth must establish its reliability, at least to a reasonable level. Acknowledging the fallibility of our intuitions is helpful, but that is no argument for their reliability. How can we be sure of our own intuitions? Intuitionists acknowledge that we cannot produce such verification, but they point out that "no such verification exists for sense perception, memory, introspection, or reason in general either." Moreover, they claim the demand is not justified: "Why should any process of cognition demand a second cognitive process directed at the first one? Why not instead hold ... that our cognitive faculties are innocent until proven guilty?"[10] This response, however, seems to presume that we can recognize their failure if not their success. It may also add depth to the question on circularity, implying that "I intuitively know that my intuition is reliable."

2. Another objection, or cluster of objections, begins with the observation that people's intuitive judgments vary widely in practice. Some critics claim that there is more moral error or variation than would be expected if intuitionism were true. Some even argue further that intuitionism makes it impossible to account for *any* moral error or disagreement. Intuitionists make several points in response. First, the extent of moral error and disagreement that exists is exaggerated. Disagreements are publicized and well known; but the broad areas of moral agreement are assumed without controversy. Many moral truths are so widely accepted as to seem self-evident: needless suffering is bad; relieving suffering is good, for example. Second, many superficial moral disagreements are actually disagreements about facts. And even when it is moral judgments and not facts that are contested, that does not make such judgments hopelessly subjective. After all, we have genuine disagreements about economic policy, about scientific matters like the origins of life and the causes of cancer, about the historical significance of certain events, about the existence of God—and these disagreements do not invalidate our *capability* of knowing the answers. Finally, moral matters are complex, sometimes among the most complex questions we face; so it is not surprising that beliefs about such matters are among the most contested. And those who claim intuitionism makes it impossible to account for error may wrongly assume that certainty is being claimed for intuitive judgments.

3. Nevertheless, critics claim, intuitionism leaves us with no way to handle moral disagreements and conflicts that do arise. This is because its radical subjectivity threatens an extreme relativism of the individual. It

also sacrifices the universalizability of moral judgments, and it provides no basis for anyone's moral intuition to have a claim on anyone else. Critics observe that, although resolving disagreements about cases between those who hold different ethical theories is often quite difficult, for disagreements between those who hold the *same* theory, that theory nearly always implies a method of resolution. Consider that for disagreeing utilitarians, the technique is to refine one's measurements and calculations; for social relativists, it takes a more careful assessment of social norms; for Kantians, there should be no disagreement, except perhaps on the matter of picking the applicable maxim. But in all these cases, disagreement implies that at least one party's judgment must be wrong. The claim is that, when ethical intuitionists disagree, however, they both may be correct—as long as they are sincere.

Those who advocate ethical intuitionism today boldly rebut all of this portrayal. Since they believe intuitions are fallible, it is quite possible that a disagreement results from error. An intuitive judgment may be wrong. Moreover, we do have ways of comparing, testing, and refining our intuitions: we may test them against other intuitions (just as we test a belief for its coherence with other, more embedded beliefs). We may stay alert to factors that tend to undermine the reliability of an agent's intuitions, such as bias, prejudice, ideology, religious doctrine, and privilege. And, we may undertake a more fine-grained examination of the particulars in the search for a refined judgment. Moreover, there is no reason for a hopeless relativism: just as our individual sensory systems enable us to live in a shared reality, so our individual moral intuitions point us toward a shared morality. Finally, universalizability is not sacrificed. Under any ethical theory, universalization is a matter of *the range of application* of a moral proposition—and this is true for ethical intuitionism. When I think about scenario B and think about whether to push the fat man, my intuition is not likely to be "It would be wrong (or right) for *me* or *for someone in my culture*"; rather, it might be "It is wrong (or right) to kill the fat man in order to spare the workers." In short, my intuition may be expressed as a universal proposition about what is right or wrong for all moral agents.

4. The fourth objection is that intuitionism is simply "too weird."[11] It postulates a dubious mental faculty for which there is no anatomical evidence, a mysterious process of moral perception, and the injunction to pay attention to particulars, without clear guidance as to what we are to notice. It is an anti-scientific theory, giving up on the grounding of moral judgments by creating a "black box" explanation. Intuitionists have responded by attempting to explicate with clarity each component

and to refute mistaken or caricatured characterizations (as in the rebuttals above). They believe that any residual "weirdness" is simply a matter of being different from other theories. In addition, the openness of the imperative to "scrutinize the particulars" is deliberate; we cannot give a prior, principled restriction to our moral perception. They would also deny that intuitionism is (ironically) counterintuitive, arguing that indeed it is built into our common discourse about moral matters. Indeed, when pressed, intuitionists may claim that we are often mistaken: we claim allegiance to, and believe we follow, some ethical theory; but underneath all our claims, in fact, we rely on our moral intuitions. We are all intuitionists.

We can test these objections and responses by examining a well-developed contemporary version of ethical intuitionism. You may recall from Chapter 10 my citation of the "disgust scale" developed by social psychologist Jonathan Haidt. I also noted that Haidt believes our reasoning tends to follow, not precede our moral judgments. In fact, Haidt has proposed a Social Intuitionist Model for moral judgment, and I will explore that as our contemporary version.

12.6 THE SOCIAL INTUITIONIST MODEL

In a crisp summary of his position, Haidt and his coauthor wrote:

> 1) Moral beliefs and motivations come from a small set of intuitions
> that evolution has prepared the human mind to develop; these
> intuitions then enable and constrain the social construction of
> virtues and values, and 2) moral judgment is a product of quick and
> automatic intuitions that then give rise to slow, conscious moral
> reasoning. Our approach is therefore some kind of intuitionism.
> But there is more: moral reasoning done by an individual is usually
> devoted to finding reasons to support the individual's intuitions,
> but moral reasons passed between people have a causal force.
> Moral discussion is a kind of distributed reasoning, and moral
> claims and justifications have important effects on individuals and
> societies. We believe that moral judgment is best understood as a
> social process, not as a private act of cognition.[12]

It is this combination of an evolutionary view of intuition with a social view of moral judgment that is distinctive in Haidt's approach. His Social Intuitionist Model (SIM) of how we make moral judgments has at its core four "links."

Link 1: The Intuitive Judgment Link. When we observe an act of compassion or of violence, "we experience an instant flash of evaluation"—an intuition. Haidt defines an intuition as *"the sudden appearance in consciousness, or at the fringe of consciousness, of an evaluative feeling (like–dislike, good–bad) about the character or actions of a person, without any conscious awareness of having gone through steps of search, weighing evidence, or inferring a conclusion."*

Link 2: The Post-Hoc *Reasoning Link.* Citing his agreement with Hume, Haidt writes, "moral reasoning is an effortful process (as opposed to an automatic process), usually engaged in after a moral judgment is made, in which a person searches for arguments that will support an already-made judgment." .

Link 3: The Reasoned Persuasion Link. This is the step in which one seeks to frame one's judgment in persuasive terms. "The reasons that people give to each other are best seen as attempts to trigger the right intuitions in others." Our rhetorical skill is honed to persuade those in the community in which we live and work.

Link 4: The Social Persuasion Link. "There are, however, means of persuasion that don't involve giving reasons of any kind," Haidt says. Many studies have shown that simply acting with authority and confidence, for example, can be persuasive to others. Expressiveness can trigger mimicking in others. As Adam Smith said, we desire "fellow-feeling" and naturally seek harmony with the opinions of others.

More needs to be said about our evolved intuitions—those that we have evolved to be "prepared to develop." In one study, Haidt offers four: suffering/compassion, reciprocity/fairness, hierarchy/respect, and purity/pollution.[13] Empirical studies suggest that human beings have evolved an innate responsiveness to these "moral modules," and that we are universally prepared to react to striking situations in which they occur. Our perceptions of these situations elicit intuitive judgments embodied in moral emotions. For creatures living in complex societies, such patterns of responsiveness have survival and coping value.

For Haidt and his colleagues, evolutionary psychology can reveal the source and sanction of our moral judgments; it can redraw our image of the role of perception and reason in moral judgment. Does this theory imply that we can *never* really reason·about moral matters in an open-minded way, considering alternative viewpoints? No. In fact, many of us recall instances in which we changed or determined our mind on an issue by thinking it through, reflecting on it in private. Haidt believes such cases are rare. He develops two additional "links" to account for these oddities: *Link 5: The Reasoned Judgment Link*, in which people "reason their way to a judgment by sheer force of logic, overriding their initial intuition." And *Link 6: The Private Reflection Link*, in which, "in the course of thinking about a situation a person may spontaneously activate a new intuition that contradicts the initial intuitive judgment."[14] Role-taking, absorbing a film, mulling over aspects of a situation—these and other events may trigger the new intuition. These rare links are not the norm, however.

Interestingly, Haidt describes philosophical study as providing "training in unnatural modes of human thought." He says it is not our natural mode to examine a contested moral issue honestly, seeking to articulate the reasons for differing points of view. That is, of course, what philosophers, including students of moral philosophy, do. Haidt says, "If you are able to rise to this challenge, if you are able to honestly examine the moral arguments in favor of slavery and genocide (along with the stronger arguments against them), then you are likely to be either a psychopath or a philosopher. Philosophers are one of the only groups that have been found spontaneously to look for reasons on both sides of a question ... they excel at examining ideas 'dispassionately.'"

12.7 CONCLUDING REFLECTIONS

Intuitionism reminds us that all explanations must presume something—something that we assume to be true in order to explain something else—whether what we are explaining is factual or normative. We use the laws of thermodynamics to explain boiling water; we use our values commitments to explain our choices. Sometimes we are asked to explain what we have presumed to be true, but eventually we come to something so fundamental we must simply *accept it as true*. The recognition of intrinsic value, the adoption of a moral principle—these are *commitments*, not inferred conclusions. The ideas in this chapter therefore direct us to the foundational questions of metaethics we will examine in the next chapter. We have, toward that goal of securing a foundation for ethical judgments, traveled a long path in this book: from God to Nature to culture, to aspects of the self—including self-interest, reason, character, moral emotion, care, and now intuition. It may seem that intuitionism represents a failure of ethical theory, a last resort of moral theorists to find a sound basis for moral judgment. Intuitionists argue, of course, that intuition is in fact that foundation. But it may also be that our moral intuitions provide only a starting point, the content to which we apply rational reflection. If the aim of studying ethics is reflective equilibrium (Chapter 1), we must make the continual adjustment of our intuitions to our theoretical considerations.

The view that we should act according to our moral intuitions certainly affirms the importance of autonomy or self-determination, but it advances a special, nuanced conception. Autonomy is not a matter of choosing for oneself the principles on which one will act. It seems to be less a matter of choice and more a matter of self-discovery or self-formation: one discovers or forms one's intuition. Thus, one's intuitive judgment carries an aspect of *authenticity*. Foreign to intuitionism is the sense of "following" a moral code or "obeying" extrinsic commands or imperatives. But this authenticity has to be more than sincerity—if intuitionism is to avoid a "hopeless subjectivism" and function successfully as a moral theory. After all, history's most horrific moral villains have been quite sincere in their villainy. Intuitionists have understandably tended to focus on showing how one's moral intuitions are valid and deserve an epistemic status. What intuitionism also requires is a cogent and explicit account of how one's intuition can be *wrong*—and be recognized as wrong.

The defensive claim that intuitions are not "simply" emotional reactions is persuasive. But our emotional responses do reflect our intuitions; though they may be immediate and spontaneous, they may also be considered. Emotions, like intuitions, are not generated by facts alone, but they are responsive to facts. So, righteous indignation may reflect an intuition about injustice; remorse may reflect an intuition about moral guilt. As I noted discussing moral sentiment theory (Chapter 10), our emotions reveal our values; moral emotions reveal moral values.

Finally, let us return briefly to the hapless person passing by the trolley tracks. If she or he were sitting in an ethics class considering the runaway trolley, the advantages of time for reflection, considered judgment, and the thoughts of peers, would shape a thoughtful response. If, while walking along the tracks, she or he were engaged in adjusting reflective equilibrium, thinking seriously about "what one should do when one sees a runaway trolley," a sense of moral agency would be fully present. But that is implausible. What is more likely, of course, is that he or she is a passerby, a bystander, thinking his or her own thoughts, until—yeow!—the runaway trolley comes into view. For most of us, once the situation is grasped, the response would be instinctive, not "considered." For many, there would be a moment of choice: the decision to "get involved" which moves us from bystander to moral agent, from spectating to acting (to use Smith's terms). That is a significant moment. Some may remain a bystander—uncertain of what to do, paralyzed by the spectacle, frightened of taking responsibility for the outcome, or simply slow to realize the possibility one's moral engagement—perhaps not realizing that switching the tracks is possible. (This is quite different from being a moral agent and deciding it is right not to change the course of events.) Pretending one didn't see the trolley, fleeing the scene—these aren't morally excusable escapes. Indeed, the habitual attempt to avoid situations in which one will be held morally responsible is itself a vice. Many theorists would hold that we are always, at every moment, moral agents fully responsible for what we do or fail to do. Being preoccupied with our own thoughts, being a bystander or a passer-by does not remove our moral responsibilities. But I am inclined to push back on this claim, at least far enough so as to note and honor the moment of choosing to get involved. We all know the shameful cases of bystanders who do nothing while someone screams for help. "I didn't want to get involved," is often an inexcusable excuse. But there are sometimes legitimate prudential concerns: *Do I understand what's happening? Do I know what should be done? Am I competent to do what should be done?* Various jurisdictions have established "Good Samaritan Laws" to protect a well-meaning person from liability for unintended consequences when attempting to assist someone injured or in danger—though most such laws will not protect the person from grossly misunderstanding the situation or from clearly exceeding their competency. But the law does have a moral purpose: to encourage and protect those who accept the mantle of moral agency and try to help. In many real-life situations, the second moral intuition, the first moral choice, is simply to engage our moral agency and do something.

QUESTIONS FOR DISCUSSION

1 What are your intuitions about Trolley scenarios A and B? If they are different for the two cases, can you explain why?

2 The Doctrine of Double Effect is sometimes used to make a moral distinction between killing and letting die. Explain how the doctrine might be used by advocates of euthanasia? Why would this doctrine be contested?

3 Discuss the strengths and weaknesses of using novels or films to examine moral situations versus using specially constructed philosophical scenarios or thought-experiments.

4 Explain why "obtuseness is a moral failing." Do you agree? Why or why not?

5 Do we have *moral* perception? For example, when you see a video of a passerby suddenly pushing a pedestrian into the path of a bus or when you watch videos of terrorist acts, do you *perceive* the wrongness of the acts? Or is your judgment something you *infer* from the facts on the screen?

6 "Suffering is bad," it is said, is a self-evident moral proposition; it is known intuitively. Can you refute this claim? If not, are there other moral propositions that have this status?

7 What is (are) the most telling objection(s) against ethical intuitionism, in your judgment? Explain why—and why the intuitionist response fails as a rebuttal.

8 What factors would keep our ethical disagreements from being "hopeless"—i.e., unresolvable?

QUESTIONS FOR PERSONAL REFLECTION

1 What steps could you take to increase your moral sensitivity?

2 Have there been occasions when you "pretended not to notice" something going on so you wouldn't "have to get involved"? Do you think your motive was fear, laziness, just wanting to be left alone, or what?

SUGGESTED SOURCES

Audi, Robert. *The Good in the Right: A Theory of Intuition and Intrinsic Value* (Princeton, NJ: Princeton UP, 2004).

Blum, Lawrence. "Moral Perception and Particularity," *Ethics*, 101 (July 1991): 701–25.

Dancy, John. *Ethics Without Principles* (Oxford: Oxford UP, 2004).

Edmonds, David. *Would You Kill the Fat Man? The Trolley Problem and What Your Answer Tells Us about Right and Wrong* (Princeton, NJ: Princeton UP, 2014).

Haidt, Jonathan. *The Righteous Mind: Why Good People Are Divided by Politics and Religion* (New York: Vintage, 2013).

Huemer, Michael. *Ethical Intuitionism* (London: Palgrave Macmillan, 2005).

Moore, G.E. *Principia Ethica*, ed. T. Baldwin (1903; Cambridge: Cambridge UP, 1993).

Nussbaum, Martha C. *Love's Knowledge: Essays on Philosophy and Literature* (Oxford: Oxford UP, 1992).

Singer, Peter. "Ethics and Intuitions," *The Journal of Ethics* 9, nos. 3–4 (2005): 331–52.

NOTES

1 Philippa Foot, "The Problem of Abortion and the Doctrine of the Double Effect" in the *Oxford Review* 5 (1967); reprinted in Foot, *Virtues and Vices* (Oxford: Basil Blackwell, 1978).

2 The wording of her original example is as follows: "A pilot whose airplane is about to crash is deciding whether to steer from a more to a less inhabited area. To make the parallel as close as possible it may rather be supposed that he is the driver of a runaway tram which he can only steer from one narrow track on to another; five men are working on one track and one man on the other; anyone on the track he enters is bound to be killed." Ibid.

3 See Judith Jarvis Thomson, "Killing, Letting Die and the Trolley Problem," *The Monist*, 59, no. 2 (1976): 204–17; and "The Trolley Problem," *Yale Law Journal* 94, no. 6 (1985): 1395–1415.

4 The recent "zero tolerance" policy regarding immigration on the southern US border, which resulted in thousands of children being separated from the parents and held in makeshift facilities, is widely regarded as an example.

5 Aristotle, *Nicomachean Ethics*, 1126b2–4.

6 Martha C. Nussbaum, "'Finely Aware and Richly Responsible': Literature and the Moral Imagination," in *Love's Knowledge: Essays on Philosophy and Literature* (Oxford: Oxford UP, 1990), 148.

7 Jonathan Dancy, *Ethics without Principles* (Oxford: Oxford UP, 2004).

8 Robert Audi, *Moral Perception* (Princeton, NJ: Princeton UP, 2013), 171.

9 Jorge Luis Borges, "Funes, His Memory," in the *Collected Fictions*, trans. Andrew Hurley (New York: Viking P, 1998), 131–37. Quotations from pp. 135–37. The story has usually appeared under the title "Funes the Memorious."

10 Michael Huemer, *Ethical Intuitionism* (Houndsmills: Palgrave Macmillan, 2005), 236.

11 The phrase is Huemer's. Ibid., 239. He offers a similar rebuttal to mine.

12 Jonathan Haidt and Fredrik Bjorklund, "Social Intuitionists Answer Six Questions about Moral Psychology," in Walter Sinnott-Armstrong, ed., *Moral Psychology: The Cognitive Science of Morality: Intuition and Diversity* (Vol. 2) (Cambridge, MA: MIT P, 2007), 181. Haidt has been the lead author with many different coauthors and has written single-authored books. I credit only him in my text, but honor the coauthors in these notes.

13 Jonathan Haidt and Craig Joseph, "Intuitive Ethics: How Innately Prepared Intuitions Generate Culturally Variable Virtues," *Daedalus*, v. 133 (Fall 2004): 4:55–66. Compare the "axes of moral concern" I identified in Chapter 1.

14 These and subsequent quotations in this section are from Haidt and Bjorklund, *op. cit.*

CHAPTER THIRTEEN

Metaethics

In December 2014, the US Senate Select Committee on Intelligence released a 6,000-page report on the Central Intelligence Agency's use of torture between 2001 and 2006. It prompted a national debate about whether torture is ever morally permissible.

Some advocates denied that what the CIA did constitutes torture, preferring instead the term "enhanced interrogation techniques." But others have accepted the term and have argued that torture is morally justifiable—permissible or even obligatory—when it is used to extract information relevant to immediate national security threats or to the saving of innocent lives. (Dick Cheney, who was Vice President during the disputed events, called the report "a bunch of hooey" and said that the questioned tactics were "absolutely, totally justified.") Others, however, say that torture is an absolute wrong, regardless of the purposes for which it is used. President Barack Obama subsequently ordered the prohibition of torture and all forms of "enhanced interrogations." President Trump has advocated a reversal of that order.

13.1 MORAL JUDGMENTS AND DISAGREEMENT

The torture debate presents us with conflicting moral judgments. But what are the parties really disagreeing *about*? Is the debate, at least in principle, resolvable? Perhaps their conflicting judgments are just fall-out from differing political ideologies. Maybe, but let's imagine that at least some participants put their political commitments on hold, consider the issue reflectively and seriously—and still disagree in the end. How can we explain the disagreement?

There is, we have seen, a disagreement about terms: some call waterboarding torture, while others say it is not. They disagree over whether the practice fits a standard definition of "torture." But that is not the whole story, because one might say, "*Whatever* you call it, it is morally wrong" (or "... morally right in certain situations"). The debate, in short, seems to be deeper than an argument over terminology.

Perhaps the disagreement is about certain facts: for example, some may believe that torture is not effective in eliciting valuable information, while others believe it is. Presenting accurate data about the informational value of torture might change the opinions of some, but this fact—and others like it—may not settle the issue. After all, one might maintain that even if torture often yielded valuable information, it is still morally wrong.

What is at issue is the moral *permissibility* or *wrongness* of torture. But what, in principle (independent of whether it actually convinced people), could settle the issue?

To answer this question and to understand ethical debate and disagreement in general, we turn at last to metaethics, the inquiry that examines the nature of ethical claims and the possibilities for justifying them. In a sense, metaethics is about what we are doing when we think and debate about morality. The focus is not directly on guiding moral action or practices, but on the existence of moral truths, the sources of normativity, the appropriate methods of moral inquiry, and the concepts and status of moral discourse.

13.2 COGNITIVISM

Making ethical claims and moral judgments is a basic element of human life. We judge individual acts and practices (like torture) to be morally right or wrong; we judge various things to be good or bad; and we judge people to be virtuous or vicious, worthy of praise or blame. When we make such judgments, especially if they are thoughtfully considered judgments, we commonly take them to assert beliefs that are true. Those who sincerely assert, for example, "Torture is morally wrong," likely assume they are making a meaningful claim about the practice of torture, a claim they believe to be true. The same applies, of course, to those who hold the opposite view about torture. Such claims are, at face value, factual; the existence of opposing views about torture means that people have conflicting judgments, differing views about the facts or their implications.

The very term "judgment" reflects this intuitive view. Judgments are *about something* that is judged; they are based on relevant facts about the thing judged; they are reasoned conclusions. Framed as an assertion, a judgment itself seems to make a factual claim about something, a cognitive claim that is true or false.

This view of moral discourse, a view I am claiming to be intuitive and common, is known in metaethics as **cognitivism**. Speaking broadly, cognitivism affirms that moral judgments are cognitive claims; they contain beliefs that are true or false, and at least some of them are true; they can indeed conflict but their content is subject to reasoning. Cognitivism views moral discourse as yielding genuine knowledge. **Moral realism** is a parallel term that views moral discourse as making existential claims about values. Moral realism asserts that objective moral values and moral facts exist and are independent of our actual beliefs and attitudes.

Cognitivism and moral realism may be assumed in our common speech, but their pre-theoretical, metaethical understanding of moral discourse has been challenged. Indeed, the challenges have engulfed all normative discourse, not just the moral. To investigate these challenges, let us start by comparing these two statements:

- *Torture is morally wrong.*
- *Torture, often resulting in serious mental harm, was used by the CIA on many suspects who were later found to have been improperly detained.*

In form, both are declarative statements. They both assert something that could, in principle, be denied: "No, that's false," would be a sensible reply to each. But the second statement is a claim (actually, two interrelated claims) based on implied empirical evidence that would support it. Assuming some definition of "torture," one could test its truth by finding out whether the CIA did in fact torture many suspects who were improperly detained, and whether that torture did serious mental harm to them. Now that the report is public, anyone can examine the evidence for the claim. It is the sort of claim that can be proved true or false by research.

But what research, what empirical evidence would prove or disprove the first statement? What fact(s) would validate it? Where does one look to justify normative judgments? Is the claim that "torture is morally wrong" factually true or false—or neither?

There does seem to be some sort of connection between the two statements about torture. If the second sentence is true, torture causes significant harm and is often misapplied (at least in the CIA cases). The upshot might be that to inflict "serious mental harm" on the wrong person is unjust, which means it is morally wrong, which means it ought to be eliminated or prevented. That inference alone is not the whole story of course: there are many other facts about torture that could be added to the argument, not merely from this CIA case but also from the long history of torture—such as whether it is actually effective in eliciting valuable information. These points do seem relevant to deciding whether torture is a morally objectionable practice. Although no single such fact would prove that torture is wrong, perhaps if we assembled enough facts, we would have such a proof—or so we might think.

Unfortunately, David Hume dealt that strategy a major blow. You may remember Hume's claim (Chapter 10) that moral judgments are not rational judgments based on empirical facts (or on conceptual relations). Even with murder, Hume asserts, "examine it in all lights, and see if you can find that matter of fact, or real existence, which you call vice." He would say the same with torture: you cannot find a fact about torture which is its moral wrongness.

13.3 FACTS AND VALUES

In his landmark work, *A Treatise of Human Nature*, David Hume surveyed the major theories of morality of his day and decided that they all embodied a basic error of logic. He writes:

> In every system of morality, which I have hitherto met with, I have always remark'd, that the author proceeds for some time in the ordinary way of reasoning, and establishes the being of a God, or makes observations concerning human affairs; when of a sudden I am surpriz'd to find, that instead of the usual copulations of propositions, *is*, and *is not*, I meet with no proposition that is not connected with an *ought*, or an *ought not*. This change is imperceptible; but is, however, of the last consequence. For as this *ought*, or *ought not*, expresses some new relation or affirmation, 'tis necessary that it shou'd be observ'd and explain'd; and at the same time that a reason should be given, for what seems altogether inconceivable, how this new relation can be a deduction from others, which are entirely different from it.[1]

In other words, Hume claims that moral arguments typically line up a lot of facts, use them as premises, and (voila!) deduce a normative claim, a conclusion about what ought to be done. They purport to derive an "ought" from an "is"—which is a fallacy. Hume says we cannot deduce the normative from the descriptive; facts are facts; they cannot by themselves yield an obligation—which would involve a "new relation." We could, in short, pile up facts about torture, even 6,000 pages of them, and we would still face a logical gap to get to the conclusion that torture is wrong. Hume's doctrine is known as the **Fact-Value Dichotomy**.

Hume's point is incisive, and it has been influential in subsequent moral philosophy. Many philosophers have accepted it, though they discern different implications of this wedge between facts and values. Some have tried to find a way "to derive an 'ought' from an 'is' and get away with it."[2] Others have directly challenged whether this dichotomy is as sharp as

Hume asserted, arguing either that values may be reduced to facts, or that "facts" are always tinged with values.[3]

Metaethics, which studies the foundations and concepts of morality, has been absorbed by the question of how facts and values are related. Hume's sharp wedge seems to prevent our values from having any grounding in the real world, the world as it is in fact. This is puzzling because facts about torture, for example, are surely *relevant* to the moral claims about it. When people disagree about the ethics of torture, they are likely to cite facts. Indeed, it is a sign of practical rationality that our judgment responds to relevant facts. And yet, what we value seems to transcend the facts; what we ought to do is quite distinct, importantly distinct, from what we actually do.

Hume's doctrine cuts two ways. If we cannot derive an "ought" from an "is" (or any number of facts), then: (1) we may not reduce a normative statement to any set of descriptive statements; and (2) just how the facts are relevant to our values is unclear. If he's right, facts and values are not tightly tethered to each other.

A similar argument was put forward by the intuitionist G.E. Moore in his 1903 work, *Principia Ethica*.[4] Moore chose to make his point first with regard to the concept of *goodness*, but his argument applied to all key terms of moral evaluation. "Goodness," he asserted, is not analyzable. *Good* is a simple property, without parts or components. It cannot be reduced to a set of natural properties, observable empirically. To attempt such reduction is to commit the **Naturalistic Fallacy**.

Moore offered a technique to detect the Naturalistic Fallacy and demonstrate the uniqueness of goodness that he called the **Open Question Test**. Suppose we are told something is good because it has a certain property; let's say, it is pleasurable. We may then ask, "It is pleasurable, *but is it good?*" If we can meaningfully ask that question, then the question of its moral goodness is still "open," and we see that being pleasurable does not capture the quality of being good. That's not to say that the question has no answer; it may be that torture is in fact always wrong (or always permissible). But the fact that we can still meaningfully pose the question shows that "torture is morally wrong" means something different from and more than "torture causes serious mental harm."

Suppose we are told "Torture is wrong because it causes serious mental harm." It would not be nonsensical to ask, "Torture does cause serious mental harm, *but is it wrong?*" The question of its *wrongness* is still open. Moore claims that whatever property or set of properties (natural facts) we use, the wrongness of the act would still be an open question. "Torture involves the deliberate infliction of pain, *but is it wrong?*" "Torture is a form of aggressive domination, *but is it wrong*?" Despite these and other facts about torture, one can still reasonably ask the question of its wrongness. Since the only way to foreclose the question is to make it a tautology—"Torture is wrong, *but is it wrong?*"—it is clear that only wrongness itself (or goodness itself) can capture the idea of wrongness (or goodness). Our moral values are not merely sets of natural facts.

13.4 NON-COGNITIVISM AND MORAL ANTI-REALISM

One response to the Fact-Value Dichotomy is to embrace it and adopt the position of **non-cognitivism**. Non-cognitivism denies what cognitivism affirms. Non-cognitivism is the view that ethical statements have no cognitive content. Despite their syntactical form, claims like "torture is wrong" do not make factual assertions about the world. Such moral judgments do not assert beliefs that are true or false. But, one might wonder, if moral judgments are not cognitive claims, what are they?

That question was tangential to the work of a group of philosophers and scientists who met regularly in Vienna, Austria, in the 1920s and 1930s. Chaired by Moritz Schlick (1882–1936), the group is known as the Vienna Circle. Its members were strongly impressed by the success of the sciences and were steeped in mathematical methods and logical analysis. They valued the objectivity of scientific investigation, which they interpreted as "value-free." A scientist aims to discover what is true about the world, regardless of the scientist's own values and desires. Proper scientific knowledge, they thought, is uncontaminated by values; it simply presents facts that may be empirically verified. This approach created a movement called **Logical Positivism**. One of its basic tenets is that the meaning of a statement is its method of verification. Except for tautologies—statements like "*A* is *A*" or definitional statements like "a bachelor is an unmarried man"—for a statement to have meaning, it must be empirically verifiable. This doctrine is known as the **verification principle** or the Principle of Verifiability. A statement such as "This block weighs four pounds" is meaningful because we can use our senses to measure its weight. The same is true of the statement "Torture may inflict serious mental harm," provided we are quite clear on what counts as "torture" and "serious mental harm." We could verify this assertion (or refute it) empirically through clinical research and documentation. It states a belief; it is a factual, meaningful claim that is either true or false.

Values claims, however, are not factual. Moral claims are not verifiable, according to the Logical Positivists; there is no way to prove empirically that "torture is wrong." By their doctrines, since moral judgments are not verifiable, *they are not even meaningful*. (By extension, no arena of value discourse is meaningful—not religious claims, not aesthetic judgments of beauty, and not normative ethics.) Their rather austere doctrine is that declarations like "torture is wrong" are meaningless utterances incapable of justification; it is neither true nor false that torture is wrong, because it is not a claim about the world. Reason cannot operate in the realm of values; only a kind of nonrational commitment lies behind values claims. Values claims are outside reason; they are non-cognitive.

This position entails a form of **moral anti-realism**, which holds that moral facts are not real. If moral concepts, such as rightness and goodness (and their opposites), duties and rights, do not exist, or at least do not exist independent of our minds, then truth-claims about them are worthless. If they exist only in our minds, then, as Hamlet says, "there is nothing either good or bad, but thinking makes it so."[5] But some anti-realists deny even this mentally conjured status: moral facts are not mind-dependent realities; they are not real, period. When I make the claim that slaughtering innocent infants is cruel and morally wrong, it is not factive, not true *or* false, because cruelty and wrongness are not real; that is, they do not exist except in human judgments. We do not "discover" what is right, because there is nothing awaiting our discovery.

This is a breathtakingly radical view. It would dispose of our common view of moral discourse and reinterpret moral phenomena in counterintuitive and problematic ways. The debate about the morality of torture—indeed all moral debates, under this view—are unresolvable in theory and pointless in practice. The debaters aren't disagreeing about facts, about real things; they are not saying anything meaningful about torture at all. The partisans are at best simply revealing their personal, nonrational commitments. Similarly, moral deliberation would not be a rational process. Trying to decide whether torture is always wrong would not, in fact, be about the practice of torture or its consequences; but what *would* it be? A spouting of unfounded prejudices? A mistake or a folly? What meaning could it have? Non-cognitivism, if correct, thus challenges the entire enterprise of normative, philosophical ethics.

But if non-cognitivism fails to give a convincing account of moral deliberation and debate, it does seem to grasp the frustration of unending moral disagreement. No wonder we become exasperated with moral conflicts: we mistakenly think we are disagreeing about facts or something in the world. The only hope of agreement is to persuade others to share our values commitments—yet we can offer them no relevant reasons for doing so! All our pronouncements about normative ethics are a sham, a linguistic façade that disguises them with a status they do not have.

13.5 EMOTIVISM AND PRESCRIPTIVISM

Soon after graduating from Oxford, the British philosopher, Alfred J. Ayer (1910–89) spent a year with the Vienna Circle. A while later, he authored the first presentation of Logical Positivism in English, titled *Language, Truth and Logic* (1936). In that iconoclastic little book, Ayer applied the Principle of Verification broadly, along with the resulting non-cognitivist metaethics. Ayer wrote:

> We begin by admitting that the fundamental ethical concepts are unanalysable, inasmuch as there is no criterion by which one can test the validity of the judgements in which they occur.… We say that the reason they are unanalyzable is that they are mere pseudo-concepts. The presence of an ethical symbol in a proposition adds nothing to its factual content. Thus if I say to someone, "You acted wrongly in stealing that money," I am not stating anything more than if I had simply said, "You stole that money." In adding that this action is wrong I am not making any further statement about it …
>
> If now I generalize my previous statement and say, "Stealing money is wrong," I produce a sentence which has no factual meaning—that is, expresses no proposition which can be either true or false.[6]

But Ayer did not let matters rest there. He must have been keenly aware that it is not only shocking but implausible to dismiss as meaningless such important areas of human discourse as ethics, religion, and aesthetics. After all, values seem tightly connected to the meaningfulness of our experiences. Moral claims like "torture is wrong" are not gibberish; they do not seem to be nonsense, not even nonsense in sophisticated form. Ayer decided that moral statements must serve a "special" non-cognitive function.

Ayer was also influenced by Hume. When Hume drove a wedge between facts and values, he stated that moral judgments are derived not from reason, but from our feelings or emotions, our moral sentiments. Ayer developed this insight further: he claimed that ethical statements express our emotions, a theory called **emotivism**. To be clear, Ayer is not saying that ethical statements *report* our emotions—that would make them factual statements about the speaker's emotional state. Rather, ethical statements are emotionally expressive. (For that reason, this theory is sometimes called *expressivism*.) He writes:

> For in saying that a certain type of action is right or wrong, I am not making any factual statement, not even a statement about my own state of mind. I am merely expressing certain moral sentiments. And the man who is ostensibly contradicting me is merely expressing his moral sentiments. So that there is plainly no sense in asking which of us is right. For neither of us is asserting a genuine proposition.[7]

Ayer also notes that in addition to expressing feeling, ethical terms may be "calculated also to arouse feeling." So, for Ayer, although moral judgments do not have cognitive meaning, they possess what is called "emotive meaning"—a form of meaning better understood as the rhetoric that expresses and incites emotion.

Suppose you are at a basketball game and, angry with a referee's calls, you yell, "Boo!" That utterance expresses your emotion. But if someone on the other side were to respond by saying, "Hey, that's not true: 'Boo!' is false!" you would find it very odd (and perhaps move a few seats away). "Boo!" is not the sort of utterance that is true or false; it merely expresses your feeling. It is not a claim to be denied. On Ayer's theory, saying "torture is wrong" is essentially saying, "Torture! Boo!" Saying it is morally right is like saying "Yay for torture!" Utterances like "Boo!" and "Yay" display our emotions and may incite our emotion in others.

A.J. Ayer's emotivist theory is a type of non-cognitivism and so inherits all its problems. Moral debate becomes a futile exercise of emotional venting, "boos" *versus* "hoorays." There is no place for reasoning in discussing ethical matters; no possibility that moral judgments assert beliefs. Moral education loses its rationale: there is no deep rationale why your child should learn to do what is right, except that you, the parent, have a positive emotional attitude toward it. Nearly all the ethical theories we have explored in earlier chapters would be misguided. On the other hand, Ayer seems correct to see a connection between our moral values and our emotions, and moral claims are often laced with emotion. But is emotive expression their only or predominant function?

A slightly more moderate version of emotivism was advanced by Charles L. Stevenson (1908–79) in *Ethics and Language*.[8] Unlike Ayer, for whom moral discourse held little philosophical import, Stevenson believed emotivism could generate a morally insightful theory. Stevenson acknowledged that moral statements have an emotive aspect that is not cognitive, but he also claimed they often had multiple aspects that included cognitive elements. "Torture is wrong," for example might express emotion ("Boo! Torture!"), report one's emotion or attitude ("I disapprove of torture"), and might imply a description of other qualities (torture inflicts pain, causes serious harm, is ineffective, etc.), according to Stevenson. Both Ayer and Stevenson suggested that moral statements may have an additional function: they may be *prescriptive*. Despite their declarative appearance, they may function as imperatives: they prescribe, advise, or command. To say "torture is wrong" may also be to say, "Don't torture!"

Richard M. Hare (1919–2002) developed this idea into a theory called **prescriptivism**. In his book, *The Language of Morals*,[9] Hare asserted that moral judgments are not true or false; rather, they are prescriptions. Nonetheless, they do, he thought, have a descriptive aspect and display a certain logic: they invoke principles and prescribe for everyone conduct that matches one's own attitudes. When I say "torture is wrong," I am also uttering a prescription, declaring, "I live in a way that rejects torture, and I urge you to do the same." For Hare, moral disagreements are best understood as attitudinal differences that have resulted in divergent prescriptions for conduct. The giving of moral advice is no longer a distinctive moral phenomenon; it is the implicit purpose of *all* moral discourse. Moral debates are characterized by conflicting prescriptions. Perhaps prescriptivism seems most plausible in interpreting moral education: when I tell my child "Honesty is the right way to act," I am really saying "Be honest!" Although Hare acknowledges the importance of moral principles, he does not explain why one is better than another. We need principles to guide our conduct, yet we appear to be free to choose whatever principles we want, so long as we commit ourselves to them. Many critics have pointed out that Hare offers us nothing to distinguish trivial principles and imperatives from those that are serious moral ones; indeed, the profound aspects of morality can elude his theory altogether.

13.6 CRITIQUE OF NON-COGNITIVISM

The members of the Vienna Circle elevated the methods of science and mathematics as the standard for all knowledge. Those fields that deal with values could not meet that standard: their claims were not cognitive because they failed the verification principle; they could not be proven empirically; having no factual content and no truth value, they were meaningless. Gradually, non-cognitivist philosophers—Ayer, Stevenson, Hare, and others—managed to locate purposes other than description. They allowed that ethical judgments carry some other sort of meaning, emotive or expressive or prescriptive. But these metaethical theories are really theories of *how moral judgments function linguistically*. They can offer no rational validation of judgmental content but can only point to individual psychology to explain why one has whatever moral commitments one has. This is a serious limitation, but one that advocates may accept. There are, however, significant and more direct lines of criticism.

1. The Principle of Verifiability works like a powerful chainsaw to trim a statement and reveal its meaning. It pruned away all moral statements and those of other values domains. Critics have noted that, ironically, it does not meet its own test: *we cannot verify the Principle of Verifiability empirically*. Yet it seems to have a clear meaning—and its advocates certainly didn't treat it as a non-cognitive utterance!

Beyond that curious point, however, there are several ways in which non-cognitivism contradicts common moral experience:

2. According to non-cognitivism, moral deliberation and debate, moral reasoning that attempts to discern the right course of action, moral judgments and ascriptions—all of these are not what we think they are. Our judgments are not about the thing judged; there is no truth-bearing assertion being made in moral discussions; moral reasoning is a kind of verbiage that mimics genuine reasoning. There is no correct answer to moral questions. But when I ask sincerely, "Is torture morally wrong?" I seek an *answer*—not a venting of emotion, not advice, not persuasion to someone else's subjective viewpoint.

3. Normativity, the idea that one thing can be better than something else—not just in ethics, but in any normative field—is reduced to unjustifiable attitudes, recommendations, preferences, prescriptions, or meaningless jibber-jabber. There is, in short, no rationally valid basis for ethical requirements or values; there is no grounding for guiding conduct. At best, our moral claims are prescriptions for conduct—perhaps intended to apply universally and therefore subject to certain requirements of convention and logic—but they give us no objective way to decide between, for example, prescriptions like "Execute murderers" and "Do not engage in capital punishment."[10]

4. The focus of non-cognitivism is on the language of moral discourse—as is found in many metaethical theories—not on moral action. For non-cognitivists, however, the structure of our language misleads us into a systematic error: we talk and write as though we have (correct or incorrect) beliefs about what is morally right or wrong; but we don't, and

we can't. Our pre-theoretical cognitivism is misguided. This claim of an error theory implies systematic mistakes of enormous proportions.

Let's look at the combined implications of these last three points for a real case. Mohammed Emwazi, a British Arab, was labeled "Jihadi John" in the media. During 2014–15, he made videos in which he beheaded captives—journalists, aid workers, a taxi driver, and others—in the name of ISIS. Most of the world was horrified: the act was cruelly immoral, barbaric. If stark non-cognitivism is true, the terrorist is no worse than his victims, or at least we have no grounds to claim so, for there are no objective moral truths; we cannot offer compelling reasons against such brutality, because our purported reasons have no traction in facts; and our entire legal system is based on a mistake or mere convention, so there is no objective reason why the terrorist should be punished rather than his hostage. If non-cognitivism is true, we have no moral grounding to argue against practices like female genital mutilation or beheadings or torture. Non-cognitivists would reply that we can, nonetheless, reason about moral matters guided by our values, consider implications and consequences, and engage in ethical debate with the serious purpose of persuasion.

5. One of the odd implications of non-cognitivism concerns values claims that arise in a context of reasoning. For example, suppose I offer this simple argument to an emotivist:

> Premise 1: *It is wrong to inflict severe pain on others for whatever reason.*
>
> Premise 2: *Torture of terrorists involves the deliberate infliction of severe pain on suspects to elicit information.*
>
> Conclusion: *Therefore, torture is wrong.*

Emotivism accounts for the "wrong" in the first premise as mere expression of emotion; but it cannot similarly account for the "wrong" in the conclusion. The conclusion does not seem to be an expression of emotion since it is, after all, reached through valid, logical reasoning. As such, it seems to carry a truth-value. The appearance of moral judgments within contexts of reasoning appears to defy non-cognitivism; it requires special explanation or the radical rejection of such reasoning as specious.

6. Finally, there is the stubborn point that facts do seem relevant to moral judgment. Non-cognitivism has a special problem of explaining this sense of relevance and why certain facts are relevant and others are not in making certain judgments. The tendency is to resort to psychological

and sociological explanations regarding the one making the judgment, not to the relationship between what is judged and the judgment itself. For example, when Stevenson pursues the question of how one determines the ethically right thing to do (personal moral reasoning); he concludes that it is "a matter of systematizing one's actual and latent attitudes in a way that gives them definite direction." Aren't the facts relevant? Yes, but only insofar as they shape one's attitudes; facts become reasons when they may serve to alter one's attitudes."

Although the rigidity of Logical Positivism has greatly reduced its popularity over the years, metaethical non-cognitivism has had a recent resurgence in popularity. It has evolved from a stark and dismissive theory to versions that are subtle, sophisticated, and more closely allied to versions of cognitivism. These new versions often acknowledge that moral judgments are, in part, descriptive (and therefore cognitive); but they choose to emphasize other functional aspects of our discourse—aspects such as persuasion or prescription or attitude—that mark it as distinctively moral. They find a purely cognitive metaethics unnecessarily narrow, since we use language for so many other purposes than merely stating facts. Nonetheless, in explicating moral theory in this book, I have taken stark, unadulterated non-cognitivism to be a metaethical theory of last resort. Our language and common practice reflect cognitivism, so we should proceed on that assumption until proven wrong.

13.7 ERROR THEORY AND NON-NATURALISM

Some philosophers are prepared to accept one aspect of cognitivism but not another. They grant that ethical statements have meaning and make cognitive claims that are "truth-bearing." But they deny that *any* such claims are true. This is like saying that moral judgments are about moral facts; but no such facts exist. John L. Mackie (1917–81) advanced this view. He acknowledged that when we make a moral judgment, we believe we are correct—that is, we are saying something we take to be true—and therefore stating a moral fact about some aspect of the world. *But we are always wrong!* We regularly and systematically make this error. As he baldly stated, "There are no objective values."[12]

Mackie's position is an example of **Error Theory**, the doctrine that human beings unwittingly make systematic errors. He believed that all normative moral claims go astray in this way and are false. His view of moral discourse is similar to the way in which an atheist might think about theological discourse: theologians make genuine claims, but they're all false because God does not exist. This version of an error theory constitutes a form of **moral skepticism** (or moral nihilism), which doubts the validity and truth of any and all moral judgments. Though this is, technically, a cognitivist position—given the sort of claims moral judgments make—it undermines normative ethics just as dramatically as non-cognitivism.

A quite different approach was championed by G.E. Moore. Yes, he charged anyone with the Naturalistic Fallacy who attempted to reduce moral evaluations to natural facts. But he also argued that moral judgments were indeed cognitive; they were factual, but they were a special sort of fact: a *non-natural* fact. "Goodness" is a simple, unanalyzable property, he said, but it is a *property* of good things—a *non-natural* property. When we assert that torture is painful, we refer to a natural property; but when we claim that torture is wrong, we mean that acts of torture possess the non-natural property of "wrongness." Whether torture has this property is true or false. When we debate the morality of torture, we are debating about moral properties of torture—not just venting our emotions or urging others to follow our advice. And such moral assertions are neither meaningless nor false by necessity.

Since a "non-natural property" seems to be undetectable scientifically—that is, by our five senses assisted by special instruments—how can we detect non-natural moral properties? Moore's answer, in brief, is that we use our moral intuition; we engage our intuition to discern rightness and goodness and their opposites. We discussed intuitionism in the last chapter, but here it is Moore's **non-naturalism** that we should note. It is a clever approach that allows him to avoid the Naturalistic Fallacy while still grounding moral judgments in facts. In that respect also, there are critical questions.

1. First, and most basic: a non-natural property is a queer thing, and there is no sharp delineation or characterization of the class of such things. The description is given primarily in negative terms: non-natural, not accessible to science, not sensory, unable to affect causally any physical properties. The appeal to non-natural facts might therefore seem to be a desperate dodge, a last resort of cognitivism.

2. If, in Moore's theory, moral facts and empirical facts are quite distinct—the one non-natural, the other natural facts—how do they relate? *How is the fact that torture causes severe pain relevant to the claim that torture is wrong?* The natural and the unnatural properties need not be completely severed. One way to reconnect them is to apply the concept of *supervenience*. It is an abstract concept that describes a dependency relationship between two things or two sets of properties: A "supervenes" on B (or, "is supervenient to B") if A is dependent upon or emerges from B.

But *A* is not reducible to *B*, nor does *B* cause *A*. If we claimed, for example, that biology supervenes on chemistry, we would mean that biological phenomena and explanations emerge from and are dependent on the laws and phenomena of chemistry. Without chemicals, life could not exist. Yet we cannot reduce biology to chemistry. That is, we can't fully explain living creatures by the laws of chemistry alone; they are more than just collections of chemicals—or so we would be claiming. Moreover, biological interactions do not alter the chemistry that underpins them; just as chemical changes do not alter the physics that underpins them.

Similarly, we might claim that values supervene on facts: our moral judgments depend upon and emerge from the facts, but are not reducible to them. This would mean that judgments of goodness and rightness depend upon natural facts, but they are not themselves natural facts.

Moore concludes that non-natural properties supervene on certain natural properties (though the term "supervenience" was introduced later). If something is "good," its non-natural property of "goodness" supervenes on its relevant natural properties. If indeed torture is wrong, it has the non-natural property of "wrongness," which supervenes on various natural properties, such as "causing severe pain." Its moral disvalue would be dependent on and arise from such natural facts. Supervenience would thus explain the felt relevance of natural facts to moral judgments. It does not, however, explain which facts are relevant to a particular moral judgment and why, and in that regard it is incomplete.

One approach remains: an important view that claims moral judgments are cognitive and moral truths are real, but rejects the odd notion of "non-natural properties." Moral properties are natural ones, on this view—that is why it is called naturalism. You will recall the discussion of naturalism (Chapter 4), which derived moral judgments from facts of human nature. Among these were several normative theories that usually rest on a naturalistic foundation: egoism and utilitarianism, for example, which hold that the concept of goodness may be defined as pleasure, or happiness, or other natural properties. We can now place these in a metaethical context.

The metaethical stance called moral **naturalism** may be interpreted in several ways. The simplest is its assertion that moral properties such as goodness and rightness are reducible to natural (non-moral) properties, such as pleasure or satisfaction of desire.[13] Moral properties are therefore real and objective, not dependent on anyone's beliefs and moral judgments—and therefore yield cognitive claims. As you would imagine, this account openly defies Moore's Naturalistic Fallacy of deriving an *ought* from an *is*, since that is precisely what the theory says we do;

but it also denies any need to resort to Moore's concept of "non-natural" properties. Furthermore, it denies Hume's dichotomy between facts and values, asserting that values are but shorthand ways of referring to sets of facts. This reductionist approach drains the mystery from moral properties. Moreover, it disputes the Open Question Test. If let us say, "right" just means "happiness-producing," it would be pointless to ask "That act made people happy, but was it right?" The question "Was it right?" is settled, not an open question. For some reductionists, ethics is fully comprehended by the facts of sociology, anthropology, evolutionary biology, or some other science. Of course, theorists may (and do) disagree about which facts are relevant.

13.8 THE GROUND OF MORALITY

Every normative ethical theory we have studied is linked to a particular metaethical theory, though for some that link is more explicit than with others. After all, we are not only interested to know what things are good and which acts are right or wrong—we want to know why. We want a way to ground our own judgments and a valid rationale to justify ourselves to others. At the outset (Chapter 1), I described five possible grounds for our moral affirmations, and I used these broadly to structure the book. Let's revisit them now in light of the metaethical concepts of this chapter. To derive our morality, we may turn to these five sources:

1. **God.** When one believes that God is the (only) source of moral values, there is no meaning of the moral outside of God's will. The Divine Command Theory (Chapter 2) looks to God's will, whether found in sacred texts, authoritative pronouncements, or revelation. In principle, then it is a cognitive theory because it makes a true or false claim about what God wills. The rightness of an act is independent of what people believe to be right. In this case, however, the moral facts are not ultimately natural or non-natural, but supernatural. Unfortunately, conflicts arise because the facts of just what God wills are not easily verified. Disputes about God's will can't be settled. As it threatens to deteriorate into subjectivism, Divine Command Theory can easily fall prey to non-cognitivism, and the view that claims about God's will are meaningless or at least not aimed at a truth.

2. **Nature, especially Human Nature.** We discussed (Chapter 4) the attempt to ground moral judgments in the facts of human nature. Egoism (Chapter 5) and utilitarianism (Chapter 6) reduced the good to pleasure, self-interest, or happiness. Ethical egoism sometimes claims support

from psychological egoism. These theories, focused on consequences, are guided by moral facts; they desire a strong connection between values and facts and would defy the Naturalistic Fallacy. After all, if the facts of the matter do not justify one's actions, what does? Nothing is intrinsically right or wrong for the consequentialist (only the good and bad are intrinsic). So, if we wish to determine whether torture is wrong, we most likely begin by acknowledging that it causes pain and often does lasting damage. The question is whether the pleasure, or well-being, or self-interest of others increases as a result and how significantly. In this approach, these theories are typically reductionist, naturalistic, and cognitive. That is: they make claims about the world that are true or false, using moral concepts that are defined in terms of facts about human nature and about intended action.

3. **Culture.** The theory that "X is right" = "X is approved by my culture" is clearly cognitive, because the meaning of "right" is cashed out as the factual claim of cultural approval (Chapter 3). Since the theory goes no further to require a basis for moral approval, it is the fact of cultural approval or disapproval that decides the issue. Since this is a reduction of values (rightness) to facts (cultural approval), this is, in the metaethical sense, a naturalistic theory as well.

But there are subtleties to consider. Is a cultural relativist a moral realist; that is, does a cultural relativist believe that moral facts are real? I would say, "Well, yes, they believe that moral facts exist and are independent of the belief of any one individual." But, of course, they do also believe that moral facts are human creations, artifacts of cultural mores. So, the reply might justifiably be, "No, they exist only as social sanctions that are dependent on human beliefs; they are not independent facts of nature."

4. **Reason and Its Instruments.** For Kant (Chapter 7), morality is a practical implication of rationality. Though moral action takes place in the world and moral judgment applies to the world, it does not derive from empirical facts. It derives from reason alone; moral truths exist and are known *a priori*—that is, logically prior to and independent of experience. Moral judgments are certainly cognitive, true or false, claims. If we instead root our morality in an artifact of reason, in what we owe each other as a result of a Social Contract or special agreements (Chapter 8), ethical judgments become factual claims about the contract or other artifacts of consent. But, to be cautious, it is human nature as revealed in the state of nature that justifies some versions of Social Contract Theory, such as those of Hobbes and Locke.

5. **The Self.** We have studied several theories that locate the only valid source of morality within oneself or aspects of the self. For virtue ethics,

it is character; for moral sentiment theory, it is in our emotions; for an ethics of care, it is in our capacity to nurture and protect; for particularism, it is in our abilities to discern and appreciate; for intuitionism, it is our faculty of intuitive judgment (Chapters 9–12). If any of these theories appears to flirt with non-cognitivsm, it is probably moral sentiment theory: the emphasis on emotion might link it with emotivism, of the sort promoted by Ayer. But that would be misguided. Neither Hume nor Smith nor any of the later theorists would have written such long and detailed books of normative ethics if they believed that all moral judgments were merely expressions of emotions, neither true nor false. They defined moral judgments in terms of emotions of approval or disapproval, and whether a person or even an Ideal Spectator experiences those is, in principle, true or false—a matter of fact. All other theories in this group, even intuitionism, claim their judgments to be cognitive. And the theories that emphasize context (virtues, care, particulars) retain the force of making claims about the moral value of acts; the moral judgments made may reflect the situation and identity of the agent, but they are nonetheless claims about the world. Here, too, some versions of the theories may ultimately ground our moral judgments in aspects of human nature— especially as they reach toward universal human capacities as a bulwark against subjectivism.

Moral philosophy requires that we link a normative theory, which tells us what acts and practices are right and wrong, what things are good and bad, and what obligations we have, with a metaethical theory that tells us what those ethical terms mean and what constitutes the basis for those judgments. This study presumes that theories may be more or less adequate; that beliefs may be true or false, warranted or not; and that judgments may be valid or mistaken.

This brief recapitulation of theories may be a helpful review, but where does it leave us? *What is the relation between the normative and the descriptive, between our values and the facts?* We have, I believe, four possibilities: (1) We can accept the Fact/Value Dichotomy stringently as an unbridgeable gap. That leaves morality casting about for its moorings (supernatural will, non-natural properties?) and unable to gain purchase in the world. (2) We can deny the separation, assure a realism and cognitivism, by accepting the reducibility of moral values to facts. This embeds morality so firmly in the state of the world that it seems to lose its normative force. The world simply "is what it is." (3) We could propose that facts are reducible to values. Perhaps this seems to be suitable for a so-called "post-truth" society that embraces "alternative facts"; that sees no difference between belief and knowledge. But this ignores the stubbornness of reality, the harsh push-back of inconvenient facts despite our beliefs. (4) Finally, we could acknowledge the distinction in principle between facts and values, but also affirm a relationship of supervenience or a non-reducible, relational quality between them. This is, I believe, the appropriate choice. What connects the facts regarding torture to moral values are relational properties like moral relevance and importance. This is the domain of judgment.

QUESTIONS FOR DISCUSSION

1 What difference does it make to call a practice "enhanced interrogation" or "torture"?

2 When deciding the morality of torture, is the record of its effectiveness in eliciting useful information relevant? Why or why not?

3 Why is it important to justify moral judgments? To whom must we justify them?

4 Consider this argument: "We shouldn't eat pigs because pigs are relatively intelligent creatures." Does that argument violate Hume's Dichotomy? Does it commit the Naturalistic Fallacy? Explain. How might one apply the Open Question Test to this claim?

5 What is the strongest argument in favor of non-cognitivism?

6 Explain how each of the following would interpret the judgment, "Torture is wrong": emotivism, prescriptivism, moral error theory, and Moore's non-naturalism.

7 Explain the observation that theories such as moral sentiment theory, virtue ethics, care ethics, and intuitionism "may ultimately ground our moral judgments in aspects of human nature— especially as they reach toward universal human capacities as a bulwark against subjectivism."

QUESTIONS FOR PERSONAL REFLECTION

1 The debate about the morality of abortion is one of the most vigorous in contemporary society; viewpoints have hardened, and discussion is often emotional. It has led to violence. Do you think this moral disagreement has a correct answer? Is it either true or false that abortion is an immoral practice?

2 In Chapter 1, I asked which of the five sources of value was the one to which you tended to turn. Has that changed during your examination of these theories?

SUGGESTED SOURCES

Ayer, A.J. *Language, Truth and Logic.* 2nd edition (New York: Dover, 1952).

Fisher, Andrew. *Metaethics: An Introduction* (Lanham, MD: Routledge, 2014).

Hare, Richard M. *The Language of Morals.* Reprint edition (Oxford: Clarendon Press of Oxford UP, 1991).

Miller, Alexander. *Contemporary Metaethics: An Introduction* (Malden, MA: Polity P, 2013).

Moore, G.E. *Principia Ethica* (Cambridge: Cambridge UP, [1903] 1966).

Stevenson, Charles L. *Ethics and Language* (New Haven, CT: Yale UP, 1944).

Urmson, J.O. *The Emotive Theory of Ethicsa* (Oxford: Oxford UP, 1969).

van Roojen, Mark. *Metaethics: A Contemporary Introduction* (Lanham, MD: Routledge, 2015).

NOTES

1   David Hume, *A Treatise of Human Nature*, edited by L.A. Selby-Bigge (1739; Oxford: Oxford UP, 1978), 469.

2   Kohlberg (Chapter 11) did precisely this in Lawrence Kohlberg, "From Is to Ought: How to Commit the Naturalistic Fallacy and Get Away with It in the Study of Moral Development," *Cognitive Development and Epistemology* (1971): 151–235.

3   See, e.g., Hilary Putnam, *The Collapse of the Fact/Value Dichotomy and Other Essays* (Cambridge, MA: Harvard UP, 2002).

4   G.E. Moore, *Principia Ethica* (1903; Cambridge: Cambridge UP, 1966).

5   William Shakespeare, *Hamlet*, Act 2, Scene 2. This quotation is used in this context by Richard Joyce in his excellent article, "Moral Anti-Realism," in the *Stanford Encyclopedia of Philosophy*, revised February 11, 2015: https://plato.stanford.edu/entries/moral-anti-realism/.

6   Alfred Jules Ayer, *Language, Truth and Logic*, second ed. (1936; New York: Dover, 1946), 107.

7   Ibid., 107–08.

8   Charles L. Stevenson, *Ethics and Language* (New Haven, CT: Yale UP, 1944).

9   Richard M. Hare, *The Language of Morals*, reprint ed. (Oxford: Oxford UP, 1991).

10 Hare's theory that moral judgments are universal prescriptions, for example, claims that moral judgments are subject to rational conditions because they project a universal scope—so consistency, application to similar cases, and so on, are required. But the ultimate ground of these prescriptions is an attitude toward what is prescribed.

11 Stevenson, op. cit., 227.

12 J.L. Mackie, *Inventing Right and Wrong* (New York: Penguin, 1977), 15.

13 Or, that moral properties are *natural* and supervene on other natural properties.

CHAPTER FOURTEEN
Moral Theory and the Good Life

Kimberly Brown-Whale grew up in the 1950s–1960s in a family that was plagued by alcoholism, violence, and plain bad luck. But Kimberly seemed to be a bright, happy, and loving child. Her father said she had a Pollyanna personality—always thinking people were good and expecting things to work out for the best. She noticed suffering and tried to help. Kimberly was always doing sponsored charity walks, giving away her baby-sitting money to street people, and being moved to help however she could.

She found her calling in religion. Though she hadn't come from a religious family, she realized the connection between her altruistic impulses and God's love—and she decided to become ordained. While studying for the ministry, she met and married Richard, who would soon embark on a PhD degree with the hope of teaching in a seminary.

Their bishop posted them to missionary work in Anguilla, then in Grenada, then in Mozambique and Senegal. This was hard, complicated service, but Kimberly felt her capacity for love growing through this work. They arrived with two toddlers—a biracial girl adopted from foster care, and their biological son. Later they also adopted a girl whose brain had been damaged by a violent father. But they faced misunderstanding, considerable resistance for cross-racial adoption, and personal violence—Richard was assaulted, robbed, and left for dead. But they were doing God's work.

Finally, a pastorate opened in the US and she was called home to Maryland. Here too there was resistance to a female pastor, objections to her efforts to attract the young and grow the congregation. Kimberly still gave joyfully of herself, empathetic to all in her care, and full of ideas for doing good. When the crisis of homelessness grew in her neighborhood, she decided to move the family out of the personage, and set it up as a shelter. The move was easy: they owned virtually nothing—not even a sofa. Many people in her congregation think she does too much; some think she's just too giving.

One day, Kimberly read a local story about a woman who needed a kidney transplant. She volunteered. She knew what a blessing a new kidney could be for someone who desperately needed it. She was not a good match. But when the nurse got the results, she asked Kimberly if she would be willing to donate her kidney to someone else. "Why not?" she thought—she didn't know the first patient anyway. So, she underwent the operation, donated her kidney, and eventually met the recipient. But the hospital required her to undergo a psychological exam beforehand. With such an altruistic act, the hospital needed to be sure that the donor was not being coerced and was not mentally ill.[1]

14.1 MORAL SAINTS

The literature of morality includes many stock characters. Among the *dramatis personae* are the villain, who acts according to malevolent plans, and the reprobate, who is plagued by vices and acts unethically. Both represent moral failure. Standing in contrast is the **moral saint**, who is the exemplar of extreme devotion to moral concerns. The term "saint" is more at home in religious, especially Christian, contexts, of course. One thinks of St. Peter, St. Francis, St. Teresa, and so on—people of extraordinary holiness. But *moral* saints may not be Christian or even religious. They are also different from **moral heroes**—ordinary people who do extraordinary things, who are morally motivated to perform supererogatory acts—people like Didar Hossain, who rescued the injured in Rana Plaza (Chapter 5) or the two men who attempted to rescue the child from a burning car (Chapter 7). By contrast, moral saints are people who live *lives* of extraordinary morality. They may be engrossed in a moral project to promote good or avoid evil, or they may be fully engaged in responding to ongoing moral debilitations, such as oppression, bigotry, suffering, or cruelty—people like Sojourner Truth, Mohandas Gandhi, Oskar Schindler (of *Schindler's List* fame), Martin Luther King, and Nelson Mandela—and perhaps, at least in aspiration, Kimberly Brown-Whale. Moral saints act from deeply held moral ideals and convictions, and they pursue the good doggedly, despite hardship, danger, imprisonment, and loss. Their prodigious moral energies are obsessive, committing the saint to renouncing self-interest, to a life in which many personal plans, opportunities, relationships, and joys are foregone. Those close to them may not claim their primary care and concern. They are not perfect; even the best of them has unworthy desires or character flaws that affect other aspects of their lives, but these vices do not stain or constrain their moral project or diminish the personal sacrifices it required. They "give their all" to the greater good.

Søren Kierkegaard, the Danish philosopher (Chapter 2), valorizes such a life in a little tract translated as *Purity of Heart Is to Will One Thing.*[2] Though Kierkegaard was a religious existentialist who worked within a Christian theology, his concept applies to moral sainthood: essentially, it is a life in which moral value takes precedence over every other sort of value at all times. To make every action the best possible whatever one's theory—to act always and only for the welfare of others, to act on a special principle without exception, to care without ceasing and will only the good of another—these commitments display what Kierkegaard called "purity of heart" and honor moral imperatives as ubiquitous and dominant.

Do iconic moral saints exemplify the epitome of morality? Are we *all*, in fact, called by morality to be moral saints; or are moral saints *special* people who recognize *special* duties that do not apply to the rest of us? Are we non-saints just shirking our moral obligations, living a life that is much less than it should be? Isn't there some less-demanding life, some point between the extremes of sainthood and villainy, in which one is *good enough*? Most of us certainly aren't moral saints; most of us doubt that we are capable of living such a life. This leaves us with only three possibilities: (1) the extremist model of moral sainthood is indeed the ideal of morality for all, and nearly all human beings are moral failures; (2) there is a less morally rigorous life that meets the requirements of morality—though moral sainthood is encouraged as supererogatory; or (3) moral sainthood is not in fact the best life, or (more radically) not even a good life.

Two contemporary philosophers who argue for the extremist model are Shelly Kagan (b. 1954) and Peter Singer (b. 1946)—both happen to be consequentialists. Kagan states, "Morality requires that you perform ... that act which can be reasonably expected to lead to the best consequences overall." Furthermore, "If the claim is correct, most of my actions are *immoral*, for almost *nothing* that I do makes optimal use of my time and resources; if I am honest with myself I will recognize that I constantly fail to do as much good as I am able."[3] Peter Singer has been a tireless advocate for animal rights, food ethics, social justice, and commitment to a better life, advanced in books with titles such as *The Life You Can Save: How to Do Your Part to End World Poverty* and *The Most Good You Can Do*.[4] These thinkers are like moral prophets, lamenting our widespread moral failure and urging us to higher expectations for living ethically. The core message: *you must change your life*. No doubt, they inspire many; many of those lapse; and many are morally lazy or dejected by their inevitable failure. And though these philosophers are both consequentialists, the extremist view can be taken within nearly every moral theory we have examined. But before we judge this extremist view, let's look at the other possibilities.

14.2 GOOD ENOUGH

The second possibility—that we might be fully moral without becoming a saint—Kagan calls *ordinary morality*. This is the common, if unexpressed view, that although moral considerations may outweigh others, morality also has its limits. It enables us to sort possibilities for moral action into three categories: the prohibited, the obligatory, and the permissible.

Permissible actions are neither morally compelled nor immoral. Extremists deny us the category of the permissible; because the extreme position is that "the demands of morality pervade every aspect and moment of our lives."[5] Our actions are either required or prohibited. In denying us the permissible, extremists eliminate a range of options for our lives, of choices that are not matters of moral obligation but are not wrong. John Stuart Mill once wrote of the French philosopher, Auguste Comte, "M. Comte is a morality-intoxicated man. Every question with him is one of morality, and no motive but that of morality is permitted."[6] Such extremists would take away our freedom to pursue interests and relationships of our own, projects that may or may not have some benefit, but to which we could devote time and energy without moral guilt or remorse.

In reaction to the extremists, some people—perhaps Trent, the self-proclaimed free-rider (Chapter 8)—would support a *minimalist* position in which morality simply prohibits certain actions, like a set of "thou shalt not" commands. The only moral requirement would be to avoid whatever is prohibited. As long as I don't murder or kill or lie or steal or whatever, I have met my moral obligations. After all, essential to morality is the drawing of a line somewhere regarding acceptable conduct. But one need not be so chary of the moral domain.

Let me introduce yet another stock character of morality: *the **decent person***, who seldom causes harm or does wrong (and never in a major way), who isn't a free-rider, who usually acts with kindness and compassion, who cares deeply for loved ones, and who occasionally makes sacrifices for the general good. Such decency is simply not "good enough," according to those who take the extremist position.

The story of Oskar Schindler, who saved over 1,100 Jews from the Nazis, is true.[7] As the horrors of the war unfolded, he seemed to change from a decent man to one who felt strongly the call of an extreme morality. Near the end of the film, *Schindler's List*, there is this powerful dialogue:

> *Oskar Schindler*: I could have got more out. I could have got more. I don't know. If I'd just ... I could have got more.
>
> *Itzhak Stern*: Oskar, there are eleven hundred people who are alive because of you. Look at them.
>
> *Oskar Schindler*: If I'd made more money ... I threw away so much money. You have no idea. If I'd just ...
>
> *Itzhak Stern*: There will be generations because of what you did.

Oskar Schindler: I didn't do enough!

Itzhak Stern: You did so much.

Oskar Schindler [Looking at his car]: This car. Goeth would have bought this car. Why did I keep the car? Ten people right there. Ten people. Ten more people. *[Removing Nazi pin from lapel]* This pin. Two people. This is gold. Two more people. He would have given me two for it, at least one. One more person. A person, Stern. For this. *[Sobbing]* I could have gotten one more person ... and I didn't! And I ... I didn't![8]

The good he *might* have done and didn't is devastating, overwhelming him in remorse. He wasn't good *enough*.

Still, most of us resist this demand. We demur, saying that we don't live in the dramatic moral circumstances of the Third Reich. We protest that we don't have the immediate opportunities for saving lives. (*Really? You haven't noticed the opportunities to sponsor orphaned children, feed those starving from famine, or defray the cost of life-saving medication?*) We may cite Aristotle's confession about the best possible life (Chapter 9)—"Such a life would be too high for man; for it is not in so far as he is a man that he will live so, but in so far as something divine is present in him"—and forget that he urged us to aspire to it nevertheless, to "strain every nerve." As the poet and critic Matthew Arnold once inscribed in a volume of Emerson's *Essays*: "Gods are we, bards, saints, heroes, if we will." We turn away.

Harriet McBryde Johnson (1957–2008), a disability rights advocate, who suffered from a neuromuscular disease that put her in a motorized wheelchair, once debated Peter Singer. Confronted with Singer's unrelenting adherence to promoting the greatest good—which entails that Singer favors the euthanasia of infants with significant disabilities such as hers—McBryde Johnson wrote that she needed "a shield from the terrible purity of Singer's vision."[9] Here we take up the third option instead: the life of the moral saint is not, in fact, the good life. The extreme moral vision is, indeed, terrible. Susan Wolf (b. 1952) has argued that moral sainthood is not a commendable life. She says "there seems to be a limit to how much morality we can stand." She wonders "whether the moral saint isn't, after all, too good—if not too good for his own good, at least too good for his own well-being." There are times when non-moral reasons should outweigh moral reasons. "In other words, a person may be *perfectly wonderful* without being *perfectly moral*."[10]

It is the personal costs of moral extremism that fill the pages of Larissa MacFarquhar's recent book, *Strangers Drowning*—as her subtitle explains: *Grappling with Impossible Idealism, Drastic Choices, and the Overpowering Urge to Help*. The life stories she features are real, including the account of Kimberly Brown-Whale. MacFarquhar says that "Do-gooders are different from ordinary people because they are willing to weigh their lives and their families in a balance with the needs of strangers. They are willing to risk the one for the sake of the other ... It's not that they value strangers more: it's that they remember that strangers have lives and families, too."[11] But it is difficult, often a matter of luck, to do such good for strangers without sacrificing so many other things of value that life offers and without damaging the lives of those close to you. Lives of extreme morality are often dysfunctional in other aspects. And some display moral *hubris* or self-righteous arrogance. But when we call exemplars of moral extremism "do-gooders," we demean them and their work. When we call them "moral saints" we set them apart, a different species, quite different from "normal" people like us. Both terms help us resist their claim on us.

Perhaps we should think about the universalizability of the extreme ideal: what if everyone were to be a moral saint? Genuine moral saints indeed do good and inspire many. The people I cited are responsible for world-altering changes, moral reforms that have benefited generations. Their work has caused huge numbers to emulate them in ways of large and small impact—but all add to the world's goodness and progress. Nonetheless—setting aside the question of whether everyone is capable of moral sainthood—if everyone were to become moral extremists, other aspects of the world would suffer. No one would attend to all the other of life's callings, such as family life, art, the mastery of a craft, the pursuit of a profession, the advancement of research—unless it directly served the moral project in the best possible way. Isn't the ultimate purpose of the obsessive moral projects of extremists the creation of conditions under which people can live *decent* lives? As MacFarquhar puts it: "They don't mean a world in which helping is the only life there is."[12] So let's deepen our examination of the possibilities and parameters of a decent, worthy, moral life.

14.3 DECENCY, FLOURISHING, AND MORALITY'S DEMANDS

The difference between the decent person and the moral saint cannot be summed up by saying that one is merely less moral, less good, than the other. The decent person recognizes limits to morality by *honoring other values in addition to the moral.* Genuine pluralism in values implies that moral values do not always and everywhere override other values. The Australian philosopher Raimond Gaita (b. 1946), an advocate of moral decency, puts the issue this way: "The most significant of the distortions of the morality system is its tendency to claim for itself all value that seriously conflicts with it. It goes very deep in us to believe that a morally serious person cannot freely and lucidly be claimed by value that conflicts with moral value."[13]

What other values does a decent person honor? The answer is complex and variable, because, although some values are foundational, the array is personal. Gaita proposes that honoring *love,* a concept that has deep connections to morality, may ironically lead us into conflicts with morality. We may value personal relationships in general—family, friends, and neighbors. Care ethics made the nurturance and protection of such relationships the core of morality (Chapter 11). But moral projects—fighting oppression, aiding refugees, battling social injustice, and so on—may so engross us in the helping of strangers that our family relationships fray and our love fades. A good life, as Aristotle claimed (Chapter 9) includes family and friends. Love is partial. To seek love and to protect it when one has it surely does not diminish one's moral goodness.

Another such value might be *health.* Acting for the greater good requires a certain level of health; so when a moral project requires destroying one's health, a very special rationale is needed. Well-being may not be the only aim of morality, as utilitarians would have it; it may not be irrelevant to morality, as Kant seems at times to make it; but attention to one's own well-being should not automatically be seen as a failure of one's moral energy and a lapse into a self-centered immorality. Moral exhaustion is a hazard for all who are consumed by good causes, whose life has narrowed to one relentless moral project.

Opening the range of permissible actions permits self-investment in personal projects—and "personal" does not mean "self-absorbed" or "egoistic." For many, having a professional career is one component of a good life. Honoring professional values and commitments will regularly take time and attention from moral projects. We may, of course, choose a "helping profession," such as pastor, doctor, nurse, firefighter, counselor, teacher, physical therapist, and so on; yet every aspect of the work is certainly not about doing the most good for someone else. We may do our work in other professions with a sense of their contribution, if less direct, to people's well-being and betterment: being a lawyer, a coach, a grocer, a taxi driver, an architect, a locksmith, and so on. But honoring one's craft or profession will nearly always involve less attention to advancing the greater good than would be otherwise possible. But it is itself a good. At times it takes precedence over moral values. Of course, murdering, thieving, and lying for career advancement are not part of decency. Immorality is not an option, and it is harshly moralistic to call someone immoral who seeks a balanced life.

Beyond health and career and love, personal interests vary widely. Creating beauty, pursuing knowledge through scientific research or scholarship, designing and building bridges or buildings, generating hearty laughter, becoming a fine cook, discovering the range of one's own potential—there are, in short, multitudes of worthwhile activities that may legitimately claim time and energy within a good and decent life. They will inevitably conflict with moral values only if we take on the extremist interpretation to moral life.

We might say that the vision of moral decency rejects the complete usurpation of our lives by the demands of morality. Such a life is good, we might suggest, when it has a proper balance between competing values, conflicting claims. Saints—whether moral or religious—are not concerned with balance. The ideal of a balanced life is more pagan than Christian—perhaps because it implies polytheism, the need to respond to many gods. (There are pagan sages, but no pagan saints.) But the images of balance and trade-offs among our values takes us nearer but only so far. We need to *integrate* these irreducible values into a coherent life that actualizes many forms of goodness. Under the proper conditions, a decent life is a flourishing life. But a flourishing life will surely have busy days, on which the most good one can do is quite modest—a gesture of kindness or compassion, an expression of thanks or encouragement or forgiveness.

And yet, I believe a morally good person hears at least a distant call for active, moral engagement. We should respond to social injustice and people in need. A good and decent agent is prepared to accept the mantle of moral responsibility when the situation requires it, even when she or he is about his own business, passing by trolley tracks (Chapter 12). A decent person has moral aspirations. Raimond Gaita tells the story of a nun who displayed "a goodness beyond virtue" as she ministered to institutionalized, mentally ill people. She had compassion without an ounce of condescension; she treated each patient as fully her equal in ways that revealed their humanity to themselves and those who observed her. Profoundly moved by her example, Gaita "came to believe that an ethics centered on the concept of human flourishing does not have the conceptual resources to keep fully amongst us, in the way the nun had revealed to be possible, people who are severely and radically afflicted"[14]—people who have no chance of flourishing.

But is the nun a moral saint, and is Gaita after all calling us to moral sainthood?

Perhaps we have the wrong model of moral sainthood. Perhaps it does not require us to "strain every nerve," to engage furiously in moral projects, or to always and everywhere pull our load with the harness of moral obligations. Perhaps the moral ideal involves, as Gaita puts it, more of genuinely seeing both our individuality and our common humanity, of understanding and responding to "the preciousness of each individual human being." To retain this demeanor in harsh conditions, to display it despite all—perhaps that is moral saintliness.

Louis P. Pojman (1935–2005), reflecting on the role of moral saints, said "It may be the case that only by having a sufficient number of moral saints in key social and political positions can our society and world be saved. They are the salt of the earth, constituting its preservation."[15]

14.4 MORAL REPAIR

Despite our best efforts, things don't always happen as we wish. We make mistakes. We fail to live up to our ideals. We do wrong unto others, and others do wrong unto us. We may know what is right but yield to temptation, having what the Greeks called *akrasia*, or weakness of will. We leave undone the things we ought to have done. Moral theories naturally aim to explicate the right and the good; they may establish responsibility and place blame. But, oddly, they seldom address the moral responsibilities that arise when we or others have done wrong. Yet there are surely times when the need for "reconstructing moral relations after wrongdoing"[16] is painfully obvious, times when morality may require acts of moral repair to fix what is broken.

When we do something wrong, the first step under any moral theory is our recognition of that fact. It is the force of that cognition we feel in guilt or remorse. The sense of moral failure is accompanied by perceiving the damage wrought, which may include inflicted hurt, offense, broken relationships, severed trust, public sanctions, and loss of self-esteem. The implications depend, of course, on the particular wrongdoing and its context. But steeping in guilt and remorse can become toxic, souring the soul, without the hope of forgiveness, expiation, atonement, or repair. We face two entangled tasks: restoring our stature as a good moral agent and making amends to those we have wronged. The need to act is both therapeutic and moral. But what should one do?

If we recognize our wrongdoing and grasp its implications, we should accept responsibility for both our action and its effects. Often, this involves a confession, an admission of wrongdoing to those we have harmed, followed by an apology. An apology is never implicit; it is an explicit, performative speech act. It requires a spoken or written "I'm sorry," or "I apologize." It also requires sincerity and moral humility; it is undone by excuses and defensiveness. Of course, it is also undone if the wrongdoing continues. An apology acknowledges those wronged and may assuage their anger and hurt; it seeks acceptance and clemency. We have all seen attempts at apologies that fail because they lack one of these conditions: the wrongdoer wasn't sincere, excused the wrong, failed to say or write the needed words, or deflected responsibility for the wrong. When a public figure says, "I'm sorry if anyone took offense at my remarks," it subtly blames those who are offended as though they are hyper-sensitive, rather than owning the responsibility for having made offensive remarks.

Offering a genuine apology does not guarantee its acceptance; and accepting an apology does not entail forgiveness. Forgiveness has its own conditions as well. There are some acts so horrendous and malevolent that they may be unforgivable. And only certain people are entitled to forgive any forgivable wrongs. I cannot forgive Janet for the wrong she did to Conrad if I have no intimate connection to him; only Conrad, only those wronged, can rightfully forgive. Harboring resentment may not be good for the soul, but forgiveness cannot be demanded; it must be freely given. Like mercy, forgiveness is not owed; it is a kind of supererogation— an act of moral value that is beyond one's duty or obligation. Forgiveness may, however, be conditional, requiring that certain conditions be met. It is a decision to let the wrong rest in the past; it re-humanizes the wrongdoer, acknowledges the frailties of human nature, and serves to restore the wrongdoer's self-respect and membership in the moral community. It is the victim's role in attempting moral repair.

The moral task does not end with apology and forgiveness. What is still needed—depending on the sort of damage done and available options— may be expiation, atonement, making amends, reparations, or restitution. Restitution attempts to restore the state of affairs prior to the wrongdoing: Ted stole $100; he returns the $100, perhaps including interest. Often, however, what is broken or lost cannot be restored; there is no *reset* possibility. We may then turn to making reparations, compensating those wronged with something else of (ideally, at least equal) value. Expiation and atonement ("at-one-ment" with others) open other possibilities to rebuild our moral relations; these are activities of value to those wronged, representing a sacrifice to the wrongdoer. The most effective activities bear some connection to the wrong itself. For example, imagine that a ten-year-old boy steals a model airplane from a toy store. Later he confesses, apologizes to the store owner, and returns the toy unharmed. Bringing the owner a bouquet of flowers might be nice, but it seems more relevant if the boy offers to clean the storefront and windows or to sweep the floor: it's an activity that honors the value of keeping the store and its contents in good order.

The passage of time is often a necessary factor in forgiveness and atonement. It is unfortunately true that betraying a trust may take only a moment, while restoring that trust may require a long time—even when all the rituals of apology, forgiveness, and atonement have been performed. The break may never heal. Moral repair between specific individuals may simply not be possible. But the moral obligation to seek it, to undertake its requisite efforts, remains.

Sometimes the lasting damage is to the wrongdoer. **Moral injury** refers to moral and psychological trauma that result from witnessing, failing to prevent, participating in, perpetrating, or being victimized by acts that violate one's own moral values and beliefs. In times of war, combat soldiers and prisoners of war are particularly vulnerable to such injury. So are hostages and victims of rape and abuse. Moral injury is frequently a dimension of post-traumatic stress disorder (PTSD).[17] Tragic errors, excessive force, transgressive acts, collateral damage, and atrocities— these may result in a paralyzing guilt, shame, withdrawal, self-harming, self-sabotaging behavior, disorientation, and a loss of one's moral compass. The common moral rituals of apology, forgiveness, and atonement may be beyond reach. Forgiving oneself may be more difficult than forgiving others. But it remains an essential step in the reconstruction of one's moral agency and relationships.

14.5 IMPOSSIBLE CHOICES

The most wrenching situations are those in which one faces an impossible choice—a morally impossible choice. Not only is no morally right act possible; all possible acts are morally wrong. This occurs when circumstances are dire: moral action is required; yet because of terrible constraints, natural or constructed, there are no morally good actions possible.

Didar Hossain certainly faced a wrenching dilemma when, in trying to save earthquake victims he was forced to choose between leaving a small girl to die in the rubble and amputating the child's hand. But in this situation, the latter choice also meant saving the child's life. This was not the very worst. The very worst occurs when there is no morally good reason, no redeeming consequence. Recall the case of Josh (Chapter 6), who is told to select and kill a captive in the terrorist encampment or all the captives will be shot. The "good" that would result from his killing—all the remaining captives would be released (or so the terrorists say)—is a consequence wholly constructed by the terrorists from an unnecessary evil.

A frequently-cited example is the moral tale by William Styron, *Sophie's Choice*. In the novel (and film), Sophie is a young mother who is sent to a Nazi concentration camp with her two children, a son and a daughter. An SS officer confronts her and orders her to choose which of her children will die. If she refuses to choose, both will be killed. In anguish, she chooses her daughter, who is sent to her death. Sophie survives the camp, but is forever haunted by this moral catastrophe. There is no transcendent good here. No morally correct decision. No way to displace the responsibility to chance or luck. As Lisa Tessman has pointed out, moral theory fails us in such "situations of inescapable moral wrongdoing."[18] The attempt to identify factors that would determine the choice rationally is an ugly evasion. For Sophie, for those caught in such impossible situations, the real issue is devastating moral damage.

14.6 THE ROLE AND THE LIMITS OF MORAL THEORY

In this book, we have examined the nature of morality and various theories of moral knowledge and justification (metaethics), and of moral action and value (normative ethics). We have tested each of these theories against an initial sense of what an adequate moral theory should do. Our goal, you will recall, has been to undertake the development of a reflective equilibrium in which our theory and our judgments about cases and practices coincide. We look to our judgments because human experience is the wellspring of ethical concerns, and its domain seems wider, more complex, and more dynamic than any theory. We look to moral theory to give consistency, coherence, and warrant to our moral judgments, and to guide us when perplexed.

Moral theory, like other theories, aspires to "adequacy" or "correctness" in some sense. This sets our judgments in the realm of the impersonal, the impartial, and the universal. It addresses ethical questions in generalized form: *What is the good? Do we have an obligation to treat strangers and family members equally? What is wrong, if anything, with lying?* It uses moral reasoning to bring the answers to these abstract but significant questions under a comprehensive moral vision—a principle or minimal set of principles, a unitary approach or method, a tidy set of justified guidelines. When moral theorizing loses its tether to human experience; when it becomes a closed intellectual game, disconnected from the contexts and richness of actual situations; when it ignores the voices, stories, emotions, and direct experience of individual human beings—such moral theorizing may become *moralistic*, presumptuous, even arrogant in its claims. Keeping that tether is not easy. But each of us needs to use moral reasoning to address *our* ethical questions: *What should I do now? Should I authorize the removal of life support for my mother? Do I owe my friend an apology? Should I tell a hurtful truth?* The ways of working things out that we use in personal situations also constitute a form of moral reasoning— and they may or may not involve the application of theory (let alone the application of principles or rules). They may take the form of arguments, but they may also simply be our stories, our accounts. In this usage, they are not opposed to moral theory; on the contrary, they are a source of the vitality of theory. (This is why I have opened each chapter with the telling of a story, which becomes, under theory's purview, a case in point.)

Because I have presented a critique of every theory, you may be inclined to think that any ethical theory is as good as another—which means that none is really worth adoption or that the choice is arbitrary. That would be a sad and cynical outcome—and a mistake. The tests of adequacy (Chapter 1) asked five questions:

1. *Is the theory clear and coherent?*
2. *Can the theory guide practice?*
3. *Does the theory rest on a plausible account of human nature?*
4. *Does the theory give a plausible account of commonly recognized moral phenomena?*
5. *Does the theory harmonize the different spheres and roles of our lives?*

There are, I believe, six additional questions that we should ask to distinguish among ethical theories:

1. *What are the core concepts and central insights of the theory?*
2. *What domain of human relationships is natural to the theory, and in what contexts is its application awkward?*
3. *What are the criteria for being a moral agent and for having moral standing?*
4. *What does the theory require of us, and what does it permit and prohibit?*
5. *What human qualities or skills are privileged in its requirements for moral agency, and what are therefore the implications for moral education?*

6. *What is the theory's conception of "doing ethics" and its answer to why should I be moral?*

Any temptation one may have to think that we could pluck the best bits from each theory and fuse them into a single grand theory is diminished, if not destroyed, by answering these six questions. The theories are quite distinct, and some are unalterably incompatible with others. What *is* possible is a *refined pluralism*. This means that one could employ refined versions of more than one theory. The versions must be "refined" because one must buffer their claims to sole and complete authority. Such **pluralism** is not an easy relativism, either cultural or situational. Rather, it asserts that no single ethical theory is adequate to capture our moral experience (similar to the view that no single theory of human motivation is sufficient to account for all actions). But, as we have seen with a plurality of principles, values, and duties, pluralism creates the possibility of conflicts and requires a ready-to-hand, justifiable procedure or hierarchy for occasions of conflict. Just as a physicist must know when to employ Newtonian physics and when Einsteinian theory is required for explanation, so the moral pluralist must know when the insights and imperatives of a particular theory hold sway. Pluralism is an open but still hard road to follow. But otherwise, the moral thinker must choose a unitary approach, a single theory, and work to resolve its difficulties.

Because moral philosophy embraces its long history of theorizing, you may also be drawn to the conclusion that ethics makes no progress. But theories evolve in light of critiques and counter-arguments—and human experience. We have seen examples of this process: the ways Mill refines Bentham's hedonism and utilitarianism; the way feminist voices have amended the focus on justice with the need for care; the way contemporary scholars work to correct the austerity of Kantian moral philosophy while retaining its power and vision. As I said early on, mastering ethical theory does not, unfortunately, make one act morally. Theory has an impact, an important one, but it is subtler and less direct. Few people are immediately transformed by rational argument or deft theorizing. Nonetheless, despite the horrors and regressions of the world, there is moral progress. The American philosopher, Richard Rorty (1931–2007), spoke of our moral development in this way:

> The view I am offering says that there is such a thing as moral progress, and that this progress is indeed in the direction of greater human solidarity. But that solidarity is not thought of as a recognition of a core self, the human essence, in all human beings. Rather,

it is thought of as the ability to see more and more traditional differences (of tribe, religion, race, customs, and the like) as unimportant when compared with similarities with respect to pain and humiliation—the ability to think of people wildly different from ourselves as included in the range of "us."[19]

QUESTIONS FOR DISCUSSION

1   Kimberly Brown-Whale's story is included in a book subtitled *Grappling with Impossible Idealism, Drastic Choices, and the Overpowering Urge to Help*. Does it fit that description? Does she "go too far" with doing good? How might you judge whether such a life is a flourishing life?

2   Would you want to be married to a moral saint? What does Pojman mean by saying that moral saints "are the salt of the earth, constituting its preservation"?

3   Explain the minimalist interpretation of morality.

4   Does forgiving require forgetting? What does it mean to "leave the wrong done to you in the past"?

5   Do we always owe an apology to someone who is offended by what we have said or done? Is offending a form of wrongdoing? What is the difference between "giving offense" and "taking offense" at something?

6   The film, *Atonement* (2007), based on the novel by Ian McEwan, portrays the impact of the wrong done by a child's lie and the striving for moral repair. View the film and consider both the form and the effectiveness of the atonement that is offered.

7   Has the study of ethical theories altered any of your views about morality? Which theory of normative ethics best expresses your view about what is morally right? Which metaethical theory best expresses your understanding of what "right" and "wrong" mean and how such claims are justified?

8   What moral question or issue most troubles or puzzles you? What do you think is the most significant problem for ethical theory?

QUESTIONS FOR PERSONAL REFLECTION

1   Raimond Gaita was profoundly changed by observing a nun who displayed "goodness beyond virtue." Have you known anyone who fits that description?

2   Have you done something knowing that it was wrong even as you did it—not legally or just "against policy," but morally wrong? Did you reflect on why you did it? If others were wronged, were you able to make amends?

3   In making friendships, how important to you is a person's moral reflection and behavior?

SUGGESTED SOURCES

Flescher, Andrew Michael. *Heroes, Saints, and Ordinary Morality* (Washington, DC: Georgetown UP, 2003).

Gaita, Raimond. *A Common Humanity: Thinking about Love and Truth and Justice*, 2nd ed. (London: Routledge, 2000).

Hopwood, Mark. "'Terrible Purity': Peter Singer, Harriet McBryde Johnson, and the Moral Significance of the Particular," *Journal of the American Philosophical Association* 2, no. 4 (Winter 2016): 637–55.

Kagan, Shelly. *The Limits of Morality* (Oxford: Clarendon Press of Oxford UP, 1989).

MacFarquhar, Larissa. *Strangers Drowning: Grappling with Impossible Idealism, Drastic Choices, and the Overpowering Urge to Help* (New York: Penguin, 2015).

Murdoch, Iris. *The Sovereignty of Good* (1971; Oxford: Routledge, 2001).

Smith, Nick. *I Was Wrong: The Meanings of Apologies* (Cambridge: Cambridge UP, 2008).

Walker, Margaret Urban. *Moral Repair: Reconstructing Moral Relations after Wrongdoing* (Cambridge: Cambridge UP, 2006).

Williams, Bernard. *Ethics and the Limits of Philosophy* (Cambridge, MA: Harvard UP, 1986).

Wolf, Susan. "Moral Saints," *Journal of Philosophy* 79, no. 8 (August 1982): 419–39.

NOTES

1   This story is a true case. For greater context, see my source: Larissa MacFarquhar, *Strangers Drowning: Grappling with Impossible Idealism, Drastic Choices, and the Overpowering Urge to Help* (New York: Penguin, 2015), 171–203.

2   Søren Kierkegaard, *Purity of Heart Is to Will One Thing* (New York: Harper Torchbooks, 1964).

3   Shelly Kagan, *The Limits of Morality* (Oxford: Clarendon Press of Oxford UP, 1989), 1.

4   Peter Singer is a prolific and popular author. Among his many
    books, I refer here to: *Animal Liberation: The Definitive Classic of
    the Animal Movement*, updated edition (New York: HarperCollins,
    1976, 2009); *The Ethics of What We Eat: Why Our Food Choices
    Matter*, co-authored with Jim Mason (New York: Rodale Books,
    2007); *The Life You Can Save: How to Do Your Part to End World
    Poverty* (New York: Random House, 2010); and *The Most Good You
    Can Do: How Effective Altruism Is Changing Ideas about Living
    Ethically* (New Haven, CT: Yale UP, 2016).

5   Kagan, op. cit., 2.

6   John Stuart Mill, *Comte and Positivism* (1865) in *The Collected
    Works of John Stuart Mill*, Volume X - *Essays on Ethics, Religion,
    and Society*, ed. John M. Robson (Toronto: U of Toronto P; London:
    Routledge and Kegan Paul, 1985): http://oll.libertyfund.org/
    titles/241#lf0223-10_footnote_nt_1093_ref (accessed July 2018).

7   To see the list of names of those Schindler saved, see the
    Auschwitz memorial website: http://auschwitz.dk/schindlerslist.htm
    (accessed July 2018).

8   Steven Spielberg, *Schindler's List*, Universal Pictures, 1993. Film.

9   Harriet McBryde Johnson, *Too Late to Diè Young: Nearly True Tales
    from a Life* (New York: Picador, 2006), quoted in Mark Hopwood,
    "'Terrible Purity': Peter Singer, Harriet McBryde Johnson, and the
    Moral Significance of the Particular," *Journal of the American
    Philosophical Association* 2, no. 4 (Winter 2016), 637–55.

10 Susan Wolf, "Moral Saints," *Journal of Philosophy* 79, no. 8 (August
    1982): 419–39.

11 MacFarquhar, *Strangers Drowning*, 299–300.

12 Ibid.

13 Raimond Gaita, *A Common Humanity: Thinking about Love and
    Truth and Justice*, 2nd ed. (London: Routledge, 2000), 6.

14 Ibid., 19.

15 Louis P. Pojman, "In Defense of Moral Saints," in L.P. Pojman, ed.,
    Ethical Theory: Classical and Contemporary Readings (Belmont,
    CA: Wadsworth, 2002), 377–87.

16 This is the subtitle of Margaret Urban Walker's book, *Moral Repair:
    Reconstructing Moral Relations after Wrongdoing* (Cambridge:
    Cambridge UP, 2006).

17 A profile of moral injury among veterans may be found on the
    website of the Office of Veterans Affairs, The National Center for
    PTSD: https://www.ptsd.va.gov/professional/co-occurring/moral_
    injury_at_war.asp (accessed July 2018).

18 Lisa Tessman, *Moral Failure: On the Impossible Demands of Morality*
    (Oxford: Oxford UP, 2015), 161.

19 Richard Rorty, *Contingency, Irony, and Solidarity* (Cambridge:
    Cambridge UP, 1989), 192.

Glossary

Act Utilitarianism A basic consequentialist theory that affirms that the right act is the optimific act; that is, the act that maximizes the greatest utility for the greatest number. Contrasted with *Rule Utilitarianism*.

Akrasia A term from classical Greek philosophy meaning "weakness of will" or "failure of self-control"; a character flaw that prevents one from doing what one knows to be morally right or rationally required.

Altruism Selfless concern for the interests and well-being of others—a motivation for moral action that some regard as nonexistent but is generally seen to be essential for morality.

Applied Ethics A branch of moral philosophy in which cases and practices such as abortion or gun control are reviewed in light of ethical theories; subfields have arisen for specific professions, such as medical or engineering ethics.

Aretē Greek term for "excellence" or "virtue"—a quality that is normally conducive to the fulfilling of the function or natural purpose of any person or thing. (See also *Telos*.)

Autonomy The capacity for self-determination, for rational and free choice—a concept that is key in Kantian ethical theory and, many argue, essential for moral agency. It is often a goal of moral education.

Axiology Value theory—in ethics, the theory of the good or worthwhile (distinguished from the theory of right action); in aesthetics, the theory of beauty or aesthetic value.

Care Ethics	An approach to ethical theory that places caring as the fundamental moral disposition, often presented as a "feminine" approach to ethics, either as a supplement to or replacement of traditional ("masculine") principled ethics.
Categorical Imperative	In general, an imperative that applies to all agents under all circumstances, contrasted with a hypothetical imperative that applies only under certain assumptions or conditions. In Kantian ethics, it is the supreme principle of morality: *Act only on that maxim you can simultaneously will to be a universal law.* It appears under several formulations.
Civil Disobedience	A form of resistance to a perceived unjust law or practice when channels of legal recourse have failed; typically involving: peaceful violation of the law, appeal to a public sense of justice, willingness to accept punishment.
Cognitivism	The metaethical view that there are knowable moral facts, that ethical judgments are true or false and make claims about moral phenomena. Contrasted with *Non-Cognitivism.*
Consequentialism	Ethical theories that claim that the rightness or wrongness of an act or practice is solely a function of its consequences, either reasonably foreseeable or actual. Contrasted with *Deontology.*
Contractualism	The view that morality derives from social agreement, from an implicit social contract. Various theories differ in their accounts of the parties to, motivations for, and provisions of the contract.
Cultural Relativism	The view that morality is relative to and produced by culture; specifically, the theory that the acts or practices are right within a culture if they have approval of that culture.
Decent Person	A hypothetical construct of a moral agent who does not meet the criteria for moral sainthood, but has morally acceptable, even commendable conduct.

Deontology

The view that what is right is what conforms to our moral duty, that it is the nature of the act—not just its consequences—that determines its rightness or wrongness. Contrasted with *Consequentialism.*

Descriptive Ethics

Empirical and historical studies of moral behavior and beliefs, including attempts to describe the evolution of ethical capacities and codes. Contrasted with *Normative Ethics.*

Determinism

The claim that every event, including human choice, is determined by prior events and the laws of nature; thus, every event or action is theoretically predictable and no other outcome is possible. It has implications for ethics in rejecting certain conceptions of autonomy and free-will.

Divine Command Theory

The theory that what is right is what God commands, that morality is revealed in the will of God.

Doctrine of Double Effect

A doctrine applied when an action has two effects: the good intended and incidental harm that was foreseen but not intended. It is used to explain the moral permissibility of an action that does moral harm as a side effect of promoting a greater good.

Duties

In general, conduct required by law, morality, role, or agreement; in ethical theory, it is identified with moral imperatives and serves as the key concept of deontological theories.

Egalitarianism

The view that human beings are equal and deserve equity; it implies that all individuals matter and are capable and worthy of experiencing the good, and thus deserve equal rights and opportunities.

Egoism

In general, a disposition or principle of concern for oneself over others—Contrasted with *altruism.* (See *Ethical Egoism* and *Psychological Egoism.*)

Emotivism

A metaethical theory that moral judgments are simply non-cognitive expressions of emotion; therefore, there are no moral truths.

Empathy	The ability to understand the emotions or feelings of another; it is sometimes claimed to be fundamental to effective moral agency. In contemporary usage, not to be confused with *sympathy (q.v.)* or compassion.
Error Theory	In general, the claim that human beings are so constituted as to make systematic errors in judgment or understanding regarding some phenomena; thus, all statements within a given area are false.
Essentialism	The view that concepts imply a set of necessary and sufficient properties that inhere in individual entities that belong to them; these may be said to comprise the "essence" of the concept—thus, all *human beings* are said to share a human nature, a distinctive set of properties that is unique and necessary for all creatures that are human.
Ethical Egoism	A normative, consequentialist, moral theory that asserts that the right act is whatever is in one's own self-interest, especially what maximizes one's own good; one's only moral obligation is to secure and promote one's own welfare. (See also *Psychological Egoism*.)
Eudaimonia	Greek term often translated as "happiness," but perhaps better understood as "human flourishing"—claimed by Aristotle as the highest human good and the aim of ethics.
Extrinsic Value	Instrumental value, a value that is derived solely from relation to something else; thus, the value of particular means to a desired end. Contrasted with *Intrinsic Value*.
Fact-Value Dichotomy	Hume's claim that facts and values are logically distinct, and one cannot derive a value or an obligation from facts; thus, the normative nature of morality cannot be reduced to true descriptions of the world.
Fundamentalism	A form of religion in which a literal interpretation of a religious text is taken as the sole source of moral guidance.

Good Will	In Kant's philosophy, a good will is the will to do what is right because it is right, not from any inclination or desire for benefit that may result; it is, he says, the only thing that is good without qualification.
Greatest Happiness Principle	The principle that the right action is that which produces the greatest happiness for the greatest number. It is a version of the Principle of Utility in which the good is interpreted as happiness.
Hedonism	The doctrine that pleasure is the sole human good; apparently diverse forms of good are thus reducible to pleasure. (See also *Qualitative Hedonism.*)
Heteronomy	The condition of being governed or directed by extrinsic factors, causes, or one's inclinations (emotions, desires, wishes, etc.). In Kantian ethics, heteronomy prevents morally worthy actions, which require *autonomy.*
Hypothetical Imperative	An imperative that applies only under certain conditions, it assumes a hypothetical, or "if-then," context. It cannot serve, therefore, as a universal imperative for morality. In Kantian ethics, it is contrasted with a *Categorical Imperative.*
Intrinsic Value	Inherent value, the value of something that is good in itself; thus, the value of an end, in contrast to the value of the means to achieve it. Contrasted with *Extrinsic Value.*
Intuition	A rational, non-inferential, evaluative cognition that is grounded by, but not deduced from, perception of particulars—and expressed as a moral judgment. Or, the faculty that provides such cognitions. The validity of the cognitions, and even the existence of the faculty as described, are contested.
Intuitionism	The view that moral judgments are ultimately intuitions; that they are nonetheless cognitive (true or false) and responsive to reason—and thus provide a sufficiently firm basis for morality.

Logical Positivism A philosophical stance championed by the Vienna Circle that grew from early twentieth-century science, logic, and mathematics. From the view that all knowledge is based on sensory experience (empiricism), positivists asserted that the meaning of a statement is its method of verification. It famously concluded that moral statements (indeed, all statements of values) were not meaningful, because they could not be verified through sensory experience.

Metaethics The branch of moral philosophy that studies the nature and contested existence of moral facts and the claims to moral knowledge; thus it often focuses on the meaning and justification of moral judgments. While *normative ethics* focuses on what actions are right or wrong; metaethics asks what we mean by "right" and "wrong," how we validate our claims, and whether such judgments reflect facts that are independent of our beliefs.

Moral Agents Beings capable of acting morally or immorally, who thus may bear moral responsibility. What specific capacities this requires may be different under different moral theories.

Moral Anti-Realism The view that there are no moral facts independent of human judgment or comprehension. Contrasted with *Moral Realism*.

Moral Bystander A moral agent who unexpectedly encounters a situation of moral concern that was not self-created; a witness or passer-by suddenly put in the role of moral agent, deciding what is right to do, and thus carrying unexpected moral responsibility.

Moral Hero One who performs a conspicuously supererogatory act; that is, one who performs an act of immense moral value despite risk and cost, an act that is well beyond what is required.

Moral Injury Moral and psychological trauma that result from witnessing, failing to prevent, participating in, perpetrating, or being victimized by acts that violate one's own moral values and beliefs.

Moral Patients

Beings who have moral standing and whose treatment is subject to moral judgment; those entitled to moral consideration and who are the recipients of the actions of moral agents. Note that moral patients include many beings who do not qualify as moral agents—e.g., infants or animals.

Moral Pluralism

The view that morality cannot be captured by any one universal or absolute theory; that no theory is both complete and correct. Note that this need not imply *Relativism (q.v.)*.

Moral Realism

The view that there are objective moral values and moral facts; that some states of affairs are indeed more desirable than others; and that their desirability is independent of our actual beliefs and attitudes. Contrasted with *Moral Anti-Realism*.

Moral Saints

Exemplars of moral "extremism" who recognize moral values as supreme at all times, who commit their lives to moral projects, and who are regarded by many as inspirational. Both the concept and the goodness of such a life are contested.

Moral Sensitivity

Alertness to morally relevant aspects of a situation; more generally, the virtue of noticing ethically relevant things.

Moral Sentiment Theory

The view that morality is derived from our emotionality and the judgments of approval and disapproval our emotions ("moral sentiments") convey, rather than from reason. The Scottish Enlightenment produced elaborated versions by Hume, Smith, and others.

Moral Skepticism

Systemic doubt of the validity and truth of any and all moral judgments; the view that all moral claims are false.

Natural Law Theory

The belief that moral principles and proper laws are derived from Nature and may be discerned by an application of reason.

Natural Rights

Entitlements and protections that are grounded in human nature (interpreted as endowed by God or as inherent in evolved humans); because they are possessed by and apply to all human beings, and thus they have universal application and deserve legal protection whether they are officially protected as legal rights or not.

Naturalism

In metaethics, the view that moral judgments are cognitive and refer to natural properties—the sort of properties studied by the sciences. More specifically, the claim that "X is good" = "X is in according with human nature"; that moral properties such as goodness and rightness are reducible to natural (non-moral) properties, such as pleasure or satisfaction of desire, or that they supervene upon such properties.

Naturalistic Fallacy

The allegedly fallacious attempt to reduce goodness or other moral properties to a set of natural properties, as defined by G.E. Moore; or (more loosely) to derive an "ought" from an "is."

Non-Cognitivism

The view that ethical statements have no cognitive content, and therefore cannot be true (or false).Contrasted with its opposite, *Cognitivism*.

Non-Naturalism

In metaethics, the view that moral judgments refer to non-natural properties discernible by intuition—and yet therefore cognitive judgments.

Normative

The quality of assertions, judgments, or theories that focus on what ought to be, rather than what is; that separate better from worse.

Normative Ethics

The branch of moral philosophy that aims at a general account of what things are genuinely good or bad, what acts are morally right or wrong, and which traits of character are moral virtues or vices.

Objective Judgment

In ethics, a moral judgment is objective if the evidence or basis for it is claimed to be independent of the judge; if its truth or falsity is independent of opinion; if its verification is, in principle, open to scrutiny by others.

Obligation
A duty or requirement; in ethics, it refers to actions and states of affairs required by moral considerations.

Open Question Test
A technique proposed by Moore to reject naturalism: when any natural property is proposed to replace a moral property, one can see whether the moral question remains open: for example, if the proposal is "pleasure is the good," and we can still ask the meaningful question "X may be pleasurable, but is it good?"—then we know that being pleasurable does not (fully) capture the concept of being morally good.

Optimific Act
In Utilitarian theory, that act which produces the greatest good for the greatest number; it is therefore the act one should do.

Original Position
In John Rawls's account, a theoretical situation of fairness from which basic principles of social justice may be chosen; it pictures rational agents who must enter a social contract from behind a *Veil of Ignorance (q.v.)*.

Particularism
In ethics, the view that one must scrutinize the particulars of a situation to determine proper moral judgment, rather than relying on the application of a principle or set of rules; it elevates the normative value of details.

Perfectionism
The view that we are called to perfect certain qualities of our nature; that morality is directed to the fulfillment of our nature, the perfection of the sort of creature we are; that who we ought to be lies within the potential of who we are.

Pluralism
In moral philosophy, it is the view that no single ethical theory is adequate to capture our moral experience. Not to be identified with *Relativism (q.v.)*.

Practical Wisdom
Translation of the Greek term, *phronesis*; practical reasoning done with excellence. Some argue it is required for virtuous conduct that harmonizes individual virtues.

Prescriptivism
In metaethics the theory that moral judgments are not true or false, but are prescriptions: to say "X is good" is really to prescribe "Do X."

Principle of Universalizability	The principle of moral theory that requires any moral principle or judgment to be valid for everyone in morally similar circumstances.
Principle of Utility	The principle that we are morally obligated to maximize the good (utility).
Prohibitions	Acts or practices that are morally prohibited or wrong, as contrasted with those that are permissible or obligated.
Psychological Egoism	The descriptive claim that self-interest is our only possible motivation; thus, acting altruistically is impossible given our nature.
Qualitative Hedonism	The view that, although pleasure is the good, some kinds of pleasure are more desirable and valuable than others because of certain qualities. Identified with John Stuart Mill's form of utilitarianism.
Reflective Equilibrium	A state of moral coherence in which the ethical beliefs one has (ethical principles or theory) and one's intuitions (or considered judgments) about specific cases coincide.
Relativism	In ethics, the view that what is right and wrong varies in relation to something—for example, in relation to culture, era, individual, or situation. Contrasted with *Universalism*.
Rule Utilitarianism	The form of utilitarianism in which utility is determined with reference to rules not acts; thus "*X* is right" = "*X* is prescribed by one of a set of rules, which, if followed, would produce the greatest good for the greatest number." Contrasted with *Act Utilitarianism*.
Social Contract Theory	A theory of political philosophy that holds that the legitimacy of government derives from the consent of the governed; it seeks to explain the content and process of such consent, using a contract model.

Standpoint Theory	The social theory that individuals and groups who experience various forms of cultural marginalization and oppression acquire an identifiable and distinctive epistemological standpoint, a "take" on the world that may include distinctive values; the implication is that such standpoints make essential contributions to knowledge and social practices.
State of Nature	A theoretical construct of human life without or prior to the installation of government; described as the situation from which humans would consent to the *Social Contract*.
Subjective Judgment	In ethics, a moral judgment is subjective if the evidence or basis for it is dependent on the judge if its truth or falsity is determined by opinion; if its verification is, in principle, inaccessible to scrutiny by others.
Subjectivism	In ethics, the view that what is right (or wrong) is whatever one sincerely believes it is.
Supererogation	Actions of moral worth that are not obligated but are above and beyond duty; morally good acts that are freely given, not required.
Supervenience	A relationship defined as follows: A "supervenes" on B if A is dependent upon or emerges from B. But A is not reducible to B, nor does B cause A.
Sympathy	A capacity for "feeling with" another person, for sharing emotions or even for feeling the emotion of another. The term is used today to mean "compassion" or even "pity." Earlier writers, such as Hume and Smith, use the term to refer to a capacity closer to *empathy (q.v.)* and taken to be essential to moral agency.
Telos	Greek term for the end, goal, purpose or fulfillment of a thing; Aristotle claims that, for human beings, it is *eudaimonia*.
Transcendental Argument	Identified and used by Kant, it is an argument that proceeds by unearthing the necessary presuppositions for something; for example, assuming there are moral agents, what conditions are necessary for moral agency to be possible, to function?

Universalism	It ethics, it is the doctrine that what is right and wrong is so for everyone (in the same situation), at all times, and in all cultures. In general, it asserts that some property is the same in all times and places—as one claims that what is truly beautiful is "timeless." Contrasted with *Relativism*.
Utilitarianism	An influential cluster of closely-related consequentialist ethical theories that claim the only moral requirement is to produce the most good.
Veil of Ignorance	A theoretical construct introduced by John Rawls as a condition of the *Original Position* in which basic principles of justice may be chosen fairly; it imagines rational agents who do not know their identity, their values, their place in society, or their life plan, but are aware they will have such individuality when the "veil" is lifted and they take their place in society.
Verification Principle	Or, **Principle of Verifiability**. A principle of Logical Positivism which claims that for a statement to have meaning, it must be empirically verifiable, and its meaning is indeed the process of verification.
Vice	A morally negative character trait; for Aristotelians, any disposition that tends to hinder or prevent one's achieving the good; vice is conceived as a tendency to excess or deficiency. Contrasted with *virtue*.
Virtue	A morally positive character trait; for Aristotelians, any disposition that tends to promote or assist in one's achieving the good, conceived as a tendency to act with proper proportionality, to do the right thing for the right reasons, and in the right way.
Virtue Ethics	An agent-centered approach to ethics that identifies "What kind of person should one be?" as the central question of morality; it focuses on virtues and vices that define moral character.

Index

From the Publisher

A name never says it all, but the word "Broadview" expresses a good deal of the philosophy behind our company. We are open to a broad range of academic approaches and political viewpoints. We pay attention to the broad impact book publishing and book printing has in the wider world; for some years now we have used 100% recycled paper for most titles. Our publishing program is internationally oriented and broad-ranging. Our individual titles often appeal to a broad readership too; many are of interest as much to general readers as to academics and students.

Founded in 1985, Broadview remains a fully independent company owned by its shareholders—not an imprint or subsidiary of a larger multinational.

For the most accurate information on our books (including information on pricing, editions, and formats) please visit our website at www.broadviewpress.com. Our print books and ebooks are available for sale on our site.

broadview press
www.broadviewpress.com

This book is made of paper from well-managed FSC® - certified
forests, recycled materials, and other controlled sources.

 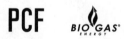